Value, meaning and social structure of human work

European University Studies

Europäische Hochschulschriften
Publications Universitaires Européennes

Series XXIII
Theology

Reihe XXIII   Série XXIII

Theologie
Théologie

Vol./Bd. 282

PETER LANG
Frankfurt am Main · Bern · New York

Obiora F. Ike

Value Meaning
and Social Structure
of Human Work

With Reference to »Laborem Exercens«
and its Relevance for
a Post-colonial African Society

PETER LANG
Frankfurt am Main · Bern · New York

CIP-Kurztitelaufnahme der Deutschen Bibliothek

Ike, Obiora:

Value, meaning, and social structure of human
work : with reference to "Laborem exercens" and
its relevance for a post-colonial African society /
Obiora Ike. — Frankfurt am Main ; Bern ; New York :
Lang, 1986.
(Europäische Hochschulschriften : Reihe 23,
Theologie ; Bd. 282)
ISBN 3-8204-9640-8
NE: Europäische Hochschulschriften / 23

BT
738.5
.I42ø
1986

ISSN 0721-3409
ISBN 3-8204-9640-8

© Verlag Peter Lang GmbH, Frankfurt am Main 1986

D E D I C A T E D

TO

my father Richard Maduabuchi Ike

and

my mother Lucy Magbafo Ike
whose deep commitment in life
and unswerving devotion to
the Christian Social Principles
of Human Work, inspired me,
their son, to read, write and
research on HUMAN WORK

PREFACE

This work was written under the directorship of Professor Dr. Lothar Roos
in the Institute of Christian Social Ethics and Pastoral Sociology of the
Theological Faculty of the Friedrich-Wilhelms-University, Bonn, Western
Germany. It was submitted in May 1985 to the Faculty of Catholic Theology
as inaugural dissertation and fulfilment of the partial requirements
needed to obtain the doctorate in Theology. It was accordingly accepted
later in the year by the Faculty.

The publication of this work now as book does not imply that substantial
changes have been made in the original form of the work. Infact, this publication is in its original form, and except for some minor corrections as
suggested by the Directors, no substantial parts of the work have been
removed, and new additions have not been made. Such a task would be the
result of another research now under study with the aim of studying @Human
Work and Human Rights in Africa -Christian Social Ethics en-route@, and
would be published as book later.

Here, I desire to record my obligation and gratitude to a multitude of scholars,
friends and institutions who have helped me in one way or another in the
writing of this work.

I desire to express utmost thanks to my moderator, Professor Dr. Lothar
Roos who generously inspired me to undertake research in the area of Human
Work. He not only moderated and guided the work, but made available to me
many books, as well as proposing in a human way, some amendations to the
work. I thank the co-moderator, Professor Dr. Hans Waldenfels SJ, director
of the Institute of Fundamental Theology for his concern in seeing that the
work had a contextual argumentation.

My friend Alfons Herweg, director of the @Deutschordens Wohnstift -Konrad
Adenauer Köln@ merits my special gratitude for he invited me, while I was
still a student in Innsbruck, Austria, to come to Germany and take up the
work of Chaplaincy of the Old Peoples Home and to study in Bonn with a
guarantee for financial security. In the years in which we have worked together, we were able to form an organisation in Cologne, the @Nigerianisch-
deutsche Kontakte@ - a step which has not only drawn us together, but has

intensified our interest and awareness of the problems facing humanity in
the North-South hemispheres. I hope that the constructive engagements begun
thereby will remain with us for many more years to come.
Likewise, do I extend thanks to Winfried Muller, also one in the club of
friends, Mr. Friedl Herweg (director of Caritas, Leverkusen), Mr.Hermann
Haeck (Dipl. Kfmn), the Catholic Nuns of the @Deutschordens Wohnstift@
for their warmth and the inmates of the Home whose problems and joys
became mine too. The pastoral and human experiences gathered here let me
test practically the claims of Christian Social Principles.
Professor Charles Rogers SJ, Oxford, gave me initial encouragement in 1982
while I was developing the scope of this thesis in London. He may not believe
it, but those hours with him strenghtened me and his book was intellecually
stimulating. Likewise do I thank my junior brother Chinedu, who in constant
telephone calls, letters and discussions counselled me to eliminate visitors
and extra-curricular activities in order to finish the work on record time.

Special gratitude goes to the Missionswissenschaftliches Institut, Aachen,
and to all the nice people who work there for kindly accepting to grant me
part-financial assistance to supplement the large expenses involved in such
a project. I thank particularly Dr. Thomas Kramm and Mrs. Maly Krebs for thei
efforts in getting the financial burdens alleviated within their means.

The Nigerian Students Union in Cologne of which I am President, offered me
moments to seriously reflect with my fellow country-men on the problems of
Nigeria and Africa in general. In this context too, I extend warm regards
to Mr. Anerobi Ngwube, Father Goddy Odigbo, Miss Petra Hagerdorn, Mrs.Renate
Bock, and the Nigerian sisters of the Daughters of Divine Love, living in
Cologne. Their constant advice, prayers and solidarity were a source of
moral strenght to me.
Mrs. Nma P. Okamgba of the Nigerian Embassy in Bonn together with her husband
Frank merit the bulk of the credit for helping out with the typing of the
manuscripts.

III

My parents merit my utmost and special thanks and gratitude for granting me very early in life, all that necessary training required both in theory and practice to pursue science and to inquire further.

Last but not least, I thank His Excellency, my bishop, Rt. Rev.Dr.Michael Ugwu Eneja, Bishop of Enugu, who sent me to Europe for further studies and has constantly written to find out my situation and to assure me of his solidarity and prayers.

There are of course many others who in one way or another contributed immensely to the success of this work, but since I cannot mention all by name here, my gratitude goes to everyone with whshes and prayers for God's guidance for all.

O.F.I.

CONTENTS

SECTION TWO (II)

VALUE, MEANING AND SOCIAL STRUCTURE OF HUMAN WORK
IN LABOREM EXERCENS AND IN CHRISTIAN SOCIAL TEACHINGS

XV

Page

SECTION THREE (III)

THE RELEVANCE OF "LABOREM EXERCENS" TO POST-COLONIAL
NIGERIA

INTRODUCTION

"Though the Church's first care must be for souls,
how she can sanctify them and make them share in
the gifts of heaven, she concerns herself too with
the exigencies of man's daily life, with his livelihood and education, and his general welfare and
prosperity".

                    Pope John XXIII, Mater et Magistra, n.3

This thesis derives from a fundamental concern with the present state of affairs on the continent of Africa - politically, socially, economically and religiously. It takes Nigeria as an example, Igboland in its strictest sense - only as a paradigm of that which happens or can happen elsewhere.

The attempt to research into the past, is seen in the context of the historical methods of research as aid towards understanding how the present came into being and thereby to help us fashion out the trends for the future.

This thesis is therefore both a modest and an ambitious project. It's modesty is seen in its attempt to provide a factual presentation and analysis of the basic tenets of Christian Social Principles, specifically, to lay bare the contents of the Social Encyclical of Pope John Paul II on human work, namely: "Laborem Exercens" in its historical and traditional context, and thereby to reconstruct from what are in many instances the most compressed and least of familiar of sources, the teachings of Social Ethics as a response to the so-called "Social Question".

At the same time, this thesis is an ambitious project because it attempts
to create new avenues for the African world, by seeking elements from
Christian Social Principles, acceptable and adaptable to Nigeria and
Africa for the solution to many of the problems facing the nation.

As is largely known, in most developing countries today, people are
deeply engaged in decrying the great anomalies facing the society -
poverty, injustice, corruption, exploitation (both internal and external),
coups and counter-coups, ignorance, alienation and cultural degradation,
hunger, the loss of moral and spiritual values, and the mounting loss
of faith in God, infact, a loss of faith in life itself and its meaning.
Many worried, honest and truth-seeking persons have called on the discipline c
Theology for action.

This work is an answer to this call, but it does not claim to solve
all these problems, rather, it takes note of them, exposes them and
goes beyond them by seeking the main causes of the problems and by
offering from the perspectives of Christian Social Principles relevant elements towards a solution.

We have therefore chosen for our research the thesis topic:
"Value, meaning and social structure of Human Work with reference to
Laborem Exercens and its relevance for a post-colonial African society".

Scope, aim and relevance of thesis:

A fundamental dimension of man's life on earth is Human Work.
Human work is the key to the whole "Social Question" as the Popes
maintain, and this refers to all the problems which have arisen for
each one of us, for our society and for the world at large with the
development of industrial manufacture. It is through work that
man can renew the face of the earth, because through work, man creates,
builds and organises the society and the world .

Human work is the guiding thread through which all political, social,
economic, religious, cultural aspects of man's life in society is co-
ordinated. We might even say that everything that is , is a product of
work, the food we eat, the house we live in, the roads, cars, books,
education, the family and society, religion and culture - for behind all
these stand the reality of work.

Now, it is clear that work, understood in its right meaning, value and
social structure, helps man to find adequate solutions to the problems
already pointed to above. On the other hand, when the right meaning of
work is lacking, there is disruption of the right order of values in
the society as priorities are wrongly placed.

The issue of human work in recent times has been fundamentally linked up with human rights. To work is a basic human right. It is a primary duty of society to create work for the greatest possible number, if not all, of its able citizens, since work is not only a means of livelihood, but an important necessity for human respect, self-fulfilment and self-realisation. Certainly, members of society must try to be self-reliant in the area of work, but when some cannot achieve this and society cannot give them job, they become marginalised and damaged in their personality.

In the world of work, it must be made clear that human work is not a commodity to be bought or sold depending on the dictates of the market price. Human work must be seen to be worthy and above rigid capitalistic conceptions. Above this, human work should be seen to be in the interest of the community and its welfare. Therefore, the worker should be seen as a person, a child of God and not simply as statistics or "a cog in the wheel" of the entrepreneur. The well-being of a country does not depend on money than on persons who make money possible. Therefore, the right set of values should once again be re-asserted that wealth and money are the products, not the origin of developement.

From the aforesaid, the first charge which Catholic Social Ethics makes on the industry and buisness as a whole is to see that there is an adequate provision for the worth and livelihood of those who are engaged in the industry. Their wages should be determined by the criteria of the need for the people to live fully as human persons and to satisfy, not only basic demands of life, but also to fulfil their obligations as bread winners for their families and thereby live with human dignity. Beyond this, Catholic Social Ethics warns that investment and the demands of economics should not simply be seen as pure economic affairs but also as moral issues.

The Fathers of the Second Vatican Council emphasised in the decree "Gaudium et Spes" the need to see political, social, cultural, economic and other related areas in the light of the Gospel of Love preached by Jesus. All kinds of discrimination which distort the fundamental rights of man and negate it, be it social or cultural, whether based on sex, race, colour, class, party, language or religion should be regarded as contrary to God's intent.

In this context likewise, the role of the State and government is surveyed. The buisness of the State is to help citizins help themselves to be what God intended, namely, free responsible human persons with rights and duties which help his human dignity. Since the rights of man are inalienable, no State may consider human rights as the priviledge granted citizens by the State. Human rights are transcendental and are granted man by the creator. Therefore no State may interfere with these rights. Infact, the legitimacy of government must be judged by a States ability to protect these rights of man, safeguarding the welfare of the citizens, and creating the necessary social conditions for their maintenance. We can therefore accept the principles suggested by Catholic Social Ethics as the guiding thread for guaranteeing that the rights of man, whether in the world of human work, or outside of it be protected. These principles believe strongly in subsidiarity, solidarity and common welfare. It is on these principles that the tenets and analysis researched in this thesis have their foundation.

Contextual reasoning from the point of view of Africa:

As far as I know, there is no deep research, infact no comprehensive
and adequate research by any Nigerian on the theme of Human work in its
social-ethical perspectives and from the standpoint of Christian Social
Principles. This work is therefore an original and pioneer venture in this
field as shown from the contents and the topics discussed.
But it is not only a reflection on the Social Encyclical "Laborem Exercens"
that is our concern here. Beyond this is the search for the relevance
and adaptability of this document, as well as other Pontifical Pronouncements in the area of Human work, and in its significant contributions,
argumentations and propositions for the African world, in our context,
for post-colonial Nigeria that is our proximate concern.

We are thus faced with the problems of unity and diversity. How can we
in the unity of catholicity seek for elements which are relevant for
African situations from the Encyclicals and other documents without
disrupting the unity in catholicity ? In times past, various documents
were completely taken over into the African world without seeking for
those relevant points which concerned the specifically African situation.
This was done during the missionary era, as well as their ongoing students.
This explains why this work attempts to re-translate and re-adapt the
suggestions and propositions made in "Laborem Exercens" to fit into the
situation of modern Nigeria. An attempt is also made to show what ancient
African societies had in their cultural heritage and which can today be
inculturated into the new era of evangelisation. In other words, this
thesis seeks to show that in as much as Africa has much to gain from the
universal Church, it has also much to give to the history of mankind today.

It is time for Africans to say what is and what is not ourselves.
To redefine and reverse the frames of reference. To establish relevant
values and put them in the context of our behavioural patterns without
denying the basic truths that guide man.

This new movement must make changes in the entire process of assimilating teachings from outside by giving definitions which arise from an African framework. In other words, theology talking to Africa has to be understood and translated into the realities of the African, so that the voice of Christ may be truly heared by the African without the risk of alienation. As has been sufficiently proved here, there are many interrelated aspects uniting traditional African views of life with the principles of social-ethics and society.

Pope John Paul II, who himself visited Nigeria in 1982, and who had the oppurtunity of seeing the reality of the Nigerian world of work, even from afar, made it clear in the Encyclical Letter "Laborem Exercens", as well as in many of his other addresses and speeches to Nigerians, that central to the problem of Human Work is man. Man is the being who works and who must be served by work and its products.

On "Laborem Exercens":

A profound and wide-ranging document, the Encyclical "Laborem Exercens" has over 15,000 words in lenght and was written to commemorate the ninetieth anniversary of Pope Leo XIII's Encyclical - "Rerum Novarum" (1891) - the first of the great "Social Encyclicals".
Successive Popes have also written on related problems of the "Social Question", such as Pope Pius XI (Quadragesimo anno), John XXIII (Mater et Magistra and Pacem in Terris), and Paul VI (Populorum Progressio) among others.

Laborem Exercens was intended to be publicly announced on 15th May 1981 -
the exact day of the anniversary of "Rerum Novarum". But the work bears
the date of 1st September 1981, the feast of the triumph of the Holy Cross.
This delay is due to the Pope's hospitalisation after the attempted murder by
the Turk Ali Agca and accomplices. This "extrinsic" affair with the
date gives the document a personal and spiritual originality which cannot
be easily ignored.

Exposing work as a human participation in God's creative activity, John Paul
shows that work must be the means of man's fulfilment as an image of God.
The product of labour must be worthy, the labour itself dignified because
the worker himself, is carrying out the creators' purpose as recorded in
the bible: "subdue the earth and govern it", and in so doing imaging God to
all his creation.

The document contains many technical and difficult arguments to make its
points clear, but it ends up as a directive for man - the worker.
The great social encyclicals of the Church, of which "Laborem Exercens"
is the latest, are of their nature different from doctrinal encyclicals.
While the principles which are essential to the teachings of the Church,
such as the dignity of man as a child of God do not change, nevertheless,
the circumstances to which they apply do change, sometimes very radically.
This is the situation of man in the later part of the twentieth century.
John Paul himself observes on the great revolution facing the economic
world of the twentieth century, which at the same time form the background
against which the encyclical refers to, namely:

Widespread introduction of automation into many spheres of productive
activity;
The increase in the cost of energy and raw materials;
The fact that the world is being intolerably polluted by industries;
The emergence on the political and economic scene of peoples, who, after
centuries of subjection, are demanding their rightful place among the
nations and in international decision making;
The development of informatics and telematics, and the vicious circle
of inflation and unemployment;

John Paul II goes further and makes mention of other distressing problems:
The unjust economic situation in the North - South axis of our globe, but
also the unnecessary and superfluous waste and endangerment of world peace
in the East - West squabblings and ideological power struggle;
The loss of a sense of culture and corporate work style;
The marginalisation of the agricultural sector and the massive exodus
of people from the rural areas to the urban zones and cities;
The seperation of work from its relation to the family;
The social and economic under-valuing of the vocation of motherhood;
Lastly, the fact that issues relating to work and labour are seen only
as determined by the dogmas of contemporary ideologies.

The encyclical "Laborem Exercens" addresses itself to these problems in a
new way. Inspite of its weaknesses as we shall show in the last chapter of
this work, its originality and achievement lies in the fact that the
document addresses itself to the problems of human work for man in the later
part of the twentieth century in an original and new way .

No one will overlook the achievement which "Laborem Exercens" has made within the development of Social Ethics in the Church's Social Tradition, for this is the first time that a Pope devotes an entire encyclical completely to this one theme -"Homo Laborem Exercens" - the working man. Although the Pope himself states that he does not intend to deal with human work independent of the tradition of Catholic Social Principles, yet, he treats his material in such an organic manner and originality, and maintains the tradition of the Church's Social direction.

In the first place, the choice of the theme exposes this fact. Unlike his predecessors who in their commemorations of Leo XIII's milestone achievement undertook an organic overview of the themes connected with the "Social Question", John Paul II hesitates and writes rather on the world of the working man.

The document itself is divided into five parts and contains in its original release, twenty seven paragraphs. (The original version is in Latin). Part One contains three chapters (1 - 3) and it is a reflection on the theme, as well as an introduction aimed at clarifying the concept and showing its fundamental relevance for man's daily life.
Part Two (paragraphs four to ten) discusses the details of work and man, the family and the society at large including the International arena. Here, work in the subjective and objective senses are considered .
Part Three (paragraphs eleven to fifteen) discusses the central conflicts existing since the industrial revolution regarding the right understanding of the factors of production - labour and capital - being given adequate consideration. The discussion on the conflicts existing between both leads us to abandon the wrong belief of an inherrent antinomy between them and to seek for the option of "Laborismus" which not only insists that human work comes before capital, but also pleads for participation of the employees in the ownership and decision making processes of production.

Part Four (paragraphs sixteen to twenty three) considers the rights of
workers within the context of fundamental human rights as agreed upon
by the world community of nations. Various groups of workers are reflected
upon and ethical options are offered as possibilities to better their
situation.

Part Five (including paragraphs twenty-four to twenty-seven) contains
elements for a spirituality of work - with Christ - the man of work as
the paramount example. In this section, the cross is elevated and shown
to be the way of salvation and resurrection, thereby identifying human
work as salvific, even though a "bonum arduum" as stated by St. Thomas
Aquinas.

Here, John Paul's reflections are deeply rooted in the Bible, where work is
presented as participation in the mystery of creation and redemption -
its cahracteristics being that work is necessary, painful, corporate,
redemptive and creative - and all these give life more meaning.

Method and formal procedure:

Our study involves a series of methods - investigation and research,
demonstration and explanation, critique, argumentation and systematisation,
and the comparative approach which is often adopted wherever it is thought
that this will illuminate the text or point a parallel in the familiar fields
of an African culture. Here and there, the descriptive and historical
approach is used, but it is not so much an exposition of a new theory that
we are after, as an attempt to seek for the synthesis of all existing materials
in the area of our theme gathered through the methods described above,
with an analysis based on my own researched views and personal inferences
which is the basic core and method employed in this work.

Of course, Christian Social Principles employs the methods of social-philoso-
phical enquiry as well as theological reflection . In core, this is the
method we used in this research.

Structure of work:

Since this work is a virgin research in the area of social ethics
and its relevance for a post-colonial African society from the
point of view of the encyclical "Laborem Exercens", my aim has
been throughout to assemble,weigh and assess objectively and
argumentatively all the available data bearing on each of the topics
discussed. Concrete examples about the situation of pre-literary,
pre-colonial Igbo society were offered, as well as the present
state of this society in the context of colonial and post-colonial
Nigeria. The elements gathered from Social Ethics have therefore been proved to be relevant within the context of an African
Society.

The work itself is divided into three broad sections - and has ten
chapters in general. Section One deals with the traditional views
of Human Work in the context of pre-literary African society, and we
chose Igboland, not only because the author comes from this area,
and is as such personally affected, but also because Igboland suggests
in its basic views on religion,politics and general cosmology,
a suitable society for study in the context of human work.
Here, we tried to show what was, before the new came as a result
of the intrusion of foreigners to disrupt this traditional set-up.
It is shown that human work in Igboland contains many elements
which todays social ethics in its systematic method is teaching
and offering as an answer to some of the problems of modern man.
This section also exposes the situation of human work in modern
Nigeria, its problems,structures and false practices, especially
in the area of neglect for human rights.There are four chapters.
Infact, it is our belief that if the present Nigerians and
Africans would look back into their own cultures and original
world views, they would discover noble values and heritages,
which unfortunately modern life easily neglects. It is as such
an attempt to self-rediscovery and assertion.

Section Two considers the value, meaning and social structure
of human work in "Laborem Exercens" and in Christian Social
Teachings, and has four chapters also begining from chapter
five to eight. This section goes beyond documentary material
of John Paul II's encyclical letter to consider other source
material concerned with the Social Question, showing how the
problems were solved at different times. It attempts to show
the existing economic systems with their contributions and weaknesses and catalogues in a formal way, the rights of workers
as inextricably joined to the quest for fundamental human rights.

Section Three is limited in chapters nine and ten, and is the
most important chapter of the work from the point of view of
aim of entire project. It seeks the relevance of "Laborem Exercens"
to post-colonial Nigeria, applying the social and ethical principles
proposed by the encyclical to Nigeria.
Infact, section three has the future of African societies in mind,
and in this concern, pleads that "Christian Social Principles" be
made more known and more deeply studied.
In the final evaluation which marks the end of this research,
a summary of all the points already mentioned above is precisely
given, the role of the Church is re-evalued as far as the challenge
to help in renewing the face of the earth is concerned. Here, the
Church is called to be the torch bearer in the fight for human rights.
Finally, certain unsolved questions are referred to, in the light
of discussions from "Laborem Exercens" and a moderate critique is
offered with an aim to contextual argumentation.

Let me immediately remark here that my views, particularly the attempts
made in Section One to reconstruct the Igbo past, are for the most part,
not statements of an ultimately established orthodoxy, but fairly attempts
to put to paper oral traditions, faint memories and scantily documented
material of an oral traditioned society. Igboland must be differentially
treated as there was no pan-Igbo identity before the European appearance
on the scene. That section should be read with an appropriate charity
and a balanced scepticism - if necessary.

On the incompleteness or inexhaustion of the area of research treated in
this book, I can only tell my readers what a satirical French philosopher
once said:

> "One should not always exhaust a subject, and leave the
> reader with nothing to do. The aim is not to make people
> just read, but to make them think" (Montesquieu),

and I would add, to stimulate people to conscious perception of the problems
of society today with a view at rational and ethical solution.
The ideas documented in this book should only be considered as a contribution
to the problems facing mankind in Africas most populous country, Nigeria,
as well as an invitation to all men and women "of good will" to join in the
search for an answer to the problems of our times in its multi-dimensional
perspectives.

For the errors in the writing and analysis of the various schools of thought
exposed here, the author accepts full responsiblity.

SECTION ONE

HUMAN WORK IN THE CONTEXT OF AN AFRICAN SOCIETY : PRE-COLONIAL, COLONIAL AND POST-COLONIAL NIGERIA

General Introduction :

History cannot be divided into watertight compartments. Infact, there are no clean breaks in history as the events of one era have their origins in the past, and leave their influences upon generations yet to come. This knowledge, already well known and articulated in African wisdom is the basis of the historical excursion being undertaken here into Nigeria's background .

This explains why we determine from the onset, to offer an exposition into the cultural and historical situation of pre-colonial, colonial and post-colonial Nigeria. Such a research, difficult as it is in the absence of a literary tradition in the past, enables the reader to better understand the background, world view and other aspects of this African world before the European intrusions of the nineteenth and twentieth centuries.

The research into traditional society is primarily intended to awaken consciousness among many modern Nigerians of today, as well as other African societies to reconsider seriously their heritage and ancient past, rediscover those noble and high values of morality and order inherent in their religious,cultural and philosophical past many of which are today gradually disappearing in the face of the "new lifestyle", and to re-elevate these values by re-integrating them into the new "African world". It is therefore a call for an authentic African heritage.

The research into the colonial and post-colonial era attempts to expose how Africa's heritage was brutally and ignorantly destroyed during the cultural contact with Britain and other foreign elements. Infact, post-colonial Nigeria still suffers from this intrusion, as evidence abounds of a vacuum in the cultural, ethical and social arena. Since we cannot afford to perpetually groove over past mistakes, the time has come for concerted efforts to find ways of overcoming the past, facing today and successfully encountering the future.

CHAPTER ONE: WORK, LAND AND PROPERTY RELATIONS IN PRE-COLONIAL IGBO
TRADITIONAL SOCIETY

PART ONE (I) : Meaning ,value and social structure of human work -

1. Basic Views:

In this section of our work, we refer to Igboland, that is, to the
pre-literary,pre-colonial and pre-industrial Igbo society. We intend
to survey Igbo tribal society in its understanding and practice of work
before the birth of the Nigerian State. Such a historical and cultural
excursion helps us keep in line with the basic Igbo principle which
stresses that people who never look back to their ancestors, cannot look
forward to progress and posterity successfully, as this would mean a certain
negation of historical experience, or to put it in the words of the
ancient Greek philosopher: "The unexamined life is not worth living".
It is important to stress here that modern Nigeria has more than three
hundred tribal or ethnic groups merged together into the one State.
Since we cannot survey each of them singly, let it be made known that
what is said here of Igboland, might , and infact does apply to many of
the various ethnic groups inhabiting Nigeria today. A few examples are
the Efik, Ijaw, Ogoja, Yoruba, Bein, Tiv, Nupe and Kalabari tribes,
among others. Outside Nigeria, many other African societies share some
of the described characteristics including the Nuer, Tallensi, Zulu,
Nuba, Lozi (Barotse), Bantu and Azande tribes, to mention only a few.

It will become clear from our research into pre-colonial Igbo society
that certain views taught today in 'Christian Social Principles' already
existed in theory and practice in Igboland , including the principles
of subsidiarity, solidarity and common welfare. This observation
arouses more interest as it is well known that pre-colonial Igbo society
and the Social Principles of Christianity had no contact whatsoever
in pre-colonial times.

2. Igboland - General Description of Land and People

(a) Igbo is the name of the land, people and geographical area
occupied by the Igbos in Africa - on the Western Coasts of Africa, and
existing today within the large country of Nigeria, politically
carved out by the British at the height of its colonial might.
The Igbo territory is inhabited by a branch of the Negro race -
the darkskinned people who might have originated in an area
along the latitude of Asselar and Khartoum in Sudan, but who
migrated to their present sites since the second or third millenium
before Christ. Evidence has it that for 4,000 years now, the area
has been inhabited by these tribes[1].

(b) Igbo people distinguish themselves from other ethnic groups in
many forms and matters, Art being one of them. Their Art shares
the same characteristic patterns or form, never embodies or
presents suspense, essentially offers its music, artifacts,
poetry, drama, folk tales, proverbs and sculpture in such a way as
to vividly establish equilibrium and to florify harmony. Igbo
Art often portrayed society and its guiding philosophical
preoccupation has been illustrated in terms of Force. As someone
has once remarked: "Force is to the pure African, vital, a universal,
omnipotent energy to which all thought and action were related to
and exist".

---

1) The first human inhabitants of Igboland must have come from some
    point further north, probably from the area of the Niger-
    Benue confluence. But men have been living in Igboland for at least
    5,000 years since the dawn of human history, a notable fact
    being the length and continuity of Igbo history and tradition.
    Ref. Isichei, E., A History of the Igbo People, Macmillan Press,
    London, 1976, p. 3 (Donald Hartle has shown that archeological carbon
    datings show that 4,500 years ago, people in Nsukka were making pottery
    which is similar to that still made in the area today; See
    Donald D. Hartle, 'Archeology in Eastern Nigeria', Nigerian Magazine 93,
    June 1967., pp. 136 - 7).

(c) But Art points beyond itself - in the context of Igboland - Art points to Religion. Every work of Art says to the beholder: "Look beneath and beyond me for what I represent and say is more than what you see"; Igbo Art is modest, yet deeply expressive and it concerns itself with life, in faces and figures showing man in his nature and activities, in the stages of his ancestry; Igbo Art depicts the fundamental dimensions of man's existence, namely, birth, life, death, power and mystery. Here it has to be mentioned that Igbo Art is not a question of matter alone, the element of spirit which is the breadth of the divine, of God in man is always present. It has been stated time out of mind that the African is generally religious... of whom it can be said that "they eat, drink, work, bathe and dress religiously"[2]. Igbo religion permeates all the departments of life.

(d) But this Igbo traditional religion is non-institutional. It is communal in the same way that African Art products and expressions of some community is peculiar. One exists in an Igbo group through active participation in the Art, Religion and Philosophy of the community. The Igbo has no demarcation between a strictly material, sensual world and a purely spiritual world. Both are united in a complete world view which sees entire life as an entity, whether alive or dead to join the ancestors of the clan. The dualism present in many European cultures concerning existence did not exist in Igboland - Now, the communal nature of African religion has been described as communalism by many African thinkers. In this communality, participation as theory and as praxis is of crucial importance; Thereby sharing, especially of food becomes the landmark of Igbo religion, life and practice.

---

2) Leonard, A.G., The Lower Niger and its Tribes., Frank Cass and Co. Ltd. 1968, London, p. 429.

(e) Land belongs to no one in this society. Land belongs to the
people - the community. But each individual and hence the family
has the right to the sacred and profane utilisation of the Land.
Appropriation in the absolute sense however, is forbidden.
Land is seen as God's gift to man for use and it is a sacred heritage,
transmitted by the forefathers as a bond between the living and the
dead, to be held in trust by each generation on behalf and for
those not yet born. Thus, the three levels of a unitary existence is
made manifest for the Igbo, namely: the dead ancestors, the present
living generation, and the unborn people on whom the future
depends, but who in their own turn, continues the tradition of the
triune one.
(f) In such a pure Igbo society, governed by this strong belief in
the three levels of existence, multiple wives were allowed as
practice, since thereby, many children could be brought into existence,
and the present living could share a greater solidarity, achieve more,
plant more and feel a sense of belonging. The unmarried woman or the
barren woman was a curse, hence, in traditional Igbo culture,
multiple wives was a sign of wealth for the community, and a protection
for those women who otherwise would live lonely and unproductive, or
rather, be tempted to live outside the ethical boundaries allowed by the
society by going into promiscuity.

(g) But the elders as transmitters of past experiences, as the
existential links between the past and present, as the nearest
members to the other world where the ancestors are, merited high respect,
merited recognition for a war through the hazards of life's hard vicissitudes.

(h) The pure Igbo society is fundamentally egalitarian, because it
guaranteed freedom to live, to speak out, to move about and feed one's
family. It was a society where the community and the individual
complemented each other in a harmonious whole, where the aged were cared for,
the young encouraged, and the dead laid to rest. The right to rebel, to
say No and to protest was guaranteed. Therefore, there was no King.
There was equal chance as God created all men equal.

MAP OF NIGERIA SHOWING IGBOLAND

3. Attitude to Human Work in Igbo Traditional Society

In discussing the attitude of the Igbo to work in traditional society,
it must be made clear that some of those traits have disappeared
in modern times among the same people, and this is understandable.
The times have changed; influences from Europe, America and other
African and world communities have infested Igboland, and the
caption of S.Ottenberg's book "Ibo receptivity to change" is being
daily experienced among the Igbos of today. The society is no longer
strictly an agricultural one, as technique, industrialisation,
commercialisation and new government jobs, among others have invaded
the economic scene. We shall however attempt here to describe what
basic attitudes accompanied the Igbo in pre-colonial times, in his
idea of human work.

First of all, human work was understood in traditional society as
a fundamental dimension of man's existence here on earth, because,
through work, man was able to change, reorganise, and restructure
his society. Work was therefore regarded as a creative activity,
Man built his house, built up his family, the village assembly,
the village square and the places of worship - all through work.
The arts and sculptures of traditional Igbo society are all products
of work, so that work in the first place guaranteed this creativity
of man, as no other level of organic living beings, such as animals
could reach this stage.

Secondly, the Igbo understood under human work, a means to feed
himself and his family and kindred. Here, work was regarded as a
necessity of nature to keep body and soul together, without which,
the society would disappear. In this context, the Igbo in traditional
society, as Basden has tried to show, toiled "when there was a great
necessity, either hunger, or else superior force"[3].

---

3) Basden, G.T., Niger Ibos, op.cit., p.299

Leisure is very appreciated and people would not overwork when it was not called for. The so-called 'Leistungsgessellschaft'- based only on the principle of continuous production and consumption was lacking in the society. What was produced, was also consumed, because the production was necessary, and the consumer was desirously needy of whatever was produced. Summarily, there were two sole inducements to work, namely,

(a) To provide basic foodstuff for the family and the kindred, and
(b) To provide shelter for the family[4].

Thirdly, work was understood in Igboland as a corporate activity, performed by all members of the community and family. Through work a man, his wife or wives, and children were able to engage themselves in a united and concerted action to complement each other and fulfil their basic needs. Painful, though it was, work was regarded as a normal human activity in traditional society. It was a part of life, in the words of Arinze : "Nobody was called a worker because everybody was a worker. It was taken for granted that everyone did some useful work, and most of it was rural"[5].

---

4) Ibid

5) Arinze, A.F., The Encyclical Laborem Exercens in the African Context., (Paper at Symposium: 'From Rerum Novarum to Laborem Exercens-Towards the year 2000'., Rome, 3-5th April, 1982; Pontifical Commission "Iustitia et Pax", p. 208.

Seen in this way, the ramblings in Europe in the nineteenth century
concerning the situation of the "working-classes" and the "employers",
could not make any sense for the Igbo of the same period.
The "Communist Manifesto" could not have been understood, and its contents
could have given the primitive Igbo a wonderful opportunity to
console himself and release a long relaxing laugh of his own
economic strenght.

It is clear to us that among the Romans and Greeks of olden times,
manual labour were usually left to hired hands and slaves, since
it was a "mean" job for the citizens. Worthy of free men was
work on poetry, science, philosophy and the art of participation in
government. Cicero expresses the attitude of the Roman aristocrats
of his time towards manual labour thus: "All manual labourers are
engaged in a shabby business, and there is nothing noble in a workshop"[6].

Totally contrary to this attitude was the Igbo view of work, which
considered one kind of labour, namely, that of the farmer, as a noble
activity. Praises were lavished on the successful yam farmer, and he
had a noble status in the society. To show the nobility of work,
W.T. Morril is quoted by Smock to have noted of the Igbo:
"No work is 'beneath' an Igbo man's dignity. Only sloth is"[7].

---

6) Cicero, De Officiis, 1, 42
7) Smock, D and Smock, A., Cultural and Political Aspects of
   Rural Transformation: A case study of Eastern Nigeria,
   Praeger Publ., New York, 1972, p. 5

As is well noted, the traditional Igbo gave their work their finest expression of skill and talent to impress the neighbours and to avoid being labelled lazy. Through work in the farm personal effort was rewarded in the society by the former receiving acknowledged traditional titles of the village, such as: "Di Ji", "Eze Ji", "Ogbuefi", "Ozo, "Oka ome", "Ugo di na mba" and "Ome mgbe oji". But extravagant and unnecessary accumulation of wealth was discouraged. Work was thus an activity to satisfy the basic demands of life.

a) Why this Attitude to Work?

This attitude to work is understandable for various reasons.

(i) The climate was tropical, plenty of sunshine, sometimes very hard on the worker. Average temperature ranged annually to about 80^{0F} or $/27^{0C}$). The rainfall decreases from south to north and is annually about 70 inches falling heavily from the months of April to October with a pause in August called August-Break.

This shows that there are only two clear seasons: the wet season or rainy season and the dry season, which takes place from November to March annually. This clear weather division into rainy and dry seasons, makes it imperative for the Igbo to work and plant in the wet season, and to harvest and rest for the greater part of the dry season. Nature thus played a vital role in determining work tempo.

(ii)   The material needs in traditional society were not generally flambouyant. People had just the minimum for existence, as a strong sense of materialism, unnecessary amassing or accumulation of wealth was generally absent. There are many reasons for this, firstly, large wealth was not present, (that is the supply in the markets was not great), and secondly, people in traditional society did not have much money to buy themselves whatever they wanted. Contrasted with today's Igboland, one would almost be ashamed of the irresponsible and unnecessary consummerism practiced to show-off by the have-s as against the squalid situation of the have-nots. In traditional society, little property was enough: "cooking-and water-pots, a few implements, some grass mats, completed the list of necessary property. Whatever accrued beyond these counted as 'luxury'[8].

(iii)   Thirdly, the needs of the family and of life were basically on the whole easily satisfied. The farms supplied practically all the food needed for daily consumption - yams, cassava, vegetables and fruits. Meat was available through hunters' activities, and its consumption was often modest. Igboland is geographically located within five friendly agricultural or vegetational belts, namely: mangrove forest, freshwater swamp forest, rain forest, derived savana and guinea savana zones[9]. Added to this was the modest implements such as hoes, matchets and cutlass used for farm work, which made cultivation reduced barely at the minimum and necessary. Of course, there are many other reasons why the Igbo attitude to work was so but we shall reduce our research here to the already mentioned reasons.

---

8) Basden, Ibid.

9) Nwabara, N.S., Iboland - A century of contact with Britain - 1860 - 1960., Hodder and Stoughton, London, 1977, p.15

b) Agriculture - The basic Economic Sub-Structure of Igbo Society

One of the basic economic sub-structures on which traditional
Igbo societies rested was agriculture, followed by trade and the
manufacture of artworks and different types of crafts.

In tropical Africa (extending into our own times), agricultural
production was and is the main source of subsistence for the rural
and urban populations. Through agriculture also, key commodities
for the foreign trade that brings in the much-needed technology and
industrial goods that foster growth were provided.
It is therefore no surprise that the increasing failure of growth
in the agricultural sector has kept many African nations in a
continuous state of development, as modern development studies show[10].

In pre-colonial Igbo society, agriculture "was important economic
activity with regard to both the number of people engaged in it either
in full or in part time basis, and to the prestige it carried"[11].
Farming was seen as the chief occupation, and all other activities,
such as trading, were regarded as a subsidiary but not a
substitute for it. As M.M. Green has pointed out:
"Igbo society existed mainly on subsistence agriculture. This
agriculture could keep the people going because of the multiple ties
holding the agricultural family together, the joint work done with
primitive mechanisation such as hoes and matchets and knives..."[12].

---

10) Altaf Gauhar (ed)., Talking About Development., Third World
    Foundation for Social and Economic Studies, London, 1983.
11) Afigbo, E.A., Economic Foundations of pre-colonial Igbo Society,
    op.cit, p. 2
12) Green, M.M., op.cit., p.32 ff.

How ancient agriculture looked like in traditional Igboland
is a matter of great speculation and difficulty for scholars, and
Afigbo thinks that 'it is nonsense trying to explain its origin
in terms of lessons learnt from outside Africa'[13]. Surely of
course, there was an earlier period of hunting and gathering,
but this period has disappeared into mythology, understood as
"the dynamic age of Chukwu (God), when he created and dominated
the Igbo world. But with the coming of agriculture, Igbo gaze
would appear to have been switched from the skies above to
theearth below - with Ala (the Earth deity) displacing Chukwu
into remote inactivity"[14].

Professor J.E. Flint regards pre-colonial Igbo agriculture to have
been very efficient, as perhaps the most efficient in Africa", and
he thinks this was largely responsible for a big population in these
areas, for the Igbo "developed a density per acre only matched in
Africa by that of the Nile valley"[15]. Such an efficiency can be
seen in the manner Igbo's used and manipulated tools such as hoes,
cutlasses, matchets to reduce their environment, originally, a
tropical-rain-forest and mangrove region to either grassland or
Palm-bush vegetation. One would therefore agree with Professor
Afigbo who maintains that "Igbo agriculture had by the first millenium
A.D. become so advanced that it could support the civilisation with
which Igbo Ukwu archeological excavations have been associated"[16].

---

13) Afigbo, A.E., op.cit., p.3
14) Afigbo, E.A., Ropes of Sand-Studies in Igbo History, UPL, Oxford, 1981
    p.10
15) Flint, E.J., Nigeria and Ghana, New Jersey, 1966, p. 63
16) Afigbo, E.A., Economic Foundations of pre-colonial Igbo Society, p.3
    (Recently, an exhibition went through the capital cities of the
    world's biggest metropoles including Hildesheim in Germany. This
    exhibition from Nigeria's past was summarised in a book called
    'Kunstschätze aus Alt-Nigeria', Ekpo Eyo und Fran Willet (eds)
    Verlag Philipp von Zabern, Mainz, c.1983., Igbo-Ukwu findings are
    there - in explicated).

And it must have taken centuries of slow development for it to attain that stage. It is thus quite clear that Igbo agriculture is ancient indeed, so ancient that the Igbo tend to associate the coming of cultivation with the emergence of Igbo society, or even with the very creation of the Igbo world[17].

From the aforementioned, every able bodied man or woman was more or less a farmer, either as main occupation as in most cases, or as second occupation for those who were predominatly traders or artists. Families produced staple food to feed themselves, some of which included yams, coco-yams, cassava, maize, vegetables, palm products, fruits of all sorts and nuts. The larger the family, the bigger the produce of agriculture, as many hands worked together to raise the quantity of production. It is reasonable to presume, that the system of many wives having only one husband, can be explained away with this attitude to agriculture. For, to have many wives, to beget many children was, besides, the general live for children, also an economic advantage, considered as "wealth par excellence" since the agricultureal produce increased quantitatively as many hands were engaged in farm work.

The fruits of work after harvesting went first of all to the owner or owners of the farm. But since the farm-owner is not an isolated individual but has a "social personality" - as father of children, husband of wife or wives, member of an extended family, kindred group or clan, titled elder, the fruits of the farm went beyond the owner of farm alone to satisfy the communal demands for shared fruits from the earth as a result of shared labour. So was the understanding of human labour in traditional Igbo society.

_____

17) Afigbo, E.A., Ibid.

4. Sources of Labour - Family, Community, Clientage, Slaves, etc.

a) Division of Labour in the Family

We have already seen that in pre-colonial Igbo society, agriculture
was the main economic structure predominant in the community.
And because it was subsistence agriculture, whereby people cultivated
primarily to feed themselves well than to sell the products ,
the family therefore became the first source of labour for the family farm.

In the words of M.M. Green: "Labour is provided entirely by the
family - the household made up of a man, his wife or wives and
children - and these cooperated as the basic unit for the production
of food crops, although a certain amount of outside help may be
sought"[18]. Because each family did its work on the farm for itself,
large families became a valued form of societal life.
A man who wanted to prosper as a farmer had to marry so many wives
and beget many children, as these would also help maximise the
production of goods in the farm. Thus, childless women were sent
back to their parents in the form of divorce, or as was general in the
society, did not get much honour and respect. However, Polygamy and the
extended family is not fully explained by the economic phenomenon alone
as we shall later see. However, economics played a vital role, since
the 'Di Ji' (successful farmer of yams) needed many hands for his farm
to grow and his prestige in the community to be acknowledged.
Consequently, since agriculture was the fundamental and most general type
of work in Igboland, work on the family land assumed great importance,
and labour was divided up for the man, his wife or wives and the children.

---

18) Green, M.M., Igbo Village Affairs, op.cit., p. 35
     (Refer also to G.T. Basden, "Among the Ibos of Nigeria", where he
     says: "Usually, each household raised its own crop by its own
     labour and is responsible for its members". (p.151).

(i) The Men: They planted the yams and attended to it throughout
the yam season till the harvest, putting sticks to its tendrils
and digging the mounds. Besides, only the men tap palm wine
and climb trees to cut down the palm oil nuts. House building
was a man's affair, besides clearing the bush, protecting the
family from external enemies, and seeing to it that law and
order was kept by the wives and the children. He had
therefore to play a neutral role in many quarrels arising among
the womenfolk of his household, and had to control their
tempers, discipline them as well as their children[19].

The man shared out land for farming to his wives and helped
them clear the bush on it, and he saw to it that his children
also got sufficient lands to plant their own products on
family land. In clan or lineage affairs, or even in religious
matters, the man has the primary function of pouring libation
to the ancestors for his family, and of representing the
family in matters concerning the entire village.

---

19) The book written by Chinue Achebe "Things Fall Apart", portrays the
role of the man Okonkwo, marrying three wives, and his
position among his womenfolk. (Published by Heinemann,
London, African Writers Series, C.1958).

(ii) <u>The Women:</u>   It was the specified work of the woman to plant
certain crops such as coco-yams and cassava, and men were
generally kept off from these crops. For a man to indulge
himself with planting coco-yams could merit him a bad name in the
village, as "He who meddles in women's affairs". He would
even be termed "a woman" by his age grade.

The women also did the work of weeding grass during planting
season from the farms. When the men worked in the yam plantation,
she cooked food for the family, so that, it is even the primary
work of the woman to feed the household, look after the children,
and organise the internal affairs of the family, together with
her husband. When the men had cut the palm nuts, the women
worked them into palm oil. Spinning of cotton and weaving thread
into cloth was also a woman's job in traditional Igbo societies[20],
manufacture of baskets and earthenware for cooking and water pots[21].

(iii) <u>The children:</u> Children helped with farm work at an unusually early
age, perhaps, about seven years old, as the boys received yams from
their fathers to plant for themselves and to learn to feed themselves
and their families when they are grown. The girls fetched water,
washed the plates, fetched firewood together with their brothers
and kept the house tidy. As Talbot has tried to show in "The Peoples
of Southern Nigeria, Vol. II": Children are taken to farm by their
mothers from the earliest age, and begin to work as soon as they
are able to weed or to wield a matchet - say from six to ten years
old, while girls begin to fetch water at the same age and both sexes
to carry small loads from the farm to the house"[22].

---

20)   Writes Olaudah Equiano in the 18th century: "When our women are not
      employed in village with men, their usual occupation is spinning
      and weaving cotton.. They also manufacture earthen vessels of
      many kinds".
21)   Basden G.T; op.cit. pp. 325 - 328
22)   Talbot, The Peoples of Southern Nigeria, Vol. II, p. 389

b) Community Labour or Communal Solidarity Through Work:

Besides work performed solely by the family to grow its farm, there
was also another source of labour in traditional Igbo society,
namely Communal Labour. Communal labour was very commonly practised
in Igboland. This is even explained from the people's world view
which believed strongly in group solidarity, often expressed in
"Igbo Kwenu" mentality, or as the saying has it: "Igwe bu ike"
meaning that "Community is strength" This community spirit, already
discussed earlier in this work, guaranteed the spontaneous aid given
to any in need. The main social investment available to a man was
investment in personal relationships with others. Each family
under subsistence conditions is too small to support itself, and
it cannot depend simply on a sort of impersonal network. It needed
a large kit and kin, distantly and proximately related kindred,
descendants of recently living common ancestors and in-laws.

No wonder the Igbos say: "Onye nwere madu ka onye nwere ego" or
"Nwakego", meaning that "He who has people and relations is richer
and stronger than he who has merely money". Thus, a child is worth
more than money, because, a child when grown - up, can produce money.
We thus invest our wealth in gaining the right to demand goods and
services from other people, as Max Gluckman has said:

"Men acquire their rights to call on the services of others by
putting them under obligations of reciprocity, by helping them with
goods and services, and usually they do so through established
kinship relations, or by entering into marriage alliances with them.
Even trading relations are converted into quasi-kinship relationships"[23].

---

23) Gluckman, M., Politics, Law and Ritual in Tribal Society; Blackwell,
Oxford, 1977, p.13 - 14.

These relations of kinship and quasi-kinship enable a man to mobilise labour to assist him in major tasks and they are also insurance against disaster and shortage since he can call on his kit and kin and in-laws to help him when he is in need.

Gluckman has shown that in primitive societies such as in Barotséland in today's Zambia, men begin by bartering with one another, and when they have bartered a few times they strike up a compact of friendship with general obligations of hospitality and help, until they may eventually go through a rite which makes them "blood brothers"[24].

Well, in Igboland, people did not need to go through a rite to become "blood brothers". They enjoyed a natural blood-kinship, extended by the status of belonging to a village, clan and family. Thus, when a man wished to build his house or hut, or to farm a very large area of land, it is generally certain that his brothers, age-grade or other landsmen would help him in his project. He did not need to pay them any cash, but traditional courtesy demanded that he prepare some meal and arrange some palm-wine for the co-workers at the end of day as gratitude. And when they needed his help in their own work, they paid back the same compliment.

Arinze says: "Work had a community aspect. People worked as members of the family, clan, village, age-grade or other group... It also happens that a farmer obtains help for some days in his farm work from young men or women, or from his age-grade and companions. In this last case, he has to return the compliment to another period"[25].

---

24) Ibid
25) Arinze, A.F., The Encyclical Laborem Exercens in the African Context. Paper at Symposium, op. cit., p.209.

Likewise G.T. Basden records his observances in the Igbo country
as follows: "When a man plans to bu id a house, he relies on the
co-operation of his relatives and friends... No wages are paid, but
the workers are mollified with supplies of food and drink"[26].

(i) <u>Labour is Jointly Shared:</u>   When labour like clearing of the market square,
the roads, village square or places of ritual comes up, information is
given to the people on the advice of the village elders through the
town crier, who announces the details of time, place and date,
including fines for absentees. When the villages are assembled for
work, which is often shared out in groups of age-grades or hamlets or
family lineage, the work is easily and immediately carried out.
Mrs. M.M. Green observed that "a team work may be accompanied by
singing with a consequent hightening of sense of solidarity which also
finds expression in dancing of men on market days, and of women in
the market places on other days"[27].

A passer-by who sees people at work was normally courteous and greeted
them, helping out in the work for some time, before continuing
his journey. Not to do this merited for him a bad name among his people.
Nevertheless, he could always tell the workers that he would help
if he had enough time, and such an excuse would be readily accepted.
Like Arinze points out, at harvest time, a helper would be remunerated[28].

Reciprocity is thus within the village, constantly operative in
maintaining the economic and social stability of the people. Wages
were not paid as pre-condition for communal labour, and workers
who tried to cheat others merited for themselves very bad names, for
the cheaters were correspondingly treated.

---

26) Basden, G.T., op.cit., (Niger Ibos), p.312
27) Green, M.M., Igbo Village Affairs, op.cit., p.253
28) Arinze, A.F., Ibid.

(ii) Absentees and Anti-Communal Workers were Punished:

Like in every other society, not everyone adheres to the norms
or the general demand to communal duty. In Igboland, there were
members who tried to cheat when communal labour was announced. They
claimed to be either sick, or to be incapable for one reason or the
other and were labelled "Onye aghughọ ọlu", meaning "a cheater at work".
Such recalcitrants were very harshly dealt with. After the
communal labour, a group of young men from the village were asked
to search out for the absentees. Among these, those without
adequate or convincing reasons were charged of indiscipline,
betrayal of communal work-moral, or laziness. They were fined
a certain amount or had their properties seized for failing to
produce the fine. In other cases, they were punished by having
to perform the same work for which the community was fining them
for being absent. It is significant to state here that Igbo
communal consciousness did not allow the punished ones to suffer alone.
Through the solidarity of their own friends or kinsmen, they were
helped to pay up the fine or to finish tne work marked out for
them as fine by the community.

Those however, who were absent from communal labour with convincing
reasons such as death in the family, birth, marriage commitments
and such like were not levied. However, these were still expected
to manifest their solidarity by sending cola-nuts or palm-wine drinks
or sliced cassava (Mbacha) to those other members who worked.
The women prepared food and drinks as part of their contribution
to the communal work.
Incorrigible absentees ran the risk of excommunication from the society
for their uncollegial attitude and this served as a preventive
warning to all those who were lazy or tried to cheat the society.

c) Clientage:

Clients were those who enjoyed the protection and patronage of a
rich farmer for whom they worked for. In traditional Igbo society,
clientage was another source of labour for the farm workers.
The rich farmer who cultivated large barns of yams needed many hands
to help him out in his farm work. Thus, his clients were people
who had taken yams or money on loan from other people and could not
pay back at the appointed time. The rich farmer made them work for
him on stated days of the week for a given period, after which, if the
loan was taken from the 'Di Ji' himself, it was regarded as settled,
but if from other people, he either paid these workers
to pay back, or paid it back himself.

Nwakibie, in Okonkwo's "Things Fall Apart" is a typical example[29].
"There was a wealthy man in Okonkwo's village who had three huge
barns, nine wives and thirty children. His name was Nwakibie and
he had taken the highest but one title which a man could take in
the clan. It was for this man that Okonkwo worked to earn his first
seed yams..." And later in the chapter, Okonkwo is presented to
have asked for aid thus: "I have come to you for help. ... I have
cleared a farm but have no yams to sow. I know what it is to ask
a man to trust another with his yams, especially these days when
young men are afraid of hard work... If you give me some seed yams
I shall not fail you"[30].

Nwakibie had granted Okonkwo's request with the hope that Okonkwo managed
well to build up for himself and his family - some reasonable
means of livelihood. Nwakibie said: "it pleases me to see a young
man like you these days when our youth have gone so soft. Many
young men have come to beg for yams but I have refused because I knew they

---

29)   Achebe, C., Things Fall Apart., op.cit., chapter 3. pp.12 -18
30)   Ibid., pp. 15-16

would dump them in the earth and leave them to be choked by weeds...
I have learnt to be stingy with my yams. But I can trust you.
I know it as I look at you... I shall give you twice four hundred
yams. Go ahead and prepare your farm"[30a].

Achebe in this passage, does not portray Okonkwo as having worked
for Nwakibie. He was rather a borrower. But in the many
circumstances where clientage was practiced, people like Nwakibie agreed
to give yams to young farmers, on the condition that they had
worked for him for a considerable time. Thus, labour was guaranteed in
the farm work in traditional society.

d) Slave Labour (Oru - Ohu):

In times of war, slaves were captured and kept by the villages who held them.
These slaves were engaged by individuals or the community in farm
work, even though the rich farmer could not abandon his precious yams
to the hands of a foreigner - a slave who could damage these crops.
Like the Igbos generally say, he is foolish who abandones
the fate of his yams to slaves. Slave labour should therefore be
understood as a mere supplement to farm work, rather than it supplanted
the labour of the free born in their farm land. It has also been
mentioned by many European scholars on Africa that the status of a
slave within the village communities, differed greatly with the
status of a slave during the Euro-trans-atlantic slave trade.

David Livingstone who opposed the external trading of men as slaves
in Southern Africa, wrote· about the Ndebele of Southern Zimbabwe,
quoting a missionary: "The African slave, brought by a foray to the
tribe, enjoys, from the beginning, the privileges and name of a child,
and looks upon his master and mistress in every respect as his new
parents. He is not only nearly his master's equal, but he may

---

30a) Ibid.

with impunity, leave his master and go wherever he likes within
the boundary of the kingdom. Although a bondman or a servant, his
position does not convey the true ideas of a state of slavery;
for, by care and diligence, he may soon become a master himself,
and even more rich and powerful than he who led him captive"[31].

Contrary however to this humane and benevolent attitude exhibited
to slaves was their treatment under the trans-atlantic route in
the hands of European dealers. Olaudah Equiano, himself an
ex-Igbo slave in the eighteenth century records in his memoirs
these differences and his treatment as a slave under the
Europeans as terribly cruel, wicked and inhuman[32].
And the missionary quoted by Livingstone is to have said:
"neither the punctuality, thoroughness, nor amount of exertion is
required by the African slave master as by the European master"[33].

One could therefore not force a slave to work as one wanted
because he could destroy the owners farms by bad job, and nothing
could be done about it. Negotiation was thence called for. And this
negotiation was carried out by another group of workers called
'Ohe oru' who went from place to place seeking job. In modern times,
Igbos call them "Ndi ana m achio Olu", meaning those searching for job.

---

31) Livingstone, D., Quoting a Missionary who lived and worked among
the people. Refer Max Gluckman, op.cit., p.15
32) Olaudah Equiano, Equiano's Travels, op.cit.
33) Livingstone, D., Ibid.

Although not a peculiarity of earlier times, these people,
mostly young people, went away in the dry season to do farm work
or odd jobs for others in the districts or far away villages for money.
They were housed in their new places of work and paid some money.
They lived there, ate there together with the owner of farm and
jointly negotiated the price. In other words, the "Ana m acho Olu"
stated his condition of service to the far-owner, and refused to
work if his condition was not met. This is contrary to the
capitalist mode of employing labourers, which, in its roughest forms,
dictated the price for the employee who had no other alternative but
to accept the job. One could therefore contrast Igbo job takers
against labourers in capitalist mode of production. For whereas the
Igbo worker decided the conditions of work, and the master had
no choice but to accept, the nineteenth century capitalist
and its modern followers decided the price of work and the conditions
of work, and the labourer has no alternative but to accept.

5. An early form of Personalism?

It has to be said with all emphasis that in traditional Igbo economy,
workers were not merely "labour forces" or "means of production",
who were alienated from work and had no personality.
The Igbo world of work knew to cherish free time, to work
because of necessity in order to produce that which was needed for the
upkeep of the family, and finally to produce that which was
essential to the community. As Arch-bishop Arinze has said:
"There is in the Igbo world of work a personal sharing, identification
and interest by workers in the work done - whether it is their own or
that of another person. This is so because the workers are
not regarded as mere "labour force" or "pairs of hands" who are "hired" on
pay for the job. Work is not regarded as a commodity with a
price tag on it.

The "worker" shares active interest with the farm-owner, discusses
and suggests his views on the manner of work with him, and they
eat together after work. The owner would give them some of
the fruits and products of the work during the right season"[34].
In this manner, a certain sort of early personalism was developed
in Igbo culture. People worked in freedom, put in all their might,
art and strength to produce the best for themselves and for their
community. Work was not looked upon as alienation, as industrial
Europe, experience shows, but remained a means of self-realisation.

---

34) Arinze, A.F., op.cit., p.209

a) Traditional Igbo Society - Absence of the Rich versus the Poor

It is generally known that in tribal societies, they had all primary goods, and hardly any luxuries, for their farm products had to be practically consumed within a relatively short time. Foods which remained for a long time got easily rotten or consumed by mots and insects, as the natives had very simple means of storage for food. Their wears or clothes were made of animal skin or barkcloth or other material relatively simple. People lived, not in palaces or in feudal houses like in middle-ages Europe, but in mud and grass houses, skin tents and so forth. In this situation, a rich man could not easily arise who would use his wealth to raise his own standard of living or those of his neighbours. Chiefs and titled men had no palaces and no costly robes, (although the situation in the palace houses of certain kingdoms changed as soon as their was a cultural contact with either Europe or other Arabian and upper kingdoms). A man with a thousand head of cattle could not consume all the milk produced alone, nor their meat and skins. He could only use them, as happened among nomadic tribes, attract and support dependants and thus acquire power over people.

In Igbo traditional society however, there was a marked absence of rich and poor classes. People were generally farmers and they grew their own food. Since most of them cultivate the same type of food, it is to be expected that their diet would be almost identical. There was a technological limitation to what wealth could bring about to cause a class system among the people, as Max Gluckman has mentioned: "With available tools - axe, hoe and adze, spear and trap, bows and arrows, dugouts or canoes and fishing-nets, each man can produce little beyond what he himself can consume. Hence though the poor might work for those who have more, they cannot be employed to give the rich an elaborate level of life above their own"[35]

---

35) Gluckman, M., op.cit., p. 15.

Under this condition therefore, the rich could not get rich
in their production and acquisition as the possibilities for
storage were limited, nor could the poor get poorer in their consumption
of excess. Mrs. Green also observes on this point:
"Another relevant economic fact is the absence of marked differences
of wealth between one individual and another... There are of
course variations: some people have more land than others, and more
trees of economic value than others. Some are better of
in respect of more wives and children than others. A few
people own several cows, but as there is little opportunity for
the accumulation of capital, no well defined wealthy class emerged"[36].

It is thus clear that as most of traditional Igbo people
were farmers at subsistent level, so was it very difficult to
create a class of haves and have-nots, for everyone was forced to eat
the same food, and live under the same circumstances.
Max Gluckman makes this point very clearly where he writes:
'the possession of wealth in the Solomon Islands, as amongst
ourselves (Europeans) ensures prestige. But in a native community,
the same scale of comforts - or lack of them - is available for all;
everyone has to spend several hours of the day at the same kind of
work, all eat the same kind of food prepared in the same utensils
from similar raw foods, all sleep on the same kinds of mats or beds.
The house of a wealthy man may be larger it is true, and better
built than that of one who is insignificant, and he may have
several wives, but the difference is otherwise negligible.
Reputation is accordingly enhanced not by accumulating in order to use
them oneself, but by giving them away"[37]

---

36) Green, M.M., op.cit., pp. 43 - 44
37) Gluckman, M., Ibid.

We must however distinguish between the wish to be rich and
the limitations imposed by external circumstances, which
prevented the potentially wealthy from being actually
wealthy. The Igbos are highly competitive, even though
this competitive spirit was marked as co-operation.
Surely, status dominated traditional Igbo society as
people took titles such as "Ozo", "Eze Ji","Ogbuefi",
"Omemgbeoji", among others. As has already been
mentioned above, the amount wealth could bring to an individual
wishing to be rich was severely restricted by the type
of tools used, the kinds of goods produced, and the amount of
trade available. The economy was therefore egalitarian,
for the powerful and wealthy used their might and goods
to support dependants who were unable to produce enough for
their own standards and with the material available.
In this way, marked differences between a rich class and a
poor was generally absent in traditional Igbo communities.
And because the Igbos lacked a feudal or central form of
government, no one ruler or monarch demanded taxes from the
populace to make himself rich, as was the case in Europe and
many other kingly societies of the past.

b) Hard Worker Praised

A lazy worker, was, if detected, harshly dealt with, strongly
criticised, and ran the risk of having a bad reputation in
the village - the worst thing that could befall an Igbo man
in traditional society. The Igbos love a good name:
"Afamefuna" - "May my name not be lost", and so one was
encouraged to strive through work to achieve independence for
oneself and one's family. A lazy man was a burden to
others and this was a sign of weakness, just as idleness
during the working season was not admired. People suspected
an idler who had land but chose to be lazy to be a thief in
potency, and therefore a threat to the community. Proverbs
to elucidate this point abound, which consider laziness to be a
bad thing. "Ngana kpue ute aguu ekpughe ya" - meaning
that "Hunger teaches an idle man that he has to work hard".

Igbo society placed a high premium on hard work, and so, not only
valued the hard-worker but held him up for admiration. He provided
the theme for edifying songs and tales, while the lazy man was the
subject of ribald songs and jokes. The Elders often advised their
youth with admonitions to hard work, as Green has pointed out:
"Property, money, honesty are constantly recurring motiffs.
Together with emphasis on loyalty between kinsmen, they are
prominent in the only long statement I collected about the qualities
or subjects that would be stressed in the upbringing of children" [38].

Elsewhere she says: "A girl who is considered to make a good wife
is one who is not shy of work, who will go for water and firewood,
who will not cook and go to market" [39], to come back and discover
that the food and pot is burnt to ashes.

In another instance, Professor Afigbo has proved that hard workers
merited respect, honour and title in the community. The Eze Ji
title (King of Yams) was open to any freeborn Igbo who through hard
work had been able to cultivate several barns of yams, not only
to feed himself and family, but when necessary, to call a feast of
entire kindred at his own expense. Members of the Eze Ji title
served as experts in yam cultivation, and their opinions were
generally sought in disputes over yams and farming land, and young men
in the farming business contacted them for advice or for a loan
of yams - counted in quantities of four hundred seeds or Nnu [40].

The case of Unoka, Okonkwo's father in the book "Things fall Apart"
highlights the point been made here about the lazy and hard worker in
Igbo society [41]. Here, Unoka was labelled "a failure in life".

---

38) Green, M.M., op.cit., p. 89

39) Ibid., p. 90

4o.) Afigbo, E.A., Economic Foundations of Pre-colonial Igboland, op,cit.
     p. 5

41) Achebe, C., Things Fall Apart, pp.cit., pp.3 - 5

6. Women and Work:

Women have been said by certain authors to have occupied a relatively
human position for the most part in traditional life. Other
observers claim the opposite, maintaining that women had a
highly and respected position. On this point, there can be no
general opinion as various villages had various status for women.

In Ohafia, for example, which is a well-known matrilineal society
and in many other parts of Igboland such as Onitsha, the woman
played a most prominent role. She was not only mother, but was
relevant in all aspects of the people's life, especially in
religion, politics, economics and culture. There was therefore in
Igboland no unitary view concerning the role or status of women.

Basden, in his observations about the role of women in traditional
society exposes these two views. On the one hand, the women were
to be seen but not heard in affairs that pertained to men alone;
On the other hand, women were highly valued and regarded as
indispensable to society, eventhough their role was determined by
custom. Unless specifically requested to do so, women in many
Igbo villages would not present themselves before the council of
Elders or the Village Council, where issues of great external or
internal importance were discussed. It was generally believed that
women could not keep secrets - for their mouths were always open to
reveal the minutest secrets at the slightest opportunity.
This disadvantage debarred them from enjoying the village's secrets.
As Olaudah Equiano points out in his narratives:

"a rich man could buy titles for his son or initiate him into the
secrets of these societies, but this did not entitle the boy
to know the secrets of these societies as it was feared that children,
like women, could not keep their mouths shut"[42).

However, in general, women were not neglected in the geo-political
organisation of Igbo society. They played, it is said,:
"a very central, dynamic and active role in various aspects of the
village life". Although men appeared in the public and village
squares, they were usually influenced by their wives, hence women
are colled "Uche di ya" meaning "the mind of her husband"; or called
"Oriaku" meaning "she who enjoys the wealth".

The dynamic and centrally politicised role of women in Igbo society
became clearer during the colonial rule under the British. Two
incidents can be briefly pointed out here, namely :
      (a)   The Aba Women's riot of 1929, and
      (b)   The Udi women's revolt of 1940.

We shall touch briefly on the first, quoting the views noted by
British Officer Dr. K. Meek: "Towards the close of 1929 riots of an
unprecedented kind broke out with startling suddenness in two of the
South-Eastern Provinces of Nigeria. The rioters were women - not a
few enthusiasts, but women en masse - who formed themselves into mobs
armed themselves with cudgels, and marched up and down the country,
holding up the roads, howling down the Government, setting fire
to the Native Court buildings, assaulting their chiefs, and working
themselves generally into such a state of frenzy that on several
occasions they did not hesitate to challenge the troops sent to restore order.

---

42)   Olaudah Equiano., Equiano's Travels, (1794)., Edited by Norwich, p.4

The rioting continued vigorously for several weeks...but in the meantime, many of the rioters had lost their lives and heavy damage had been done to the property of the Native Administration and of numerous European trading firms"[43).

The cause of this riot of women in Aba is clear - imposition of British rule, imposition of Native Authorities and Warrant Chiefs in an Igbo community which knew no kings, introduction of direct tax, and fall of prices of native goods. The former Governor-General of Nigeria, and the man who created the Nigeria we know today, Lord Lugard had this to say on this incident: "Misconceptions regarding the incidence of the direct tax introduced in 1927, added to the fall in the prices of native produce, served to set fire to the highly inflammable material and produced the strange phenomenon of the women's riots in 1929. The Government could not afford to delay the introduction of the necessary reforms" [44), some of which included a modification of the system of direct rule, withdrawal of the tax imposition and accelerated attempt to democratise Igboland. We need no further commentaries to demonstrate the strength, power and political consciousness of Igbo women, at such an early stage.

A second example occured, though on a village level in Udi in the year 1940. The then resident British colonial officer, Mr. Chadwick, enacted an Edict, demanding of every farmer, an accurate head-count of all Palm Trees and economic trees belonging to each person. The Udi women revolted and protested, demonstrating

---

43) Meek, K.C., Law and Authority in a Nigerian Tribe, (1937), Humanities Press, Oxford, p.ix. Dr. Meek was lately anthropological officer serving Great Britain in the Nigerian Administrative Colonial Service.

44) The Right Hon. Lord Lugard, G.C.M.G., Quoted from a Foreward to Dr. Meek's book, op.cit., p.vi

furiously before Mr. Chadwick, for they saw this as an attempt to impose more taxation on them. Afraid of what might happen, Mr. Chadwick rescinded the decision.

As has been seen, women were not only house maids in traditional Igbo society. Traditional society ordered work into divisions - for men, for women and for children. Roles and functions were divided out in the Igbo world of work, and for women, particular types of activities were aportioned out to them such as to allow them be first of all wives and mothers. Besides these, women played other roles in the society. They were the greatest traders of petty articles. On this Green says: "The women are the great petty traders, spending much time and energy for what must often be a very small profit... The time and energy are considerable, and already the women have much arduous work with their farming, cooking and palm-oil making, besides looking after the children and the household"[45].

Women were also active in organising themselves into groups of meetings, age-grades, age of marriage or rather years of marriage groups, as those who married in certain years became colleagues for the purposes of dancing, music, sharing out of goods or pressing their interests through.

Women acted as priestesses of certain gods, rain-makers, diviners or herbalists, seers and prophets and joined certain Guilds in the form of a pre-trade union.

Lastly, women also tried in their own way to preserve peace in the community. The story is told that once when Amokwe and Udi were engaged in a bitter fratricidal war, and attempts at peace had been futile, the women organised themselves and moved into the war-front where their men were battling, carrying with them palm-fronts and oil-bean leaves on their heads, When their warring husbands and men saw them, they dropped their matchets and weapons and went home.

---

45) Green, M.M. op.cit., p. 39

PART TWO (II) : Property Rights, Ownership and Laws of Inheritance

> "It is Chukwu and Ani that we invoke;
> Every people in their town call upon Chukwu and Ani...
> When the Akpu plant matures it falls,
> and rots on the Ground,
> No one can see it again.
> When the Iroko tree matures,
> it falls on the Ground.
> When man matures, he falls on the Ground" -
> (Rev. R.C. Arazu)

1. Introducing the Situation:

Land is the most valuable asset and the source of continued
existence for the Igbo people, both in pre-colonial times and in
modern Nigeria. All land was believed to belong to Ala, Ani, Ana -
the Earth - deity who owns all cattle, wild products, human beings
and ultimately all land. Traditional Igbos thus looked up to
Ala for a portion of good, arable land for grazing their cattle,
erecting their houses, fishing and farming their crops. Ala is
obliged by its Children to give everyone land to live on and land to
cultivate, and She must allow every subject to fish in public
waters (except on days prohibited), to hunt game and birds, to
gather wild fruits and to use the clay, iron ore, grasses,
reeds and trees with which the Igbo mould their pots, utensils,
mats, baskets, weapons, implements, nets and traps, furniture and huts
and needed medicaments.

The Earth-Goddess however was believed to be so benevolent
that she could not dispossess anybody of land, as these for the
Igbo belonged to that area which today will be called "Fundamental
Human Rights". The Igbos on their own worshipped and sacrificed to
Ala, the Spirit-Force and Earth-deity who owned all land, regarded
to be sacred.

2. Ownership of Land in Traditional Igbo Society (Four Various Classes)

Many early anthropologists have considered the very complex theme
of land ownership in Igbo land[1]. There is no united agreement
as to the status and ownership relationship of land to the people,
for whereas, some emphasise the communal ownership of all land,
others stress the fact that individuals owned land, while some
still maintain that land belonged to no one, and was only for the use of
citizens disposed. We shall now consider the ownership of land
under four classifications:

---

1) Meek. C., Land Law and Custom in the Colonies, London, Oxford
   University Press, 1968; Green, M.M., Land Tenure in an Ibo Village
   in South-Eastern Nigeria., London, Humphries, 1941;
   Liversage, V., Land Tenure in the Colonies, Cambridge University
   Press, 1945., Elias, O.T., Nigerian Land Law and Custom, London,
   Routledge and Kegan Paul, 1961; Elias, O.T., The Nature of African
   Customary Law, Manchester, University Press, 1956, Chapter IX;
   Eastern Nigerian Region: Policy for Lands,Paper No. 3 of 1955,
   Enugu Government Printers; Chubb, T.L., Ibo Land Tenure, Ibadan
   University Press, 1961.

a)   Land which is Sacred or Taboo

This includes sacred groves surrounding the shrines of public cults
(Ihu Ani), and land regarded as 'Ajo Ofia' or evil forest which are taboo
places. No one had permission to use such lands for private or
family affairs as these lands were regarded as property of the
deities or village spirits.. A bold farmer who dared however to clear
portions of the Evil forest for farming purposes would be forwarned
of the dangers involved in meddling with land owned by the spirits.
If he however did not give heed (as many modern Igbo Christians who no
longer regard the gods of their forefathers), but went on with
cultivation of the land, the elders and community would allow
him a certain period leading up to two years during which the Spirit -
Owners were supposed to harm the intruder, but failing, in which the
new intruder became the owner of the taboo forest. Sacred forests
used for worship were hardly tampered with by anyone[2]. The new
owner would often use such areas for farming purposes and it
eventually became his permanent land to be taken after his death by
his descendants.

b) Virgin Forests -

For some reason or the other, a village might migrate to an entirely new
site, occupying a large tract of land. In the proximate occupied area,
they built their houses and shared out the land to the various
family groups. But there still remained somewhere at the
outskirts of the village, land which has remained unused for farming
because nobody has required it, or because the village has forbidden
farming there for the purposes which it serves, such as defence against

---

2) Meek, K.C., Law and Authority in a Nigerian Tribe., op.cit., p.101.
    See also: Nwabara N.S., Iboland - A century of contact with Britain
    1860., Hodder and Stoughton, London, 1977,p.35.

village enemies, or as a shade, or as a source of supplies of fibre
and wood or for other ecological reasons. Such a land
constituted what is called virgin forest. This virgin
forest may also be given the name for the mere reason that nobody
has ever cleared the grounds there - and they remained public land
for whoever could clear the ground there and cultivate therein.
If the village is not particularly meticulous about this virgin
forest, any member of the village was at liberty to clear it and
cultivate his crops therein, thereby making such cleared virgin
forest to his own property, a practice, similar to what the
Manu law of India allowed: "He who clears a piece of land is the
owner of it". If such a forest land was however strictly out of
bounds for any private use, then they remained community property.
In other cases, such land might still be declared out of bounds, but
a villager might in the face of scarcity of land, demand from
the elders who are trustees of such land to allow him plant on it.
With such a permission, he became full owner of whatever area he
cleared[3].

c) Communal Land

The basic general principle where many scholars maintain a united
stand is the observation that among the Igbos, the land is
conceived as belonging to the community which includes the ancestors,
as well as the present and future generation. This involves
'a vast family of which many are dead, or living and countless
members are yet unborn'[4]. Or as F.C. Ogbalu has said:
"land is thus a communal property, just as certain trees such as
the Iroko and Oil-bean are owned in common"[5].

---

3) Meek, K.C. Ibid., Nwabara, N.S., Ibid.
4) Elias, O.T., The Nature of African Customary Law, Manchester,
   Manchester University Press, 1956, p. 162.
5) Ogbalu, C.F., Igbo Institutions and Customs, University Publ.
   Onitscha, 1973, p. 73

Communal land is thus land owned by the entire community in common, whether fertile or infertile, and it is held in reserve for the benefit of the whole group, being formally apportioned out when necessary, to deserving farmers, or in other instances, freely at the disposal of each farmer to farm where he wants. In some parts of Igboland like in Owerri regions, there are no communally owned lands as such, but families own the land communally in place of the entire village or clan community[6]. M.M. Green in her studies among the Igbo of Nigeria came up with the conclusion that the village does not communally own any land, except a few small pieces of bush sacred to the village deities[7]. This view cannot hold water in pre-colonial Igbo society, except if we understand her description of "communal", not as the entire village generally, but the various groups or families, therefore communal groups on smaller scale inhabiting the village. And this seems really to be the sense in which she describes communal ownership, for she adds: "Ownership of land is divided up among small groups of nearly related kinsmen, branches of the various kindreds, with the exception of here and there, of a residue of land which may still be the property of the whole kindred"[8].

The idea of communal or public land might have originated in a method of land acquisition which someone has described as the "Right of First Occupation"[9]. It is thinkable that in more primitive times, land was owned by the community in general, but with the

---

6) Meek, K.C., op.cit., p.102 (Law and Authority in a Nigerian Tribe)

7) Green, M.M. Igbo Village Affairs., op.cit., p.33 - 34

8) Green, M.M., Ibid

9) Menkiti, A.G. The Chief Land Officer of East Central State Government, Land Tenure, Enugu", Unpublished Document, 11.2.1970.

increased population over the area, the community divided up the land
to the various families or groups within it to avoid conflicts
and the problems of scarcity. The families thus divided up
further the land due to them to the various individual heads of
families within it, so that it eventually became their permanent
possession for cultivation, herding and habitation. We shall hence
consider family lands as an aspect of communal lands within the
community.

(i) Family Lands - an Aspect of Communal Ownership

Dr. S. N. Nwabara has very nicely shown how family ownership of
lands might have begun in original Igbo society. According to him,
for some reason not always specified, a village might migrate to an
entirely new site, occupying a large tract of virgin land which soon
took on the name of the ancestral father. The area so occupied
would be communally owned. This village might comprise various
Umu Nna groups, each of which had received a designated area of land
upon occupation. Members of each group redivided their own share
of the land - which was again subdivided according to the number
of mature adult members, ensuring that each adult received a
portion of land, which became inalienable[10]. On this land, the
families built their compounds as it was often situated in the
village enclosure. This land belongs to the household occupying it,
and the recipient held it in perpetuity. It was however disposable
to other Umu Nna members for purposes of agriculture and pasture,
but could not be withdrawn to strangers as we shall see later.

---

10) Nwabara, N.S., Iboland - A century of Contact with Britain -
     1860 - 1960, op.cit., p. 34

For practical purposes, the system of land tenure made every free born (Amadi) to own a piece of land over which he enjoyed usufructuary Rights. However, each family had right over the land collectively, and divided it out to the children individually for use. In this sense, one would agree with certain authors who maintain that no piece of land, not even that which stood on "bad bush" was without an owner. Says Green, "The pressure of population on the land is so great that every square yard of it belongs to a small land-owning group which may consist of only three or four males"[11].

Family ownership of land thus expressed in a very profound way, the communal ownership of same, as Floyd suggests: "In most Eastern Nigerian communities, the land belonged, as it still does in the last analysis, to a group of kin, a family or a clan, the membership of which included not only the persons alive at any particular time, but persons dead, or not yet born. Land was therefore more than tangible property; it expresses the social and spiritual identity of a group of kinsmen in contradiction to other groups in other communities"[12]. In this case, the elder of the family was often considered trustee of the land to see that conflicts do not arise, and to know the border-line of family ground. In cases of land-conflict he represented his family, or was called upon by the community to witness land settlement. His age conferred this authority on him, as he was nearer to the ancestors, who in turn were the custodians of community land.

---

11) Green, M.M., op.cit., p.34

12) Floyd, B., Eastern Nigeria-A geographical Review, London, 1969, MacMillan Press, pp.199 - 200

From all that has been said, it is clear that communal as well
as family ownership of land existed in Igboland. What is highly
debatable is whether individuals could also own land absolutely?
A very difficult topic, Dr. Taslim Elias, Nigeria's former
Chief Justice maintained that individual ownership of land is not
peculiar to pre-colonial African societies, but is a modern
phenomenon since the intrusion of the Europeans. He said:

"In Nigeria, as in practically many African societies, ownership
of land in the accepted English sense is unknown. Land is held
under community ownership, and not as a rule, by the individual
as such... It is true that the impact of English ideas of property
law upon ind·igenous·conceptions has made great influences and
produced tendencies towards a partial breakup in the existing system,
and many individuals now own land in their own right, ... but the
indegenous customary law of land tenure remains essentially communal"[13].

It is good to note that in the original work of Justice Elias,
the word "communal" was not used. Rather he employs the term
"corporate" instead of "communal", by which he argues that the
'rights of the individual members often co-exist with those of the
group in the same parcel of land'. In other words, the individual
is part-owner of land belonging to the family"[14].

---

13) Elias, O.T. Nigerian Land Law, 4th Edition, London, Sweet and
Maxwell, 1971, p.7 (Originally published under the title:
Nigerian Land Law and Custom, Routledge and Kegan Paul, London,
1966, p.6).

14) Ref. Elias, O.T., Nature of African Customary Law, 1956, chapter ix,
Manchester.

Reasons given which have led to the outright ownership of land
today by individuals include:

(a) The efforts of practising African Lawyers trained in
English Law;

(b) The change from the subsistence economy of the autonomous
household or village to the market economy of cocoa and
palm-oil plantations of "Urban" areas;

(c) The increased pressure of population upon the land
consequent upon this change, which has produced tendencies
towards a partial-break-up in the existing system,
and many individuals now own lands in their own right[15].

Opposed to the views of Elias is Dr. S.N. Nwabara who maintains that
individual ownership of land existed in Igboland. For to the above
views of Sir Justice Elias he asks: "But does this communal ownership of land circumscribe the rights of the individual"? No, there
was individual rights to farm work on communal lands, there was
individual ownership of lands with all the rights attendant to it
including the right to sale of land[16].

I am myself an Igbo and come from Aguagbaja Umana-Ndiagu, a small
village in Ezeagu Local Government Area in the present day Anambra
State of Nigeria. From observations and questionnaire presented
to the people of Umana, it is clear that land in pre-colonial
times was never sold, nor was it an individual property, except in
so far as Usufructary rights of ownership were granted to it.
The thesis being presented here, proposes to support the idea of

---

15) Elias, O.T., Nigerian Land Law, op.cit., p.7

16) Nwabara, N.S., op.cit., pp. 37 - 38

Sir Elias, that in pre-colonial Igboland, land was not
understood as an individual property, but was communally owned.
Perhaps, within the context of Umu-Nna or within the confines
of the family, people could talk of individual ownership, but
generally, it was communal ownership that existed, even
into our times as a newly released constitution of Umana Ndiagu
citizens shows.

(ii)   Communal Ownership - the Example of Aguagbaja Umana Ndi Agu
       Village Constitution

In the said document, the Aguagbaja Village Union stated clearly
and I quote:

"The Aguagbaja Village Union is a Union of all Aguagbaja citizens
bound together in blood for mutual understanding,
harmonious living and peaceful development of their area. The
citizens agreed to guide themselves with the following
guiding principles or bye-laws -

"All citizens of Aguagbaja Village are members, therefore,
all males and females both young and old, married and unmarried
are members.

"Any son of Aguagbaja is permitted to build on Aguagbaja soil
where there is available space of land. That is to say that
ownership of land must not prevent one from building. Also no
amount of economic plants should prevent one from building
provided that such a citizen is a legal Aguagbaja citizen.

"Any Aguagbaja citizen man or woman is permitted to farm on
any available space of land belonging to the community. In
farming, no economic plants must deliberately be destroyed and
no compensation such as money, wine or yams must be demanded...
An offender pays to the community a fine of sixty naira and eighty
naira correspondingly"[17].

---

17)   Aguagbaja Village Union - Umana Ndi Agu Constitution, signed,
      1st September 1984, pp 1-2; Printers: Liberty Press, Nsukka,
      22 University Road.

In another document of the same village community, concerning the
ownership of community of land and the social relationships supposed
to exist in the community, the villagers bound themselves under
oath and declared:

"The entire Aguagbaja citizens gathered together today 10th June,
1984 and agreed to take an oath on the following items listed for
their mutual understanding and togetherness. This oath taken today
is bound on every Aguagbaja person both male and female, young,
old and also those to be born in future.

"Aguagbaja Community has a communal land streching from Ekpe Eze to
Ajali and from the old tract road to Akpata.
"That in this communal land, any good citizen of Aguagbaja can farm
or build without any hindrance from other Aguagbaja citizens.
"That if anybody from Aguagbaja leases or sells out any piece or
portion of the said land to either a company or the government for
his personal gain should be killed by the idol"[18].

---

18) Refer: 'The Items of Agreement on Oath Taking by Aguagbaja
Community on their Communal Land", Oath sworn on 10.6.1984, and
signed in paper for documentation by ten signatories on behalf
of their various families on 1st September 1984.

(iii) Is Igboland - A Communistic Society?

Some observers, especially Western writers concluded that traditional Igbo society, like many other tribal societies could be termed "communistic" and that individual rights in land or other goods did not exist. But Max Gluckman has tried to contradict this judgement, because implicit in it is a false antithesis between "communistic" and "individualistic", arising from the way in which we say that a person or a group "owns" a piece of land or some item of property. Says he, "we are speaking loosely when we use this sort of phrasing"[19], for a strict adoption of the principle of "communism" would have stifled individual initiative. One must understand that in Igboland, there was a peculiar combination of individualism and communitarianism to develope a system which both accommodated the interests of the individual and those of the community at large.

Like in the example shown above with Umana Ndi Agu, communal ownership of land, guaranteed the free use of the land by any "legal Aguagbaja citizen". Land did not belong to individuals absolutely yet, the individuals used the land for their various needs. In short, if we are to understand the use of land as a unit of production, we have to appreciate that it is too simple to talk of such tribal societies as marked by either communism or individualism. Clearly, land as it is ultimately cultivated, "is worked by individuals with secure and protected rights, but representatives of their families, their village, and of the clan have claims on the land. No superior or elder can arbitrarily oust a junior from his holding, and the heir of each junior enters on succession into this holding"[20].

---

19) Gluckman, M., Politics, Law and Ritual in Tribal Society, op.cit., p. 36
20) Ibid., p. 41.

Hence, when we say that a particular group of kinsmen or
family owns land, it is also implicit in such a statement that
all the members of that group have claims to exercise certain rights
over that land - may be equally with one another, may be varying
with their status[21]. We shall now consider that last type of
ownership of land in Igboland called individual ownership of land.

d) Individual Land

From all that has been said, it is now clear that individual
ownership of land could be accepted to exist within the communal
ownership. This includes as Meed has pointed out, land handed
on by father to son, or acquired by clearing virgin forest or
return for a loan. In many village groups says he,
"there is scarcely any land at all within the recognised boundary of
the group which is not held by the individual"[22].

There were other ways in which an individual could acquire land
and this was pointed out by S.N. Nwabara, namely, land
acquired through inheritance, marriage dowry, homicide
compensation, conquest, kola tenancy and land given as present[23].

An individual could also gain land under the terms of seasonal or
temporary transfer, and we shall touch on this elaborately later
in this chapter. Meek maintains that within the clan, it is common
practice for a man to pledge his land in order to cancel a debt,
pay a bride price, or even to raise the means of paying his tax.
Land which has been pledged is normally redeemable at any time and
at the same rate at which it had been pledged, and there
is an Igbo proverb which says: "Ihe ibe efughi efu", meaning that
"a thing that is pledged is never lost[24].

---

21) Ibid., p.36. (See also: Hoebel, the Law of Primitive Man, 1954
22) Meek, K.C. Law and Authority in a Nigerian Tribe, op.cit.,p.103
23) Nwabara, N.S., op.cit., p.36
24) Meek, K.C., Ibid.

Within the clan, there was marked individualism and except on
ceremonial occasions, few effective demands could be made of the
individual for the benefit of the entire clan outside his own
particular lineage or extended family. The farms were held by
mature adult male members of the family who could cultivate with
their families, a series of plots of land. Women do not own
lands. They leave their native places at marriage and henceforward
have definite farming rights in the village of their husbands.
But they are no land owners[25].

Despite this strong individual attitude and right to the
cultivation of a land, it has been suggested that what is really
owned by the individual is the claim to have power to do certain
things with the land or property, to possess immunities against the
encroachment of others on one's rights in them, and to exercise
certain priviledges in respect of them. However, in the communal
or family concept of ownership, "other persons within the
family may have certain rights, claims, powers, priviledges, immunities
in respect of the same land"[26].

We can now say with Nzomiwu that it is a peculiarity of Igbo
land tenure system that the rights of the individual members often
co-exist with that of the community in the same parcel of land.
"There is both communal and individual ownership of land in Igbo
community. Some plots of land owned on family basis, are generally
made available to individual members as house, garden or grazing land.
These individuals exercise some type of ownership over the land"[27].

---

25) Green, M.M., op.cit., p.34

26) Gluckman, M., op.cit., p. 36

27) Nzomiwu, J.P.C., The Moral Concept of Justice among the Igbos,
op.cit. p. 219.

The former Chief Justice of Nigeria put it so well by looking at
ownership of land from the perspective of right to use of land,
but not right to absolute ownership of same land, with regard
to title: "It is in a sense that of part-owner of the land
belonging to his family. He is not a leasee, he is not a licensee,
he is not a usufructuary. He pays tribute to nobody, is accountable
to none but himself, and his interests and powers transcends
those of usufructuary under Roman law"[28].

In the Oxford English Dictionary, the word "Usufruct" is defined
as "a right of enjoying the use and advantages of another's
property short of destruction or waste of substance". However,
this dictionary definition does not cover the strength of
rights of African holders; and those who use the word, with the
meaning to enjoy the fruits similarly fail to recognise
this strength. The land is not "another's Property".
Moreover in Roman law, a grant of 'usufruct' was for use of fruits
during the holders lifetime, not transmissible to heirs, as
African holding is. We are thus forced to accept that in
the context of pre-colonial Igboland, three sources interplayed
as far as ownership of land was concerned, namely, the community,
the family and the individual.

Contrary to this way of life is that practiced by the ancient
Germans and celts. Gluckman has shown that the rights of all
citizens or subjects to claim sufficient land as an inherent
attribute of citizenship, marked the political system of ancient
Germans and Celts, but not the land tenure system of feudalism.

---

28) Elias, O.T., The Nature of African Customary Law,
Manchester, 1956, p. 165

Under feudalism, a vassal entered into a special contract with his
immediate lord in which he gave service of a demarcated king in
return for control over land and those attached to it. No one
in those days however could go to the king directly and demand
land as in Africa[29].

An individual owning land would call the elders to witness the
division of land among heirs according to the laws of inheritance.
Again, the general community limits the absolute rights of the
small land-owning groups over their land. But there is no one
individual who is looked on as holding the land in trust for the
community. The situation in feudal Europe did not occur in Igboland
as there were no lords and no feuds to lord it over others.

There was no institutionalised chieftainship. Rights to control
the land rest not an individual alone, but on the entire family
together. Land was communally owned but individually utilised.
Under this condition, was it possible to sell land in Igboland?
What rights had foreigners over the land on which they lived?
Who could buy land or have it transferred it to his care?
Was such a transfer permanent or was it temporary? These and other
questions will now be considered in the following discussion.

_____

29) Gluckman, M., op.cit., p. 40

3. The Inalienability of Land

We have already seen that in traditional Igbo culture, the land stands as a basic right for every indigene on an equality with air and water. Could land therefore be sold by an individual to a foreigner who was not a member of the group?

M.M. Green attempted an answer to this question where she wrote: "Without generalisation, one can say that in the majority of cases, 'Rights of Ownership' over the land are qualified by the fact that though it can be, and frequently is leased and pledged, land cannot, according to native law and custom be sold. Can land be lost? people ask. And this prohibition is widespread in the Igbo country"[30]. She gives an account of how she deeply interviewed her interpreter, who although comes from another part of Igboland, was able to confirm this view as general among the Igbos. "This was stoutly asserted not only for Umueke Agbaja but by my Mbieri interpreter about his own village group, and he insisted that the law was universal among the Ibo, land cannot be lost, he said. Any assumption therefore by Europeans that land can be sold would cut right across the most fundamental basis of native society. The only title to permanent ownership of land is inheritance"[31].

That land cannot be lost was also attested to by Nwabara in the work sufficiently quoted already. He confirms that this statement of loosing land, depended on the party to whom it was lost. Property was not considered lost when it was transferred by Pledge or Sale to a brother or blood relations. As long as the property circulated within the Umu Nna, no sense of loss was entertained. It would be regrettable and a loss if it was transferred permanently to a "stranger", that is, to a person from another village who must not necessarily be an unknown person.[32].

---

30) Green, M.M. op.cit., p.34 (See also in her work written in 1941: Land Tenure in an Ibo village in South-Eastern Nigeria, London,p.7)
31) Ibid.
32) Nwabara, N.S., op.cit., p.35

For the Igbos, there is a strong belief that land cannot be
alienated since it does not merely belong to the current generation who are only caretakers thereof. Many anthropologists and
historians have this to say, like D. Smock reports:
"When a possibility of land consolidation was discussed with Eastern
Nigerian villages, misgivings also arose from the fact that the land
is thought to belong not just to the current generation, but also,
to those members of the family who have died and those yet to be born.
Thus they argue that the current generation has no right to make
adjustment in land owning pattern"[33].

Mrs. Green says on this: "As a general rule, land, whether community,
family or individual is inalienable and this practice is widespread
among the Igbos"[34]. And G.T. Basden who somehow represented the view
that purchase and sale of land was exceptionally practiced added
to the views already stated: "It can be generally accepted that,
under native law and custom, it is generally repugnant to alienate
land from the family, and the head acts as trustee of the property.
There are exceptions to this statement". Elsewhere he says on the
same topic: "It was and still is generally speaking repugnant to the
Ibo mind 'to make trade', that is, to regard the land as a
source of profit"[35].

---

33) Smock, R.D. and Smock, C.A., Cultural and Political Aspects of
    Rural Transformation - A case Study of Eastern Nigeria; Praeger
    Publishing Company, New York, 1972, p.161
34) Green, M.M., op.cit., p.33
35) Basden, T.G., Niger Ibos, op.cit., pp.264, 266.

a) Why was Land Inalienable?

Why was this policy of the inalienability of land adopted by the Igbos?
Surely of course, there are a lot of reasons with solid positive
consequences why land was considered inalienable in traditional
society.

(a) Out of respect for the ancestors buried on the ground,
people did not sell out land to foreigners on a permanent
basis. The ancestors handed over the land to their
successors without sale. What would the present generation
hand over to the future generation if they succeeded in
selling off their fatherland? If the ancestors had
sold the land, they could'nt have had anywhere to cultivate,
live and work on. For fear of the ancestors therefore, land
was considered inalienable.

(b) There is a general respect for the land as a fundamental
right inherited by every person within his kindred and clan
community. A sentimental attachment thus followed the
inalienability of land.

(c) The exploitative tendency of certain greedy members within
the society or outside of it was curtailed, as the sale
of land was forbidden. These greedy fellows might have
bought off all the land, latter to sell it at exorbitant
prices to others, or rather, create a class of land owners
and non-land owners, who will be permanently subdued to
slavery by working for those who have land in other to exist.
In one way or the other, this policy helped the Igbo to
prevent the extreme capitalistic and unjust situation now
existing in Latin America, where some people bought off all
the land to the detriment of the masses of the people.

(d) Land was not sold in Igboland because land remained within
     the control of the owning community, and not under the
     control of a single individual. The community might
     however, depending on definite circumstances chose to
     alienate land on a corporate basis, and the individual who
     had his personally acquired land, could only engage in
     sale of land, after due consultation with the family members,
     and a corresponding performance of required rituals.

(e) It was generally believed that all land and its products
     belong to the Earth deity - Ala, who in turn apportioned
     land to Her children. It could have been absurd if the
     Igbo engaged in marketing of the land for the purposes of
     amassing wealth. Only in extra-ordinary situations could
     land be considered alienable.

(f) Lastly, the Igbo often liked to preserve some of his land
     for his sons, and to reserve land for unforseen
     circumstances in the future.

Smock maintains that people outside the community are denied the
right of ownership of land since they are strangers, although they
could be allowed to use the land, so long as they do not control it.
"In no case would a community that has a virgin land allow someone
from another community to assume control of it, except on basis
of pledging and leasing agreement"[36].

_____

36) Smock, R.D., andSmock, C.A., op.cit., p.152

b) Foreigners and the Land

The fact that strangers were not sold land on a permanent basis does not mean that they had no right to use the land, or even to rent the land on a temporary basis - which could on the long run mean generations, and sometimes involve permanent usage.
It has already been said that land could be pledged or leased to foreigners. There were other forms of transfer of right of use of land to people outside the village, such as, seasonal transfer, temporary transfer, Kola tenancy, payment of debt, dowry etc.

We shall now examine briefly these situations under which land was transferred to strangers. M. Gluckman in this situation has already mentioned that "one frequently finds people who are not resident in the village but are working its land. This they do under a condition and law, namely, that all kinsmen, in all lines, of the main family group of a village are entitled to make use of its wealth provided that there is more than sufficient land for the members resident in the village"[37].

And Basden says: 'permission is often freely given to tenants to cultivate land or to build upon it, but the "Head" can always lay proprietary rights claim. The occupier is seldom disturbed so long as he is prepared to acknowledge the ground landlord. Rent is not usually demanded, the tenancy being confirmed by the offering and acceptance of 'Oji' (cola) at the time permission to occupy the land is granted, and on more or regular occasions subsequently"[38].

---

37) Gluckman, M., op.cit., p.39
38) Basden, T.G., op.cit., p.264.

(i) Pledged Land - In point of fact, pledged land is often that
land pledged, for example, for a sum of money, in excess of that
normally given, and so many such lands are said to remain
unredeemable for generations, for several reasons, one of which
might be, that all evidence of the original transactions has been
lost. In this way, certain rich men have acquired land
in perpetuity[39]. This is so because pledged land could
be transferred or inherited by the pledgee, but after three
generations, the pledger's descendants lost the title permanently
to the descendants of the pledgee[40].

It has also been accounted as common in Owerri area of
Igboland, where the head of a family may have to pledge a piece
of family land to pay off a debt by the previous head, and he
may insist on doing so against the wishes of the family,
especially if these have offered no assistance towards ameliorating
the paying off of the debt.[41].

(ii) Land Lease: - Temporary transfer, otherwise known as land lease
could be practised for a season or thereabouts. Rent was charged,
and this practice is age-old among the Igbo. The lease was for
an unlimited period, but recoverable by the rentor or his
successor within three generations. A man may thus lend a piece
of land to a friend free of charge, expecting merely to receive
a pot of wine - palm and a feast after the harvest[42].

---

39) Meek, K.C., Law and Authority in a Nigerian Tribe, op.cit., p.103
40) Jones. I.G., Report of the Position, Status and Influence of
     Chiefs and natural rulers in the Eastern Region of Nigeria,
     Enugu, 1957
41) Meek, K.C., op.cit., p. 103
42) Ibid.

(iii) Seasonal Transfer: Seasonal transfer limited the tenant to one
       farming season. An important condition attached to it was that
       the foreigner plants no permanent economic trees or crops
       on the land so transferred, nor should the lender harvest already
       standing palm-trees, take wine or oil from them. Such a
       transfer involved a nominal fee as rent, and the transaction
       did not involve other members of the family.

(iv)   Kola Tenancy: Otherwise called in certain areas 'izi ani', or
       'land showing',in this case, a man gives a plot of land to his
       friend or even to a slave. Title was often permanent, provided
       the occupant performed the required rituals and brought the
       required cola nuts, chicken and other demands for such a transfer.
       Nwabara suggests that in such cases of 'Kola tenancy', the
       title of transfer is permanent, and this accounts for the
       ownership of land by slaves in certain parts of Iboland[43].

(v)   Showing a Land (izi ohia): This was another form of land transfer
       in Igboland. Money or rentary transactions were not involved.
       Someone in search of land could approach an acquaintance with his
       wish. If the discussion was positive, the land owner would
       demand the normal custom of 5 cola nuts and a pot of palm
       wine. The family members were duly informed and their permission
       solicited, for this would be impossible without their consent. On
       the appointed day, rites are performed, the relations of both
       parties present, a goat is killed and the blood sprinkled upon the
       site with prayers to the ancestors for protection, peace and
       prosperity. Such a system of transfer is neither pledge or lease
       or sale, but is termed 'Izi Ani' or showing of land.

---

43) Nwabara, N.S., Iboland-A century of contact with Britain,
     op.cit., p.3

The land normally reverts to the original owner or his
descendants when the renter departs the land. In fact,
as Nwabara has noted "the title of land is not transferred
to the renter. He and his descendants could live on the
land as long as they wished, but once they quitted, the land
riverted to the owner. But should the owner for one reason
or the other force the renter to quit the land earlier,
unprepared with his house and economic trees still on the land,
then the owner of land must compensate him a very large sum,
in cash or kind for all the buildings and economic trees"[44]
erected on the site. This could be such a large amount or
involve very much costs that the original owner has to withdraw
his forced quit notice.

(vi)   Untransferable Land: : Having talked about land that was
transferable, we shall now discuss briefly land that was considered
by the family to be untransferable. Nwabara calls such land
"Ama Ochie", which means "the original home" where the
forefathers of the village lived. Title to the "Ama Ochie"
was rarely transferred to anybody outside the immediate family.
Such land was part and parcel of the family and carried some
religious sanction with it, because the incumbent has to
account not only to his posterity but also to his ancestors for the
use of the land. He is as Liversage says: "only a link
in an unbroken chain". To transfer such land either seasonally,
temporarily or permanently to a non - member of the family
was an abomination and a disgrace to the ancestors, supposed to
be buried there. It is somehow related with the belief of
certain East AFrican tribes who believe that the souls of the
ancestors are inextricably bound up with the land where they are
buried. Sale of land is therefore unthinkable.[45]

---

44)   Nwabara, N.S., op.cit., p.36
45)   Basden, T.G. op.cit., p.266

As Liversage says: "No Ibo man would, under any circumstances, suffer the graves of his dead relatives to be descecrated. In some cases, the land was vested in the head of the family, but in others, it was shared among the male adults and in time the land became extremely fragmented and smaller in size"[46] that no one could do any thing grand with it again, or think of renting it out. The living, the dead and the unborn thus placed a very interdependent role in the system of land tenure.

---

46) Liversage, V., Land Tenure in the Colonies, Cambridge, Cambridge University Press, 1945 p.7 and p.66. (Refer also Nwabara, op.cit. p. 37)

4. Ownership of Property

In traditional Igbo society, people believed strongly in and practiced
the right of private ownership of property. We shall make a brief
excurs here to consider what this right of private ownership of
certain goods mean. Basically, man from his natural instincts needs
things for his existence, he uses these things, consumes them,
and makes them his property, depending on the circumstances.

We therefore talk of ownership of property. Fagothey has defined
this ownership thus: "A thing is said to be one's own when it is
reserved to a certain person and all others are excluded from it...
an owner is a proprietor, ownership is proprietorship, and
belongings are property.. Ownership may therefore be defined as
'the right of exclusive control and disposal over a thing at will"[47].

The operative words in this definition are 'right','exclusive'.,
'control and disposal', 'over a thing', 'At will'. To own a good,
the owner must have the exclusive right of possessing the good.
A thief who has stolen a good cannot be called an owner, eventhough
he is a mere holder of the good at his possession, but he cannot
acquire a right to them. The owner, who has the exclusive right
over the good has the right to keep others off from the use of the
thing owned. We can also talk of ownership by a group or corporation,
or community joint ownership, which excludes people from outside
the group to the rightful proprietorship over it. As Fagothey says:
"Exclusiveness is probably the most prominent element of
ownership, and only by destroying it exclusiveness can the right
of ownership be breached"[48].

47) Fagothey, A., Right and Reason - Ethics in Theory and Practice.,
    CVM, Company, St. Louis, 1959, pp.445 ff.
48) Ibid.

Thus a property over which everybody claims equal rights cannot be owned at all, such as air, sun, water and heat. Property, normally defined as "that which is owned and over which one has the exclusive right of control and disposal at will"[49], can be kept by the owner, changed, disposed away by selling, using, consuming or destroying. An absolute owner of a property acts at his own will by deciding on his property, and he does not need to consult anyone on his property before disposal of it. Thus, this property which can be a material object, or actions, credit, services, talents or good-will, is solely under the authority of the owner. A trustee can have a right to control or dispose, but not to own the good.

Legalists talk of public and private ownership of property, likewise perfect and imperfect, direct and indirect ownership. A detailed study of all these various types of ownership cannot be undertaken here. But further details can be seen in the work of Fagothey, already quoted. Our basic occupation here is to consider whether the right of private ownership of property as already defined existed in Igboland.

In traditional Igbo society, the interplay between the individual and his relationship to the community of his birth and kinsmen determined the scope, extent and possibilities of ownership. This is so because, even though ownership of itself can be considered to be unlimited, limitations came from other sources, such as from Chukwu and Ala, the demands of kinship solidarity of sharing, and in more modern times, through the civil laws.

---

49) Ibid.

One can generally say that in Igboland, there was a mixed system
of property and ownership, with lands owned in common by the
community, and the individual's possession of private goods which
were under his direct control and disposal.
Therefore the Igbos' say in their proverbs and wise sayings:

'Onye na nke ya Onye na nke ya' - Each person with his own
'Nke m diri m' - May what is mine be left to me alone
Nke m bu nke m mana nke anyi bu nke anyi - Mine is mine and our's
is ours.
'Egbe bere ugo bere' - Let the Kite perch but let the Eagle perch too.
'Nke onye diri ya' - To each his due!

From these pithy sayings, we can now see that there was a valid
and basic attitude for private ownership existing in this community.
One had a right to acquire any object of value and dispose of it
at will. People could own houses, farms, crops, livestock, jewelry,
market stalls, private utensils and equipments, economic trees and
their personal 'Ikenga'. To prevent abuse however, a series of
legal and sacred sanctions accompanied the ownership of private
property. Generally however, we can posit the fact that Igbo
society owned property on three levels, namely: the village or community
level, the family - either narrow or extended, and the individual as
a person.

Writes Shapera while observing the practices of the Khoisan peoples
of Southern Africa, an observation also applicable to Igboland,
he says: "The only thing owned in common is the land...

> All portable property is generally owned by individuals,
> and theft is severly punished. People acquire the water
> they draw, the vegetable food they collect, and the game
> they kill, and though a man who shoots a buck or bird will
> cut it up, and share with the other people present... the
> dividing is done by him, and the skin, sinews, etc. belong
> to him to be done with as he pleases"[50]

---

50) Shapere, I., The Khoisan Peoples of Southern Africa, London
     Routledge and Kegan Paul, 1930, p.127 (See also:Gluckman,M, P.58)

Traditional Igbo society in its unwritten law emphasised
appropriation of produce and manufactured goods, and the dominant
right which this gives a man or woman over these. So serious was
this idea of private ownership of goods, that, 'to steal yam seeds,
death penalty or slavery could be imposed on the thief"[51].
Yam food is for the Igbos, a most precious food, it is the
"king crop", and with it is related - wealth, status, power and influence
for the rich yam producer. As Killam says: "The yam is King:
a man's wealth, status and reputation depend upon his possession of yams"[52]

51) Basden, T.G., Among the Ibos of Nigeria., op.cit., p. 148
52) Killam, G.D. The Novels of Chinua Achebe; African Publ.
    N.Y. 1969, p.20

a) Relationship Between Status and Property Ownership:

Having stated that ownership of private property was guaranteed in
traditional Igbo society, we shall now consider the relationship
between property and the status of the individual owner within
his own kindred. Gluckman as well as Mead and Evans Pritschard
have shown in their studies of the African, that "the law of
property is intricately intertwined with the laws of status.
To understand the system of property, we must investigate the system of
status relationships... Ownership cannot be absolute, for the critical
thing about property is the role that it plays in a nexus of
specific relationships. Hence in Africa, there is no clear
definition of ownership: when an African court makes a decision on a
dispute over property, it states that X stands in a masterful
position in relation to that specific object, priviledge or person,
as against some other person who is counterclaiming that is,
the decision is made as between persons related in specific ways"[53].

With all recognition of the noble achievements of the authors in
this area, we must however state that Igboland had a clear understanding and practice of private ownership. The assertion that
there is no clear definition of ownership can only be relatively
seen by the foreigner who comes from another culture with a certain
property understanding, and not seeing his Western notion of
property practiced, concludes that there was no clear cut
understanding of private property. People knew what belonged to them
as a result of the fruit of their hard work, or through inheritance.

---

53) Gluckman, M., op.cit., p. 45 ff

What the authors fail to understand is the relationship between the direct owner of a good and the use of this good by other from the family or kindred group. But this is exactly the area where African 'communal spirit' crosses with 'western individualistic systems' of property. The truth however can be seen in another perspective. Ownership of property did not mean neglect of the kit and kin. It really meant that he who has, helped those who have not from his abundance. Property rights therefore became associated with obligation of persons to persons, not necessarily to things.

As Gluckman rightly observes: "Property law in tribal societies defines not so much rights of persons over things, as obligations owed between persons in respect of things... If new relationships are being established, this is done through transfers of property, which create and define new relationships... Gifts are given at all changes of relationships, and these gifts are believed to recognise and validate the new relationship of giver and recipient"[54].

This is best illustrated in relationships of marriage, where as a symbolic way of expressing relationships, an intending husband or his family pays dowry, cattle or other goods for a bride. The man by this gesture is not purchasing the woman to be his concubine or slave as some uninformed observers say, although in modern Igboland, abuses of the bride price as a source of capital is being sadly practiced in certain areas, especially in Imo State. The Bridegroom by giving presents to the parents of the bride is validating the transfer of certain rights over the bride from her kin to himself, and establishing friendship, in-law relationship with those kin.

---

54) Gluckman, M., op.cit., p.46

The marriage gifts also signify that he accepts obligations of his status as husband, and that his own kin, who contributed to the payment, accept obligations to their new daughter or sister-in-law and the rest of her family. This practice is not limited only to the Igbo of Nigeria, it is also widely practiced in many African cultures. "When a Lozi girl marries as an ostensible virgin", says Gluckman, "her bridegroom presents two beasts to her kin. He pays the first beast to make the girl his wife, the second is for her untouched fertility. Should he divorce her and she has not conceived, he is entitled to recover the second beast handed over with its progeny"[55].

---

55) Ibid., p. 44

b) Attitude to Wealth and the Symbolic Function of Property:

The Igbo attitude to wealth in traditional society was not that
of accumulation, but that of using basic wealth to keep one's
family together and feed them, and using the same wealth to help
the less fortunate members of the community. Greatness was merited
through sharing and giving out what one has to others.

It has emerged that if there is any "communism" in tribal society,
it is to be found in consumption, rather than in production.
The rich have an obligation towards the poorer members of the
village. No selfish ownership of property was encouraged, as this
would betray the communitarian spirit of traditional society which
like St. Paul would say, express that no one lives for himself.
To get social recognition in the society, a wealthy individual
must dispose his wealth to the less priviledged, by lending out
to them, or sharing with them his food, crops and so on.
The primary function of property for the traditional Igbo was that
of supplying community needs as well as those of the individual.
The attitude of sharing with the community that which one possesses
and has exclusive control and right over, determined the spirit
behind all ownership.

Perhaps it can be asserted that accumulation was neither very
possible nor considered desirable. Food accumulation was not an end
in itself, but rather the means to build up a large following of
dependants, as Gluckman has said: "Reputation is accordingly enhanced not
by accumulating possessions in order to use them oneself, but by
giving them away"[56).

---

56) Gluckman, M., op.cit., p. 51

There is virtue in giving aid and in dispensing hospitality
and men in these societies are moved by virtue as well
as self-interest. But virtuous performance does build up one's
reputation, not only as an upright man, but also as one who cares
for others. They become his dependants, since a man can win
away the allegiance of kinsfolk from their common senior kinsman,
in order to raise his own prestige[57].

Women compose songs of praise for him. Children are trained earlier in
life to share their food or presents with others. Besides, the
child is taught quite early that there are certain relatives who
have a right to expect goods from him and an obligation to give
to him. Contrasted with the European upbringing of children,
the Igbo attitude lays emphasis on sharing, whereas the Western
child is encouraged to individual initiative and to take pride
in their personal possessions. For the Igbo child however,
"The pride here is in having to share and in being prepared to
share one's goods with others... and this situation continues
into adult life and even beyond it... Ancestral spirits expect
to share in the goods of their descendants which must constantly
be offered to them"[58].

---

57) Ibid., p. 58 (From this we can say that tribal society aimed
    not only at subsistence, but also to prestige and power.
    The imperative to extravagance seems to be a social one, as
    social obligations are allowed to override economic prudence).
58) Richards, I.A. Land, Labour and Diet in Northern Rhodesia,
    1939. London, Oxford University Press for the International
    African Inst.

No one owns food or a chattel absolutely, because his kinsfolk
and even outsiders may have claims upon it which he has difficulty
in denying. Among the Igbos, certain fruits and crops growing in the
farmyard of another could be plucked by any member of the kindred and
eaten without being charged of stealing.

During the harvesting period, the less priviledged and lazy ones
are allowed to go to another's farm in search of 'left-over'
yams, cassava, and other crops, which they could take away with them.
They are not, if seen, charged with stealing for the original
harvesting has already been done by the owner of the farm.
In this way, a poor man was not reduced to a beggar status, as this
role was very shameful in tribal society. But the poor man had to do
a little work for himself, by going into another's farm after the owner has
done the original harvesting, and taking to himself crops and
other eatables left over. Work was therefore highly recognised, as the
Igbo strongly believe like St. Paul does, that "he who does not work
should not eat". The lazy man, even if he did not produce enough food
crops to keep himself and his family, he had still to work for a living.
He thus became industrious in gathering left-overs and had the right
to dispose of the goods gathered, the way he wanted, either by selling
the excess for money, or by eating them himself.

This attitude to wealth cannot however be divorced from the real
economic situation in which the Igbo found himself. Women were
conditioned to reciprocal sharing of food, crops, and other goods with
their fellow women. A woman after cooking, would send some of it
through her child to another woman to enhance sharing, and this was
correspondingly reciprocated. Rather than accumulate, she extended her
individual responsibility outside her own household. The limitations
to wealth and accumulation made the Igbo look out to others.

c) Symbolic functions of Property

Property ownership and material exchange carried out through
it had a symbolic aspect, for material objects in Igboland have
high symbolic value. Going into the details is above the
scope of this work. Evans-Pritchard, writing about the
Nuer of Sudan recognises this fact, for he says: "People not
only create their material culture and attach themselves to it,
but also build up their relationships through it and see it in
terms of it... the poorer a society is in material goods,
the more symbolic functions these goods have to serve... a very
simple material culture narrows social ties in another was...
material culture may be regarded as part of social relations, for
material objects are chains along which social relationships run,
and the more simple the material culture, the more numerous
are the relationships expressed in it..."[59].

An example here would do: In Igboland, sharing cola-nut with
someone was a mark of friendship. Enemies could not share cola-nut
together, for the cola-nut symbolised friendship, unity and good-will.
The Ofo staff of authority which passes from father to his son,
marked the transfer of authority from father to son, and the
maturity of the son concerned to speak the truth whenever he had
his ofo. The palm-frond over a log of wood expressed ownership!

---

59) Evans-Pritchard, The Nuer, 1940, p. 89 (Refer to Gluckman for
    a thorough analysis of these assertions by Pritchard,
    op.cit., p.46).

Material property, whenever exchanged, had a high symbolic value
and there are many reasons for this:[60]

(i)   Material property stand for the range of relationships which
      form the very fabric of society;

(ii) The ceremonial goods which circulate in them may
      take on this symbolic value as expressed in ritual practices.

(iii) They represent that wider spread of peace which extends
      around borders of each tribal group, and which makes it
      possible for that group to enjoy some possibility of
      pursuing its internal objectives. Hereby is meant that
      exchange of certain goods between two societies
      helped to tighten their neighbourly relations and to
      reduce the chances of inter-village wars.

(iv) Lastly, material property served direct utilitarian
      ends, as one uses its distribution to gather for himself
      some prestige and influence over a large following.

As Gluckmann has pointed out: "The more sumptuous the presents
giving away to others, the greater the prestige of the person
involved, and a competitor who saw his rival give out presents
lavishly, would, to recover his face and regain prestige, give out
also presents in return to the rival, and prepare a greater feast
whereby he boasted of his family's prestige, rights over property
and greatness"[61].

In this way, property or its distribution led to competition for
power, influence and prestige. The competition is caused too by the
desire to acquire dependants or partners in exchange who would
regard him as a "big man" or "Ogaranya". An additional wife in
an agricultural society expressed this bigness, since it brought in
more children, more agricultural produce, and more goods to be shared

---

60) Gluckman, M., op.cit., p. 57
61) Gluckman, M., op.cit., p.60

out during feasts, either to show-off, or to obtain community
recognition. Thus within the limitations imposed by simple tools
and egalitarian standards of consumption of primary goods, there
is competition between persons in acquiring control of the means
to produce goods. In fact, those concerned have an eye to the
bargains they are making and expect their partners to make
reciprocal returns.

The fundamental point at the beginning of this chapter is thus seen
in the fact that ownership of property was not simply for accumulation, but for sharing, distribution and consumption within the
community. Like in the New Testament Acts of the Apostles,
the early christians lived co-operatively, for those who have,
shared their goods with those who have not. Property rights
existed, but these were seen as not just individual accumulation.
Kinship involved a general obligation to help and sustain one another.
The kinship system is widely extended and many distant relatives
are classed with close relatives. As a man grows up in one of these
groups, there is no enterprise to draw him away from those who gave
birth to him and nurtured him. He keeps his belongings too at
their disposal. This is the principle of communitarianism which
stresses the individual as "relevant" and "Existenzfähig" only
within the kindred. What can he do elsewhere? What more
rewarding labour is there for him outside? And should he even go
outside the clan, his soul and mind are always there with his own
kindred. Elsewhere, he will be alone and if he is injured or dies, who
will care or avenge him? Men therefore remain in the land of their
ancestors, working with them and supporting them. Western influence
has disrupted this.

5. The Laws Governing Inheritance of Property:

The phenomenon of private property as an accepted mode of
economic enterprise in Igboland is further articulated by the laws
of inheritance. One inherits a good in order to own it, or as the
case may be, in order to place the inherited good at the disposal of
the family members who are still living, dead or yet to be born.

Meeks recounts that the rules governing inheritance are consistent
with the general character of the social organisation, and at the
same time, are so elastic and based on such equitable principles that
they can be easily modified to meet changing conditions, such as
the tendency towards individualisation. Property held by virtue of
an office passes to the successor. Thus, lands or palms held in
trust by the head of a family for the family's benefit, cannot be
alienated without the consent of the family, and this must be
handed on intact, together with the official Ofo and other insignia
of office, to the next senior elder or other person chosen as the
successor of the previous office holder[62].

Generally, the governing principle with regard to inheritance is
that of primogeniture, whereby the eldest son in a family inherits
from a father - whether deceased or very old, the right over the
property of the father. Says Basden, : "a man's personal property
is inherited by his eldest son, or if he has non, by his eldest
brother or male relative"[63]. In other words, the eldest son succeeds
absolutely as a general rule (exceptions abound), to all the
property of his father. He takes over all the household.
It has to be made clear however, that, although the eldest son inherits the
major share of all property, he is bound to look after the interests
of his younger brothers, half-brothers and the widow(s) of whom he

---

62) Meek, K.C. Law and Authority in a Nigerian Tribe, op.cit., pp.319 ff
63) Basden, T.G., Among the Ibos of Nigeria, Frank Cass, London,
     1966, p. 32

becomes the social father[64]. The new heir takes over all the
properties and could keep them to himself if he wanted; but the normal
practice was that he distributed the money that they may be able
to pay their dowry, and gave the widows to other men, while
receiving the dowry from these. Old widows remained quietly
in the compound and were not disturbed by the new heir, for he
could not eject them, and they could not remarry.

Meek observes that in certain Igbo areas, widows are heritable,
and may become wives of brothers or of sons of the deceased.
An eldest son may give one of his father's widows (with her consent)
to his father's younger brother, without demanding any bride-price.
Where the woman marries out to another foreigner, the bride price
received may be divided up among the sons, proportionately[65].

It is degrading and insultive for a son to receive a bride
price on the remarriage of his widowed mother. In other cases, like
in Agwu division where a woman (widow) remains unmarried after
her dead husband, she may stay on in the home and have promiscuous
sexual intercourse which could result to children, and these latter
are regarded as the children of the dead man, or directly, of the heir.
On this issue, there is no general law in all Igbo communities.
In some cases, sons may inherit their father's widows as wives,
while in other cases, sons neither inherit nor re-marry their
father's widow, nor do brothers inherit the widows of brothers or
half-brothers.

---

64) Meek, K.C., Ibid.,

65) Meek, K.C. op.cit., p. 321

The new heir not only succeeds to his father's property; with
it, he inherits also his father's liabilities and debts, or even
debts which his dead father inherited from the ancestors. Says Basden,
the "settling of ancient debts, perhaps three generations old,
is very intricate business, and the new heir may find himself in a
big dilemma, and possibly critical position owing to his being
suddenly confronted with a debt contracted by his dead grandfathers"[66].

There are cases where the eldest son of a deceased man is too
young to inherit, cater for, and administer the property to which
he has traditional customary right towards. In such cases, the
brother of the deceased man, or the elder in the compound takes
charge of all property, whether cash or kind, and these he
keeps in trust until the rightful heir is matured. On this Meek says:

"He is bound to provide for the up-keep and marriage of his deceased
brothers sons. In due course, when the children have grown up, they
take possession of their father's lands and economic trees and any
balance of property that their uncle may have in hand. If the
uncle has squandered the property, or failed to act equitably towards
his nephews, he is liable to an action for damages"[67], otherwise
fighting and serious disputes might arise.

There are cases where a man makes his Will before death to avoid
cases of disputes over the property he left over to his heirs.
This happens especially in families where there are many wives and
children. When death draws near, a man may call on all his
children and responsible relatives and divide among them, his property.
He does this particularly, if his eldest son is seen to be irresponsible and careless and incapable of managing the household after

---

66) Basden, T.G. Niger Ibos, op.cit., pp. 267 - 268
67) Meek, K.C. Ibid. p. 322

his death, or where he notices that the heir apparent is very greedy. In this case, the man may make gifts to all his daughters, sons, and his nephew. Should the eldest son however be trustworthy and strong enough for the great household he is inheriting after his father's death, the old dying man may bequeath on his son therefore, the Ofo which is the symbol of authority and leadership with a prayer whose formular can run thus:

> "To you my eldest son, I bequeath my Ofo. You are today
> appointed to be my successor as head of the family.
> To this, your uncles and brothers have agreed. They are
> to respect you in all things, and this Ofo must remain
> with you and your descendants"[68].

When the aged father has finished his prayer, he would strike the Ofo on the ground and breath onto it with the intention of conveying his words to the ancestors immanent therein. This ceremony is very significant as the dead father will be sure that he will afterwards get a respectable burial from his son. Indeed, one of the main reasons why the father allows a larger sum of his property to his eldest son is to enable him carry out the burial rites, which is a primary duty.

In Meek's words: 'a man's foremost duty in life is to see that his father or brother is buried with as much ceremony as his means permit'. Such a successful burial merits for the young heir much respect from the villagers and the immediate family relations who confer him with social status and respect.

---

68) Meek, K.C., Ibid., p. 323. (The law of inheritance is clear. A man may express his wish while he is alive... His property real or movable belong to his sons and they take shares according to their seniority in age, Refer to Ogbalu, C.F., Igbo Institutions and Customs, University Publ. Company, Onitsha, 1973, p.18).

It is important to mention here that private cults of the
deceased are not usually inherited, and the symbols are destroyed
when the owner dies (e.g. the Ikenga). But the family Ofo is
taken over by the eldest brother as we have shown, or by the
eldest son of the deceased.

A man who dies as a result of false swearing on the oath of 'Ani'
or by the Spirit or deity of a cult may not be honourably buried.
His property is handed over to the priest of the deity and is not
used. His house might be burnt down, and possessions thrown away
into the 'Evil Forest' also called 'taboo bush', if the divining
apparatus so directs. In this case, there is nothing to inherit.

However, if an honourable man dies, all his sons, including the
sons of his slave women may have a right of inheritance, generally
equal over the heritage. The eldest son or oldest surviving
brother of the deceased does the sharing. The property so shared,
is performed in the open, in the presence of the elders of the
kindred, so that disputes of inheritance may be avoided.

Inheritance laws as it concerns women is generally little.
A woman is married into the family, a bride-price or dowry paid on
her behalf and with this transfer from her father's family to
that of her husband, she becomes a woman with very little to call
her own. Says Basden, "for the ordinary woman, the only
property that can be classed as her own are her market equipment,
her cooking utensils and her water pot, together with small odds and
ends that she has accumulated and the coco-yam tubers which she
cultivates in her garden plot"[69]. In the family, a woman
contributes her own share in providing for the needs of the family, and
her husband shows appreciation by giving her a present
occasionally, such as a piece of cloth.

---

69) Basden, T.G. Niger Ibos, op.cit., p.208

When a woman dies, her property is heritable by her children,
with the eldest son taking care of all her personal belongings.
These personal belongings cannot be appropriated by the husband of
the deceased woman, eventhough her sons may allow their father a
share[70]. The woman's goats, fowls, crops, and cooking utensils are
divided up amongst her daughters, the eldest taking the largest
share but being expected to use it for the wedding of her young
unmarried sisters. Sisters in their turn, do not inherit from
their brothers, except articles of trifling value[71].

Should a woman however not have any offsprings, her property
is claimed by her husband, and the typical feminine goods will
be sent by her husband to her sisters. Says Meek:
"The rule permitting a husband to claim his wife's property, in
the absence of children, is justified on the grounds that in this way,
he receives compensation for an unproductive bride-price"[72].

In other cases, the man still appropriates the wife's goods
even if there are children in the marriage. Such an attitude is
not however general in certain Igbo areas, and where it is
practiced, the justification is that at marriage, the woman brought
little or nothing with her into the matrimonial home. All her
acquisitions are therefore the fruits of her husband's home.
Any wealth she acquires after marriage is therefore through the
agency of her husband.

---

70) Basden, Ibid., Meek, Ibid., p. 323
71) Ibid.
72) Meek, op.cit., p. 323

In cases of divorce under native law, there is no protracted litigation or bureaucracy. A man could initiate the divorce, and thewife could also do the same. A man who divorces his wife may or may not have genuine reasons for his action. Likewise, a woman who divorces her husband would run away back to her father's compound. If after deliberations, she did not want to go back to her husband, her relations will refund the husband the bride price and the divorce is concluded. No financial commitments of keeping the woman or paying her is forseen. Should she be nursing a child, she can take the infant with her until the child has been weaned and is strong enough to exist independently in the father's compound with his other relations. In divorce, the problems of inheritance of property or of finance is not central.

CHAPTER TWO

ECONOMIC TRANSACTIONS IN PRE-COLONIAL IGBO SOCIETY

PART ONE (I) : Trade and Markets

1. Introducing the Situation:

Agriculture was the most important and basic economic activity
practiced in pre-colonial Igboland. There however existed other
subsidiary economic activities, among which we shall consider
trade and manufacture, thus rounding up the three-legged stool
on which pre-colonial economics was based.

On this, a number of earlier anthropologists to penetrate Igboland
are of one opinion. Says Mrs. M. Green: "If agriculture is the
basic occupation of these people, trading is a close second.
One might almost say that whereas they farm of necessity, they
trade not only of necessity but also for pleasure"[1].
Basden agrees to this view, for he writes: "Igbos are not
primarily traders, but the art of buying and selling is not unknown
to them"[2].

When one considers the Igbo people of present day Nigeria, one
is marvelled how a typically agricultural people have, within very
few years of the colonial and post-colonial experience, become
powerful masters in the art of trade and marketing, for Igbo
traders are seen all over Nigeria as successful businessmen and
traders. We are thus led to conclude that trade, even on a low
scale, existed in precolonial Igboland. And this trade existed
on a three-dimensional front, namely, home or domestic trade,
regional trade within, and long-range trade with Igbo neighbours
on all fronts.

---

1) Green, M.M., Igbo Village Affairs, op.cit., p.37
2) Basden, T.G., Niger Ibos, op.cit., p.334

2. The Home or Domestic Trade:

Normally described as 'Afia Uno' or home market, each village or
even quarter had a market square where they assembled on one
day of the Igbo week for the purposes of buying and selling.
The Igbo calendar is divided into thirteen lunar months of 28 days
or seven weeks. A week was made up of four days, called
"Izu nta" (small week), and the days are named - 'Eke', 'Olie',
'Afo' and Nkwo'. Two four days period of eight days made the
'Izu ukwu' (or great week)[3].

The domestic markets were generally named after the four days of
the week on which they were held. Formerly, the market places
contained no buildings and all trading activities took place under
the shade of trees, or in the open village square, or near the
shrine to whom the market was dedicated, or on any other suitable
plain field central to the community to which the market belonged.

Observing the manner of buying and selling in this home market
arena, Basden writes: "Goods are exchanged, examined, approved
or condemned and sometimes thrown down again to show contempt for
the price demanded and altogether the market appears to be a
veritable pandemonium. No article of any value has a fixed price,
exchanges are arranged only after long bouts of bargaining"[4].

The suggestion that goods were bartered in exchange for other
commodities does not hold, as the researches carried out showed.
The home domestic was primarily a woman's affair as they dominated
it. Basden says on this: "To such an extent do women dominate the
situation, that it could be said with a fair measure of truth that
trade in the Ibo country was in the hands of the women"[5].

---

3) Ibid., p. 151
4) Basden, T.G., Ibid., p. 90
5) Ibid., p. 335

The market moral laid stress more on obligation than on right.
This is seen from the fact that all contracts and trade affairs
were carried out in the atmosphere of 'utmost good faith'.
Seller and not buyer, must look to the quality of goods exchanged,
and the concept of 'latent defect' is applied more widely
and for a longer period, than say in Europe. In Europe, if one
buys a commodity of a special type, one gets some guarantee for
a certain period within which the good could be returned
to the seller for repairs or exchange. After this period, the
buyer owns up all risks. And these commodities guaranteed were
of electro-technical wares, cars, and such like. In Igboland,
it involved more - almost everything sold in the village market.

Like Gluckman has pointed out: 'If a Lozi sells a Cow to another
and it dies some months later, he must placate it.
Among some plain Indians, the seller of a Horse bore some
responsibility if it was stolen a day or two after its purchase,
or was lamed in the first race it ran for its new comer'[6].
Likewise for the Igbo was this practice normal for a cheat
in the home market was publicly disgraced, and even banned
from attending the market. In the home or domestic market, the
Igbo proverb holds valid: "Ada elebe onye uno okuko, okpa mkpirisi"
which means that "you do not sell to a fellow villager
a lame(bad) fowl".

Goods for sale include mats, baskets and other art works, spoons,
oil, chairs, bed frames from bamboo, animals, salt, pots and
other foodstuff. But the domestic markets were not only for
buying and selling - they also provided a forum for inter-social
relationships, especially for women, who were the main domestic traders.

---

6) Gluckman, M., op.cit., p. 48

In the words of M. Green: "Markets are one of the main features of
their lives. They provide a meeting point for the discussion of
common business and for the disemmination of news; they are a
social event where the spice of gossip, the recreation of dancing and
the test of a bargain relieve the almost continuing toil of
hoeing, planting weeding and harvesting throughout the year...
Trading is the breadth of life, particularly to the women
among the Ibo, and the vigor with which bargaining and haggling
are conducted is evidence of the prestige attaching to
successful commercial enterprise"[7].

The Igbo market was therefore not simply a business center.
It served other purposes as already mentioned. The meeting point of
friends and relations, sons of the soil and foreigners.
When a man or woman was tired of work at home, he or she went to
the market, normally attended in good attire (today we shall say
sunday dress), to share the latest news, to socialise, to get
entertainment and drink wine with colleagues, and above all -
the market offered some sort of relaxation from work whenever it
came up every fourth day in the village.
Basden remarks: "A woman will visit the market if she can,
whether she wants to buy or sell or not, because it is the one
sphere of entertainment in the ordinary life of the village.
There she will meet her friends... To be deprived of this
priviledge is a handicap"[8].

---

7) Green, M.M. Ibid., p. 37
8) Basden, T.G., Ibid., p. 335

On the domestic or home front, the market was basically
a woman's affair, and she controlled and governed its procedure.
A number of influential women in the village dictated the rules
and lobbied for regulations to apply in the market. They succeeded
with the support of the village elders who directed all market
problems to the committee of women. In certain cases, this
council of women had the authority to prescribe what other
neighbouring markets could associate with them, what the
rate of cowries or other means of exchange was worth, and what
articles could be sold or forbidden entry into the market
under taboo law. If they outlawed someone from the market for one
reason or the other, they made sure it was enforced.

3. The Regional Trade within Igboland:

Trade was not only limited within the domestic area, but reached
the height of inter village or even inter-clan trade. In this
way, the Igbo who were normally competitive tried to outdo
their rivals by long distance trades.

A man's internal standing often depended in the era of
trade on his role in the external exchange, so that for internal
prestige, he had to have alliances with foreigners, which he could
operate under the protection of recognising the rules of this
international trade. Blood-brotherhood or extended lineage system
enable people to move into foreign lands which in those days
was generally dangerous as cases of slave raiding and kidnapping
were rampant.

As Gluckman says: "Among the patrilineally organised Ibo of Nigeria,
a man moves to trade at a distance by going to an in-law or
maternal kinsman in a neighbouring group, and is passed on, under
the protection of this relative, to the protection of one of the
latter's relatives yet further on, till he progressed accross the
land"[9].

But why this risk? Why this long range internal trade adventures?
Simply put, the local or domestic markets could not offer
all the needs which the market consumers demanded, such as salt
which came from Uburu areas, or iron-ore and smelthing goods
which came from northern Igboland around Udi areas. There was
specialisation in the production of the various goods, and a
domestic trader was forced to move accross his own village boundary
to purchase those goods lacking in his area, and to sell it to his
own people. In the words of Mrs. M.M. Green, : "the markets are
specialised to a certain extent in the sense that one is reputed
for meat or livestock, another for pots, another for yams and so on"[10].

9) Gluckman, M., op.cit., p.63
10) Green, M.M., Ibid., p.37

No doubt, this principle of specialisation led people without
these special goods, to go out in search of them. Says
Professor Afigbo, the organisational structure for carrying on
this distance trade certainly improved with time. At first the
most likely method is that items moved in a relay fashion from
one village to another in the direction of the greatest demand...
Most people never travelled outside their village. And even
at the time when the trading system in Igboland was most developed,
it was only a small fraction of people who travelled from one
region to the other for business[11].

Among the goods traded on were salt, wooden or iron spoons,
iron pots, horses, cows, chairs, weaponry, ritual objects, beads,
cloth and ivory among others. In these distant markets popularly
known by its special name (either of the god of the place, or of the
name of the town or other nick-name), men generally dominated
since it involved inter-clan meeting for haggling and exchange,
and the risks of travelling long distances was not a woman's
challenge. There is plenty of competition, free buying and selling,
and cheating was not excluded, as such markets were not attended by
one's own clansmen alone, but by foreigners too from various villages
and clans. A sort of double standard was thus practiced, for whereas
in the domestic markets, truth and honesty were basic, in the distant
inter-clan markets, cheating and competition played a role. Such
an attitude helps us to understand the spirit of myopism existent
in traditional society. Outsiders could be treated anyhow.
Morality, good-will and justice could only be merited a-priori
by one's fellow clansman, beyond which these virtues were not binding.
The spirit of universalism was therefore lacking in pre-colonial Igbo
society, and one might say, in all primitive or tribal societies, where
village rights were merited by status, but not by being a human being.

---

11) Afigbo, A.E., Economic Foundations of pre-colonial Igbo Society,
    op.cit., p.10

4. Long-range Trade with Igbo Neighbours:

It has been stated by scholars of Igbo history and culture that very little information existed with regard to this long-range trade. And it is as yet impossible to be precise as to when this kind of long-range trade developed with Igbo neighbours to the north and the south and west. AFigbo however suggests that from the limited information available, "we have trends to show that by the ninth century, the trading system was such that one can firmly assume that both regional trade linking different parts of Igboland and long-range trade linking Igboland and the area further north (the Sudan and beyond) were already long established.. For example, the Igbo Ukwu archeological discoveries dated back to the 9th century suggest that exchange of slaves and ivory for horses, beads and bronzes coming from the north to Igboland already existed"[12].

In the context of this work however, the debate about origin of the long range trade between Igboland and its neighbours is of little relevance to the issues being raised. Important is the assertion by Afigbo that people living in Igboland, especially in certain areas were forced a long time to abandon to some extent their agricultural ways of life and turn to trade which guaranteed them a livelihood. This is so, because geographically seen or rather physically considered, a growing differentiation in ecological conditions, leading to a situation in which one part produced more kinds of goods that it could consume arose. Especially in the areas of the northern Igbo, and affecting specifically the Awka, Nkwerre and Aro peoples, worsening conditions of the soil due to overworked soil, led the people to turn to other professions, such as trading, manufacturing, medicine, and the exploitation of occult forces as ritualists and diviners[13].

---

12) Afigbo, A.E., Economic Foundations of pre-colonial Igbo Society, op.cit., pp. 8 - 9. (Refer also for full studies the work by Shaw, T., Igbo Ukwu - An account of archeological discoveries in Eastern Nigeria, London, 1970).

13) Afigbo, A.E. Ibid., p. 8

The Awka thus specialised in smithing work, using iron-ore to
produce dane-guns, hoes, matchets, pots, and other bronze or
metallic works; the Aro specialised in using rituals and
occult forces to trade on slaves, and although, these long-range
traders did not entirely abandon the art of farm work in
their villages, they became increasingly dependent on their
neighbours for the extra food with which to supplement the meagre
produce of their exhausted soil[14].

The neighbours to the north, west and south of Igboland such as the
Ijaw, Igala, Bini, and other far-off traders were able to penetrate
Igboland with their merchandise, such as fish, salt, lead, iron-ore,
horses, glass beads and bronzes, ivory and slaves and cloth.
Long-range trade did not begin in Igboland as many authors suppose,
with the slave-trade or the advent of the Europeans, but existed
in very early times. Says David Northrup: "It is therefore false
to suppose that trade began in Igboland with the coming of the
Europeans. It existed long before the Europeans showed up on the
Nigerian Coast in the 15th century, for long before this time, the
lower Niger had become an important commercial highway in which
Aboh, Edo, Igala, Ijo and Northern Igbo traders occupied an important
commercial position"[15].

---

14) Ibid.
15) Northrup, David, The growth of Trade among the Igbo before 1800.,

On this point too, Professor Afigbo observed that 'by 1903
when the British penetrated northern Igboland following the
conclusion of the Aro war (1901-1902), they found Igala and Hausa
traders in Enugu and Udi, while the Awka blacksmiths were settled
for trade reasons in Igala and Idoma. The following merchandise
reached Iboland from northern Nigeria - horses, coral beads,
cloth, dye, ostrich feathers, potash, raw cotton and native
tobacco"[16].
Thus trade in Igboland stood on three levels-domestic, regional,
external .

---

16) Afigbo, E.A., Pre-colonial Links between S.E. Nigeria and the
    Benue Valley., Nsukka, University of Nigeria, unpublished paper,
    pp. 1 - 29. (refer also to S.N. Nwabara, Iboland - op.cit., p.22)

PART TWO (II) Currency Transactions:

1. Introducing the Situation:

In the earlier part of this century, uninformed Europeans while
talking about the means of exchange in traditional society, at
times spread the opinion that trade in the African interior
was entirely or at least in the most cases by barter. Such erroneous
views became widely accepted until recent studies have shown
that values for products were measured in Igboland by a means of
exchange which is as yet impossible to trace its origin.
By the eighteenth and nineteenth centuries, much of the commercial
transactions in Igboland were done in money[1].

Earlier revelation of the use of money was already made by an
Igbo ex-slave on whom we have already said a lot in initial
chapters of this work. In his narratives and memoir,
Olaudah Equiano maintains that monetary transactions were already
established in the eighteenth century, the time of his writing.
He says that in his village there were"small pieces of coin made
from something like·an anchor"[2].
Here most probably, Equiano was referring to the Manilla currency.
We must admit that the currency situation in pre-colonial
Igboland has not been satisfactorily studied, and further researches
in the area will still be awaited. But one thing which is quite
certain is that this development preceeded the down of European
era in West African trade. From the gathered information of
the earlier part of this century, Igbo traders and peoples were
using various articles to serve as currency including
salt, Umumu, cowry shells, manillas, brass rods, and copper wires[3].

---

1) Afigbo, E.A., op.cit., p. 14
2) Olauda Equiano, Narratives, op.cit., p.12
3) Afigbo, Ibid.

In his definition of money, Robertson assets that it is anything which is widely accepted in payment for goods, or in discharge of other kinds of business obligation[4]. It is as such indices or measurement of value. There are tribal societies where values are measured in terms of some common produce, like rice, or baskets or other grain, or nuts; some other tribal societies have tokens of value which can be considered to approach money, rather than that most societies of this type should lack such an aid to exchange. Yet, where there are such tokens, which observers have thought to be money, they still tend to function in series of exchanges, specific to particular ranges of social relationships. In the case of Igboland though, the goods used as currency were rare, portable, small and extremely divisible. This guaranteed the idice of measurement of value for whatever good was exchanged.

We shall now consider the various currencies used in Igboland in the pre-colonial era. They all served as money, were means of exchange and were valid. In the words of Afigbo, "the usage of salt as currency is a phenomenon found in many communities the world over. And it is quite possible that salt was oldest currency in use in Igboland. The salt which came in earthen jars from Uburu was ground into fine powder and moulded into cones of different sizes and used in exchange transactions"[5].

Salt in pre-colonial Igbo society was not an easy or cheap commodity to purchase. First of all, there were not many salt producing areas, and the few existing ones were not open to everybody.

---

4) Robertson, D.H., Money, London, Nisbet, Cambridge Univ. Press, 1922, p.2.
5) Afigbo, E.A., Ibid., p.14

The distance to say, Uburu was very far, dangerous and the
regulations guiding the extraction of salt from Uburu lake were
very stringent; Still people needed salt to cook and to eat.
It is therefore understandable that this scarce commodity, which
was portable, divisible into sizes of big and small cones,
and desired, would be legal tender in transactions between traders,
for everybody needed salt to eat.

The next currency after salt in later times was the iron money
known as Umumu, which was perhaps minted on the regions around the
northern Igbo plateau. G.T. Basden refers to 'this novel currency
found between Enugu and Awka' where he says: "this unique currency
is formed of tiny pieces of thin flat iron, half an inch in lenght,
with one end barbed, resembling a miniature arrow head.
These 'Umumu' have the advantage of being very compact as compared with
cowries but are easily lost. Awka people used the Umumu in the
purchase of slaves and titled men always carried Umumu along.
The value in cash was at the time one Umumu to two cowries, or
compared to British money in the year 1920, fourty-five Umumu
to one penny"[6].

But probably the clearest example of an approach to using money
is to be found in the largely used West African Cowrie Shells.
It is possible that they came into existence as considerable external
trade with Europe and the Meditteranean littoral of Africa has been
in existence for many centuries, and markets are considerably
developed in the internal economy of the region.

---

6) Basden, T.G., Niger Ibos, Frank Cass, London (1938), rev. 1966,
    p. 339

Says Basden: "Cowrie Shells appear to be in use over a large part of
tropical Africa, and the Ibo country shares in the wide distribution.
A wealthy man would have a large heap of shells in his house and
these could be measured in bushel. A clean shell is whitish
and light brown in colour. The back and lip edges are crumpled.
A hole is usually broken through the crown; This enables the shell
to be threaded on a string, though this was seldom done in practice...
A simple Cowrie Shell is of the merest trifle in value, yet one is
never wantonly wasted"[7].

The most striking feature of the Cowrie Shell economy is its
rapid response to the inflationary or deflationary pressures. This
has occured over a period of years, as more Western money came in
or was reduced in quantity. Gluckman asserts that 'in some areas,
the pressures were seasonal: cowries altered their value in relation
to French currency as demand for this currency rose in the months
when taxation was due, and subsequently fell..."[8].

Seen under this perspective, the debate whether cowries should be
classed as money in tribal society does not really arise, because
they could be brought under that denotation. Afigbo has also
established that there is enough evidence to suggest that cowries
were in use in Igboland before the advent of the Portuguese.
These three means of exchange therefore, namely, salt, Umumu and
Cowrie Shells were available in small units in pre-colonial
Igboland and were used in small purchases in the local markets.

---

7) Ibid.,
8) Gluckman, M., op.cit., pp. 67 - 69

Currencies of the post-colonial period included the brass rod, manilla and copper wire. Says Afigbo: "the brass rod, manilla and copper wire came with the Europeans and were useful for large purchases, as their exchange rates were much higher than those of the pre-European currencies"[9].

Brass rods was a higher currency in those areas which carried a cash value of roughly six-pence each, according to Basden. Manillas are horse-shoe-shaped tokens used in exchange. They are composed of an alloy of brass and iron. Formerly copper was used instead of brass. They probably originated as bracelets introduced by the Portuguese. Writes Basden, 'Mary Kingsley speaks of the Manilla as a bracelet in a state of sinking into a mere conventional token. An alloy of copper and pewter manufactured at Birmingham and Nantes'[10].

Generally, all these monies were regarded as money and accepted in entire Igboland, even though, in the more southern and eastern districts, manillas and brass rods were used, while cowries were popular for generations in the northern and western parts.

---

9) Afigbo, E.A., op.cit., p.14
10) Basden, op.cit., (Lord Lugard writes about the introduction of currencies such as brass rods, manilla, English and local coinage in his book: The Dual Mandate in British Tropical Africa, reprint: 1956)

2. Taxation:

There was in traditional Igbo society, no individual at the
head of the village with the title of chieftainship to whom
the villagers paid obeisance. The popular saying "Igbo enwegi eze",
meaning "the Igbos have no kings" holds, and as such, no one
arrogated to himself the right to impose tribute or taxation
to the people.

There was no one to whom tribute was paid to, or for whom work
was performed as of right. Says M.M. Green: "any such
conception, so far as one can see, is foreign to the minds of
the people. It is therefore not surprising that the introduction
of taxation by the British government in 1927 came as a shock
to the Igbo people"[11].

The origin of taxation in Igboland came with the influence of the
British. Before then, community development projects and road
maintenance or other village affairs were jointly agreed upon by
the village elders and village assembly, who generally agreed upon
a definite amount or tribute to be levied on each mature male
member of the community. This payment or tribute was used for
the "bonum commune", and respectable titled men, the priests
of the village shrine or elders were often asked to keep the
money on behalf of the community. Any abuse was seriously dealt with.

---

11) Green, M.M., Igbo Village Affairs, op.cit., p. 37
    (Mrs. Green remarks that when she told one of the villagers
    that down back in her native country Britain, people paid taxes,
    her listener was astonished and inquired to whom the payment
    was made! This explains the situation in Igbo society where
    there was no ruler).

Various groups and institutions such as the Ozo title holders,
secret societies like Mau, the age grades, and other institutions
often imposed levy on their members for jointly agreed projects,
and once in a while, they made contributions to promote village
dance groups, market clearance or other village projects. It
was the duty of the town crier to announce the levy and tribute
for all to hear in the quiet of the night. Collections and
payments were made to one of the age grades mandated to collect
the money on behalf of the village. Failure to pay up the levied
amount was often treated by confiscation of one's goods or
ostracisation from the important community activities. In some
cases, the member who did not pay up an agreed levy was outlawed
with his entire family from certain village affairs.
In this way, an earlier form of 'taxation' was introduced into
traditional society. Whereas however, in modern societies,
taxes are legislated by the ruling executive of a nation,
in tribal society, the village assembly to which wvery male
member belonged made the levy. Thereby, people directly bound
themselves to levies without representations by anybody or organ.

3. Contracts:

In Igboland, all the economic, social, legal and ritual customs and practices converge on the nodal point of family organisation and clan structure. In fact, social life in traditional society was only possible as a moral order in so far as it reflected in the sentiments of the members of the community. Law was therefore somehow dominated by status, which described one's belongingness to a particular clan. It was one's status as a member of the clan that guaranteed him rights or priviledges. Outsiders and foreigners were not included as they were considered as "Fa, Ha" (they) in contradistinction to "Anyi" (We). So it was for contracts. Says Achike:

'The role of contract or the law of contract depends upon the nature of the economic and social system within that community. Thus in the era when legal duties or obligations were determined by the status into which a person was born, the law of contract was of minor significance. Generally such rights and duties were not easily changeable by agreement"[12].

Dr. H. Maine follows the same line of thought of the role of contract in primitive law above where he says: "The point which before all others has to be apprehended in the constitution of primitive societies is that the individual creates for himself few or no rights, and few or no duties. The rules which he obeys are derived first and foremost from the situation into which he is born, and next from the imperative commands addressed to him by the chief of the household of which he forms part. Such a system leaves very smallest room for contract"[13].

---

12) Achike, O., Nigerian Law of Contract., Nwamife publishers, Enugu, (c) 1982, p.9
13) Maine, H., Ancient Law, 1959 (ed), p. 259

From these assertions, we are somehow led to believe that
Igbo traditional society did not have a notion of Contract as a
legal institution, even though they might have had a notion
of contract as a social institution. This explains why contracts
between two parties were often conducted under the seal of oath
known as "Igba ndu". Says Achike: 'An ancient society was
dominated by formalism and fiction: thus the only enforceable
type of agreement freely employed by the primitive society
was 'contract under seal'[14], which agrees to Maine's idea of law
in ancient society. At first, nothing is seen like the
interposition of law to compel the performance of promise.
That which the law arms with its sanction is not a promise, but
a promise accompanied with a solemn ceremonial[15].

---

14) Achike, O, op.cit., p. 3
15) Maine, H., op.cit., p. 260

a) Did Contracts Exist in Igboland?

From the aforesaid, it is not clear whether traditional Igbo societies had a clear law of contracts, or was it simply 'status' and 'good-will' in the name of contracts. We may begin by defining contract!

Generally, there are so many definitions to the term, but we shall single out this one by Achike where he says, that "a contract is an agreement which the law recognises as binding on the parties and which is enforceable by law"[16]. There are thus two elements involved in such a definition, namely 'agreement' and 'obligation'.

Since a contract involves two parties, there must be a substance on which they want to contract or agree upon, without which the contract cannot take place. Likewise, a contract must involve at least two persons or parties for it to be legally valid and reasonable, since a person cannot with himself. One contracts always with another. The basis of this contract is then an agreement between the contracting parties which normally serves as the grounds for its legal obligation. "Since there must be an agreement to every contract", says Achike, "the duty of the court is not to discover and enforce the intention of the parties but to discover and declare the legitimate expectation of the parties...
Secondly, there must exist an obligation which is reciprocated by the other party to the contract; that is, each party should be legally bound to discharge his own party of the contract"[17].

---

16) Achike, O., Ibid., p. 10
17) Ibid., What is an obligation? What is an agreement in contractual law? The word "Obligation" was used by the old Romans to express the right to a remedy, which arises from the conclusion of an actionable bargain. It is not every obligation that gives rise to an enforceable bargain. Thus a moral or social obligation will not support an action on contract; the obligation necessary for the formation of a contract must be one that will be legally enforceable. The word "agreement" includes such mutual assent by the parties to agreement which may or may not give rise to a cause of action. (Refer Achike, Ibidem).

We can now proceed to consider the situation of contractual law
in pre-colonial Igboland from the above background. Surely,
contract so understood, did not exist. Just like in the early law
of Europe, most of the transaction in Igboland in which men and
women are involved, are not specific or single transactions
involving the exchange of goods and services between relative
strangers. Instead, men and women hold land and other property,
and exchange goods and services, as members of a kindred or
hierarchy of political groups and as kinsfolk or affines.
Pre-existing relationship of status linked people together in
transactions with one another. Says Maine, "the movement
of the progressive societies has hitherto been a movement
from status to contrayt"[18]. Status determines the law of
property, and the position of persons. Thus, most of the law of
contract, dealing with transactions, is similarly involved in the law
of status. Under this kindred and clan structure as already mentioned
above, contracts could not exist in the way we understand them
today as obligatory agreemtns before the law.

In the words of Maine: "the separation of the law of Persons from
that of Things has no meaning in the infancy of the law... the rules
belonging to the two departments are inextricably mingled together,
and the distinctions of the latter jurists are appropriate only to
the jurisprudence"[19].

_____

18) Maine, H., Ancient Law, op.cit., chapter Five: 'Primitive
     Societies and Ancient Law".
19) Ibid.

Achike speaks out more clearly on this where he writes:
"Under traditional customary Igbo law, there was no law of
contract properly so-called. But the notion of binding
agreement pervaded all the economic and commercial transactions of
the indegenous community. An agreement meant a promise of
the parties to it, which promise they regarded as binding on them.
In other words, parties to an agreement were bound to carry out
in good faith the obligations assumed under it. It is therefore
submitted as erroneous to speak of customary laws of contract
since by definition, the modern notion of contract generally
presupposes the element of actiona-bility with the attendant legal
remedy where one of the parties causes a breach of it"[20].

He gives an example where an agreement between two parties
was not honoured by one of the parties, and because there was no
legal machinery to carry out the enforcement of the contracted
obligation, the contract did not work out as planned, therefore
rendering its contractability redundant. 'A' may agree to
exchange his yam for 'B's pot of palm-oil. 'A' may be ready and willing
to perform his part of the agreement, but the agreement may
not be executed should 'B' have a change of mind. Here, 'A'
has no remedy for there was no machinery to compel 'B' to honour
his promise. The agreement was devoid of legal backing and was
therefore no more than a 'gentleman's bargain'[21].

On the other hand however, Justice T.O.S. Elias asserts that
'indegenous legal systems was not devoid of the notion of
contractual rights and obligations'[22]. We can agree to this
assertion from the standpoint of Igbo philosophy, which believe

---

20) 20) Achike, O., op.cit., p.9 (Refer also Maine, op.cit., p.260)
21) Ibid.
22) Elias, T.O.S., Groundwork of Nigerian Law, p. 206

in keeping one's promises and in truth as life: "Eziokwu bu ndu".
From childhood, people were taught to keep promises, once they
make them, but not out of fear of the law, but out of respect
for the truth and for integrity. Contractual rights and obligations
which existed, as Elias has said, were observed out of morality.
Agreements made or obligations entered into, were also observed out
of sanctions resulting from the religious view of the world.
For example, in the field of agreements affecting the communities
interest in land, the mutual assent of the parties was usually
followed up by solemn rituals. The solemnity of these ceremonies
obliged the parties to the agreement to abide by its terms. As
Achike has said, "the sanction imposed for breach of the agreement
consisted of a fine or social taboo or restitution to 'status quo
ante' imposed on the defaulter by the community"[23].

In reality, specific contractual relationships, for exchange and loan,
and the provision of services, do exist and are most important.
One of these has been called the 'contracts of agistment' which we
shall now consider.

---

23) Achike, O., Ibid., p. 9

b) <u>Contract of Agistment</u>:

T.O.S Elias asserts that these contracts of agistments are
"agreements in stock farming communities whereby owners of cattle,
goat, or even poultry give them into the care and custody of
friendly neighbours for the purpose of being reared on a more
or less commercial basis"[24].

The purpose of these contracts in traditional society was to enable
the poorer and needy, but hard-working members of the community
who could not afford money to purchase animals for stock-farming,
to gradually build their own farms, through the help of wealthy
farmers, or other better-off members of the same community.
A contract of agistment was then entered into, whereby the borrower
of livestock accepted a certain quantity of animals such as goats,
chickens, sheep, etc. from the lender under specific contractual
agreements. Under this contract, the male animals are fed and
fattened by the borrower or caretaker until they are fully grown up.
The animal is then sold and whatever gains in terms of money
that comes from it is shared into two, or according to
other proportionally agreed terms.

With regard to the female animals, the owner of the animal and
the caretaker take alternatively the young ones produced;
the first fruits of the animal go normally to the owner first, and

---

24) Elias, T.O.S., The Nature of African Customary Law, p. 150

other issues to the caretaker and so alternatively. The
original animal continues to belong to the original owner, and
the caretaker has or may have right of possession after some time,
if this is in the agreement, otherwise, the owner reserves the
right to take back the original animal if he or she observes that
the chargee is careless with the livestock. When the animal is
no longer able to bear issues, it is sold off and the proceeds shared[25].

The basic attitude or spirit underlying this type of contract
of agistment is seen in traditional communitarian spirit which
believes that the riches of a fellow community or kindred member
is to be shared by all, on the condition that the poorer member
is willing to work for it. It is therefore the principle of
"No work no pay". Secondly, such practices increased the ties and
friendship existing between the contractual parties, as the
animal shared by both of them became a symbol for intimate
relationship and bond of nearness.

---

25) Nzomiwu, J.P.C., The Moral Concept of Justice in traditional
Igbo Society, op.cit., p.230

4. Loans:

There were no banks in traditional Igbo society, and yet the
practice of loans, either in cash or in kind took place. Loans
involved an agreement "by which a person borrows some article
or capital from another and pledges the return of same within
a specified period. Objects of this type of contract include
farm crops, money, and moveable property"[26].

It was the practice in tribal society that a member in need should
be helped if he merited it, and so the practice of long-term
and short-term loans and credit systems existed. One who needed yams
for cultivation would go to another farmer who had and borrow
from him, with a promise to pay back from the yields of his
harvest in the first year, the second year, or according to his
capacity. Misunderstandings often arose if one party to the
agreement did not keep his word, and this could lead to serious
family fighting. Damage done to a borrowed article can bring
trouble between the parties involved and this explains why
great care is taken by the borrower to return whatever he took
safely back. In many cases, a borrowed article may not be lent
out to a third party, since this third party may be an enemy of
the original owner. In cases where this has been practiced,
much has resulted.

---

26) J. P. Nzomiwu, Ibid., p. 231

G.T. Basden maintains the involvement of families in loan
affairs of this type. "Borrowing is a pronounced habit among the
Igbos... But the debtor may defer repayment of the loan,
if he prefers until the lender himself stands in need of it"[27].
Interest was not normally demanded, as the lender allowed the
debtor to use whatever gains to start off his own business.
In any case, he had to refund the capital whenever it was
demanded or at an agreed time.

There were people who incurred unforseen circumstances and
extraordinary expenditures such as through financing a funeral,
or marrying a new wife. In such a case, the debtor leases
his land to the creditor as guarantee for the required aid, and
ran the risk of loosing the land if within a specified time, he
did not pay back. But normally, his relatives came to his
rescue and got back the land. One who could not pay back a loan
or debt had another alternative of paying back physically by
doing manual labour for the creditor.

---

27) Basden, T.G. Niger Ibos, op,cit., p.107

5. Pledge:

This refers to a promise by a borrower who after getting a
loan or credit, could not pay back within the specified period.
He thus made a new pledge and promised within a renewed
period to settle his debt, supported at the same time however,
with the transference of certain of his moveable property to the
creditor as guarantee. People sometimes pledged economic trees
or even land, although this practice was not rampant.

Human labour was sometimes pledged. In this way, the creditor
obtained the usufruct of the pledged property until his loan was
paid back. In other cases, pawning was adopted, a system,
whereby the pawn would work manually for the creditor
(sometimes with his children) to pay off the debt.
His status however in the indegenous economy was protected.

Says Nzomiwu: "Pledging was carried out to assure that the
property remains within the said community and to prevent a member
being permanently deprived of his possession as would be the
case were he to sell his property to repay the loan"[28]

28) Nzomiwu, Ibid., p. 232

PART THREE (III) :   Manufacture and Industry

1. Introducing the Situation

In traditional Igbo society with all of it's harsh environments,
a man had to struggle hard to survive with his fellows.
Brave warriors, enterprising workers, gifted and artistic fellows,
all these gained in influence and status by their
industriousness.

The art of manufacturing goods by art and craftwork became
recognised profession in this typically agricultural milieu.
Through industry and manufacture, the natives involved were
offered some relief to the more strenuous farm jobs available.
They also supplied the much needed technological base of Igbo
society, and provided some of the items required by the demands
of social, ritual and political life. Manufacture requires some
sort of specialisation, ranging from the exercise of skills
and talents to a few trades such as smithing which require long
training. In many parts of Igboland, manufacturers formed
guilds of artisans for their trade with rules and regulations
to guide and protect them.

Afigbo writes: "The Igbos manufactured a wide range of items -
agricultural tools, war implements, various kinds of baskets,
cloths, earthen jars, household furniture... Some of the crafts
which produced these wares could be, and were, practiced by
anybody, but some were practiced only by selected communities,
either because only they had the necessary raw materials, or
because the crafts demanded so much time and expertise that they
could not easily be combined with full-scale farming. But by and
large it could be said that no region of Igboland lacked
specialists in at least one particular craft"[1].

---

1) Afigbo, A.E., Economic Foundations of pre-colonial Igbo society,
op.cit., p.15

The members of various crafts and industries sometimes formed guilds or associations to protect their rights, solidify their trade and to solidarise and encourage one another. Some of the many guilds available include: Metal workers, Blacksmiths otherwise known as Smith's union; carvers of sacred objects (artists); clay and pottery makers; herbalists and diviners; circumcisers; music instrument artists; the mid-wives guilds. These guilds were powerful and had power as a pressure group to influence policy in traditional society. Whereas they rendered basic and essential services, they could also deny their services to anyone who flouted their laws.

2. Smithery:

Although the basic profession of many Igbo's is agriculture,
no farmer could work without the basic implements needed for
farm work, which was the product of the blacksmiths. They
produced the hoes, knives, cutlasses, hooks for fishing, dane guns
and other weaponry, iron pots and other metallic equipments.
They were highly regarded and respected in traditional
society, and their profession was hailed as sacred.
"So important in fact that a northern Igbo legend says it
was the smith who dried up the land at the beginning of the world,
thus making smithery the first profession in Igboland..."[2].

It has been noted that of all Igbo communities which engaged
in smithery, the most famous and best organised were the
Awka, Nkwerre and the Abiriba. And their industry had a very
wide influence extending even beyond Igboland to their neighbours.

Says Basden: "Awka, Nkwerre and a few other places manufacture
nearly all the metal work produced in the Ibo country.
Apart from the agriculturist, the blacksmiths have more scope
for their activities than any other craftsmen"[3].

The iron they used for their work were mainly supplied
by the Agbaja people of Udi division and the Nsukka people
who smelted the ore partly to meet their own needs and partly
for export. In the western Igbo area, there were local smiths
who are believed to have learned the craft from the travelling
Awka master smiths. Like Elisabeth Isichei has tried to show:

---

2) Ibid.
3) Basden, T.G., Niger Ibos, op.cit., p.318

"Historians have tended in the past to take too much of a bird's
eye view of Igbo economic life, and to neglect the smaller
centres which nevertheless were dominant in the local trading
network. Thus although Udi was more famous for its smelters,
it also had a community of smiths at Agulu Umana...
These in turn looked down on their neighbouring 'Oheke' who did
not share their skills"[4]. Very artful and adaptable,
the smiths were generally competent in their trade, and could
very well imitate foreign metal wares in their reproduction of same.

In the records of Isichei concerning a missionary observation
dated at the beginning of this century:
"I paid a visit to a blacksmith's shop. It was most interesting.
With exceedingly primitive tools, and very meagre materials, these
native smiths turn out some very neat work. While I was waiting
he made a needle out of a piece of old knife. The eye and point
all complete without being filled or ground..."[5].

The smith's guilds in traditional society might be looked upon as
an anticipation of the trade unions to emerge in the country later,
because of their methods of work and their joint efforts to ward
off any hostile group. Says Basden: "The Ibo blacksmiths appear
to have anticipated the Trade Union Movement. In former days,
the rules and regulations governing the craft were rigidly enforced...

---

4) Isichel, E., A History of the Igbo People, op.cit., p.30 and 19.
5) Ibid.

On the whole, the members respect the instructions issued by
their councils, compliance with the general principles of the
institution as they apply in the different towns, is all that is
now demanded... But there is freedom from arbitrary restrictions..."[6].

In another context, he notes that the trade is controlled by
the council of the smiths in the different villages. No man may
go forth to practice until sanction has been granted by the
council under whose auspices he serves. Ceremonies have to be
observed and areas are assigned to those who are authorised to work
as journeymen in different parts of the country[7].

Infact, smithery was believed to be as mystical a profession which
established special links between the smith and the spirit world.
Consequently, it was hedged round by many taboos and required a
long period of apprenticeship. Wherever they went, Smiths enjoyed
special rights, and because their profession required much
physical strength and artistic ingenuity, people had much faith in
their artwork. The famous saying among the Igbo had a special
reverence for the capability of the smiths, namely:
"onwero ife asi onye uzu kpuo o na di akpu" - meaning: "there is
nothing a blacksmith is asked to forge that he does not achieve".

---

6) Basden, T.G., op.cit., p. 321
7) Ibid., p.318

3. The Herbalists and Diviners Guild:

These were regarded as life-giving-professionals, who are
able to cure the sick, intercede with the gods on behalf of
the community or single individuals, and deal with the
world of spirits beyond, where ordinary mortals are simply
helpless. The diviners are contacted in many matters of
social, political, religious or personal affairs. They
were just a power-base of traditional Igbo society, able
to collaborate and conceal each other and to push across
their demands on any topic.

If a person should flout their decisions, the person will
have to make sure that he does not fall sick, as the diviners
or herbalists association will not tend to him, should he need
their help.

4. <u>The Guild of Carvers:</u>

As has been recorded by Afigbo and others, the guilds of carvers
enjoyed a very lucrative occupation, where they had to meet the
various needs of religion, practical utility and of entertainment.
'Each of the myriads of gods, goddesses had its representation
in wood and owing to the ravages of white ants, these
were constantly being replaced'. No person would normally have
peace of mind if the guild of sacred carvers refused to carve
his '<u>Ikenga</u>', '<u>Chi</u>' or personal gods, or his masquerades and other
festive or ritual articles for him. It was an important profession.

It belongs also to the area of the carvers to make stools, doors,
wooden decorations, utensils, panels, domestic gadgets and art
work. In certain areas, an entire community specialised as carvers
such as the Umudioka people around Awka town[8].

'The Umudioka carvers were popular for their manufacture of ritual
objects and insignia. And they made much money from carving
various objects'.

A profession of carvers was not despised in traditional society,
because, not only was their job regarded as reasonable and
utilitarian, their job was also associated with affluence and money,
and they were also generally gifted. No wonder then, people called
them '<u>Omenka</u>' which means 'maker of Art'. People believed that one
was born an artist and not made. Thereafter however, carvers were
trained in the job and learnt to carve under a supervisor,
sometimes in far off regions.

---

8) Afigbo, A.E., op.cit., p.17

All the different guilds were able in times of dispute or
cases to be consulted because of their unity, power and
honesty, and due to the nature of their work. When they
consulted on an issue and they passed their judgement,
it was often difficult to act otherwise than to follow their
wise counsellings. To refuse to follow their
admonitions could result to denial of their services on
whoever was concerned. Other traditional
institutions sent them cases, already tried to review.
Thus, the guilds often performed as appelate courts.
There are however cases brought to their attention, which after
trying, were again referred to other traditional
institutions. Sometimes, they do recommend the consultation
of oracles or the swearing of oaths towards clearing a case.

5. The Salt Industry:

Not all trade exchanges involved craftmanship.
The various parts of Igboland were well suited, with her
neighbours, to an exchange of natural products. For example,
the swamps and waterways of the Delta were unsuited for
farming, but they were excellent for salt manufacture and
fishing.

Isichei shows that southern Igboland lacked salt and its diets
tended to be deficient in protein, relying too heavily on
starches and vegetable soup[9].

Salt however was founded in the north-eastern and eastern Igbo
areas of Uburu, Okposi and Abakaliki which had brine lakes. The
salt industry did not require any special training, nor
was much initial capital outlay necessarc. Often described as
'Nnu Oku' or 'salt in Earthenware', it was a dirty, grey coloured
salt. Isichei describes one of these salt centres:

"The other source of Igboland's salt was the salt lake at
Uburu, in the north-east, where the salt was processed by
an exclusive guild of women producers. Because of its salt,
and its strategic location for trade with the north, Uburu
developed into one of Igboland's great periodic fairs, under the
aegis of the Aro, and attracting merchants from a great distance[10].

---

9) Isichei, E., op.cit., p. 31
10) Ibid., pp. 31 - 32

Like smithery, the salt industry had a religious aspect,
and was associated with spirit forces, such as a local god,
which is believed to have given ordinances and regulations
guiding the exploitation of the salt. One of these was that
non residents may not exploit salt from the lake;
another was that only women might extract the salt
from the lake, and those having their monthly menstrual periods
were forbidden to approach the lake, lest the salt would
dry up[11].

---

11) Afigbo, A.E. op.cit., p. 16

6. Weaving of Cloth:

It might be necessary in this section dealing with
pre-colonial industries in Igbo society to mention the weaving
of cloth. Afigbo shows that the Igbo Ukwu excavations has
revealed that this industry is a long established one among the
Igbos, streching back to a period beyond the 9th century;
even before they learned to use cotton, the Igbo made cloth from
fibrous bark of certain trees, especially the Aji plant.
This type of cloth was often a man's make as it was energy
exerting. With the introduction of cotton, cloth-weaving
became a woman's business[12].

Isichei also mentions textiles in her accounts of traditional
Igbo society: "Textile manufacture was another ancient and
widely distributed craft in Igboland. Equiano's account of
mid-eighteenth century Igboland states 'when our women
are not employed with the men in tillage, their usual
occupation is spinning and weaving cotton, which they afterwards
dye and make into garments'. In the 1850's a British explorer
found elaborately woven patterned cloth on the Benue and near
its confluence with the Niger, which had been exported from
Igboland, possibly from the Nsukka area, where textile
manufacture was highly developed"[13].

---

12) Ibid.
13) Isichei, E., op.cit., p.30 (See also Olauda Equiano:
    The interesting narrative of the life of Olauda Equiano,
    abridged and edited by Paul Edwards, London, 1967, p.4)

From this, we see that cloth weaving was a time consuming industry
which women generally engaged in. Before marriage when women
were in the so called 'fattening rooms', old women or newly
married girls who are normally absented from communal work engaged
in this trade. It is noted that they produced two main colours
of this material in blue and white. Cloths were dyed blue by
steeping either the thread and or the finished woven material in
liquid preparations from local berries (<u>uli</u>, <u>uri</u>) and herbs.

As Afigbo says: "weaving is still being practiced today on a very
significant scale. It has still its advantages over imported cloth,
especially for ritual and ceremonial purposes"[14].

Isichei supports this view in her observations about the view of
an early European missionary who described the textile
manufacture in an Igbo town, west of the Niger thus:
"Every woman here weaves cloth from the cotton which grows on
the trees in abundance, and they do beautifully working
patterns..." The southern Igbo town of Akwete made textiles so
superb that imported cloth could not rival them, until finally,
foreign producers copied them"[15]. Today however, foreign
cloth is much coveted, and home made cloth would rather be labelled
with a foreign mark to be more attractive.

---

14) Afigbo, A.E., op.cit., p. 17
15) Isichei, e., op.cit., p.31 (Quotes missionary -
     F.M. Dannis, The 'Wild West', Niger and Yoruba Notes, 1903,
     p.23, re- Idumuje Ugboku).

CHAPTER THREE

AN IGBO SPIRITUALITY OF WORK

1. Religion in Igbo Traditional Society:

Clearly, religion has always been a very powerful factor in
human life and history. It is the same for Igbo people.
In ethical life, religion has played a particularly very
significant role, for it is in and through religion that moral
codes were formulated in most tribal and ancient societies and
also enforced. The Mosaic law which forbids and binds actions
with DO's and DONT's is a clear example.
No doubt, religion has been well used or misused by very many
societies. The Igbos are no exception to this.

a) Chukwu (God) - the supreme Spirit :

With regard to the religious conceptions of the Igbo people, it may
be shortly said that it is a universal belief, circumscribed
in their world view that a Supreme Spirit known as Chukwu (God)
exists. Chukwu is all powerful and surpasses all other existing
things, whether organic, inorganic or transcendental. In his
creative aspects, Chukwu is described as 'Chineke' - the God who
creates; 'Chukwuoke' or 'Chi okike' meaning creator;
'Osebuluwa' - the God who fashions the world; he is the author of
all life including man. He sends rain, makes the crop grow, and
is the source from which men derive their Chi or Soul.
As a merciful and just God, he grants favours to mankind in
general (Chidiebere, Chinenye, Chukwuka, Chinwe). Wrong doers
are adequately punished by the smaller gods and spirits on behalf
of Chukwu. "He is thus the creator of, and father of other

122

revered spirits, such as 'Igwe' - the sky; 'Amadi Oha' -
Lightening; and 'Ala' - the Earth-deity.

Sacrifices are not usually offered to Chukwu, but he is
regarded as the ultimate recipient of all sacrifices"[1].
The Supreme Being 'Chukwu' is never represented in symbols or
figures, for He is pure spirit. He is thus referred to as
'Obasi di n'elu' - God in the heights.

It is still under debate among scholars of Igbo religion, if
man, had anything to do with God directly. Surely it is
Chukwu who ordered and created the universe as we know it,
but after this work, he withdrew into solitude so that man has
hardly anything to do with him directly. This explains perhaps,
why, besides the existence of God as Supreme, Absolute, and
Just Being, the Igbos believe in the existence of a series of
deities and spirits, living on the supernatural plane,
but however dealing with man and his environment on the natural
plane. These include 'Ala' (the Earth-deity); the smaller
divinities and spirits who are agents of 'Chukwu' and
carry man's prayers, wishes and offerings to Him. So we have
the 'Sun-god' - (Anyanwu); the god of weather and lightening -
(Amadioha); the gods of fertility, food production and yam
production - (Ihejioku); there is also the 'Alusi' - meaning
the spiritual forces surrounding the village and from whom
Oracles, oaths, swearing, worships and sacrifices were determined;
then, there are the ancestors - 'Ndichie' who are now dead and
have joined the world of spirits to intercede for man before 'Chukwu'.

1) Meek, C.K., Ibo Law., (From Essays presented to C.G. Seligman,
London, Kegan Paul and Co., 1934, pp. 209 - 226).

Belief in devil - 'Ekwensu' also existed, as he was always
understood to be opposed to God's plan for man and to destroy
the harmony within the community. Every Igbo village worshipped
one divinity or another and they erected places of worship for it,
either in the forests, or around a river, on a hill, in a cave, or
on the village square (Ilo). We shall now give a little summary
review of the core of Igbo belief in these various religious and
cultural phenomena in traditional society.

b) Ekwensu or Devil: Belief in 'Ekwensu' - the architect of all
evil and perpetrator of wickedness among men existed. Ekwensu is
always opposed to Chukwu, and although subordinate to Him,
(like all other spirits) tried continuously to free man from God's
ways, to deceive him into mischievous and disharmonious
activities. The Igbos regard all mischief as works of the devil,
(olu Ekwensu) and Ekwensu is blamed for most of men's worst ills
and pestilences. No sacrifice was made to Ekwensu, nor did the
Igbo worship him. But they tried to free themselves from his
control by going to the Alusi and making their sacrifices
as demanded by the 'Dibia' - native doctor or diviner, or still by
going to the priests or priestessess of the deity - 'Ezeani' and
demand for placative sacrifices to drive out the evil forces of
Ekwensu. Personal responsibility for individual actions were
thus referred to the devil.

c) Alusi or Village Spiritual Forces and Shrines:

The Alusi as has already been shown above were strong spiritual forces
in the village, often residing in a shrine, and having the power
of blessing or destruction according to circumstances.
Unlike Chukwu whose attribute was goodness and benevolence, the
Alusi was responsible for externalising Chukwu's powerful
qualities, but also for punishing social offenders, and those who
unwittingly infringe their benefits.

Hence, the <u>Alusi</u> was worshipped in Igboland. Sacrifices were made to placate it, and the Diviners - '<u>Dibia,ogba-afa</u>', and priests - '<u>Eze-udo</u>' or '<u>Eze-ani</u>' were involved in interpreting the wishes of the <u>Alusi</u> and placating it for the general good of the community[2].

2) Isichei, E., op.cit. p.25

2. 'Ala' or 'Ani' - The Earth-deity:

Obviously central to the entire existence of the Igbo, it seems,
is the soil, the land or the earth which is of the utmost
importance. It is in it that a succession of the ancestors
are buried, and their souls rest in it. Life springs
from the soil - plants, animals and men are nourished by the
soil. On the soil grow yams and cocoyams, vegetables and all
sorts of fruits. So we speak of the soil as "Mother Earth" for
it is sacred for the Igbo. To commit a crime
forbidden by tradition was an 'Nso ani', that is, an abomination,
for it polluted the spirit of the Earth (Ala, Ani), and
threatened the entire community. Punishment included death or
abdication.

Ala, writes C.K. Meek, "is the most powerful and important deity
after the Supreme Being 'Chukwu'. She is the Earth goddess,
who exercises very great influence on Igbo morality, as she is
the divine female principle who guards the 'Omenala'
(customs of the land), believed to have been handed down to
the ancestors from time immemorial"[3].

The concept of Ala is believed to have originated in Chukwu
even though, she is the wife of Igwe (the sky) a son of Chukwu.
Just as a husband fertilises his wife, so Igwe, in the form of
rain, fertilises Ala[4].

---

3) Meek, C.K. Law and Authority in a Nigerian Tribe,
   Oxford University Press, London, 1937, p.25
4) Ibid.

Anthropologists D. Forde and G.I. Jones while documenting their
research findings in Igboland noted on the <u>Ala</u> :
"<u>Ala</u>, earth spirit, is the most prominent deity and is regarded
as the queen of the underworld and the owner of men whether dead
or alive.. She is the source and judge of human morality and
accordingly exercises the main ritual sanctions in disputes and
offences...[5]

The priests of <u>Ala</u> are guardians of public morality; the cult of
Ala is one of the most powerful integrating forces in Igbo
society". Since she has all these noble attributes especially
of being the source of human morality, Ala is in consequence the
main legal sanction. The Earth goddess is believed to share
in the justice of the Supreme God (Chukwu) in great measure,
being nearest to him. Laws are made in her name, and oaths as
well are sworn through her. The Igbos believe that <u>Ala</u> cares
and loves her children, and the laws issued by her are for their
well-being and happiness. So people see in her punishment
for offenders, a warning to the innocent and a sign of
corrective measure. Nonetheless, <u>Ala</u> does not punish so easily,
but waits till the criminal has become incorrigible at heart.

In this case however "<u>Ala</u> deprives evil men of their lives
and her priests are the guardians of public morality... <u>Ala</u> is in
fact the unseen president of the community, and no group is
complete without a shrine of <u>Ala</u>. The common possession of a
shrine of <u>Ala</u>, is indeed one of the strongest integrating
forces in Igbo society"[6].

---

5) Forde, D, and Jones I.G., The Ibo and Ibibio speaking peoples
   of South-Eastern Nigeria, International African Institute,
   London, 1950, p-25
6) Meek, C.K. Ibid.

Some Igbo anthropologists have sounded sentimental in
regarding man's relationship to Ala as that between mother and
child. This might be an over-exaggeration, in figurative
sense however, it is correct. After Chukwu, all other minor
deities and the ancestors buried in her bowels under the
earth are subject to her. Yet, Ala remains the nearest and
dearest, maintained to be a merciful mother, who increases
the fertility of the soil and makes the fruit of the earth
available to man's livelihood. No wonder, M.N. Okoro writes:
"Ala is a great spirit and man, having got his Chi from God,
is in the custody of Ala"[7].

The Earth Spirit, Ala, as the mother of the Igbo people, is
characterised by sacredness and peacefulness. Therefore, man
being made from the clay of the Earth, also bears the
sacredness of the Earth-Spirit. Plants, animals and humans go
back into the womb of the Earth, and the dead ancestors play
their peculiar role in the world of the living from yonder - in
the Ala.

Generally in Igboland, the "Cult of Ala" is very common, as each
of the hamlets or villages composing a village group has a
shrine and a priest of Ala, but there is always a senior shrine,
namely, that of the particular hamlet or village which originally
occupied the locality[8]. People worship her as the sustainer of
life, champion of justice and defender of the weak or innocent.
Respect and fear of the laws of Ala make people fair in their
dealings with others, for Ala as the custodian of morality
and the giver of 'Omenala' demands good deeds and prohibits evil,
which is termed 'Nso-Ala'.

7) Okoro, N.M., The Igbo belief in man's continued existence after
   death - It's influence on the society, Unpublished Thesis,
   Rome, 1971, p.39
8) Meek, C.K. Ibid.

In this manner, law and order was guaranteed in traditional Igbo
society and legal sanctions were imposed generally in society
on the people from the world of the sacred. Heinous social
crimes were forbidden and major offences against native law
and custom were punishable under the sanction of Ala.
Some of these crimes included "Homicide, kidnapping, poisoning,
stealing, adultery, giving birth to twins or cripples or
abnormal children"[9].

Death alone or banishment was not considered enough punishment
for some of the above crimes, and in certain cases, an offender
was denied ground for burial, being thrown into the evil forest,
one of the greatest social humiliations and condemnations
a native of Igboland could ever suffer. Such a soul found no
rest among the ancestors. It might be compared to the
Christian idea of hell.

But the action of an individual alone could bring punishment down
on the whole community, who did not prevent the crime by
ommision or also by commission. In such a case, the whole
community was bound to make propitiatory and expiatory
sacrifices through the priests of Ala, so that the entire
community do not suffer lack of fertility or productivity in
their farms, or other pestilences in the community. In this
manner, social responsibility for the evil actions of an
individual became the communal attitude. This communitarian
spirit made people swear their honesty by Ala, but they could
also, as was often the case, gather together in the village on
extended family level to impose a curse or blessing through
the Ala on offenders or peacemakers correspondingly.

---

9) Meek, C.K., Ibid.

And people did swear through Ala to explain their innocence.
One discovers until today, in Igbo villages, elders advising
younger ones not to perform evil deeds considered
as 'Nso Ala', as these may bring down the wrath of Ala on the
entire family or community. An individual's action thus
becomes a communal responsibility. No doubt, a certain
amount of individual freedom got lost in this way, as decisions
and actions were only encouraged if they contributed to the
general good of the community. It was thus not an Egocentric
or "I" society, but rather a strongly accentuated "We"
society. J.S. Mbiti made this point clearly where he
described the relationship between the individual and the
community in traditional African societies. In his book:
African Religions and philosophy, Mbiti concludes:
"I am because we are; and since we are, therefore I am".
Nzomiwu has noted in his thesis that "one very readily sees how
Igbo religion sustains and enriches Igbo sense of justice.

Igbo belief in the Earth goddess thus enhances and enforces
social justice. Whether one acts out of fear or love of the
Ala, who is a 'merciful mother', the result is the same, namely,
the effecting of social justice within the community"[10].

---

10) Nzomiwu, J.P.C., The Moral Concept of Justice among the
     Igbos., Unpublished Dissertation, Academia Alfonsiana,
     Rome, 1977, p.161.

Although other minor deities could be rash in their
judgement and punishment, the Earth goddess was the opposite
as she was slow to punish, having granted the offender
enough chances. "She is supposed to see the thoughts of all
and thus can measure the depth of the malice of each action.
In this way, her judgements and punishments are considered as
proper... The Earth goddess can thus give life or destroy it,
she loves immensely, but it is true also that nobody can
hurt more than she. But her justice is believed to be next to
that of Chukwu, because, she, like Chukwu, weighs all the
circumstances sorrounding an action"[11].

And Uchendu confirms this view too where he writes:
"Minor deities may not take action against an Igbo without asking
Ala to warn her children, but no spirit can intercede or
interven when Ala herself has decided to punish. But she does
not punish in haste, she gives many signals of her displeasure"[12].

Land is not sold in original Igbo traditional society as
land belonged to the community and not to an individual.
It has been suggested by scholars of Igbo culture that the
main reason why land remained unsellable was because, it
portrayed disrespect to the Earth goddess to sell land.
And where there was a sale of land in latter years,
especially after the foreign influence in Igbo culture, the
Earth goddess had to be ritually purified if the transaction
was to be accepted as consumated. Said Uchendu:
"The Igbo feel ashamed and guilty to have to sell the land"[13].

---

11) Ibid., p. 159
12) Uchendu, V.C., The Tgbo of South Eastern Nigeria.,
    Holt, Rinehart and Winston, New York, London, 1965, p.96.
13) Ibid., p.25

Finally, we must mention the fact that the Igbos, being an
agricultural people, performed a lot of rituals through the
priests of Ala during the various planting reasons, harvest period,
first fruits, and in all major yearly celebrations.
Ala was thus correspondingly respected, acknowledged and requested
to guide and care for her children here below, being steadily
pacified by the incessant prayers of the ancestor.

We shall highlight this section by relating a typical prayer
made often by the people to Ala, thus:

> "Ala, our Mother, on behalf of my dear people I make
> this sacrifice to you as thanks for the good harvest.
> You have brought us rain and have given us a good
> harvest. Let your children eat grain of this harvest
> calmly and peacefully. Do not bring us any depression
> or surprises. Guide us against illness of people
> and our herds and flocks, so that we may enjoy this
> season's harvest in peace of mind. Remove death and
> anything that will bring misfortune to your children.
> Give us good health to enjoy the fruit of our labour
> which we received from you"[14].

 With this sort of prayer, we can observe that in traditional
Igbo society and religion, ritual helps man find himself in a
cosmic infinity, for it is, as Wole Soyinka has said,
"through the drama of ritual that African Societies search for
harmony in their universe, and for the formulation of social
standards and moral verities"[15].

---

14) Iloanusi, A.O. Myths of the Creation of Man and the Origin
       of Death in Africa"., European University Studies,
       Peter Lang, Frankfurt/Main, 1984, p.95.
15) Soyinka, W., Myth, Literature and the African World, Cambridge,
       1976, (In Africa Studies Review, Vol.26, nos.3/4, sept. -
       Dec. 1983, p.126)

The African world is striving for harmony. Man, the community, and nature are concentric circles, and their consonance defines a structure of moral order. A breakdown in one area must affect the others, and the consequent disharmony is potentially catastrophic. In this way, the sickness of one individual is no isolated phenomenon, and may be seen as the sign of general malady. Individual fertility cannot be separated from the regenerative promise of earth and sea.

What emerges is thus 'an idiomatic African World, age-old and valid in its antiquity, but also fresh and forward looking, ready to face the future, to absorb what is new and useful'. In our own times, such a world view if resuscitated, would help the Igbos in their present search for a cultural direction; it would restore a noble character of continuity and harmony, thereby raising the qualities of his world view, which aims at considering the cosmos as a seamless whole.
Avoided will be a compartmentalisation of emotions, phenomena, institutions and scientific observations, as is often the case in Western societies. We might finally say that interdependence existed in Igboland uniting the economic and social relations, politics, law, morals and ritual into a harmonious whole.

3. Work and Religion:

Traditional religion influenced work in Igbo society. In the words of Archbishop Arinze: "Farm work was particularly permeated by prayer to the spirits for rain and fertility and by sacrifice of first fruits. Work was regarded as a type of link with the ancestors, whose heritage was taken over by the present generation. Even blacksmiths, midwives and herbalists had particular spirits who were regarded as their patrons. Work in traditional African society was not a purely secular affair"[16].

And as we have already seen above, most of work in Igbo society was work on the land. Any tribe is obviously dependent on its land around which are surrounded the shrines and rituals of the tribe. Land and its products are the focus both of general tribal interests, and of competition between individual natives. This is so because the prosperity of all depends on the land as a whole, being fertile and providing game; The Igbo belief in the land has been shown to be the basic reason why general feeling for peace in the village prevailed. They staged rituals to purify the soil after an abomination. They combined together to pray for rain, and to celebrate first fruits and harvest at certain shrines which we may here call 'landshrines'.

Thus, lack of respect for a landshrine or disrespect or des-ecration of it by a villager or foreigner was enough reason for a war or a general penance in the community. Porfessor Afigbo offers as one essential reason why the land was very regarded in Igbo cosmology in these words: "In the absence of the deliberate use of artificial manure as a means of fertility of the soil, the people resorted more and more to the religious worship, veneration and ritual purification of the Earth"[17].

---

16) Arinze, F., op.cit., p. 209 - 210
17) Afigbo, A.E. Economic Foundations of pre-colonial Igbo society, op.cit., p.10

Whether this suggestion is serious enough to be given consideration
in this chapter is outside the scope of our aim. But surely,
Igbo cosmology and religion surrounding the Earth, in as much
as it could be explained by economic factors, went beyond the
merely economic to pure philosophical and theological reasons.
We shall however, rather now consider the ritual importance
attached to agriculture and the mythological stories
surrounding the fruits of the land, such as yam, cocoyam, and
other crops as it has been handed down in the Nri legends
among others.

a) Ritualisation of Agriculture

A highly ritualised economic activity in Igboland was
agriculture. This is so because it was an important
occupation that had its roots in antiquity. The various
stages of agriculture were ritualised as Afigbo notes:
"The beginning of the farming season, the date of which varied
from one part of Igboland to another for ecological reasons,
was a formal occasion marked by a festival and ritual.
It was the same with the beginning of the harvest season
which was marked by the important New Yam festival..."[18].

b) Crop's Ritualisation

Crops were also ritualised, and prayers, taboos and
religious practices were observed with regard to certain crops,
especially yams and cocoyams which 'constituted the
backbond of Igbo agriculture'. People believed that all
these crops had spirit forces behind them, which laid down
the specific code of conduct of cultivating, harvesting,
cooking and eating them.

---

18) Afigbo, Ibid., p.4

c) The Yam and Cocoyam Legends:

This is the crop which is regarded as the 'King' of Igbo
crops. The legends relating to its origin expose this
important position. We shall narrate three of such myths here
to highlight the religious role of the cultivation,
harvesting and eating of yams in traditional Igbo society.
Basden narrates for example:

> "In the olden times, there was nothing to eat, so
> "Eze Nri" (King of Food)considered what should be done
> to remedy the defect. He took the drastic course
> of killing his eldest son, cutting the body
> into small pieces and burying them. His
> daughter shared a similar fate. Strange to say,
> five months later, yam tendrils ("ome Ji")
> were observed to be growing at the very places
> where the disembered parts of the son's body had
> been planted. In similar fashion "edde"
> (Koko-yam) began to grow where the remains of the
> daughter had been buried. In the sixth month,
> the "Eze Nri" dug up fine large yams from his son's
> grave and "edde" from the place where he had buried
> his daughter. He cooked both and found them sweet.
> At this time, the King was unable to rest or
> sleep during the day. On one occasion, one of the
> children of the village came along seeking fire.
> "Eze Nri" gave a piece of cooked yam to the child who
> ate it, went home, and promptly fell asleep.
> The child's people were surprised and, when he awoke,
> asked him to relate what had happened. He

replied that he did not know what it was
that "Eze Nri" had given him to eat. So the
process was repeated, and it happened again as at
the first instance. Then the people asked for
yam and "edde". The king demanded a great price
and then handed out a supply, at the same time
giving instructions how to plant. From that time
yams and "edde" spread throughout the country"[19)
This is the first legend relating to the yam tuber.

A second legend about the yam is related by Northcote Thomas, thus:

"Chukwu gave them (Eze Nri and Ezadama) each a piece of
yam; yams were at that time unknown to man, for
human beings walked in the bush like animals.
After eating his portion, Ezadama went to ask
for more. Chukwu gave him another piece and
instructed Ezadama to tell Eze Nri to send his
eldest son and daughter. The Eze Nri sent
them to Chukwu who told them to bring a big pot,
which he sent back again. The Eze Nri was to
plant this pot wherever he chose and no one
was to look into the pot for twelve days; when
they looked in and saw yams growing they went to
Chukwu and told him, and Chukwu said, 'Plant
them, put sticks, and lift up the runners!"[20).

19) Basden, T.G., Niger Ibos., op.cit., p.389
20) Northcote W. Thomas, Anthropological Report on the Ibo-Speaking
    Peoples of Nigeria, Part I, Law and Custom of the Ibo of Awka
    Neighbourhood., London, 1913, p.50

The third legend or myth on the yam crops is recorded by
M.D. Jeffreys: According to this corpus of myth which also
refers to the cocoyam,

> "When Eri died this food supply (from heaven)
> ceased and Ndri at Augleri complained to Chukwu
> that there was no food... and Chukwu told him
> he was to kill and sacrifice his eldest son and
> daughter... This killing of eldest son and daughter
> was carried out and the bodies buried in separate
> graves. Three native weeks later shots appeared
> out of the graves of these children. From the grave
> of his son Ndri dug up a yam... The next day Ndri
> dug up Koko-yam from his daughter's grave...
> For this reason, the yam is called the son of
> Ndri and Kokoyam the daughter of Ndri"[21].

---

21) Jeffreys, M.D.W., The Umundri traditions of Origin.,
African Studies, Volume 15, No. 3, 1956., pp 22-23-

4. Analysis of the Religious Aspects of the Legend:

There are certain elements which serve the religious aspects
of the yam and coco-yam from the above legends, and it might
be useful to mention a few of them here, namely:

(i)   Yam and cocoyam are crops which existed in very ancient
      times in Igboland, when men still talked naturally to
      Chukwu. It is thus an original and traditional food,
      whose origins in Igboland is very difficult to
      trace, as the legend says: "In the olden times..."

(ii) The yam and cocoyam are crops given to the Igbo by Chukwu
      himself, hence its highly religious meaning.
      As one of the legends says: "Chukwu gave them a piece
      of yam each....", and instructed them to plant
      these crops thus: "plant them, put sticks, and lift
      up the runners'. It is thus a crop, which has
      ritual value because of its religious origins.
      Here, all things are seen to come from God - Life,
      nature, food; God gives man food to eat and
      shows him how to plant it.

(iii) Thirdly, the yam is a crop associated with sacrifice and
      the suffering belonging to the human predicament. In the
      narrated legends, men are portrayed as having nothing to
      eat. There was famine. A typically religious phenomenon,
      for it is really in such situations when people are
      suffering, empty, helpless, and needy that they often
      turn to God, recognise their limitedness and appeal
      to transcendence for aid. The yam is thus a crop

which was the result of man's suffering in famine and his
dependence on God. But not only this dependence, for God
asks man to sacrifice to him before their wishes can be heard.
"...And Chukwu told him he was to sacrifice and kill his
eldest son and daughter...". The fruits of sacrifice is
yam and cocoyam. The king of Nri (Eze Nri) offered his son
and daughter as sacrifice to Chukwu and got in return "Ji na Edde"
(yam and cocoyam). Sacrifice is a topic on which very much has
been written about- whether in the Old Testament or in the New,
where Jesus Christ himself becomes the sacrificial lamb.
The higher the gift sacrificed, the greater the reward for mankind.

Sacrifices of simple cola-nut, chickens, a few amount,
goat, sheep or cow are always gradingly regarded, and are by all
forms lower than the sacrifice of a human being. When "Eze Nri"
sacrifices his son and daughter, it is clearly certain that
something greater will result out of it. Thus the yam which
results is the most favourite food for the original Igbo, just
as potato is the typical Irishman's diet. There is no substitute
for the yam, and its shortage or lack is a cause of very much
distress to the village community.

The yam is cherished, as well as the cocoyam, and the value
accorded to it makes it the food of the rich, the food for big
village occasions, and the food which has the greatest
ritual value. In many cases in traditional society, it was a
capital offence to rob a farm of its yams whether they were newly set
seed or the mature roots. Death or banishment often followed as
punishment for a yam thief.

(iv) Finally, we must mention the fact that two principles
here are present as in most affairs affecting Igbo
cosmology, namely, the male and female principle. For the
Igbo's, there are always two principles in each reality, which
go to make the whole. Thus, we speak of Igwe (heaven)
and Ala (Earth). It is in this vein also that the
legends concerning the basic diet of the Igbo in ancient times and
continuing into our own time, speaks of the yam and cocoyam. These are characterised as growing out of the graves of
"Eze Nri's" son and daughter. Yam grew out of the son's
grave, and cocoyam, out of the daughter's grave. No wonder
then, in the Igbo world of work, there are roles to be
played by the female and male sexes in cultivation and
harvesting. The relevance of this is that yam is a male's
crop, while cocoyam is a female's crop. Both of these
crops make up the world of work and show the balance in
in God's creation.

a) Cocoyam:

The Cocoyam (edde) had its own spirit force, known as
Njoku-ede. There were however fewer rules guiding the
treatment of Cocoyams as Ihejioku had for yams. As Afigbo says,
in many Igbo societies, the Cocoyam had its own festival,
largely an affair of the women. Husbands could help their
wives in the cocoyam work on that day and be feasted for their help[22].

---

22) Afigbo, A.E., op.cit., p.4

b) The Palm Tree and Bread Fruit (Ukwa) Legends:

As M.D.W. Jeffreys records in his "The Umundri traditions",
the palm-tree, which is a very important economic tree in
Igbo society has a legend regarding its origin. The legend says:
"Ndri also had a male and female slave killed and buried in
separate graves, and in three native weeks, there sprang from the
grave of the male slave, an oil palm, and from the
female slave, a bread fruit tree"[23].

From the palm tree, food, drinks in the form of alcoholic palm wine,
oil for eating and rubbing on the body, as well as for
medicinal purposes, brooms for clearing the compound, rope,
rafia for art work and for roofing the house, wood, etc.
resulted. The palm tree served a multi-purpose. It is
surprising that the legend here quoted proposes the origin
of the palm tree to be of servile origin, and this means, as
something not incarnated in the community as it is the result
of slaves, just like its counterpart, the bread-fruit.

However, the myth narrated, depicts how religiously, almost each
crop or plant had its spirit force. Other crops such as beans,
grains, cassava, maize were thought to be generally possessing
a spirit force, just as the Igbo believed every individual
thing, including stone to have its own 'Chi' or 'guardian spirit'.

_____

23) Jeffreys, M.D.W., op.cit., p.123

5) The Religious Aspects of Trade:

Just as the Igbo believe that Chukwu institutionalised agriculture, gave man yams, cocoyams and other crops to plant and eat, so also does the Igbo believe that trade and market, as well as the crafts of industry and manufacture were originated and institutionalised by Chukwu or one of his deputies. Thus, the market in Igboland which has four days, are named after four heavenly fishmongers each of whom went round the Igbo country, establishing markets bearing his spiritual name. As M.W.D. Jeffreys records in his legends and myths, we shall recount that concerning the markets and show its religious significance, thereby supporting the thesis that there existed a religious view of work in traditional society, which can today be elevated to a 'theology or spirituality of Igbo work'. The legend says:

"In the beginning, the days of the week had no names,
for there was no way of counting the days because the sun
was always shining and no one slept. Then four strangers
arrived at Aguleri with four baskets. Ndri asked Chukwu
where they cam from. Chukwu refused to say, but said he
would send a person who would divulge their names and
tell where they came from. A wise person (Okpeta) was
sent to Ndri. Okpeta brought a rat with him. At night he
tied a string round the rat and told the rat to enter the
first basket: the rat did so and made a noise therein.
One of the unknown visitors shook the owner of the basket
and said 'Ekke, Ekke', and told him that something was
making noise in his basket. When Ekke was about to get up

and find out the cause of the noise, Okpeta pulled
the rat away. So when Eke looked in he saw nothing to
cause the noise. Ekke went to sleep, Okpeta noted the
name, and sent the rat into another basket to make a
noise therein and the next man woke up and
called to the owner of thebasket saying, 'Oye, Oye',
something is in your basket. Okpeta did as before
and so on for the other two baskets and
secured the names of the owners, namely 'Afo' and
'Nkwo'... These four men founded four markets, and
that is how the Igbo got their four-day week.
These four strangers were sent by Chukwu, and their
baskets contained fish..."[24].

From this legend, Afigbo concludes that the Igbos regard the
origin of the market and trading in their society as ancient
indeed, going back to those far-off-days, 'when the world was
young', and men held discussions directly with Chukwu. It shows
the religious and ritual attachment to the market, and
explains why taboos, laws and ceremonies accompanied so many

---

24) Jeffrey, M.D.W. Ibid., pp. 124 - 125

business affairs in traditional society. Says an early
anthropologist to Igbo land:
"The smallest village has its market (afia), and each market
has normally a patron in the "spirit world" who guides and
leads it to prosperity. This patron, otherwise, the
"Alusi" (spirit force) of the village gains more popularity
even beyond the village if the market prospers, and looses prestige
if the amrket declines.

No wonder, some of the markets which hold in one of the
four days of the Igbo week: 'Afo, Nkwo, Eke, Orie' are also
called or named after the Alusi. Dr. E.A. Afigbo agrees to
this for he writes:"Each market in Igboland was believed to
have its own spirit-force and the more successful the market was
the more powerful this spirit-force was believed to be. And it
was widely believed and known that to attack or enslave
anybody going to or coming from such a market was to cause
disaster, as such a trader was believed to be the client of the
spirit-force that owned the market... Though the exploitation
of these beliefs and institutions, the professional traders
and other specialists built up their business in long
range trade"[25].

---

25) Afigbo, A.E., Economic Foundations of Igbo society,
    op.cit., p.12

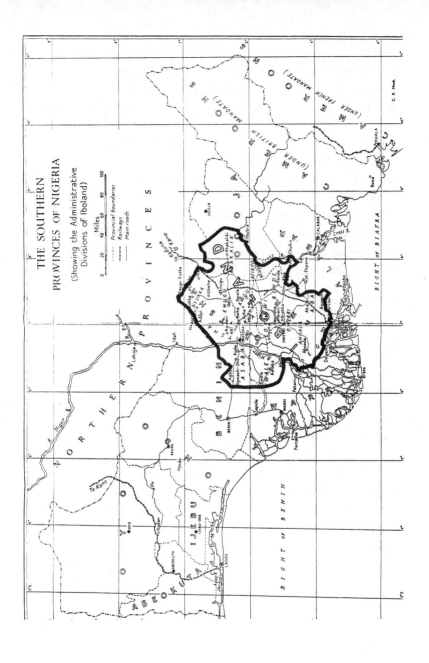

THE SOUTHERN
PROVINCES OF NIGERIA

(Showing the Administrative
Divisions of Iboland)

Miles
0   20   40   60   80   100

———— Provincial boundaries
-+-+-+- Railways
———— Main roads

C. K. Meek.

6. Conclusion:

We have now come to the end of this study into the
economic way of life in pre-literary, pre-colonial and pre-
industrial Igbo traditional society. With such a historical,
cultural and philosophical background, we have been enabled to
understand better the thesis that all social, legal,
economic, ritual and political practices in Igbo society
converged on the nodal point of family organisation,
religion and the clan structure. We have also been able to
see that life in traditional Igbo society can be analysed
in terms of factors of production, organisation of labour,
entrepreneurship, principles of distribution and payment,
and of exchange and value.

Even though most transactions are conditioned by general
social, rather than specific economic advantages, we can say
that it is possible and profitable to apply the standard
techniques of economic science to the life of tribal society, and
this has been surely demonstrated cogently in the preceeding
chapters.

There are similarities between economy in a tribal and a
civilised economy. Differences which exist cannot be due to
any difference in the character or intelligence of the peoples
existing in these two types of economic systems. Differences can
rather be said to be 'imposed' by the types of productive tools,
the predominance of primary goods, and the restricted scale of
the communities and their external trade connections.
So we see for example that Igbo economics in pre-colonial times
had more elements of general social and community considerations
dominating over the simple, specific economic calculations.
We can thus apply the words of Firth to the Igbo situation:

"It will probably be agreed... that the differences
between a primitive economy and a civilised
economy, as far as the 'spirit' of the relationships
is concerned, are quantitative rather than
qualitative. To some degree, the elements
characteristic of tribal economics can be paralleled
in modern industrial life"[26].

Surely, of course, these elements which can be paralleled
from tribal economics into modern industrial life formed
the foundations on which the Igbos met the British at the
beginning of this century.. Many books have been written about
'Igbo receptivity to change', and their wholesale embrace
of Western ways of life. In many cases, these western ways of
life in the area of economics, politics, social life and
culture, did not embrace at the same time, a sound
religious and ethical world view, authenticated in the Igbo
'Omenala'.

As a consequence, the Igbo at the time of the European-Igbo
contacts ran the risk of exchanging his culture with a foreign one.
He became acculturated, westernised and alienated from his own
basic philosophical and religious past. The break was abrupt,
and the consequences for the Igbo in the context of Nigeria
today are quite clear to many informed persons interested in
the problems of the "Third World". People are living a life
that does not correspond to their historical past and does not
coincide with it.

The basic principle which in Igboland says that 'people who do not
look back to their ancestors cannot look forward to progress and
posterity' has been abused.

---

26) Firth, 'Primitive Polynesian Economy, 1939, p.355

CHAPTER FOUR

NIGERIA IN THE COLONIAL AND POST-COLONIAL ERA - A SOCIETY
IN TRANSITION

PART ONE (I) : From British colonial territory to independence

1. Background information and history:

The period that opened up towards the end of the 15th century has been
described by historians as the "Age of Exploration", and this description
covers many events that followed, namely, slavery, colonialism, evangelisation and europianisation. A new impulse to exploit the natural
resources , raw materials and commodities which Europe did not have,
the desire to counteract muslim expansionism, the avarice for power,
and the wish to explore the so called "unknown world", pushed the well-
to-do-classes of Western Europe to look outwards into the world and thereby
to seek for the supplies of such luxury commodities which the Asian
and African world possessed, such as silk, ivory, gold, precious stones,
spices, pepper, oil and other such goods.

The markets of Syria, Egypt and Asia Minor were almost without exception
in Islamic hands following the crusades, and thus made it difficult for
merchants from "Christian Europe" to venture directly to the sources of
supply for these goods beyond the medittarenean and Black seas.
By the fifteenth century, direct commercial relations had been opened
by sea not only between West Africa and Europe, but also with the newly
discovered American continent . In 1472, the first Europeans visited
Benin, an ancient African kingdom in today's southern Nigeria and tried
to establish commercial relations there.

For the next three hundred years however, entire West Africa and beyond
was to discover that this contact was the begining of a nefarious trade
on human beings as slaves, captured to work in Europe and its "newly
discovered continent" on the other side of the Atlantic. The story is
brutally known that millions of Africans were carted out annually to
work in the white man's plantations as slaves[1].

---

1) Captain John Adams, "Remarks on the country extending from Cape Palmas
   to the River Congo", London, 1923,p.129 (Ref. Isichei,E., op.cit., p.43)

For both economic, philanthropic and other reasons, and moved by the impulse that the African had been misused and brutalised in the centuries of the trans-atlantic nefarious slave trade which involved dealers from almost every European country, especially Britain, Germany, France, Portugal, Holland, Danemark, Brandenburg,[2] certain noble Englishmen of calibre including William Wilberforce, Granville Sharp, the Duke of Gloucester, Thomas Clarkson, Thomas Babington Malcmulay led a movement for the abolition of the slave trade, which had thrown entire Africa into a crisis, depopulated the continent, robbed it of all its able-bodied men and women, and almost distorted completely its history, culture and heritage.

In 1807, the British outlawed slavery, and, to effect it's observance, supervised coastal trading for the next fifty years. France and other Europeans powers outlawed slavery half a century after Britain.

Colonialism took over from slavery. Indeed, the year 1885 stands eloquent in the history of Africa as the year of the official "scramble and partition of Africa" by European powers. Under Bismark of Germany in 1884, the Berlin conference was summoned, among other things, to help the French and the Belgians effect a cessation of British activities in the Congo-Basin, activities being carried out by Baptist Missionaries and merchants from Manchester and Liverpool.

---

2) Fage J.D., A History of West Africa, Cambridge, London, 1969, p.68

In this, Bismark got his way, for Germany soon annexed Cameroun.
Not wishing to push Franco-German conspiration too far, the
conference had little hesitation in allowing Britain to be
responsible for the Niger River regions. The result
of all this internal European conflict and rivalry was the
shameful Berlin Act, which provided that

> "Any European Power which could show
> that it had a predominant interest in
> any African region would be accepted as the
> administering power in that region, provided it
> could show that it's administration was a reality"[3].

Since the British outlawed slavery in 1807, coastal trading in
other tropical products began, especially with the
establishment of coastal trading centres from 1857 onwards.
Subsequent attempts to penetrate into the interior from
the coasts of Lagos were resisted by native middlemen.
However, Sir George Goldie, a British magnet and successful
trader united in 1879 his fellow countrymen trading at the
coasts against their French rivals. Sir George Taubman Goldie's
efforts and the manoeverings of other European powers in the face
of the impending Berlin conference made the British Government
recognise an amalgamation of European Firms trading on the
Western coast of Africa into one single Firm, namely, the
'National African Company', later renamed the 'Royal Niger Company'.

Through this company, the British Government ruled the Protectorate
of Lagos until 1900 when the Company handed over power
officially to the British in what has been termed "Flag follows
trade", complementing what the missionaries on the other hand
did for Britain in the other aspect termed: "Flag follows Cross".

---

3) Frederick Forsyth makes reference to this historical misnoama
   in his book on the Nigerian - Biafran civil war: 'The making
   of an African Legend: The Biafra Story', London, 1969, p.15.

Lord Lugard Frederick, a seasoned British soldier and colonial servant of Her Majesty was sent by his Home Government's Colonial Office in 1897 to experiment in the newly conquered zone. He needed one year to push out the French influence and although war with France was threatened, the Anglo-French agreement of June 1898 established the basis of the new territory's borders. Besides, Lugard spent three years subduing the North of Nigeria, conquering with his tiny force one emirate after another. Having subdued the sultan's firepower, Lugard began the conquest of the southern hinterland with the Aro-wars which led to the annexation of Igboland.

As an "act of administrative convenience", Lugard amalgamated the North and the Southern Protectorates in 1914, and a system known as "Indirect Rule" was imposed on the natives, during which Britain was interested in exploiting from its new colony whatever it could. Like British born writer Frederick Forsyth mentions:

> "Britain had gained a colony. It had not been
> conquered, it hadn't really been explored.
> It had no name, so later Lord Lugard's
> girlfriend gave it one - NIGERIA"[4].

Britain's colonial policy remained exploitative and orthodox: "maintain law and order, stimulate the production of raw materials, create demand for British exports, and raise taxes to pay for colonial rule"[5]. This policy lasted until 1960 when Nigeria became independent.

---

4) Forsyth, F., op.cit., pp.14 - 15
5) Ibid., p.20

2. Nigeria at Independence - 1960:

In 1914 under Lord Lugard's colonial policy, Britain had amassed
a large land with an area of 913,072.64 square kilometers, well
watered by the two rivers of Niger and Benue and their tributaries.
Lying within the tropics between latitudes 4 and 14 degrees
north of the Equator, and longitudes 3 and 14 degrees of the
Greenwich Meridian, Nigeria remains bounded on the North, east and
west by the former French colonies of Niger, Cameroun and Benin,
all republics now and independent, and it is washed on the
south by the Atlantic ocean. A tropical climate with an average
temperature of about 25 to 32 degrees celsius and two well-marked
seasons - the dry season (from November to March) and the rainy
season (from April to october), Nigeria remains a land of
contrasts with diverse peoples (over 400 tribes), languages
(over 250), cultures, and religions[6].

---

6) For further information refer to: Nigeria - Background
    Information; Published by the External Publicity Division,
    Office of the President, Lagos, 1981. (Nigeria's population
    in 1984 was estimated to lie somewhere between 100 and 110
    million. It is as such the most populous country in entire
    Africa, as well as the most sophisticated).

153

Like Forsyth says: "Nigeria at the time of the colonial lordship
had never been more than the amalgamation of peoples wielded
together in the interests and for the benefit of a European Power".
Nigerian elites fought without violence for the independence of
the colony from Britain, and on 1 October 1960, Nigeria became an
independent and Federal Republic, with a British - styled
Constitution, and was admitted within the United Nations.
She enjoyed this period only too shortly, just sixty three months,
before the tiny veneer that hid the basic disunity burst into
a tribal war between the predominantly Hausa-Fulani north with the
support of the Western Yorubas, against the predominantly Igbo
Eastern region. The war to subdue and retain Biafra
(Igbos and entire eastern region) within the context of a
colonially carved out Nigeria lasted from July 1967 till January 1970,
with a balance of over two million people dead, fourteen million
homeless and three million wounded in battle or otherwise, besides
loss of property, poverty, psychological terror and societal
disorder.

In tracing the root cause of this war, many authors and opinions
maintain in the words of Forsyth, that

> "although the immediate cause of the
> war had been the political, the fundamental
> spark had been the tribal hostility embedded
> in this enormous and artificial nation... for
> Nigeria was essentially a British, not a
> Nigerian experiment[7].

---

7) Forsyth, F., op.cit., p. 34

Chief Obafemi Awolowo, one of the strongest and outspoken politicians of Nigeria had this to say in 1947, even before the creation of Nigeria into an independent nation:

> "Nigeria is not a nation: It is a mere geographical
> expression. There are no Nigerians in the same
> senses as there are English or Welsh or French.
> The word Nigerian is merely to distinguish those who
> live within the boundaries of Nigeria from those who
> do not"[8].

In the same tone, Nigeria's first Prime Minister at independence in 1960, Alhaji Abubakar Tafawa Balewa confirmed what Awolowo already referred to above, namely:

> "...Since the amalgamation of the Southern and Northern
> Provinces in 1914, Nigeria has existed as one country
> only on paper... It is still far from being united,
> Nigerian unity is only a British intention for
> the country"[9].

Infact, it is held by many political scientists, that one main problem of African nations rests in the creation of artificial boundaries which the Berlin Conference legitimised during Europe's Colonial might and expansionist trauma. This artificial creation of boundaries, the indiscriminate division of peoples, cultures and clansmen into different spheres of influence, just for the benefit of the colonialist countries concerned, has constituted a major obstacle to the economic, political, social development and well-being of many African countries today.

---

8) Awolowo, Obafemi, 1947, published in "The Punch", Nigeria, Friday, 12.12.1982, Vol.8. No. 13, 819., pp.12 - 13
9) Balewa, T. Abubakar, op.cit.

In the context of Nigeria, the colonially imposed government
with its federal structure coincided with Britain's
dreams, without proper consideration of the historical realities,
the wishes of the various ethnic groups occupying the area,
and was therefore from its inception unworkable and
politically unrealistic as history has tried to prove in the
twenty-five stormy years of the nations existence. What the
future has with regard to the political destiny of the nation is
still unknown and unclear, but Britain's imposed governmental
pattern and "divide and rule" policy is unfortunate as is often
observed by respected opinion on African studies.
It lies now on Nigeria itself to decide its fate by choosing
between its commitment to pan-africanism, or by deciding for
the purposes of short run political realities to go apart.

3. The Problems of Nigeria

a) Colonial Heritage and the Crisis of Values

It is a marathon task to attempt within the context of our
research to offer an exposition of the problems of Nigeria.
This section can only in a very brief form make reference to this
issue, as many books have already been written on the topic, and
many more are being published daily[10].

In making reference to the problems of Nigeria, we are thereby
attempting to locate the context and milieu in which the
Encyclical Letter of Pope JOhn Paul II is being applied in its
relevant message. As has already been shown from the preceding
descriptions, the traditional society described in the entire
second section of this dissertation has already or is rapidly
disappearing, following the intrusion of foreign powers into the
political, cultural and social life style of the natives.

---

10) Books and articles already published on the problems of Nigeria
     are numerous. Among the most recent are: Achebe, C.,
     The Trouble with Nigeria., Fourth Dimension Publishers, 1983;
     Chukwudum, M.A. Nigeria: The Country in a Hurry, John West
     Publ. Ikeja, 1981, Nwankwo, A., Can Nigeria Survive.,
     Fourth Dimension Publ. Enugu; 1981. Amadi, E., Ethics in
     Nigerian Culture, Heinemann, Ibadan, 1982; Nigeria in
     Transition - A critical examination of the main Political,
     Economic and Social aspects of the Nigerian society;
     (Seminar Report at Kaduna, 11th - 13th September 1979);
     Federal Government Printers; 1210/480/5,000 (OL/29971)
     And a host of articles in all the national Dailies of the country.

Infact, Nigeria today is undergoing a massive change in all
spheres of life, be it economic, social, political, religious
or otherwise, and this situation has to a very large extent
also changed the original attitude to work in traditional society;
it has changed the organisation of work, as well as the type
of work done.

For many Nigerians, work is ceasing to be rural or subsistent
and is becoming urban and white collar jobs. Instead of hoes and
matchets, people today work with paper and bics, dressed in
French or British suits to match. Like Cardinal Francis Arinze has said:
"The changes have been sudden in Africa. What took about
centuries in Europe in the pre-industrial, industrial and
post-industrial eras are being cramped into one century in Africa.
Changes that took several generations in the West are being
witnessed by one person within his lifetime in Africa. In the
same community, some people may be living a simple and rather
primitive form of existence, while others are in steady contact
with the products of the post-industrial western revolution"[11].

The implication of all these very fast and hurried changes are
imaginable. There is a very big confusion as regards to values,
and there is a big crisis in digesting the new colonial heritage.
A well known Nigerian novelist Prof. Chinua Achebe has written
two books titled: 'Things Fall Apart' to portray that the old
order has changed giving place to the new, and another book
titled: 'No longer at ease', to portray the internal situation in
which the people today find themselves. Of course, this
difficulty in adjusting to the massive pressure of the space age,
the moon age, the technological and computer age, for people who are
still unable to read and write, who live in huts in the villages and
are still harassed by the vicissitudes of life in traditional society
has brought much discontent and disarray.

---

11) Arinze, F., The Encyclical Laborem Exercens in the African Context.,
     op.cit., p.210

Pope Paul VI well knew of this situation, for, in his Encyclical Letter
"Populorum Progressio", he says:
"The conflicts between traditional civilisations and the new elements of
industrial civilisations breaks down structures which do not adapt
themselves to new conditions. Their framework, sometimes rigid, was
the indispensable prop to personal and family life; Older people
remain attached to it, the young escape from it, as from a useless barrier,
to turn eagerly to new forms of life in society. The conflict of the
generations is made more serious by a tragic dilemma: whether to retain
ancestral institutions and convictions and renounce progress, or to admit
techniques and civilisations from outside and reject along with it, the
traditions of the past and all their human richness. In effect, the moral,
spiritual and religious supports of the past too often give way without
securing in return any guarantee of a place in the new world.
In this confusion, the temptation becomes stronger to risk being swept
away towards types of messianism which give promises but create illusions.
The resulting dangers are patent - violent population reactions, agitation
towards insurrection, and a drifting towards totalitarian ideologies.
That is the situation. It's seriousness is evident to all"[12].

In these words, Paul VI uses adequate picture to describe the transition
mood which characterises the situation of many nations of the developing
world in its relationship to new technologies from outside.
Nigeria, or specifically Igboland, like many other tribal societies is a
clear case in point.

_____

12) Paul VI, Populorum Progressio, n.10 -11

Such a difficulty in adjusting to new changes in the Nigerian
world has affected work, families, national development, labour
relations and productivity. It has affected the world views
of the Nigerians as many people today read and write English,
think English, French, German, American or anything exotic,
but have practically forgotten the traditions of their own
native soil. So we can say today that the area of culture is
existing in a sort of 'cultural bazaar'.

A wide variety of ideas and values drawn from different
civilisations, compete for the attention of potential Nigerian
buyers. This marketing has brought Nigeria the infamous name
of a nation of 'consumers'.

The pervasive impact of this neo-colonial exploitation
(decades after colonial independence) remains as strong as ever
especially as it has developed a hydra-head - with local
people changing places with or collaborating actively with
former exploiters, whether from the western world or from
the Arabian world. An Igbo author analyses this cultural
bazaar where he says: "any people who have been controlled or
ruled by a colonial system have a hard time re-establishing
themselves. The systematic repression of original ideas through
many hidden and open facets, and the gradual influence such
repression has on the man and his children and society, lead
the person toward self-condemnation and produce complexities
and confusions not easily noticed or analysed"[13].

---

13) Njaka, N.E., Igbo Political Culture, Evanston, North
Western Univ. Press, 1974., p.xii.

The issue of values in general, and particularly that of
cultural and socio-political values has become a central
issue in treating any topic related to the solution of the
Nigerian societal chaos. This vital problem demands a
creative policy based on a hierarchy of values in the same
way that their foundation and substantiation cannot be acquired
with old conceptual instruments. It is no more the season
of asking "to be or not to be", but rather, of asking
"if to be what to be and why to be". This is the decisive
question towards solving Nigeria's 'drifting' society.

General Obasanjo, former Head of State in Nigeria pointed this
value crisis out in an interview he granted in early 1979 before
handing over power to a democratically elected Government.
He said among other things: "ostentatious consumption,
the wastefulness in looking for foreign made, but non-essential
goods, extravagance and lack of a sense of thrift in regard
to local, state and federal government spending"[14],
all these have become the bane of Nigeria.

Many of those in power since independence were, as employees of
the British in pre-independence days, antagonistic to the
people's interests because of private gains. Some were
responsible for misleading the peasants and masses into
accepting values and cutting their coats above their sizes,
in the interest of the coloniser.

---

14) Obasanjo, O., Foundation for stability., Transcript of a
    Television Interview, Jan. 16 - 18 1979., Publ. by the
    Federal Ministry of information, FMG, Lagos.

Like Chinua Achebe has said: "When you went into a university to read in those days, it was not really very much related to your interests (or to your people). If you were lucky, the two might coincide, but you were simply looking for the shortest, the quickest avenue into the "senior service",,, colonialism meant: a loss of initiative in one's own history, just have no say in who you were, your own self development"[15]

Professor Soyinka made the same experience during his school days in London for he notes in an interview:
"I took one look at our first set of legislators...when they visited the UK and talked to students... I realised that the first enemy was within... They could not wait to return home and get a slice of 'independence Cake', because that is all independence meant to them... step fast in the shoes of the departing whites before other people got there"[16].

---

15) Achebe, C., Interview in 'West Africa' Magazine, London, 5.11.1984, ed. Kaye Whiteman., p. 2211
16) Soyinka, Wole., Interview on 50th Birthday by Biodun Jeyifo, publ. in West Africa, London, 27.8.1984., p.1729

From all that has been said, we have been able now to show that
colonialism in Nigeria left terrible psychological and
political woes on the colonised. For not only was it an amalgamation of varied peoples into one nation without consultation,
it succeeded in brainwashing the colonised into rejecting
their own skin, their own culture, their own relations, and
in replacing for all these - the eccentric, the new, the vague
values from Europe. No doubt, many Nigerians bought over this
manipulation under which the country now suffers and have themselves
become colonialists to their people. It is common knowledge
that the developing nations suffer from internal colonialism.
A small group of rich and powerful people maintain its power
and wealth at the expense of the misery of millions of
population. Many governments are still semi-feudal, with a
semblance of a 'patriarchal' system, but in reality a total
absence of many personal rights; the situation is sub-human
and undignified, as we shall come to show in the pages ahead.

b) The Political, Social and Economic Spheres

With seven past administrations, both civilian and military
to her record between 1960 and 1985, (and the military staging
at least four successful military coups and several
unsuccessful ones), Nigeria, like many other developing nations,
could easily qualify as a country that is unstable,
difficult to govern and in political transition.

People may differ as to the reasons. However each new
administration pledges to remedy the mistakes of the past, blames
the previous government for all the ills of the nation, and
almost always receives the good will of the masses who look
forward to a regime that would fulfil their aspirations for
a human life with dignity and satisfaction. The rulers
themselves announce blueprints of action to correct the ills
of the society, issue decrees upon decrees, and perhaps with
some determined effort, attempt to put the country once more on
the path of true greatness to play its role towards
helping entire Africa to true liberation in all its aspects.

The question to finding a formula to redeem the country from
complete political, economic, social and moral collapse has been
uppermost in the minds of many Nigerians, both high and low,
rich and poor, public officers and private employed, students,
teachers, churchmen, civilians and military men. Some have been
content with mainly exposing the ills of our society, solutions
have been sought, ideologies propounded and moral orientation
schemes initiated, such as the "Low Profile",
"Otu Olu Obodo", the "National Ethical Re-orientation programme"
and the "War against indiscipline".
One may however ask: But why all these measures? What is wrong
with Nigeria? A cursory reflection into the daily realities of
the country will do here.

If we consider the economic sphere, the economy since independence in 1960 to the present date has not shown the expected results towards breaking the inertia to economic development. In many states of the Federation, development efforts are floundering; the reliance of foreign assistance is increasing overtly or covertly; industries are operating at extremely low capacity, and above all, exports are declining while basic health services, agricultural extension, roads, transport, and other infrastructures are deteriorating. Moreover, there is a lack of basic technology and enough trained man-power which would be required for a rapid diversification of the economy. Worse still, the institutions addressing these issues are bloated, inefficient, and costly.

Thus the economic problems are structural, complicated and need long-range solutions. Furthermore, dependency relationships compounded by ill-thought government policies and political instability have added its stuff to retard economic success. Nigeria is bedevilled by what a writer has described as 'gargantum, inefficiency, corruption, and general social malaise'.

The population of the country is growing at an astronomical rate. In 1963, the country's population was reported to be about fiftysix million. In 1985, approximate estimates has placed the population to anywhere between eighty to hundred and ten million peoples. The issue of an accurate population count has become the issue of a failure in leadership, and a lack of political will. With this dire population growth, Nigeria must have a lot to go through, as many more mouths will be fed, more people housed, more jobs created, and more facilities for education, health, recreation and fundamental human requirements are needed.

The lack of an adequate technological base to satisfy the new
demands will bring its own social crisis with it.
Arthur Nwankwo observes:

> "the Nigerian economy is highly incompetent...low
> productivity in the industrial sector, with technically
> fixed production functions and a declining agriculture,
> which because of the primitive subsistence nature of
> cultivation, is facing constant diminishing returns in
> production. Unemployment and underemployment abound
> with an ever-increasing rural-urban migration"[17].

He asks:

> "Can a country be truly independent while its banking
> and insurance systems, distribution networks,
> manufacturing sectors, indeed nearly every facet of its
> commercial life, are controlled by foreign nationals?...
> Foreign monopolies adversely militate against all
> efforts by developing countries to achieve take-off
> into sustained growth. They invest capital in ex-
> -tractive industries and to a significantly lesser
> extent, in productive industries. As a result,
> the lion share of the economic surplus generated from
> the extractive industries goes to the countries of the
> foreign monopolies; thus the determination of these
> developing countries to have industries that will
> generate forward and backward linkages in the economy
> is frustrated"[18].

---

17) Nwankwo, A., Can Nigeria Survive? Fourth Dimension Publishers,
    Enugu, 1981, p.109
18) Ibid., p.xii,pp. 2ff

Of course, the Government looks at this state of affairs as
a challenge. When the Buhari military group took up power
on new years eve in 1984, they seemed to summarise the
enormity of the economic chaos in the country, for they
charged the government before it (and each military government
levels the same charges on its predecessor) of the following:

(i)   lack of food at reasonable prices
(ii)   workers being owed salaries in arrears
(iii)   corruption and indiscipline
(iv)   weak and inept leadership
(v)   lack of respect for the law and the constitution
(vi)   deteriorating education
(vii)   mismanagement of the economy
(viii) reduction of hospitals to mere consulting clinics, without
        enough drugs and adequate medical equipment[19].

Buhari's Military Junta promised among other things, to heal the
nation of all these social malaise, and people are really expecting
results that are positive for all. However, "within the first
three months of getting onto power, over 150,000 workers were
sent on compulsory retirement and by the end of January 1985,
(just one year), over three million workers were made redundant"[20].

---

19) Refer to Head of States Speech on 1st January 1984 broadcast
     on Radio and Television in Nigeria. Buhari's speech is also
     published in many newspapers. (Refer for example: 'Talking Drums'
     1st April 1985, pp 5 - 9., publ. in London., Editor:
     Elisabeth Ohene).

20) Surajo Mohammed Agoro, in 'Talking Drums', op.cit., p.9

The Journalist Surajo Mohammed Agoro accuses the Government of not
putting into practice what it promised the people.

> "One would have thought they are going to right the wrongs.
> Instead after more than a year of their stay in power
> Nigerians have never had it so bad. We have witnessed
> a year of vicious and destructive military regime,
> which has more than doubled unemployment, increased
> poverty, presided over the wholesale destruction of
> jobs and decimation of industries. Food now costs three
> times what it used to cost before they came to power,
> while hospitals are now mortuaries because doctors
> have now decided to stop treating patients with
> infectious diseases.,."[21].

The Military Government consoles itself daily with its self-analysis
of its achievements so far. There is surely a big economic
quagmire which has affected the political, economic and social
climate.

---

21) Ibid.

c) <u>Conclusion</u>:

One could go on listing the ills of the Nigerian society, but for the purposes of this research, we shall limit this endless list by summarising this section thus: Although Nigerians are not different from other people in other continents and nations, we must note that the peculiar situation of their history has in a very deep way, strongly affected their political, economic and world outlook. The Western European influence during the colonial era and after has left its indelible mark on the situation of Nigeria, and has inherently become the origin of all problems associated with the nation Nigeria. This does not mean that the external causes alone are responsible for the situation.

Infact, there are also internal problems which have no doubt joined to maximise the contradictions. The problems of corruption, embezzlement of public funds, laziness, the tendency to materialistic wooliness and self-centred pedestrianism coupled with selfishness, the absence or total lack of intellectual rigour in dealing with issues, the cult of mediocrity, lack of exemplary leadership, the lack of fair play and the neglect of public utilities, added to the situation of "get rich quick", armed robbery whether by single individuals, groups, or by public servants and elites, the cult of waste, consumerism, lack of efficiency, the exploitation of the weak and lowly, and above all, the indiscipline in public and private life, - all these join hands together to make what we today call the 'bane of the Nigerian society'.

Inspite of all criticisms on external powers and on the past, Nigeria today needs authentic values to appreciate the actions of its citizens and judge their conduct, but these values cannot be solely created by western society and then applied to Africa. Africa's values must and has to emanate from the realities of Africa, and it is only when committed individuals decide for this option that the new society ideally aiming at restoring the dignity of the human person can be created. The time has come for such a revival.

It is my contention that "Christian social Principles" with all its dynamism, accompanies men in their quest towards solving their problems and allowing life to be spent more humanly. Even if it does not intervene as Pope Paul VI says: "to give authenticity to a determined structure or to propose a prefabricated model, it does not confine itself just to recalling some general principles. It evolves by means of a reflection that matures in contact with the changing situations of this world, under the impetus of the gospel as a source of renewal, since its message is accepted in its totality and its requirements..."[22]

Nigeria, in its present situation will surely need the contributions of "Christian Social Principles" as aid towards solving its problems.

---

22)   Paul VI., Encyclical : Octogesima Adveniens, n. 42.

PART TWO (II): Consequences of the "Nigerian Situation" for Human Work and the Worker

1. Attitude to Work Today:

It has been sufficiently demonstrated in the preceeding pages that Nigeria's history is one of colonialism and extended economic exploitation, both from outside and from inside. Because of the colonial economic system with foreign firms such as UAC, UTC, BP, Shell, John Holt, Royal Niger Company, National African Company, all operating within the territory and carting away its raw materials to Europe, independent Nigeria inherited an economy that was in 1960 structurally engineered to be dependent on, and manipulable by the International Money markets of Western Europe. This dependence and the vulnerability attendant to it, made many young Nigerians see in Government work, even after the colonial era - service to a bourgeois institution that does not merit it.

Government work is looked upon only as a source for "getting one's share of the national Cake", and therefore many people are prone to look at what is government's as "no mans land" and "no man's property", and people render unsatisfactory service to it. There is strong negative"utilitarianism" in people's attitude towards national service and government work. The reasons are clear, and in the historical situation understandable. Cardinal Arinze commenting on this state of affairs said:

> "The colonial power was not loved and was served with
> less than total dedication. Government business was
> regarded as nobody's business. Government funds were
> considered to be limitless. This mentality had a
> damaging effect on work attitudes"[1].

---

1) Arinze, F., op.cit., p.211

Behind this assertion lies the principle that work which serves
the good of a foreign power primarily, and not that of the workers
runs the risk of being half-hazardly done. After the British arrived
to Nigeria, certain things happened for example in the agricultural
world of Nigerian farmers:

(i)   Cotton, a basic crop grown in Northern Nigeria, was no
        longer to be grown exclusively for home use and manufacture
        but primarily for export.

(ii)   Export crops were being emphasised in every part of Nigeria
        such as groundnuts, cocoa beans, cashew, and peanuts.

(iii)   New roads, railways and transport possibilities were being
        constructed in a way that disregarded the old links in
        traditional communication systems. Instead, new systems of
        transportation and waterways were brought into existence so
        that the Nigerian economy could easily be directed into
        channels directly leading to Europe. These roads connected only
        the areas where there were raw materials for Europeans markets.
        A look into the old maps of Nigeria even into our own time
        prove this.

(iv)   Lastly, a discontinuity emerged between the old economic system
        and the new colonially imposed system.

The consequences for the natives was that new classes of people gradually came into existence with nothing to sell other than their labour. Surely, they did not like this labour and would easily neglect it, but for the fact that their daily bread depended on it.

These hired labourers were fired anytime, badly paid, sometimes beaten by the colonial masters, and they on their own, have bad reminiscences of these times. National work was therefore looked upon with suspicion - as work for a foreign body. This attitude however, is gradually changing with the many appeals to patriotism by the post-colonial governments, but much has still to be done. The famous slang "O ga e me m pay" (Will it pay me, or rather, is it to my gain) often heard in post-colonial Igboland is a product of this situation. When attitude to work remains only utilitarian, only to get daily bread, but not to become more, not to help in nation building, not to build up a corporate body, that is, a community of workers, not to get spiritual fulfilment; when work is considered simply as a task to be done and get quick money, then we are away from the mark. Pope John Paul has a lot to offer the Nigerian worker in his attitude to work.

2. Man - The Subject of Work?

In Laborem Exercens, John Paul II wrote:

> "Man is a person. He is the subject of work.
> He takes decisions about himself. His work must
> serve him and make him better. His work is for him,
> not he for his work. The dignity of his work comes
> primarily from himself. The primary basis of the
> value of work is man himself, who is its subject"[2].

How is this statement understood in the Nigerian world of work?
Is man considered the subject of work? Do people even
know what this implies? Without going too far, it is clear
that in the Nigerian society of today, human work, whether in the
industry or in the home, whether in the mines or in the
government institutions, human work for the greater part is often
looked upon simply as a "Meal Thicket". Many people do not work
to fulfil their potentials and personalities as men, as persons,
as individuals. They see in their work mainly a means to
existence.

Work, (and this is contrary to all that traditional societies
taught the natives) is considered alienating, especially paid
jobs. Therefore there is no personal engagement or interest in
the work done for others. And so, many Nigerians employed to
work for an entrepreneur or for the government, engage likewise
in private work which can give him personal fulfilment or bring
him nearer to his private wishes.

---

2) John Paul II, Laborem Exercens, n. 6

During employed working hours, many people play, eat, chat,
prepare for exams, trade on other goods, but they do not work
adequately for that which they are paid for unless this is
adequately controlled. The booklet on 'National Consciousness
and Mobilisation Crusade' titled "WAR AGAINST INDISCIPLINE",
and systematically carried out by the Buhari military junta
has a lot to say on the point mentioned here[3].

Slogans often heard during work hours include 'Na me be Nigeria?',
'Me I no go die for dis kind work', meaning simply that many
workers do not identify themselves with the work they do.

Is man the subject of work? Surely yes, man is the subject of work,
because all work is for man, and not man for work. Through work,
man becomes more human, developes himself and perfects himself.
Would that many Nigerians knew this! Laborem Exercens has a lot
to teach the working world on this subject.

---

3) On Tuesday, March 20, 1984, Chief of Staff Supreme Headquarters
   Brigadier Tunde Idiagbon launched the War Against Indiscipline
   at the National Theatre in Lagos to mobilise national
   consciousness on the bane of the Nigerian Society today.
   (Pamphlet published by NIS, WSL, European H/Q London, 1984.)
   Let it be noted that Brigadier Idiagbon and his military colleagues
   came into power through indiscipline, for they overthrew a
   constitutionally elected civilian Government.

3. The conflicts between Labour and Capital - The Poor and the Rich

We spent enough time to explicate the ideological conflicts
existing between the production factors of labour and capital.
In the Northern hemisphere of our world, this conflict has
led to the dividing line between the two super-powers and the
ideologies guiding them. Soviet Russia emphasises Labour and the
worker.Western America and Europe emphasise capital and entrepreneur.
The conflict has reached intolerable limits, and the clear
divisions of the world into two, the "Mauer" (Wall) through the
German city of old Berlin is a symbol of this evil.

How is the situation in Nigeria? Is there an ideological conflict
existing between the world of labour and that of capital?
The answer is clear and simple. Such a conflict does not exist
ideologically in Nigeria. Both the capitalist and the worker
are all workers and cannot be separated. Surely, there is a rich
few and a poor mass of peasants. But this is not yet an ideological
warfare in the proportions seen in Europe. We noted in original
traditional society that everybody was called a worker and these
categories of labourer and employer did not exist. We also noted
that work in traditional African Society had dimensions that
were at once human, communitarian and religious.

It was taken for granted that everyone did some useful work for himself,
his family and his village or town. With the colonial era, much of this
has changed. Work for many is gradually ceasing to be
predominantly subsistent and rural. Many people in Nigeria today
have to work in a labour system somewhat like the western pattern.
Industries of various sizes are growing everywhere.

Oil refineries and big car assembly plants have been put into
action and production. The multinationals are present with
their structures, money, pollution and urban congestion has
become the order of the day. Lagos which was almost one
million population in 1960 is today almost eight million
people. Workers today are learning to work with machines
of various sorts and sophistication, and they work in shifts.
Modern Nigeria is faced with the situation which can easily
generate a conflict between capital and labourer, as a few
millionaires are coming up, amidst great poverty of the masses.

Cardinal Arinze sees this danger too in the Nigerian context
of today and describes his observations thus.

> "The phenomenon of the worker who has no farm of his
> own, who is just paid a salary and who can suddenly lose
> his employment and become jobless, is now common.
> More and more people are compelled to maintain
> themselves and their families by the "sale of their
> labour". Many of them work for the Government which,
> even though it has changed into African hands, is
> still unconsciously regarded as a symbol of the
> colonial oppressor which should not normally expect
> an honest deal, since Government business is often
> regarded as nobody's business. Other workers sell
> their labour to individuals or groups of entrepreneurs
> who replace the exploitative merchants of the
> colonial times and who may in some cases have formed a
> partnership with them"[4].

---

4) Arinze, F., op.cit., p. 210

Tendencies are clearly noticeable whereby many people in the villages rush to the cities to gain from the new economic structure, but those they left behind in the villages continue to live in their traditional patters, untouched by these recent technological changes. In other words, whereas some people in Nigeria are living in the post-industrial, computer and technological age, other Nigerians are living in the pre-industrial, primitive society. It is clear that two classes of citizens are being created.

For those living in the townships, whereas some, infact just a few have all they need, many, the masses have not even got a place to lay their heads. These few are the owners of the industries who control the private sectors of the economy. The great mass of people receive only minimal incomes, if at all; they lack good housing, are ignorant, poor, have no good health care, and run the risk of being marginalised into the slums of "Ogui - urban jungle' in Enugu, or the "Ajegunle squalor" in Lagos.

In the New African Yearbook of 1979, this situation was well depicted with the words: "Just as there are wide inequalities in the country-side, between the wealthier farmers and those who farm merely to feed themselves, there are further inequalities within the towns and cities, between the well established commercial and professional classes and the poor, often homeless, unemployed, undernourished masses.

There is 'poverty amidst plenty'! These inequalities are often
disguised by the continuance of the extended family system
whereby the wealthier members of a family or clan subsidise
the less fortunate members. But inevitable such social
structures are being eroded in the expanding urban environment.
Nigeria's size and population cover other social inequalities too,
between the towns and the villages and between the regions.
Such divergencies have been somewhat reduced by deliberate government
measures to spread the new found oil-wealth throughout the
Federation, but there are strong economic forces that inevitably
concentrate growth and development in the already favoured areas"[5].

This quotation suggests the type of situation that existed in
early capitalistic, class societies of Europe when Pope Leo XIII
wrote in 1891 the Encyclical "Rerum Novarum".
Such a situation if allowed to continue unarrested and unchecked
may prove to develope into a real class warfare for the Nigerian
society in the future. A lot therefore has to be done, both by
state, church, and private or group entrepreneurs with concrete
suggestions of a way out of this dilemma.

Revolutions are well carried out in such breeding grounds like the
one we have tried now to portray about Nigeria. In a country where
the number of the poor fluctuate widely, where the majority live at
subsistence level, without enough savings and no social security
to help them in case of distress, in such a country where the
growing youth are destined to look at work from the outside
because they may be unemployed, exactly in such a situation does
'false messianisms' arise which promise a lot, even though they
may never fulfil them. But action has to be taken by all those
responsible for government and society, by the professions, but
especially by the Church in its social principles to guide and
protect the rights of the citizens, guarantee more justice, more
social welfare and act as buffer before the tide of revolutions
overcome entire society.

5) New African Yearbook 1979; IC Magazines Ltd. London., p.259
publisher Afif Ben Yedder.

4. The Rights of Workers

There are fundamental human rights which a worker deserves and merits and which must be protected and granted him, whether by government, or by various other institutions for which the individual works. These rights are human and just, and to deny them would mean to act inhumanly and unjustly. Some of the rights of workers include the right to just pay for job done, the right to adequate rest or leave, the right to social securities of various sorts - health, education, pension, insurance and so on.

Above all, there is also the right of workers to come together in the form of unions for the protection of their rights in the spirit of solidarity, as well as the right to strike when all other peaceful means have been tried; the right to employment, and all the rights which the United Nations, the Organisation of African Unity, the Worker's Charter of the International Labour Organisation, and the Nigerian Constitution has honourably codified and accepted to grant its citizens for the good of all.

In this section, we wish to survey three of such rights as it exists in the Nigerian community of today, namely, the right to work, the right to form trade unions for the protections of workers' rights, and other basic rights of workers.

a) The Right to Work

Surely, the right to work stands as the most fundamental of all
rights in the labour world, for it is only to the working
individual, that all other rights descend upon. To be out of job
means to be out of the means of livelihood. One might even say
that unemployment is not only an evil in the general sense in which
everybody describes it, it can in certain senses also mean the
negation of existence, especially in the context of Africa and
many of the developing nations, where to be unemployed does not
automatically guarantee social security, like in many European
countries of today. How is the situation in Nigeria?
How does the government guarantee the right to work?

Unfortunately, there are no statistics available to buttress the
exact number of Nigerians without work[6]. But it is reasonably
acceptable to state that about fifteen to twenty percent of the
capable working population of Nigeria are without work.
The situation is a terrible one. Majority of Nigerian citizens,
both skilled/unskilled - workers are thrown out of job, by
private, public and government sectors.

_____

6) A funny release which lacks comprehension by the Central Bank
    of Nigeria, in its half-year report in mid-1984 stated that,
    the total number of registered unemployed persons in Nigeria
    stood at 154,409 persons at the end of March. The statistics
    said that 69% were low-grade-workers and 30% were school
    leavers without experience (Ref. West Africa Magazine,
    publ. in London, 5. November 1984, p. 2238).

It is agreeable that in a country with about 80 million
to 110 million people [7], at least 40 to 50 million people
must be engaged in work, or should be in thegroup capable of
working. If that is so, let us take for granted that
50 million are capable of work , it means that for 20 percent
to be out of job, ten million Nigerians are jobless.
This is a modest and unpretentious statistics because the number
could well be more. It is a sociological fact that
African nations as well as other developing nations are growing
in population. There is the love for children. But there is
also the ignorance for family planning, as well as good health care.
In such a growing continent, youth make up more than eighty
percent of the population, and here I refer to youth as those who
have not crossed the age of 45. The situation is therefore
alarming and calls for urgent action.

At the moment, there is a military government in Nigeria and
within the last two years of their regime, from January 1984
till April 1985, sufficient newspaper records abound as to
how they have dealt with the problem of unemployment.
It is generally clear that instead of employing new workers,
more of those already in work have been sacked for various
reasons, than those who have been granted jobs. Newspaper
reports gives the breakdown as follows:

---

7) In July 1984, the National Director of Nigeria's Population
   Bureau, Mr. F. Falodun, said in Lagos while speaking at the
   closing session of a micro-computer programme for data processing
   and analysis in population and development planning, that
   Nigeria numbered 94 million people. He estimated that Nigeria
   would exceed 150 million people by the year 2000. (Ref. West
   Africa, 24.9.1984, p. 1965)

900 Lose Jobs in Ogun: (daily Times of Nigeria, Thursday,24.5.1984,p.1)

"900 public servants (Beamten) in Ogun State have been relieved
of their posts in a purge announced yesterday. In the exercise,
260 officials were retired, 580 had their appointments terminated,
while 60 were summarily dismissed. A government statement in
Abeokuta said it had become inevitable to remove officials who
were fraudulent or whose productivity had declined. The purge
would be a continuous exercise in the effort to foster discipline
in public offices. The statement said that the action would
ensure the development of improved work ethics as well as help
to rid the public service of bad eggs".

3 million Unemployed: (Talking Drums, April 1. 1985, p. 9 London)

"...The military came to power complaining that the level of
unemployment was too high; within the first three months of
getting into power, over 150,000 workers were sent on compulsory
retirement, and by the end of January 1985, over 3 million people were
made redundant".

54,000 Purged: (West Africa Magazine, London, 9.July 1984, p.1416)

"The figures of those either sacked, retrenched or dismissed since
February from available records, showed a total of 54,826 workers
at both the Federal and State levels, according to a report of the
Daily Times of Nigeria... The figures for Federal departments are:
National Assembly 2,100; Police 1,600; The Nigerian Airport Authority
238; and the Federal Capital 275".

Purge of Civil Servants: (Talking Drums, London, June 4 1984, p.21)

"About 2,076 civil servants have lost their jobs in Ondo and Ogun
States following purge exercises carried out by the two state
governments. In Ogun State, about 900 civil servants have been
removed following purge exercises. 260 of them were
retired, 580 had their appointments terminated while 60 others
were dismissed from the service.
In Ondo State, a total of 1,176 civil servants were retired,
dismissed or had their appointments terminated".

9,444 Teachers Retrenched in Bendel: (West Africa, London, 29.10.1984,
p 2193)

"A total of 9,444 teachers have been retrenched by the Bendel State
government. In a press briefing the State Commissioner for Education,
Dr. Abel Guobadia, said that the teachers were sacked in order to
raise the standard of education by utilising qualified teachers
only. The Commissioner however said, that the removal of the teachers
had created serious shortage of teachers in many schools..."

NET Purge: (West Africa, London, 29.10.1984, p.2192

"The Nigerian External Communications Ltd. (NET) has experienced a
purge breeze. The District Manager of the North, Mr. Bayas,
was among the 200 senior officers swept away by the 'breeze'..."

8,000 Textile Workers lose Jobs: (West Africa, 6.8.1984, p. 1604)

"About 8,000 textile workers in the country have lost their jobs
this year, Chief chinyah Ubur, National President of the Textile,
Garment and Tailoring Senior Staff Association of Nigeria, has
revealed. He said that more workers might be retrenched before
the end of the year... He urged the bank to aid the textile industry
by making appropriate representation to the Federal Military
Government on behalf of theworkers to ensure security of employment
of Nigerians 'who make their living from these industries' .

28,000 Dock Workers to Lose Jobs: (West Africa, 6.8.1984, p.1602)

"More than 28,000 Dockworkers will lose their jobs when
the Nigerian Ports Authority (NPA) introduces "manning scale", a new
mechanical device for handling goods from ships, in September...
The sources said the introduction of the device would leave only
7,000 of the 35,000 dockworkers at the port..."

Anambra retires 2,535 Civil Servants: (West Africa, London, 23.7.1985, p.1513

"The Anambra Military Government has announced the immediate
retirement of 2,535 more civil servants in the State.
In a statement in Enugu, State Governor, Navy Capt. A. Madueke, said
that the action was a follow-up of the May 22 retrenchment exercise
in which 1,385 civil servants lost their jobs".

Imo to Reduce 46,000 Teachers by 30 Percent: (West Africa, 3.12.1984,
p. 2499)
"The Imo Commissioner for Education, Professor Adiele Afigbo, has
said in Owerri that the government was planning to reduce its
46,000 teachers by 30 percent... He said that the ratio of teachers
to students in the state was one to 26 instead of the
normal ration of one to 30..."

Rivers State-cutback in Civil Service: (West Africa, 7.1.1985, p. 33)

"The authorities in River State have further purged the civil
service by 20 percent and the parastatals by another 30 percent,
despite official denials of plans to reduce staff in the state's
civil service... Letters sent to victims at the State School of
Basic Studies, gave reasons of 'present unfavourable economic
situation and compliance with the directive from the secretary to the
Military Government and Head of Service of State..."

More Civil Servants Retired: (West Africa, London, 28.5.1984, p.1140)

"The Federal Civil Service Commission has announced another list
of 471 officers either dismissed or retired. More than 400 of
the affected officers are from the Ministry of Aviation and
parastatals under it, including the Nigerian Airport
Authority; Similarly, 81 senior and junior workers of the Nigerian
Security Printing and Minting Company have been retired with
immediate effect..."

3,000 Federal Civil Servants Dismissed: (West Africa, London, 23.4.1984,
p. 901)

"About 3,000 Federal Civil Servants of various cadres have been
retired or dismissed while 15 other have been re-deployed as
at April 9... A statement signed by the Chairman of the Federal
Civil Service Commission said that age, declining
productivity, length of service and ill health were the criteria, among
others used in the purge..."

184 NET Officials sacked: (West Africa, 30.4.1984, p. 950)

The authorities of the Nigerian External Telecommunications (NET),
have dismissed 184 junior workers in a recent house-cleaning
clamp-down... Those affected were mainly on level 101 -06.
The list of those to be retrenched from level 07 and above is still
to be sent by the Ministry"...

116 Diplomats Dismissed:(West Africa, 20.2.1984, p.412)

"The Minister of External Affairs, Dr. Ibrahim Gambari, has
confirmed the compulsory retirement of 116 senior officials of the
Ministry... He said that the officers were retired on the
orders of the Supreme Military Council, using the criteria of
"effectiveness, previous disciplinary record and public interest...""

673 Policemen Retired: (West Africa, 26.3.1984, p. 691)

"Another group of 673 Police Officers have been retired. The
grounds for their retirement range from age, disciplinary
measures, to decline in productivity; 34 senior officers were
retired in January..."

64 NSO Officers dismissed: (West Africa, 13.2.1984, p.355)

"The house cleaning exercise embarked upon by the Federal Military
Government has swept away 64 senior officers of the Nigerian
Security Organisation (NSO)... Already 17 Permanent Secretaries
in the Public Service, 34 Police Officers etc. have been relieved
of their posts. Last week Major General Muhammed Buhari,
Head of the Federal Military Government, said that the
retirement would be a continuous exercise".

We could continue the catalogue of Nigerian workers thrown out
of job by a government, whose sole purpose is among others,
to guarantee that workers maintain their jobs, and thereby their
means of existence. There are reasonable and actual grounds
offered by the government and its officials to explain
away such a catastrophic mass purge of its citizens from the labour
world. General Buhari, who is head of government told a group
of Roman Catholic Bishops who were worried by the mass purge, and
who discussed these issues with him in State House that

> "the retrenchment of workers by the present administration
> was absolutely necessary, because we don't have money
> to pay people for doing nothing, and this is a
> process where you can't eat your cake and have it"[30].

---

8) A delegation of Catholic Bishops led by Cardinal Ekandem visited
General Buhari in Dodan Barracks, Lagos and presented to him a
memorandum concerning actual political issues facing the nation.
Refer to report in 'West Africa', 18.6.1984., p.1283.

The protest of the Bishops was although gentle and constructive,
not accepted by the Government. This is not the place to
debate the real issues for or against the mass purge, dismissal
and complete retirement of workers, often without any benefits,
pensions or remunerations, not to talk of alternatives in the
labour market. Criticism of this exercise is very high, and
editorial opinions in newspapers advised the government to stop
the purges:
"On no account should government seek to frighten workers through
purges and re-organisations apparently designed to reduce
cost and balance government accounts", commented the New Nigeria,
and the Nigerian Union of Journalists stated that "the
retrenchment of workers could not be defended, for the exercise", in
the words of the unions secretary, Mr. Jola Ogunensi, was
"not only a negation of a recent pronouncement of the Chief of
staff, Supreme Headquarters, but also a violation of an
agreement (referring to workers sacked from the Federal Radio
Corporation, Nigerian FRCN) that the Union would be informed
before letters of termination were served on workers".
The Journalists went further to affirm that "the time
was ripe for security of employment to be guaranteed to all
Nigerians, particularly when, the Head of State has said in his
budget speech that the economy was picking up"[9]

The Nigerian Labour Congress also called for the suspension of the
mass purges and threatened a head-on-collision with the government.

---

9) Refer to news in'West Africa', 21.1.1985, p.123

From all that has been pointed above, we have been able to
expose the lack of "Rights of workers to work" existing in
present day Nigeria. We have been able to show that the
government which is the central apparatus for upholding and
guaranteeing this Right has not upheld it, but rather, used its
powers to throw out those already within the labour world.
In as much as one might appreciate the actual problems
pressing the government to such a move, unemployment can never
be regarded as a good.

Pope John Paul II called the inability of people to find job, when
they want it "an Evil". The situation in the private sector
is no less better, for here, indiscriminate and arbitrary
sacking of workers, underpaying workers, exploiting labourers
without any rights or benefits exists in various forms.
This is why the Encyclical on Human Work "Laborem Exercens",
becomes for the Nigerian worker and employer, an indispensable
charter for a direction, a purpose, an ethics of work,
and above all, towards guaranteeing man's Human Rights.

b) The Right to Form Trade unions:

Trade Unions operate within Nigeria, but their bargaining power is weak, their leaders sometimes very rich and corrupt, and the Unions politicised. This situation led to a series of pressures within Nigeria to rationalise Nigeria's diffuse trade union system. The culminating point of these pressures was the promulgation of decrees under the Military Government in 1977 and 1978 which banned the four former trade union federations and eventually reduced the number of unions from several hundred to fourty-two. Ostensibly, this trend, which began under the Gowon government, was designed to eliminate corruption in the unions and protect them from foreign influence in the form of financial aid from the ICFTU (Brussels) and the IFTU (Prague)[10].

There is no doubt that some union officials were corrupt, held several posts in several unions, and used these positions for their own advantage. But suspicion grew among the populace that the unions were gradually becoming a puppet of the government, without its own will, bargaining power, and ability to speak out in defence of the toiling, labouring workers. Critics of the new system, finalised in a trade unions (amendment) decree in mid-1978, alledged that it was designed to bring the unions under Government control.

A new union federation, the Nigerian Labour Congress (NLC) was formed to replace the four bodies banned in 1977, grouping some 70 organisations, 28 of which are professional, management or employers associations[11].

---

10) New African Year Book, 1979, IC Magazines, London, p.270
11) Ibid.

The amendments decree bringing the NLC into birth in 1978 under
Obasanjo did not go unchallenged. The response of
workers, suffering under the twin scourges of inflation and the
long-standing wage freeze, was not favourable and soon after
publication of the new decree there were a number of strikes
(still illegal under a decree dating from the beginning of the
civil war).

At least two of these strikes, led by officials of the newly-banned
company unions, resulted in violence. Cars were damaged, and
managers beaten up in a dispute at Volkswagen Nigeria outside
Lagos which resulted in closure of the plant. At Cadbury Nigeria,
several workers were shot by police called in to disperse
demonstrators, although no fatalities were reported[12].

These incidents probably represented a widespread mistrust of
the new system among wage-earners aware that the new structures
had been set up by the Government and were being run by
Government appointees. Assurances that the NLC was meant to
represent the interests of the workers failed to convince them,
especially in view of the then long-standing wage freeze and
declining standards of workers.

General Obasanjo was asked in a television interview why the
Nigerian Labour Congress was set up. Was it set up to suppress
the demands of workers instead of bettering their situations?
Was it set up to manipulate the trade unions to become an agent
of the government, instead of an agent for the rights of workers?

---

12) Ibid.

To the above question, Head of State, General Obasanjo replied:

> "I think we have instituted a few things that
> should make us put "workers strike" under control.
> One is the new National Labour Congress itself...
> they will be able to exercise greater control and
> restraint on the workers on the basis of understanding
> and communication between workers and employers...
> We have a system which does not allow you to wake up
> one morning, if you follow the rules, and just describe
> yourself as being on strike. You must go through
> a certain process and in going through that process it
> allows for conciliation, reconciliation, arbitration
> and all sorts of things, in the hope that at every
> stage, there will be a dialogue... and it is in making
> sure that we use this established process in settling
> any dispute between workers and employers that the
> salvation lies. I believe that the NLS will have a very
> important role to play in this when they settle down"[13].

When no less a person than a Head of State declares that trade
unions are created by Governments, we have nothing else to add.
It has shown us how weak and inconsequent Nigerian trade unions are.
General Obasanjo accepted in the same television interview that:
"there is a weakness of the union leadership in the country..."
In such a situation, how can the legitimate rights of workers be
guaranteed and defended? The International Labour Convention
in Article 98 declares that there must be an application of the
principles of the rights of workers to organise and bargain collectively.

---

13) Olusegun Obasanjo, Transcript of a Television Interview,
January 16 - 18, 1979; Published in "Foundations for stability",
Federal Ministry of Information, Lagos, FMG, 1979, p. 28 - 29

In Nigeria as elsewhere, to minimise exploitation by employers,
the hired labourers should come together in trade unions to achieve
the advantages of collective bargaining. But how can Nigerian
workers achieve this right in view of the control by
government and the inherent incompetence and corruption of the
union leaders themselves? Cardinal Arinze observes:

> "Bribery, corruption and embezzlement of funds are more
> attractive to weak human nature than hard work as a
> means of acquiring wealth. Workers' unions often employ
> their newly-acquired bargaining power to organise strikes
> at the least provocation without understanding or
> observing of all the rules. To make matters worse, some
> employers who look only on one side of the African workers,
> are suprised when these band together to demand a better
> deal. They react to the workers' demands with exaggerated
> and sometimes infuriating paternalism, if not sacking of
> some of the workers also"[14].

There is therefore, as we have seen, a big confusion, a lack of
good trade unions for the objective representation before employers,
of the basic rights of the workers.

Recently, the Nigerian Labour Congress in Nigeria, supposed to speak
out for the working classes, was advised by government to suspend
negotiations with government for one year on bilateral issues.
The news report reads: "Labour Unions in the country have been
advised to suspend for one year, negotiations for new collective
agreements. The appeal was given by the Federal Ministry of Labour,

---

14) Arinze, F., op.cit., pp.211 - 212

Employment and Productivity... Reacting to the statement in Lagos, the second Deputy President of the Congress, Mr. Kailu Ibrahim said: "This means labour should not talk to the management, because when we meet at the negotiation tables, we do not only discuss Naira and Kobo, but also mutual co-operation between us,..."[15].

Now, here is a government advising workers to keep quiet and not to appear before the management table for normal discussions, talk less of demanding their legitimate rights. In such a situation, strikes may be the only way out, for if the workers' unions cannot talk with management, they can at least go on strike. But even then, in Nigeria, to strike might be dangerous for the worker's security. There are multiple examples where workers striked and were given automatic sack by their employers like the following recent incidents within Nigeria will prove:

Pilots strike and are sacked: (West Africa, London, 2.4.1984, p.746)

"Nigeria Airways' operations were paralysed for most of this week by a strike of its pilots, Flight engineers and cabin crew, which started on March 23. The air crew went on strike to protest at cuts in their night allowances. In reaction to the strike, the airlines management, on Saturday, March 24, dismissed all the striking employees, including the company's 287 pilots and flight engineers and the cabin crew. The management said that it viewed their refusal to return to work as abandonment of duties, "the consequences of which is summary dismissal". However, the sacked employees were given the option of re-applying for their jobs, not later than 8.00 a.m. on March 26,... By the Monday deadline, the pilots were still on strike, and refusing to recognise the Management's sack notice. The dispute continued as we went to press, on March 29, although government officials were hopeful that it will be resolved later in the day..."

---

15) Sunday Times, Lagos, Nigeria, 7.10.1984, p.5

Pilot Strike Ends: (West Africa, London, 9.4.1984, p.793)

"The strike by Nigeria Airways pilots, flight engineers and cabin
crew ended on March 29, and the airline was able to resume full
services the same day. By March 28, most of the 287 striking pilots
who were sacked after they went on strike, had re-applied for
employment, according to the airline management. Among the conditions
specified for their re-employment, were that they should sign
letters of undertaking to be of good behaviour and not go on strike
in future. In the end, of the 224 who re-applied the airline
re-employed only 177 of them, dropping 47 among who was the Pilot's
Association President, Captain Augustine Okon. Sixty-three pilots
had not applied because of the conditions attached to
their employment..."

Government intervention in Trade Unions: (Nachrichten aus Nigeria,
publ. in Bonn, No. 1, March 1985, p.8)

"The Nigerian Medical Association (NMA) and the National Association
of Resident Doctors (NARD) have been proscribed. The Federal Military
Government announced this in a statement in Lagos on Thursday,
21.2.1985. The statement directed all doctors who were on strike,
or had withdrawn their services in any way, to resume normal work
at 7.30 a.m. on Friday, 22.2.1985, or failing to do so, should regard
themselves as dismissed. Those who failed to comply with the
directive were ordered to vacate their residential quarters within
24 hours..."

It is a matter of fact that after the strikes had ended, the
Government went so far as to dismiss 64 of the striking doctors, as
reported in 'Concord', a Nigerian National Daily of April 29, 1985.

<u>100 Trade Disputes in 1984:</u> (Nachrichten aus Nigeria, publ. in Bonn, No. 1, March 1985, p.14.

"Of the 100 recorded trade disputes for 1984, 49 resulted in strikes involving 42,046 workers. The Minister of Labour, Employment and Productivity made this known in Lagos while addressing the Press.

Major General S. Omojokun pointed out that most of the issues at dispute centred on non-implementation of conditions of service, wrongful dismissal and termination of appointments, and other usual Trade Union grievances. He disclosed that 60 of the total amount of disputes recorded were settled through mediation and intervention".

An attempt has been made to show how weak the Trade unions are in Nigeria, how intolerant the government is towards them, and how it controls them; we have been able to show also that the Trade Unions have under the circumstances not arrived at the expected goal where they could without bias, represent the interests the working masses place on them in order to obtain their rightful Rights.

During the political party era of President Shagari, the trade unions were interested in active party politics and really, left their strict area to join political parties. This no doubt brought them into issues of unnecessary debate with other parties. In a newspaper report in Nigeria, 'the National Executive Council of the Nigerian Labour Congress decided to support in the 1983 elections, all pro-labour political parties. It was also agreed at the meeting that henceforth, the Nigerian Labour Movement would resist any attempt to prevent it from being actively engaged in politics...'

Of course, the working class movements has its rightful share of responsibility in the construction of a new society and a new order. But this cannot be achieved by being the associate of a political party. This can only be achieved by objective, unprejudiced and impartial engagement in the labour question for the good of the working masses and the defence of their Rights.

The Encyclical 'Laborem Exercens' has a lot to offer the Nigerian Trade Unions in guidelines and basic principles as we shall later show. Meanwhile in Nigeria, there is a hard effect on the labourer due to the integrating effect of labour on the individual, the family, the community and society at large. Many workers stand the risk of economic chaos and stagnation because of a denial of their rights. Urgent action is needed now.

c) Other Basic Rights:

There are fundamental Human Rights which all free Nations have agreed to adhere to as contained in the charter of the United Nations of December 1948. Other Charters on regional basis also exist, such as the Organisation of African Unity's charter, the West European Nations' charter, the organisation of American States, among others, In the background of all these rights are to be found, the right to life, to freedom of movement, speech, thought, and above all, the respect due to the individual's human dignity. It is in the context of the Nigerian worker that we want to shortly review if some of these rights are observed, above, all, the right to protect the citizen and respect him as a worker in his field. In the last two years, but already earlier, cases abound of mishandling of workers, caning of highly placed civil servants or giving them military drilling for one fault or the other, unnecessary suspension of workers, cutting their monthly salaries, or not paying them at all for months, denying workers their due wage increases or allowances, or denying them of their fringe benefits, pension, insurance guarantees to health and so on. National occurences in this area has been reported in many newspapers:

Popoola's Recipe for Discipline: (West Africa, London, 30.4.1985, p.951)

"Governor Oladayo Popoola of Oyo State has said that the civil
service rules and procedures would be suspended to make
punishment of erring civil servants easier. He said the suspension
of the civil service rule would also make it easier to stamp out
corruption from the service... The Governor warned that public officers,
especially women, who were fond of travelling overseas to buy
goods for sale in their offices, would be dismissed if
caught... He said that he had authorised the reintroduction of
caning in schools and given Headmasters greater powers to
discipline teachers..."

Civil Servants Drilled by Military Personnel: (West Africa, 30.1.84, p.244)

"Hundreds of civil servants in Ibadan are reported to have been
locked out of their offices. The lock-out order was given by the
Military Governor of the State, Lt. Colonel Dayo Popoola...
Very senior officers were included in the lock-out. They were not
allowed to go to their respective offices until they were drilled by
military personnel, who ordered them to hold their ears and keep
jumping for many minutes. Addressing the late-comers later,
the Governor said he could have sent them home, but for the pity he
had for them and their families, calling them idle, indolent and
advising them to be ashamed of themselves.

63 Suspended for not Reciting National Anthem:(West Africa, 15.10.84, p.2100)

Sixty-three civil servants attached to the Governor's office have
been suspended indefinitely because they could not recite the
National Anthem. The suspension order was handed down by Governor
Oladipo Diya during a suprise swoop on workers in his office.
The suspended officers will be reinstated as soon as they can
recite both the National Anthem and the pledge fluently".

35 Television Employees Caned: (west Africa, 27.2.1984, p. 473)

"Ondo State Military Governor Commodore Bamidele Otiko has
denied that he ordered the caning of some employees of the
Nigerian Television Authority Akure who came late to work.
He told the News Agency of Nigeria that he did not also order the
sacking of a messenger of the company, Mr. Remi Adesunloro, who
sacked for 'showing disrespect' to the governor. The governor's
denial leaves unsolved the mystery of who ordered the caning of
35 employees of the Television station".

Civil Servants to Lose Fringe Benefits: (West Africa, 7.1.1985, p.33)

"Civil servants in a number of Federal Government Ministries will
either have their fringe benefits suspended or cancelled as from
the beginning of January 1985, the Lagos Guardian reported,
quoting a cabinet office circular of december 21, signed by the
Head of Service, Mr. Gray Longe. The paper said, in all,
15 categories of allowances will be affected. According to the
circular, 'Revision of some fringe benefits,' leave
allowances are to be cut by half while housing in government
quarters will become more costly. The payment of
no-accident bonus to motor drivers and driver mechanics, facilities
to visit family at government expense during courses abroad to
be suspended. Other benefits cancelled are incidental expenses,
allowances to officers on Grade Level 07 and above and henceforth
official local journeys undertaken within the officer's duty station
will receive no fringe benefits. Warm clothing allowance which
was given to officials travelling overseas, is to be withdrawn".

Salary Increase Unrealistic: (West Africa, London, 9.4.1984, p.793)

"Head of State, Major-General M. Buhari has said that it is
unrealistic to demand a salary increase for workers because the
economy is too weak to sustain such an expenditure..."

Earlier on in March (West Africa, 12.3.84., p. 582)
Mr. Buhari said that 'a real wage policy' aimed at shifting
emphasis to what workers' could buy would be adopted.   'If your
money wage can buy 10 loaves of bread and we manage to reduce
the price of bread so that the same money wage can buy
20 loaves of the same size of bread as before, your real wage has
doubled'..."

d) Underline Conclusion:

There are many more incidents of denigration, disrespect, and
brutal discipline of workers by their employers.
This situation leaves much to be desired, keeping in mind, that
Nigeria, as well as many other nations have signed to abide
by the charter of the World Body towards respecting the
freedom and dignity of the human person and individual. It is
apparent that many workers do not get their desired rest or
leave holidays with all attendant benefits as is basically
agreed upon by Right.

Many private officers expect money before they do the work
for which they are paid, or in order to omit doing their work.
Those in authority sometimes demand payment by their subordinates
to execute the rights, not just privile-ges of these subordinates.
There is an upside-down situation of the right order of values
in the labour world in Nigeria, as is perhaps the case in many
regions.

It is now known that this government attitude to their
employed workers, as well as private entrepreneurs
attitude, has often not motivated labourers and workers to work
with their mind and heart and dedication.

Like Cardinal Arinze observes:

> "There are reports that schools and hospitals
> run by government are inefficient. Airways,
> motor transport, banks, mine, posts, furniture
> companies, construction companies and other such
> public corporations accumulate heavy yearly deficits.
> But similar companies run by private individuals
> in the same towns render good services and make
> good profit. The reason has to be sought in the
> people who work and in the conditions under which
> they work"[16],   Is this an example which goes to
> support the theory of 'personalism' in social ethics?

It is the teaching of Christian Social Principles that man's work concerns not only the economy, but also personal values. The Encyclical Laborem Exercens tried to elaborate on these issues elaborately and to offer each community elements for translation into its societal apparatus.

The next chapter is devoted to the application of "Social and Economic Ethics" in the context of Nigeria, using the criteria set out in the Encyclical Letter - "Laborem Exercens".

---

16) Arinze, F, op.cit., p.214

SECTION TWO

VALUE, MEANING AND SOCIAL STRUCTURE OF HUMAN WORK IN LABOREM EXERCENS
AND IN CHRISTIAN SOCIAL TEACHINGS:

CHAPTER FIVE: Work in General - Aspects and Functions

PART ONE(I): Basic views:

In attempting to research on the meaning of Human Work as stated by
Pope John Paul II in the encyclical "Laborem exercens", our aim is to
portray what the Holy Father understands under the term Work,
that is, its significance, aim, purpose and intent. Such a research is
a basic foundation for further enquiries into the Pope's philosophy
and theology of work, and consequently, into the main reason for the
contents of "Laborem exercens" and thereby for its justification,
adoption or rejection. Before going into the pope's specific
definition and meaning of work, it is necessary to undertake a general
survey of the meaning of work, to distinguish it from that which it is
not, and clarify its relationship with its synonyms, thereby arriving at
a suitable basis for the pope's definition and writing on Human work.

1. Definitions of Human Work:

Work is a very general term, usable in a variety of contexts. Although
used often synonymously with occupation, labour, toil, business and
drudgery, work differs from all these because of its specific broader
connotation and wider application. Work may or may not suggest
laborious, burdensome, onerous expenditure of energy, like drudgery,
toil or labour might do. Occupation may indicate the trade, craft,
vocation, or profession which one has chosen and prepared oneself for
and which one is apt usually to follow. It may indicate also whatever
occupies one's time and energies quite purposefully as a means of
livelihood or less so as an avocation of interest.
Labour differs from work in often being limited to purposive,
necessary expenditure of effort, usually, of a fatiguing or onerous nature.

Analysing the distinction between labour and work made by the philosopher
Hannah Arendt in her book: 'The Human Condition', she defines labour as
that necessary, essential, and useful activity of doing what is required
to keep alive. It produces nothing that lasts. Its products are
consumed as soon as they appear. It is a basic natural activity
in tune with the rhythm of nature.
Work, on the other hand, she defines as something beyond
this. She describes man as busy at the work of fabrication, making
tools, using skills to produce more than he needs just for himself,
creating something durable, with an existence of its own.
By its mastery and lordship over nature, work becomes the source of
man's confidence and his maturity.[1]
Toil indicates fatiguing prolonged work, for example the labour of
sifting, constructing, combining, correcting, whereas drudgery
applies to continuing dull, menial, irksome work.
Work however as a concept, is broader in its application than its synonyms.
It may be defined as: "an activity in which one exerts strenght or
faculties to do or perform"[2], and there are five aspects of this
activity, namely:

1. sustained physical or mental effort valued as it overcomes
   obstacles and achieves an objective or result (in contrast to play).

2. the labour, task, or duty that affords one his accustomed means
   of livelihood.

---

1) Work and the Future, 10 Publishing Church House Bookshop;
   Great Smith Street, London, 1971.   See also: Unemployment and the
   Future Work; Document published by the Church of England General
   Synod, Board of Social Responsibility, Industrial and Economic
   Affairs Committee; December 1982, London, Chapter 5, p.3.

2) Websters Third New International Dictionary of the English language,
   Vol. 3, S-Z, (1768); published by Encyclopedia Brittanica, Chicago,
   1982, p.2634.

3. strenous activity marked by the presence of difficulty and
   exertion and absence of pleasure.

4. occasional or temporary activity towards a desired end.

5. a specific task, duty, function, or assignment often being a
   part or phase of some larger activity [3].

From the aforesaid, we are enabled to distinguish work from that
which it is not. Work is not play, it is not leisure nor is it
pleasure. Work is an activity of man which sometimes corresponds
to one's calling, vocation or profession.
In many cases work is remunerated through payment and here we speak of
paid job. However, not all work is rewarded through payment in cash or
kind, as there are people who are not employed by anybody but are self-
employed.
Pope John Paul II took out time in his Encyclical letter "Laborem
Exercens" to discuss the various related meanings of human work.
It is these views that we shall now proceed to consider.

---

3) Websters Third New International Dictionary of the English
   language, Vol.3,s-z, (1768); published by Encyclopedia
   Brittanica, Chicago, 1982,p.2634.

It is important to note here what the writer Cathrine A. Mackinon
says on human work: She defines it as "the social process of transforming and shaping the material and social worlds,creating people
as social beings as they create value. Work is that activity by which
people become who they are. Class is its structure,production its
consequence,capital its congealed form,and control its issue".
(Publ. in Signs: Journal for women in culture and society,1982,Vol.7,3).

2. The Pope's Definition of Work:

In the encyclical letter of Pope John Paul II - "Laborem exercens",
the Holy Father defines work as "any activity by man, whether
manual or intellectual, whatever its nature or circumstances;
it means any human activity that can and must be recognised as work, in
the midst of the many activities of which man is capable and to which he is
predisposed by his very nature, by virtue of humanity itself"[5].

This definition of work and its meaning as given by the Pope
has a very wide and broad scope. Work is referred to by the Pope as
an activity. In the book of Genesis, man is presented as the only
creature in all creation created in the image of God. "So God
created man in his own image" [6], and gave him the command to
"subdue and fill the earth" [7]. This command contains within it an
invitation to participate in the creative activity of the creator
through Work. Says the Pope: "From the beginning therefore he is
called to work"[8]. Man is called to work and to activity in the
biblical words of the creator: "Be fruitful and multiply, and fill the
earth and subdue it; and have dominion over the fish of the sea and
over the birds of the air and over every living thing that moves upon
the earth". Commenting on this biblical words, the Pope says: "even though
these words do not refer directly and explicitly to work, beyond any
doubt they indirectly indicate it as an activity for man to carry out
in the world. Indeed, they show its very deepest essence...
In carrying out this mandate, man, every human being, reflects the
very action of the creator of the universe" [9].

---

5) John Paul II, Laborem exercens., Encyclical on Human Work, London Catholic
6) Genesis 1 : 26   Truth Society, 1981, printed by Tee and
                                     White,
7) Genesis 1: 28   n. 1 (preamble) Henceforth for
                                     Laborem Exercens we shall indicate LE)
8) John Paul II, LE, Ibid;
9) Ibid., n.4, 2

Through work, man benefits from past generations and works for
the benefit of generations yet to come. Work is thus a transitive
activity: It originates from the human subject and is directed
towards an external object. However, it does not follow from this
that work's external purposes are of the first importance,
necessary though it is that all should be pursued. The Second Vatican
Council teaches that 'as human activity proceeds from man, so is
it ordered towards man'. The essential purpose of man's work is to
perfect himself than to change the world in which he lives, though he
must change the world. In changing the world man supplies the
material for human progress but that material cannot of itself bring
human progress about.

a) Work - A Specifically Human Activity Uniting all Mankind (Corporate)

The Pope makes it clear that work is a specifically human activity.
Just as man is a "homo sapiens", "homo loquens", so also is he a "homo
laborem exercens". This peculiarity of work as an attribute of the
human species alone raises the dignity of work. Animals do not work;
their natural movements and activities is not and cannot be regarded
as work, but is rather best explained by their instinct for self-
preservation. Man however, beyond the instinct of self-preservation
seeks self-realisation which work offers. In the words of Pope John II,
"Work is one of the characteristics that distinguish man from the
rest of creatures, whose activity for sustaining their lives cannot be
called work. Only man is capable of work, and only man works, at the
same time by work occupying his existence on earth" [10].
Since work is a specifically human property, it is therefore a
uniting factor for all men. This universality of work suggests the
unity of mankind whether among men or among women of every race and nation,
who speak different languages, represent diverse cultures, and profess
different religions.

---

10) John Paul II., LE, n. 1

Addressing the general assembly gathered for the 68th Session
of the International Labour Organisation in Geneva, Switzerland
nine months after the publication of the encyclical "Laborem exercens",
the Pope spoke on the universality of work. Said he: ..."In its
fundamental characteristics, the reality of work is the same all over
the world, in every country and in every continent; the reality
of work is the same behind a multiplicity of forms",[11]
whether manual or intellectual, whatever its nature or circumstances.
Without concealing the specific differences which may be observed here
and there in the world of work, the reality of work unites all men in
an activity which has the same source and the same significance.
As a consequence, work cannot therefore be looked upon as mean,
infradig or superior, since all work, done by man, gains its
dignity through man.

There are various forms and types of work: "manual work and brain
work; work in farming and work in industry; work in the
service sector and work in research; the work of the craftsman,
the technician, the educator, the artist or the housewife; the
work of the factory operative and the work of the supervisors
and managers... In the diversity and universality of its forms,
human work unites men because every man seeks in work 'to realise
his humanity, to fulfil the calling to be a person that is his by
reason of his very humanity"[12].

---

11) John Paul II; The Way of Solidarity, Address to the International
     Labour Organisation in Geneva, Switzerland., 68th Session,
     Tuesday, 15th June 1982. Published by the Catholic Truth Society;
     "The Pope Teaches", 1982/7, London, p.282
12) John Paul II, The Way of Solidarity, op.cit., p.282 - 283.
     (Refer also: John Paul II., LE, n. 1 and n. 6".

208

It belongs then to the meaning of work, according to the Holy Father, that work bears the stamp of "unity and solidarity". With respect and regard to and for this meaning of work, the Pope paid tribute to all work, and to each and every man or woman engaged in it, irrespective of its specific content and this includes physical and intellectual work; irrespective of its particular purpose, and this includes creative or reproductive work; and irrespective of whether it consists of theoretical research providing a basis for the work of others, or in any activity aimed at organising the conditions and structure of such work or, again, the management or actual performance, by workers, of the tasks involved in carrying out programmes.
"Work in any of its forms deserves particular respect because it represents the output of a human being and because behind it there is always a live subject: the human person" [13].

b) A Means of Livelihood and Existence (Necessary)

The second meaning of Human Work, dictated by the Genesis story: "in the sweat of your face you shall eat bread...", [14] and often quoted and elaborated upon by John Paul II is the concrete fact that work, is a means of existence, assures a livelihood, sustains family life and helps the working person earn some wages to satisfy his material and spiritual needs. The Pope acknowledged this fact where he wrote: "Through work man must earn his daily bread and contribute to the continual advance of science and technology"[15].

---

13) John Paul II, The Way of Solidarity., op.cit., p.279
     (Refer also: John Paul II., LE, n.1 and n. 67.
14) Genesis 3 : 17 - 19
15) John Paul II, LE, n. 1 . (It is important to stress here that human work in the Pope's views is not necessarily paid job alone. His idea is deeper for he includes as work, "all work", paid or unpaid, domestic or mental, private or public.)

Work assures man's life and health, either directly, whereby man grows
his own food as farmer, or indirectly, whereby man does some job which
earns him money to buy his needs. Man's life, personality and
development are shaped and dignified by work. The nature of work
changes, the Pope says, with human progress, and that is why new
problems must be constantly faced. The present age is faced by the
problems of automation and new technologies. It is faced, too, by the
rising costs of raw materials and by a concern for the limited resources of the
earth. Work is thus as a human issue, at the very centre of the
"Social Question". As John Paul II says: "It is probably the essential
key to the whole social question, if we try to see that question
really from the point of view of man's good ... making life more human"[16].
Since through work, man earns his daily bread, it is therefore
as the Pope suggests, the church's convinction that work represents
"a fundamental dimension of man's existence on earth"[17], not only
because the practical life of man shows this daily and the
various sciences have confirmed it, but also because the revealed word
of God suggests it as the Bible records: "In the sweat of your face
you shall eat bread". A new and extremely important feature of the
social question which has come to the fore only in the second half of
the twentieth century is the plight of the poor and hungry in some
of the so-called "Third World Countries". While a small group of the
human family enjoys a standard of living unknown to the world in the
past, most of the human family eke out a precarious existence and
almost 40,000 people, mostly children, die each day from sheer starvation[18].
These countries want a New International Economic Order, which will
mean profound changes in the balance of wealth between nations.

---

16) John Paul II, LE, n. 3,2.
17) Ibid., n. 4,1
18) O'Mahony J.P., The Fantasy of Human Rights., Mayhew-McCrimmon;
    London, 1978, p.25

Pope Paul VI noted this same fact in 1967, in the great Encyclical letter:
"Populorum Progressio". There he wrote: "Today, the major fact that
everyone must grasp is that the social question has become
worldwide in character... Today the peoples in hunger are making
a dramatic appeal to the peoples blessed with abundance.
The Church shudders at this cry of anguish and calls each one to
give a loving response of charity to this brother's cry for help"[19].
And Pope John Paul II has this to say:
"The world economic crisis, with its repercussions throughout
the globe, compels us to recognise that the horizon of the problems
is increasingly a world horizon. The hundreds of millions of
starving or undernourished human beings, who also have the right to rise
up out of their poverty, should make us realise that the fundamental
reality today is mankind as a whole. There is a common good which
can no longer be confined to a more or less satisfactory compromise
between sectional demands or between purely economic requirements.
New ethical choices are necessary"[20].

A new attitude to work has to be developed for it will transform
unjust structures into just ones, and make possible the dream of the
Church's Social Teachings a reality, namely, the realisation of
justice and peace on earth, and the removal of the foundations of
hatred, selfishness and injustice, which have too often been erected
into ideological principles or as a vital law of life in society [21].
The Holy Father admits that this is not an easy task. Infact he
admits that while it is true that man eats the bread produced
by the work of his hands - he eats this bread by the "sweat of his
face"[22], that is to say, not only by personal effort and toil
but also in the midst of many tensions, conflicts and crises, which,
in relationship with the reality of work, disturb the life of
individual societies and also of all humanity[23].

---

19) Paul VI., Populorum Progressio., 26th March 1967., n. 3
20) John Paul II, The Way to Solidarity., op.cit., p.287
21) Ibid., p.286
22) Genesis 3: 19
23) John Paul II, LE, n. 1,2.

This sweat, effort, and toil is something that is universally
known, for it is universally experienced. It is familiar to
those doing physical work under sometimes exceptionally conditions,
to farmers who spend long days working the land; to workers at
the mines and quarries; to steel workers at their blast furnace;
to those who work in builders' yards and in construction work, often
in danger of injury and death. Toil is familiar likewise to those
on intellectual work; to scientists and to all those who bear the
burden of grave responsibility for decisions affecting society.
Toil is familiar to all workers, and as the Pope says, "since work
is a universal calling, it is familiar to everyone"[24].

c) Work Gives Meaning to Human Life and Existence on Earth

In the Encyclical "Laborem exercens", the Pope brought to light
one fundamental meaning of human work, stating clearly the fact that
work reveals to man the true meaning of his existence.
"The problem of work has a very profound link with that of the
meaning of human life. Because of this link, work becomes and indeed
is a problem of man's spiritual nature"[25]. As one of those aspects
connected with the 'inscrutable mystery of man's Redemption in Christ',
work presents itself as a fundamental aspect, one that is always
relevant, demanding renewed attention and decisive witness. In his
first Encyclical letter "Redemptor Hominis", the Holy Father stressed
the fact that "man is the first road which the Church must travel in
fulfilling its missions; man is the first road and the fundamental
road of the Church, mapped out by Christ himself..."[26]. Man's dignity is
an elevated one, because of the saving work of Christ and so also is
man's work. For not only does work bear the imprint of man, but it
reveals to man the true meaning of his existence - work considered
as a human activity regardless of its concrete content and circumstances.
Work is endowed with this "basic dimension of human existence",
through which man's life is built up every day [27].

---

24) John Paul II, LE, n. 9,2
25) John Paul II, The Way of Solidarity., op.cit; p.283
26) John Paul II., Redemptor Hominis; 1979, (Ref. CAtholic Truth Society,
     London, Do 506)
27) John Paul II., The Way of Solidarity., op.cit., p. 281

For the Pope, the Church is convinced that 'work is a fundamental
dimension of man's existence on earth' and the reason for this
belief is above all because the Church 'believes in man'.
Continuing, John Paul II maintains that this observation enables
us to set human work, in whatever way it is performed by man, within
man himself, in other words, in his innermost being, in the essence of his
nature, in what makes him a man and therefore destined to work.
"The convinction that there is an essential link between the work
of every man and the overall meaning of human existence is the whole
foundation of the Christian doctrine of work - one might say
the foundation of the "gospel of work"[28].
In attempting to support the view that the link between work and
the very meaning of human existence bears constant witness
to the fact that man has not been alienated from work, or enslaved
especially as Karl Marx asserted, John Paul II, opposing the
identification of work and alienation, uses the same logic
of his predecessor, Paul VI who addressed the International Labour
Organisation in Geneva in 1969. He writes: "Never again will work
be against the worker; but always work will be in the service of man.
If work must always serve man and his welfare, if the programme of
progress can only be carried out through work, then there is a
fundamental right to judge progress in accordance with the following
criterion: does the work really serve man? Is it compatible with
his dignity? Through it, does human life achieve fulfilment in all
its richness and diversity?"[29].
And in answer to these questions, John Paul II confirmed that work
has become the ally of man and humanity, which helps him to live
in truth and freedom in a freedom built on truth, and which enables him
to lead, in all its fulness, a life more worthy of man [30].

---

28) John Paul II., The Way of Solidarity., op. cit., p.283 - 4
29) John Paul II., The Way of Solidarity; op. cit., p.284
30) Ibid., 285

As far as the Pope is concerned, that which gives a real meaning
to the life of the worker is right and good work.

We have the right and the duty to consider man not according to
whether or not he is useful in his work, but to consider work in
its relation to man, to each man, to consider work according to
whether or not it is useful to man. We have the right and duty to take
account, in our approach to work, of the various needs of man, in the
spheres of both the spirit and the body, and to take this approach to
human work in each society and in each system, in areas where well-being
prevails, and even more so, in areas where destitution is widespread.
We have the right and duty to take this approach to work in its relation
to man - and not the reverse - as a fundamental criterion for assessing
progress itself... In a word, one must constantly ask oneself whether
the work helps to fulfill the meaning of human existence... [31]

Without work, man is unfulfilled. Since work is 'any activity by man,
whether manual or intellectual', it follows that to lead realised and
fully human life different from that of vegetative animals, man must work.
From the beginning, 'man is called to work'[32] and all work is hence
not only a necessity, but a duty and a task. It is man's vocation to
work and thereby to "contribute to the continual advance of science
and technology, and above all, to elevating unceasingly the cultural and
moral level of the society within which he lives in community with
those who belong to the same family"[33].

---

31)   John Paul II., The Way of Solidarity; op. cit., p.284
32)   Genesis 3 : 19., 1 : 28
33)   John Paul II, Laborem exercens; op.cit., p. 3

PART TWO (II): The Objective and Subjective Aspects and Values of Work

1. Introduction:

What is meant by the objective sense of human work?

Work in the objective sense as shown by Pope John Paul II refers
specifically to human activities carried out according to ever changing
and new modalities in order to subdue the earth; It refers to the
instruments used by man for his work including the techniques of
modern science, machinery and industry, the domestication of animals
in order to obtain from them food and clothings and the transformation
of the earth through products developed by man's brain. It differs
in its emphasis from "work in the subjective sense", which has man
as the centre, the operator, the "subject of work". Work in the
objective sense suggests like the Pope himself said, that "it is the
machine which works and man merely supervises, making it function and
keeping it going in various ways"[1].

Being endowed with manifold faculties to act on and within the
cosmos, and in accordance with the biblical precept[2], man is called to
participate in the remaking of a more perfect creation, while by
transforming and dominating the world, he in a sense, becomes "partner with God".
Through his work he regains his true greatness as God's collaborator
and ensures the continuation of the divine creative action.
For this reason work is necessary. How he goes about it can be
considered from two perspectives - the objective one and the
subjective one. In both cases, the dignity of work and the working
agent, that is, the human person are to be placed in the centre of
all considerations.

---

1) John Paul II, LE, n. 5,1.
2) Genesis, 1 : 28

2. Work in the objective sense:

The creator has given the earth to man so that "he may subdue it
and upon this dominion of man over the earth he based man's
fundamental right to life"[3]. Therefore, "man's dominion over the
earth is achieved in and by means of work. There thus emerges the
meaning of work in the objective sense, which finds expression in
the various epochs of culture and civilisation"[4].
The Holy Father elaborates more on what he means by work in the
objective sense by going further to explain the various ways, in
which man during the course of the centuries, has tried to dominate
the earth and find fulfilment for his personal life and that of
entire society. He highlights three specific areas where work in the
sense already explained has been undertaken by man, namely:

a) In domesticating animals, rearing them and obtaining from
    them, the food and clothing needed by man;
b) In agriculture, whereby man cultivates the earth,
    transforms its products, and adapts them to his own use;
c) In industry, which consists in linking the earth's riches--
    whether nature's living resources, or the products of
    agriculture, or the mineral or chemical resources - with
    man's work in the physical and intellectual plane to
    produce goods needed to qualitatively and quantitatively
    better and increase his production, and thereby renew the
    face of the earth.

---

3) John Paul II, Sermon at Holy Mass at Nowy Targ, Poland.,
    8th June 1979; L'osservatore Romano, English Edition,
    16. 7.1979, No. 29, p.7
4) John Paul II, LE, n. 5, 1.

Through this analysis, the Pope presents a historical data of
the progress of human work through its various stages - from
a nomadic sphere through an agricultural sphere till the present day
industrial and post-industrial technological age.
The Pontiff gives credit to this progress for he says:
"In industry and agriculture man's work has today in many cases ceased to
be mainly manual, for the toil of human hands and muscles is aided by
more and more highly perfected machinery. Not only in industry but
also in agriculture we are witnessing the transformation made
passible by the gradual development of science and technology"[5].
Work in the objective sense has caused great changes in man's
way of conceiving the universe and man's conception of work generally.
The introduction into the field of human work of the products of
science and technology, highly perfected machinery, service industries
whether applied or pure research, electronics, microprocessors, the
computer and the miniaturisation gadgets, all these have in
one way or the other, presented advantages for the working man,
nonetheless presenting problems and dangers.

Pope John XXIII expressed the same views 20 years earlier in his
Encyclical letter "Mater et Magistra" where he said:
"In the field of science, technology and economics we have the
discovery of nuclear energy, and its application first to the purpose
of war and later, increasingly, to peaceful ends; the practically limitless
possibilities of chemistry in the production of synthetic materials,
the growth of automation in industry and public services; the
modernisation of agriculture; the easing communications, especially
by radio and television; faster transport, and the initial conquest
of interplanetary space".[6] All these show that a radical
transformation, both in the internal structure of the various states
and in their relations with one another has been introduced.
This is no less true in the field of human work and in the tools
used by modern man in his work.

---

5) John Paul II., LE, 5.

6) John XXIII, Mater et Magistra, n. 47

And in our times, John Paul goes on to show that in some instances, technology can cease to be man's ally and become almost his enemy. He demonstrates the various ways in which technology can be the enemy of man. He shows this both in the Encyclical Letter "Laborem Exercens", and in his address to the General Assembly of the United Nations gathered in New York.

Technology can cease to be man's ally and become almost his enemy, "as when the mechanisation of work supplants him, taking away all personal satisfaction and the incentive to creativity and responsibility; when it deprives many workers of their previous employment; or when, through exalting the machine, it reduces man to the status of its slave"[7].

With the same tone, the Holy Father made it clear that a critical analysis of our modern civilisation shows that... "it has contributed as never before to the development of material goods, but that it has also given rise ... to a series of attitudes in which sensitivity to the spiritual dimension of human existence is diminished..."[8].
Here he makes it clear that although man depends on the resources of the material world for life, he cannot be their slave, but must be their master. The words of the book of Genesis are a primary and essential directive in the economic process.

Work should help man to be more human. It should be the expression and measure of his dignity. Hence the urgency of eliminating the consequences of all obsessing and alienating work, of technology becoming man's master instead of the tool for his labour, of work that limits and restricts personal freedom and thereby reduces the dignity of the working man.

---

7) John Paul II, LE, n.6
8) John Paul, Address to the General Assembly of the United Nations,
    2 October 1979., English Edition, L'Osservatore Romano,
    15 October 1979, No. 42, pp. 10, 11.

Agriculture, industry, technology and other forms of aid to man the
worker should be in reality an aid to man who is the subject of work.
Looking at work in the objective sense, the Pope agrees that
 "the recent stage of human history, especially that of certain societies,
brings a correct affirmation of technology as a basic coefficient
of economic progress",[9] and so it should be! As a basic coefficent
of man, these tools should therefore be truly at the service of
man in his choice of goods to be produced, in the production methods and
timing, in the just distribution of the goods and in the production
process. But the task is not an easy one as the Pope rightly
remarks, for the relationship of the machine to man has placed men of
authority in a great dilemma, especially in our own time. The Pope
knows this and so says: "These questions are particularly charged with
content and tension of an ethical and social character.
They therefore constitute a continual challenge for institutions
of many kinds, for States and governments, for systems and international organisations; they also constitute a challenge for the church"[10].
The call to "subdue the earth" is a challenge to man, and in his
attempt to conquer the universe, man has created new tools to
help him lessen the manual nature of the job. But these new tools
have brought their own challenges with them, such as the problems
already mentioned above, not to forget the equation of man as a
"Robert" in the computer programme. Like all changes facing man, this
one is within man's reach to conquer and to be the master of his own
house, and 'the Lord of the universe'. The Church in Her social
teachings has guidelines for this task. It depends on man's choice and
freedom.

---

9) John Paul II, LE, n. 5
10) Ibid.

3. Man - The Subject of Work

In treating work in the subjective sense, and man as the subject
of work, Pope John Paul's aim should primarily be understood as an
attempt to unmask the basic failings of various systems of thought which
view human relations in the area of work as solely and purely economic.
The Pope on the other hand, viewing work from the Christian way of life
suggests other relations which could integrate or rather, regenerate the
myopic standpoint of the ideologists. Says he: "First Man, then the rest".
With this assertion, the Pontiff shows that man is the first value in
the cosmos - and that we cannot deny him his essential projection towards
transcendency. He opens the section on 'work in the subjective sense' with
the words: "In order to continue our analysis of work, an analysis
linked with the word of the Bible telling man that he is to subdue the
earth, we must concentrate our attention on work in the subjective sense"[11].
What words of the Bible are here referred to? Exactly this, the
words found in Genesis where God gave man the commission to
"be fruitful and multioly, and fill the earth and subdue it, and have
dominion over the fish of the sea and over the birds of the air and over
every living thing that moves upon the earth"[12].
This commission, this task and vocation is the starting point for the
Pope in discussing 'man as the subject of work'. And so he says:
"Man has to subdue the earth and dominate it, because as the image of
God, he is a person, that is to say, a subjective being capable of
deciding about himself, capable of acting in a planned way, and with
a tendency to self realisation. As a person, man is therefore the
subject of work. As a person he works, he performs various actions
belonging to the work process; independently of their objective content,
these actions must serve to realise his humanity, to fulfil the calling
to be a person that is his by reason of his very humanity"[13].
The basic thesis postulated by the Pope is a simple one to understand:
"In the first place, work is "for man" and not man "for work"[14].
In other words, man is the subject, not the object of work.

---

11) John Paul II, Laborem Exercens, n. 6

12) Genesis, Chapter 1, Verse 28

13) John Paul II, LE, n.6

14) Ibid.

The value and dignity of human work does not depend on the kind of work done, but on the fact that it is a human person who does it. In the subjective dimension of considering work, labour must not be treated as a merchandise, as a commodity that can be bought and sold, as it was in the nineteenth century societies of Europe, and is still today in many countries in the world. We must seek the sources of the dignity of human work primarily in its subjective dimension, not in its objective one.

It is important to note that methodologically, the Pope had treated 'work in the objective sense' in the section preceeding his treatment of the subjective dimension. He hoped thereby to contrast two modes of approaching human work, in order to order them in their right chronology after contrasting them both. God has called man in the work of participation in the creation and ordering of this universe. The mandate to "subdue and dominate the earth" since it first became man's vocation, had often led to clashes of whether it was a domination in the objective or in the subjective sense. The Holy Father takes a position on this dilemma where he says: "this 'dominion' spoken of in the biblical text being meditated upon here refers not only to the objective dimension of work but at the same time introduces us to an understanding of its subjective dimension"[15]. From John Paul's attempt to a solution of the dilemma, we can see that work really has these two dimensions - an objective and a subjective one. But a question stands out: Which dimension is higher in the hierarchy of values concerning human work? John Paul does not waste time to answer this question because for him, man's dignity as a Person, created in the image of God, lightens any complex problems and acts as criteria towards providing exact answers. First of all, the Pope clarifies what the subjective dimension of work entails, and then gives an answer to our question. Work in the subjective dimension is understood by the Pope as a process whereby man and the human race subdue the earth according to the biblical concept, and man manifests and confirms himself throughout the process as the one who "dominates"[16]. But to our basic question,

---

15) John Paul II, LE, n. 6
16) Ibid.

the Pope gives the answer as to which of the two dimensions is higher
in the hierarchy of values. He says: "This dominion, in a certain
sense, refers to the subjective dimension even more than to the
objective one, for it conditions the very ethical nature of work.
Infact there is no doubt that human work has an ethical value of its
own, which clearly and directly remain linked to the fact that the one
who carries it out is a person, a conscious and free subject, that is
to say that decides about himself"[17].

The high position given to man by the Pope is not simply his own
peculiarity of writing and thinking but corresponds to the
fundamental and perennial teachings of Christ and the tradition
of the Church. The Church Fathers in the Second Vatican Council,
in the Constitution "Gaudium et Spes" devoted much time and
attention to man. Chapter One of this document begins with the sentence:

"Believers and non believers are practically agreed
that man is the centre on which all things on earth focus -
the apex of nature. But what is man?... The
scriptures teach that man is created 'in the image of God',
capable of knowing and loving his Creator, established
by him as the Lord of creation to rule over and use
created things for God's glory..."[18].

Right here, man is placed at the apex of nature, as the King and
noblest creature. Pope John Paul in his first Encyclical letter
'Redemptor Hominis" followed this ageless tradition of the Church
and wrote that: "Man is the primary route that the Church must
travel in fulfilling her mission; he is the primary and fundamental
way for the Church, the way traced out by Christ himself"[19].

---

17) John Paul II., LE., n. 6
18) Second Vatican Ecumenical Council; Constitution of the Church
    in the World of Today (Gaudium et Spes), Chapter 1,12.
    (Cf. CTS London, Do 363, p.15 ff)
19) John Paul II, Redemptor Hominis., n. 14.

With these basic statements, in which he stresses man's centrality
in a particularly loving and impassioned way, John Paul affirms
that human dignity is not only illuminated and strenghtened by
the mystery of Christ (christological anthropocentrism), but is
also closely connected with the church's mission to serve and defend
man's entirety and full dimension (ecclesiological anthropocentrism).
In fact, if the Church's fundamental task throughout the centuries,
and especially in our times, is to be at the same time "a sign and
a safeguard of the transcendence of the human person"[20], she cannot
abandon man, but has to be aware "in an always new manner of man's
situation"[21], endeavouring to follow and assist him with particular
pastoral solicitude, so that he may live and grow in dignity and
freedom.

It is in an attempt to impress it upon a materialistic world
that the Pope repeats over and over again the primacy of the person
over things, the priority of ethics over technology, and the
superiority of spirit over matter. Carried over into the world of work,
it is the Pope's basic postulation that the "primary basis of the value
of work is man himself, who is its subject". Pope Pius XII shared
these same views for he said : "man is as such, far from being the
objective, passive element in society, its subject, its basis and its
purpose; and so he must be esteemed"[22].

Similar thoughts were shared by Pope John XXIII speaking on the
dignity of the human person and subject where he wrote:
"...man's personal dignity involves his right to take an active
part in public life, and to make his own contribution to the
common welfare of his fellow citizens"[22b].

20) John Paul II, Redemptor Hominis., n. 14 (Gaudium et Spes, 76)
21) Ibid.
22) Pius XII., Broadcast Message, Christmas 1952, A.A.S.XLV, 1953, pp.33 -
    46; Refer also John XXIII., Pacem in Terris, n 26, n. 83,
    (London, 1963., CTS London, S 264, p. 14)
22b) Ibid., John XXIII Pacem in Terris, n. 26.

No less a great Pope like Leo XIII spoke out also on this issue where injustice and systems negate the supremacy of man as a person and a working subject. Leo made it clear that "if we turn now to things external and material, the first thing of all to secure is to save unfortunate working people from the cruelty of men of greed, who use human beings as mere instruments for money making. It is neither just nor human so to grind men down with excessive labour as to stupefy their minds and to wear out their bodies"[23].

All these sayings of the Pontiffs show how unanimous the Church's Social Principles is on matters concerning the centrality of man as subject of work. In an admonition, worded with strong warnings which John Paul II gave to Christian Union Entrepreneurs and Managers in Italy sometime in 1979, the Pope told them: "The entrepreneur and managerial staff must do everything in their power to give a hearing, due hearing, to the voice of the worker in their employment and to understand his legitimate demands for justice and fairness, overcoming all selfish temptations to make the economic factor a law into itself... Any lack of attention in this sector is culpable, any delay fatal"[24].

---

23) Leo XIII., Rerum Novarum, 1891, n.33. (Cf. English translation "The Workers Charter, CTS London, 1976, S 219, p.31).

24) John Paul II, Address to Christian Union of Entrepreneurs and Managers, 24.11.1979. L'osservatore Romano English, 24.12.79, Nos 52-3, p.3.

The Holy Father defends the working man by making it clear to his
August hearers who themselves are employers and often run the
risk to place their workers on the level of objects:
"You are not unaware of the situation of so many factory workers
who, if obliged to live fenced off, as it were, in an artificial
structure, run the risk of feeling atrophied in their interior
spontaneity. Machines, with their rigid automatism, are unrewarding
and offer little satisfaction... and the machinery of production,
distribution and consumption often forces workers to live in a
"standardised" way, without initiatives, without choices.
This level of dehumanisation is reached when the scale of values
is reversed and "productivism" becomes the only parameter of the
industrial phenomenon, when the interior dimension of values is
neglected, when the aim pursued is rather the perfection of the
work than the perfection of the one who carries it out, giving
preference in this way to the work as compared with the worker,
the object as compared with the subject"[25].

With the above reflections, we have attempted to create an avenue,
whereby with John Paul, we can rightly conclude the pre-eminence
of the subjective meaning of work over the objective one.
With such a conclusion and on the basis of the social teaching
clearly elaborated in John Paul's "Laborem Exercens", the differentiation of people into classes according to the type of work
done disappears. The difference between slave and master, menial
job for slaves and noble work of counting money for masters also
disappears. This is the aim of John Paul II when he considers
work in the subjective sense. His arguments against the economistic
and materialistic trends which treated human work as a mere

---

25) John Paul II, Address to Christian Union of Entrepreneurs and
    Managers, 24.11.1979. L-osservato Romano,
    English, 24.12.79, Nos. 52-3, p.3.

instrument of production or a merchandise gain in weight, in
sound reason and common sense, and mankind is shown a new way
towards removing the class struggles and en-mity existing between them.
With"Laborem Exercens"we can say that "given this way of
understanding things, and presupposing that different sorts of
work that people do can have greater or lesser objective value, we
shall show that each sort is judged above all by the measure of the
dignity of the subject of work, that is to say the person, the
individual who carries it out... In fact, in the final analysis,
it is always man who is the purpose of the work, whatever work
it is that is done by man - even if the common scale of values
rates it as the merest "service", as the most monotonous, even
the most alienating work"[26].

Having arrived at this point where we view man as the subject of work,
we shall then conclude by saying that work must serve man.
This observation enables us to set human work, in whatever way it is
performed by man, within man himself, in other words, in his
innermost being, in the essence of his nature, in what makes him
a man and therefore destined to work.

---

26) John Paul II, Laborem Exercens., n. 6.

4. Three Spheres of Values - Personal Dignity, Family, Nation -

a) Dignity of Human Work and Personal Dignity

The Encyclical 'Laborem Exercens' had not yet seen the light of day
when the Pope, while visiting his homeland Poland in 1979 articulated his
views on the dignity of human work. In a homily delivered at Holy mass
before thousands of workers, the Pope made these statements which
content he later repeated in 'Laborem Exercens':

"The problems being raised today - and is it really today? -
about human labour do not, in fact, come down in the last analysis -
I say this with respect for all the specialists - either to technology
or even to economics but a fundamental category: the category of the
dignity of work, that is to say, of the dignity of man. Economics,
technology and the many other specialisations and disciplines have their
justification for existing in that single essential category.
If they fail to draw from that category and are shaped without
reference to the dignity of human labour, they are in error, they are
harmful, they are against man. This fundamental category is humanistic.
I make bold to say that this fundamental category, the category of work
as a measure of the dignity of man, is Christian. We find it in its
highest degree of intensity in Christ"[27].

With the above basis, the Holy Father specifically elevates the
dignity of human work, because this work is done by man, and he
thereby brings down any other dimensions of human endeavour under this
category. The primary basis of the value of work is MAN. Man is
the fundamental category from which all work derives its dignity.
Without man, there is no work, and therefore no dignity!

---

27) John Paul II, Homily at Mass at Nowa Huta, Poland, 9 June 1979;
In L'osservatore Romano, English Edition, 16. July 1979, No. 29,
pp. 10 - 11.

i) Work is a "bonum arduum" - (good hardship):

Several times in the Encyclical 'Laborem Exercens', John Paul stresses
that, in spite of the heavy toil that sometimes accompanies work,
work is a good thing for man. "It is not only good in the sense that
it is useful or something to enjoy; it is also good as being
something worthy, that is to say, something that corresponds to man's
dignity, that expresses this dignity and increases it" [28].

For the Holy Father, this ethical meaning of human work defines more
clearly the dignity of work. Says he, "even though it bears the
mark of a "bonum arduum", in the terminology of Saint Thomas Aquinas,
this does not take away the fact that, as such, it is a good thing
for man"[29].

But why is work a good thing for man, when we notice how injustices
have been heaped upon man by man through work? How is work a good
thing when God imposed on man the mandate and order to work after the
biblical fall? For there it is written:
"And to Adam he said, "Because you have listened to the voice of
your wife, and have eaten of the tree which I commanded you not to,
cursed is the ground because of you; in toil you shall eat of it
all the days of your life; thorns and thistles it shall bring forth to
you; and you shall eat the plants of the field. In the sweat
of your face you shall eat bread till you return to the ground....."[30].

How can the Pope say that work is a good thing when millions of
people die in their places of work, when workers live outside
their homes - without family security and in loneliness?

---

28) John Paul II, Laborem Exercens, n. 9.
29) John Paul II, LE, n. 9 (Cf. Thomas Aquinas, Summa Th. I-II, q.40, a.I.c)
30) Genesis, Chap. 3, Verse 17 - 19

228

John Paul II knows these questions and even expressed them himself in
his writing where he made reference to the words of God to Adam
quoted above, and said: "These words refer to the sometimes heavy
toil that from then onwards has accompanied human work; but they do
not alter the fact that work is the means whereby man achieves
that "dominion" which is proper to him over the visible world, by
"subjecting" the earth. Toil is something that is universally known
for it is universally experienced"[31]. But is this enough?
The Pope knows that this is not enough an answer, and so goes on to
talk on the consequences of work; on all that which man through work
has been able to achieve; on the co-creation and reproduction which
human work has made possible. Here lies the goodness of work.
"Work is a good thing for man - a good thing for his humanity -
because through work man not only transforms nature, adapting it to
his own needs, but he also achieves fulfilment as a human being and
indeed, in a sense, becomes "more a human being"[32].
Without this consideration says the Pontiff, it is impossible to
understand the meaning of the virtue of industriousness.

---

31) John Paul II, LE n. 9
32) Ibid.

ii) Human Work transcends all ideology and class struggle:

In his attempt to elevate the dignity of work in a world where
ideologies have reduced its meaning to mere slogans and to class
struggles, the Pope ends up in a eulogy for work, sometimes giving
room for mere sentimental outbursts. Addressing thousands of workers
at "Jalisco" Stadium Guadalajara in Mexico on his first international
tour as Pope, a visit to an unjustly treated and exploited
continent, the Pope spoke to the masses thus:

"Dear workers.... I arrive here in the magnificient setting of
Guadalajara, where we meet the name of him who wished to be known
as the carpenter's son... I wish to express to you, right away, how
happy the Pope is that this is a meeting with workers, with working
families, with Christian families, which, from their places of work,
know how to be agents of social welfare... in the workshop, in the
factory, in any house or place... Work is not a curse, it is a
blessing from God who calls man to rule the earth and transform it,
in order that the divine work of creation may continue with man's
intelligence and effort. I want to tell you with all my soul
and with all my might that I suffer at the lack of work..."[32b].

Yes, the Pope suffers at the lack of work, like many other millions
of people the world over who are willing to work, but are unable to
find paid work - the unemployed people. In this convinction that
work has a dignity, and that the working man becomes more fulfilled

---

32b) John Paul II, Address to Workers at Jalisco Stadium,
Guadalajara, Mexico, 30 January 1979, L'osservatore Romano,
English Edition, 12 February 1979, No. 7, p.11

through his work, the Pope, showing his respect for human work
accepted the noble invitation of the International Labour
Organisation and addressed them in Geneva, thus:
"In addressing you ladies and gentlemen, I wish first of all, through
you, to pay tribute to human work, whatever its nature and wherever in
the world it may be performed - a tribute to all work, and to each
and every man or woman engaged in it... Work in any of its forms deserves
particular respect because it represents the output of a human
being and because behind it there is always a live subject -
the human person. That is the source of its value and its dignity"[32c].

The earth is entrusted to man, and through work man has dominion
over it. As such, work has for man a significance that is not
merely technical but ethical. It can be said that man "subdues"
the earth when by his endeavour he becomes its master, not its slave,
and also the master and not the slave of work.

John Paul gave these views more force and support when he preached
to workers of Jasna Gora in his native Poland. He did not lack
words to remind the masses listening to him that:
"The riches of the earth, both those that appear on its surface
and those that we must seek in its depths becomes riches for man
only at the cost of human labour. This work, in its many forms,
both intellectual and manual, is necessary for man to fulfil the
magnificent mission that the creator has entrusted to him, the
mission expressed in the book of Genesis with the words "subdue the
earth and have domination over it"[33a].

32c) John Paul II, Address to the International Labour Organisation,
Tuesday, 15 June 1982, Geneva; Published in CTS, 1982/7, p.279.
33a) John Paul II, Homily at Mass for Workers of Jasna Gora, Poland,
6 June 1979, L'osservato Romano, English Edition, 16 July 1979,
No. 29, pp. 3 - 4.

iii)Work helps in personal maturity :

The dignity of human work lies therefore on this, that "work helps
man to become better, more mature spiritually, more responsible in
order that he may realise his vocation on earth both as an
unrepeatable person and in community with others, especially in
the fundamental human community constituted by the family...
Work must make it possible for this human community to find the means
for its formation and maintenance"[33b].

The same views were articulated by the Pope in Nigeria during his
meeting with workers at the Holy Cross Cathedral, Lagos on 16 February
1982. He told them in a homily: "People who work enjoy a God-given
dignity. God could have created everything on earth in its final
form, but he decided differently. For God wants us to be associated
with him in the improvement of things he has made. By our work
we share in God's creative dignity"[33c].

The consequence of this view of human work and the dignity conferred
on work because of man, make it urgent and absolutely necessary,
that all obsessing work which sees work just as the 'only means of
expression' of one's personality, of work that limits and restricts
personal freedom and man's dignity, all these have to be eliminated.
Workers are to be treated as mature persons, capable of taking care
of their own interests and of responsibly contributing to the
common welfare.

33b) John Paul II, Homily at Mass for Workers of Jasna Gora, Poland,
      6 June 1979, L'osservato Romano, English Edition, 16 July 1979,
      No. 29, pp. 3 - 4

33c) John Paul II, Homily at Mass in Holy Cross Cathedral, Lagos to
      Nigerian Workers: L'osservatore Romano, March - April 1982, p.26
      Special English Edition.

iv) Work has a social and creative value:

Work should not therefore be considered only as a mere "necessity" and source of one's livelihood, but also as a "service for brothers", a real vocation.

Work has a high creative and social value. Not only does it offer man an opportunity for self-realisation and self-improvement as a person, it also encourages him to commit himself with the whole community. This is how vocational commitment becomes an active co-efficient for the development of the worker's personality, as an individual and as a responsible element in his community, whereby his social, civil, moral, cultural and also spiritual perception will improve.

The dignity of work lies in the fact that man becomes more man. Work should be the expression and measure of man's dignity, as John Paul says:

> "We should create a world unpleasant to live in if
> we aimed only at having more, and did not think
> first and foremost of the person of the worker,
> his conditions as a human being and a son of God
> who is called to an eternal vocation, if we did not
> think of helping him to be more 'man'"[34].

For this reason it is all the more important that in work, "whereby matter gains in nobility, man himself should not experience a lowering of his own dignity"[35]. All this, according to the Pontiff, pleads in favour of the moral obligation to link industriousness as a virtue with the social order of work, which will enable man to become, in work, "more a human being" and not be degraded by it.

---

34) John Paul II, Address to Workers at Monterrey (Mexico), 31 January 1979; L'osservato Romano, English Edition 19. February 1979, No. 8, pp 6 - 7.

35) John Paul II, LE, n. 9

Human beings cannot subsist, feed, and develop themselves without their manual and intellectual work. Work is a factor of human fulfilment, and is a "bonum arduum". Without working, the human being cannot realise and make himself respected as a person; whereas through his work, he conquers nature, as willed by the creator, and gains a part of the riches of the earth.

Already in his first Encyclical letter "Redemptor Hominis", Pope John Paul II asserted in very clear terms that work exalts and magnifies man who works. He stated that work "does not only develop potentialities inherent in the universe, but it exalts and magnifies man himself, by making him more mature spiritually, more like God, since through his work he participates in the divine mission to radiate and instil kindness into human beings. But he should not become a threat for the natural environment, whose recources are limited and often incapable of reproduction, nor should he create such environmental situations as may be harmful to vegetal, animal, and human life, nor turn himself into an instrument whose sophisticated techniques divert man from the love of nature, and alienate him of his relations with nature"[36].

Unfortunately, mankind, especially in the industrialised nations as a consequence of misguided historical and materialistic development has reached a stage where human dignity is precarious because of alienating work, and where also, the disregard for ecology in a mad rush for industrialisation has led to the fear of destruction and the future of history. The Pope articulated these fears where he intentionally refers to the precarious situation of mankind: "Today", he says, "man is in danger: a serious threat bears upon him as the result of the work of his hands, and even more so, of the work of his intellect and the tendencies of his will"[37].

---

36) John Paul II, Redemptor Hominis, n. 15
37) Ibid.

Man lives in fear for he is afraid that what he produces could be
used against him. This evidence leads the Holy Father to come
back on the subject and to insist, as he does, in an address he
delivered to participants at the convention of the Italian
Federation of Knights of Labour:
"...Authentic progress, in fact, is only that which helps man
become more mature spiritually, more conscious of his dignity,
more open to others, and freer in his choices: that is to say,
a progress aiming at forming a man who knows the "whys" of things,
and not only their "Hows". Never has man been as rich in goods,
means, and techniques, as he is now, but never has he been as poor
in indications about their utilisation"[38].

There is therefore an urgent need to give back to man the
consciousness for which he lives and works;   Such task may be
carried out only by those who believe in the "priority of ethics
over technology, in the primacy of the person over things, in the
superiority of spirit over matter"[39]

---

38) John Paul II, Address to Participants at the Convention of the
     Italian Federation of Knights of Labour, 11 May 1979,
     L'osservatore Romano, Italian Edition, May 12, 1979, p.2
     (Translated into English by the Pontifical Commission for
     Iustitia et Pax., Vatican, The Social Teachings of John Paul II,
     Human Labour, Number Series 5, p.51)
39) John Paul II, Redemptor Hominis, n. 16.

b) Work and Family

In the second Chapter of the Book of Genesis, the author
records that the Creator noticed a mistake in the creation of
man alone without a helpmate. But it did not take the Lord God time
to see that this imbalance was not the best natural state for man
whom he had created and placed in the garden of Eden to "till and
keep it"[40]. Man had animals, trees and plants around him but he
had not his like in the whole garden. God is quoted in this Yahwistic
tradition as having recognised this imperfection in his creation
and to have said:

> "It is not good that the man should be alone;
> I will make him a helper fit for him"[41]... "So the
> Lord God caused a deep sleep to fall upon the man,
> and while he slept took one of his ribs and
> closed up its place with flesh; and the rib which
> the Lord God had taken from the man he made
> into a woman and brought her to the man"[42].

The man's exclamation when he saw his partner and the words of the
author thereafter is the first biblical and generally orthodox account
of the history of man in the universe. It is as such the origin of
the family, which has continued into the Judaic-Christian tradition.
The account records: "Then the man said: This at last is bone of
my bones and flesh of my flesh; she shall be called Woman, because she
was taken out of Man"[43]. And the author concludes thus:
"Therefore a man leaves his father and his mother and cleaves
on his wife, and they become one flesh"[44].

---

40) Genesis 2: 15
41) Genesis 2: 18
42) Genesis 2: 21 - 22
43) Genesis 2: 23
44) Genesis 2: 25

Later in the New Testament when Jesus was confronted with the problem of the family and the case of divorce, he did not waste time according to the writers of the New Testament to refer to this Old Testament standard [45].

No sooner however, the first man and woman fell into temptation, disobeying God, and as consequence, they must work all their lives: "In the sweat of your face you shall eat bread"[46].
The command marks the first connection between work and family.

In his Encyclical Letter"Laborem Exercens", John Paul II referred to three basic spheres of values necessarily linked to work. The first sphere we already considered under "Dignity of Work and Personal Dignity". The second sphere of values linked to work is the family, and the third is the Nation.

Considering the value of work and the family, the Holy Father says: "Work constitutes a foundation for the formation of family life, which is a natural right and something that man is called to. These two spheres of values - one linked to work and the other consequent on the family nature of human life must be properly united and must permeate each other"[47].

In fact, the family basis its being, development, and union on work as its fundamental factor, since work conditions its life, gives meaning to the family, determines its social status, impresses rhythm and character upon it, and represents an essential element of order, cohesion and stability.

---

45) Mathew 19: 5; Mark 10:7; 1 Cor. 6:16; Ephesians 5:31
46) Genesis 3: 19
47) John Paul II, Laborem Exercens, n. 10

For this reason, work has a high creative and social value
which role for the family can hardly be overemphasised;
John Paul II makes this point very emphatic when he writes:
"In a way, work is a condition for making it possible to found a
family, since the family requires the means of subsistence which
man normally gains through work"[48].
As we already made clear in the initial chapters, work is
necessary for human survival. In more primitive times, mankind
would have died out without the hunting, fishing and gathering
which enabled him to feed and clothe himself. At a later stage of
development, herding flocks, farming the land and making useful
objects like tables and chairs were also essential aspects of the
struggle to survive. Without them there could have been no family
or communal life. In many parts of the world today these basic
activities are still just as vital. We can therefore assert that
work is part of the givenness of existence. St Thomas Aquinas
developed this idea as part of his exposition of the natural law.
From this has come the idea of everyone's "right to work" which is
so deeply engraved in our legal constitutions and individual consciousness.

While addressing young people attending the 1982 meeting for
friendship among people's in Rimini, the Pope took the
opportunity to refer to Work and the Family, maintaining that the
family is a fundamental resource of man. He continues:

---

48)   John Paul II, Laborem Exercens, n. 10

"Man works to support himself and his family. If to work is
to take care of one's being, co-operating in the creative work
of God, this general principle becomes evident and existentially
concrete for the greater part of men in the fact that by working man
takes care of his loved ones. If it is certainly true that man, as all
the animals, feels the instinct for self-preservation, it is also true
that it is not right to posit as the principle of work an intention that is
only utilitarian and selfish. Even the instinct for self-preservation
exists in man in a specifically human, personalistic form as the
will to exist as a person, as the will to safeguard the value of the
person in himself and in others, beginning with his loved ones.
This fact defines the limit of every utilitarian and economic interpretation of human work"[49].

From the above, the Pope attempts to show that even though
work is necessary for the family's existence, it should not be
reduced to the level of simple animalistic instincts or to work from
purely utilitarian purposes. Above that, work should be a means of
our humanisation and therefore belongs to the fulfilment of our
potentials in the family.
Beyond subsistence, "work and industriousness also influence
the whole process of education in the family for the very reason
that everyone "becomes a human being" through work"[50].

49) John Paul II, Extracts from the Pope's Address on 29th August to
     young people attending the 1982 meeting for friendship among
     the People's in Rimini; Published in The Pope Teaches, 1982/9, CTS,
     (Address and Homilies of John Paul II, London), pp. 347 - 348.
50) John Paul II, LE, n. 10

Exactly provocative but completely correct is the Pope's thesis
that "the family is simultaneously a community made possible by work
and the first school of work, within the home, for every person"[51].
Work has therefore two aspects in that it makes the upkeep of the
family possible, and secondly it makes education possible, which
"is one of the purposes of the family".

The teaching of the Church has always devoted special attention to
this question. The social Teachings of the Popes and the Decrees of
the Council Fathers - also made clear and direct statements on
this issue[52]. There is a basic Christian conception of man and
the family which believes in the individuality of the Person and his
fulfilment only among Persons. Pope John XXIII confirms this
teaching once again when he wrote: "We are bound to consider as ideal
that form of enterprise which is modelled on the basis of a community
of persons working together for the advancement of their mutual
interests in accordance with the principles of justice and
Christian teaching"[53].

---

51) John Paul II, LE, n. 10
52) Vat.II, Decree "Gravissimum Educationis"
    Vat.II, Gaudium et Spes, (48 - 50)
    Pius XI, Divini Illius Magistri (On the Christian Education
    of youth), Dec. 1929;
    Pius XI, Casti Connubi (On Christian Marriage), 30.12.1930
    John Paul II, Familiaris Consortio, (CTS, 1982).
53) John XXIII, Pope, Encyclical "Mater et Magistra", n 142 - 3

Commenting on the implications of this Encyclical of Human Work
of John Paul II in reference to Work and the Family, Lothar Roos adds:

"Hier steht offensichtlich nicht das Bild einer in
verschiedenen Individuen zerfallenden, lediglich
noch durch äußere Zwecke zusammengehaltenen Familie
vor Augen, sondern die gerade bei einfachen Menschen
fast selbstverständlich anzutreffende Vorstellung,
daß alle Familienmitglieder gemeinsam füreinander
einstehen und sich miteinander eine Lebensexistenz
erbauen. Gerade darin liegt eine fundamental
erzieherische, das ganze Leben eines Menschen
prägende Aufgabe"[54].

Described as "the fundamental dimension of man's life on earth",
work must help man individually and the family collectively to
become better and more mature spiritually in order to achieve his
vocation on earth as an unrepeatable person and in community
with others, especially in the fundamental human community
constituted by the family. By joining together in this very
community, whose character was established by the Creator himself
from the beginning, a man and a woman give life to new human beings.

---

54) ROOS, L., Laborem Exercens - Sinn and Sozialgestalt der
menschlichen Arbeit; Hrsg. Katholischen Sozialwiss.
Zentralstelle Mönchengladbach; Nr. 86,
Verlag Bachem, p. 8.

Work must make it possible for this human community, the family,
to find the means necessary for its formation and maintenance.
Like the Pope said in a homily at Mass in his native Poland,
"the reason for the family is one of the fundamental factors
determining the economy and policy of work. These keep their ethical
character when they take into consideration the needs and the rights
of the family... I wish your work not to cease to be the source of
your social strenght. Thanks to your work, may your homes be strong...[55].
With this postulation, the Pope affirms the value of the family
in the nation, for man, and the society. He rediscovers a new
meaning for work and its necessary link to the basic value
represented through the family. As such, "the family constitutes one
of the most important terms of reference for shaping the social
and ethical order of human work"[56].

Having said this, he goes on to consider the third sphere of values
linked to work, namely the Nation and the family of Nations.

---

55) John Paul II; Homily at Mass for Workers of Jasna Gora (Poland)
6 June 1979; L'osservatore Romano, English Edition,
16 July 1979, No. 29, pp 3 - 4.
56) John Paul II, LE, n. 10

c) Work, Society and Nation

The third sphere of values with regard to work according to the
Holy Father, "concerns the great society to which man belongs on
the basis of particular cultural and historical links"[57].
Man combines his deepest human identity with membership of a nation,
and should intend his work also to increase the common good of society,
together with his compatriots, realising in this way that work serves
to add to the heritage of the whole human family and of all the
people living in the world.

The basic point which John Paul makes in this context is that
since work is a social fact, it requires various forms and modalities of
cooperation to establish a relation of solidarity among those who
work together. Even when personal and individual aspects seem
to necessarily prevail over the community and co-operative aspects,
work will appear as the outcome of an ongoing process of cooperation,
that is to say, of a work community.

Commenting on this passage, Lothar Roos sees the writing hand of the
Pope from Poland for whom 'cultural and historical links' mean much.
He writes in his commentary on Laborem Exercens:
> "Er verweist damit auf einen für uns Deutsche, keineswegs aber
> etwa für die Polen völlig verblaßten Wertzusammenhang, nämlich
> auf die „Volksgemeinschaft", auf die „Gesamtheit" der
> „Kultur einer bestimmten Nation", in der er „auch eine große
> historische und soziale Inkarnation der Arbeit aller
> Generationen" sieht[58].

---

57) John Paul II, LE, 10
58) Roos, L, Laborem Exercens - Sinn und Sozialgestalt der
menschlichen Arbeit., op.cit., p.8

This differentiation and interpretation of the strong cultural ties
to the past and to history, as presented by the Pope leaves little
impression on the German reader who has a different milieu, a
different economic system and historical past.

Man lives in a society, he is a social being, and society influences,
moulds and educates the individual. Says the Pope, "This society
is not only the great "educator" of every man... it is also a
great social incarnation of the work of all generations"[59].
The work of each generation leaves its stamp on the oncoming group.
Says he: "Work, through which man subdues nature, is the work of
the entire human community throughout all its generations.
Everyone of these generations has its obligation to take care of
the earth in order to hand it over to future generations, still
and ever more fit to be man's home... When the bond of solidarity
that must bind men among themselves and with future generations is
broken, this care of the earth is lessened. So the ecological
catastrophe that is threatening mankind today has a deep ethical root
in the for-getfulness of the true nature of human work and
especially of its subjective dimension, its value for the family
and social community"[60].

No better words could the Pope use to express the historical and
cultural link of human work than these addressed to the young in Rimini.
He thereby succeeds perfectly to regard work and to teach
it as a communal or corporate activity. It brings us into

---

59) John Paul II, LE, n 10

60) John Paul., Extracts from the Address to the young people
attending the 82 meeting for friendship among People's in Rimini;
(Cf. The Pope Teaches, 1982/9; p. 347, CTS London).

relationship with other people . It is a major means of
integrating us into community, of giving us a place, status, belonging
and value. For man in the industrial milieu of twentieth Century
European Society, this teaching has to be emphasised and overemphasised for it to make a strong impact. In the industrialised
nations of Europe, the danger and tendency is there to disregard
this corporate dimension, also because the individualism based on
the philosophy and culture of this society has left its mark already
on the society. To counteract this influence, the Holy Father says:
"Man combines his deepest human identity with membership of a nation,
and intends his work also to increase the common good developed
together with his compatriots, thus realising that in this way, work
serves to add to the heritage of the whole human family, of all
the people living in the world"[61].
With this assertion, two new perspectives are opened to humanity
through work: Firstly, work unites man with fellow men;
Secondly, work leads to the interdependence among nations - It gives
room for Solidarity; and herein lies its advantage.

    (i) <u>Work Unites Man</u>:   John Paul considering work as a unifying
        factor among men has this to say: "It is characteristic
        of work that it first and foremost UNITES people. In this
        consists its social power - the power to build a community.
        In the final analysis, both those who work and those who
        manage the means of production or who own them must in some
        way be united in this community"[62].

---

61) John Paul II, LE, n. 10
62) John Paul II, LE n. 20

After reflecting carefully on these words of the Pope, nothing else needs to be added for he articulates in a clear manner the role of work among peoples - that of unity. When members of a nation put in their energy into creative work, much is produced in this society. With that which is produced, entire population gains from the goods. Whereas some work on the intellectual bench and others in the factory; whereas some work in the coal mines and others pilot the affairs of the nation; whereas some trade and others cultivate, in work and through work, the goods of each party is perfected and by distribution reaches all the members of the society and nation. Those who receive salaries are enabled with their wages to buy the goods produced by others and out of it pay taxes to provide a range of services such as Defence, transport, Housing, Environmental services, Law and Order, Education, the Arts and Sciences, Health, Personal and Social services, Social Security, Amusements and other public services which all together constitute the "social wage"[63].

The realisation of this situation should lead us both to be concerned about the right creation of wealth and its just distribution. Creation, Yes, but not by any means or at any cost to people or to the environment. Distribution, Yes, but with special concern for the weak, the handicapped, the poor, the young and the sick.

---

63) In England for example, in 1982/3, total public expenditure was about 115 thousand million pounds, of which 89 thousand million pounds was used on items just mentioned above, or if we divide that by the 55 million people inhabiting the UK, 1600 pounds a year or 31 pounds each week. (Ref. Board for social responsibility, Church of England Synod, London 1982), Working Paper - Industrial and Economic affairs Committee, chap. 5, p.4).

Pope John XXIII already spoke on this matter when in his Encyclical "Mater et Magistra" he stated that "as history testifies with ever increasing clarity, there can be no such thing as a well-ordered and prosperous society unless individual citizens and the State co-operate in the economy. Both sides must work together in harmony, and their respective efforts must be proportioned to the needs of the common good in the prevailing circumstances and conditions of human life" (paragraph 56).

In modern work, the need for new attitudes towards social solidarity is also being emphasised. This requires a tissue of closer and more conscious human relationships, which may lead, through the indispensable and often complex functional divisions of production, and through the collaboration of all concerned, to a more united and harmoniously operating society.

(ii) <u>Work and Interdependence among Nations</u>: Addressing the World International Labour Organisation in Geneva sometime in summer 1982, the Pope spoke in unequivocal terms about work in the international context. He made it clear that not only does work unite mankind, the reality of work leads to the inter-dependence among nations.

"The need for man to safeguard the reality of his work and free it from any ideology in order to bring out once more the true meaning of human effort, becomes particularly apparent when one considers the world of work and the solidarity it calls for in the international context. The problem of man at work today must be set against a worldwide background which can no longer be ignored. All the major problems of man in society are now world problems! They must be approached on a worldwide scale, in a realistic spirit of course, but in an innovative, critical spirit as well"[64].

Certainly, one of the principal characteristics which seem to be typical of our age is an increase in the inter-dependence and inter-relationship among nations, societies and political regions in the world arena. The progress of science and technology in every aspect of life has led, particularly today to increased relationships between nations, and made nations more and more dependent on one another. As Pope John XXIII said: "No single State has sufficient resources at its command to solve the more important scientific, economic, technical, social and political problems which confront it at the present time alone. These problems are necessarily the concern of a whole group of nations, and possibly of the whole world"[65].

As such, work, which is a basic human activity has become a unifying factor for entire humanity and for the family of the world's independent nations. The nations therefore must work together for the mutual development and perfection of its peoples. They can help

---

64) John Paul II, Address to the International Labour Organisation, Geneva, Switzerland, Tuesday, 15 June 1982., (Ref. The Pope Teaches, CTS, London, 1982/7, p.286)
65) John XXIII, Encyclical Letter 'Mater et Magistra', 1961, par. 201.

themselves only in so far as they succeed in helping one another.
This explains why international understanding and solidarity are
so necessary.

Among those forms of associations and activities which have increased
international understanding among the worlds peoples and nations
may be included: scientific and technical gadgets, greater
productive efficiency, modern means of communication such as the
radio, television, the Cinema, Press, periodicals and daily newspapers, travelling, and no less, the growing universal knowledge
of Christ and his Church that excludes no one and embraces everyone.
Christ proclaimed to us the Gospel from which we know that God is
love, that He is Father, and that entire humanity are His children.
Through the above means in all their variety, the trend and phenomenon
of "ONE WORLD, ONE HUMANITY, ONE DESTINY" has been developed as
the past had never known it.

One basic reason for this growing interdependence was given by
John Paul in his address to the International Labour Organisation:
"Whether we are dealing with the problems of natural resources,
development or employment, a satisfactory solution can be found
only if the international aspect is borne in mind.... The world
economic crisis, with its repercussions throughout the globe,
compels us to recognise that the horizon of the problems is
increasingly a world horizon. The hundreds of millions of starving or
under-nourished human beings, who also have the right to rise up out
of their poverty, should make us realise that the fundamental
reality today is mankind as a whole"[66].

---

66) John Paul, Address to ILO, op.cit., p. 286 - 287

Important however in our entire context is this fact which the Pope reminds us, that it is work, human labour which contributes to this interdependence, thus realising that in this way "work serves to add to the heritage of the whole human family, of all the people living in the world"[67]. The regular functioning of human society requires many services and duties performed by the various branches of labour. An idle society can neither subsist nor progress. In 1967, Paul VI noted in his Encyclical Populorum Progressio : "Today, the major fact that everyone must grasp is that the social question has become worldwide in character" (n 3). This is why the common good can no longer be confined to sectional demands or purely economic requirements alone.

Like John Paul said: "Each of us, without denying his origins and his membership of his family, his people and his nation, or the obligations arising therefrom, must regard himself as a member of this great family, the world community... we must ensure that nations complement each other in their efforts to develope their own spiritual and material resources, on the other hand, we must proclaim the demands made by universal solidarity and the structural consequences it implies"[68]

---

67) John Paul II, LE, 10
68) John Paul II, Address to ILO, op.cit., p. 287

(iii) <u>Conclusion:</u> This solidarity and interdependence brought about by and through work has many advantages for mankind as Pope John XXIII tried to show [69]. The interdependence makes it possible for the individual to exercise many of his personal rights, especially those which we call economic and social, such as the right to the indispensable means of obtaining a livelihood, preserving good health, receiving further education and a more thorough professional training. The social relationship through work also leads to the security of other rights, such as the right to housing, work, suitable leisure and recreation. Nations gain from each other on cultural and spiritual values, besides the economic gain. The underdeveloped Countries which supply much of the raw materials to the industrialised nations will also have much to gain as far as technological know-how and transfer is concerned. Friendship is cultivated among persons all over the world, and the basis for a just and peaceful society is guaranteed through work.

According to John Paul II, the three dimensions and value spheres discussed above, namely work and personal dignity, work and the family; and work, the Nation and the Society, are of very great advantage. Since man is the subject of work, "there is realised, first of all, that "dominion" over the world of nature to which man is called from the beginning according to the words of Genesis...
This is an advantageous and positive phenomenon, on the condition that the objective dimension of work does not gain the upper hand over the subjective dimension, depriving man of his dignity and inalienable rights or reducing them"[70].

---

69) John XXIII, Mater et Magistra, n. 64
70) John Paul II, LE, n. 10

CHAPTER SIX:

THE SOCIAL STRUCTURE OF HUMAN WORK

PART ONE(I)Certain economic schools of thought

1. Liberal Capitalism and Adam Smith

One of the most important controversial issues in economic
principles which have agitated the minds of men and nations in the
past, and also in our own times are important,concern the theories
postulated by liberal capitalism. After nearly two centuries,
Adam Smith remains a towering figure in the history of economic thought.
Two of his books "On the theory of moral sentiments" (1759), and
"An inquiry into the nature and causes of the wealth of Nations"
(1776), are classics which classify him as the founder of the modern
science of economics, although his ideas were developed in the
context of the previous history of economic thought centuries before him.
One question in particular interested Smith in the Theory of
Moral Sentiments, concerning the source of man's ability to form
moral judgements, including judgements on his own behaviour, in the
face of his seemingly over-riding passions for self-preservation
and self-interest. Smith's answer, at considerable lenght, is the
presence within each of us of an "inner man" who plays the role
of the "impartial spectator", approving or condemning our own
and others' actions with a voice impossible to disregard.

As professor of logic and moral philosophy at Glasgow and Edinburgh,
Smith's theory may be seen as part of his general philosophy.
He saw man as a creature driven by passions and at the same time
self-regulated by his ability to reason, and no less important -
by his capacity for sympathy. This duality serves both to pit men
against one another, and to provide them with the rational and moral
faculties to create institutions by which the internal struggle can be
mitigated and even turned to the common good. His basic view in
his book "The Moral Sentiments" was repeated in "The Wealth of Nations":
that "self-seeking men are often led by an invisible hand... without
knowing it, without intending it, to advance the interest of the society".

He assumed a certain natural harmony in man's economic life, having
been influenced by the natural sciences - the Copernican revolution,
Newtonian Physics and the development of mathematics. As
Roger Charles notes: "Men were fascinated by the order in the working
of the physical world and, in the way that culturally dominant
ideas influence other areas of thought and life of their time, the
belief that this same harmony was at work passed over into the
developing science of economics - even though it is not directly
comparable with the physical sciences in data, purpose or degree of
scientific predictability and accuracy"[1].

The first country to make the transition to modern industry and
economic growth was Britain. The reasons for this primacy were
partly material, partly social and institutional. Britain was
favoured by its oceanic position, which gave the country access to the
overseas markets and suppliers; by its modest size and population
(about 1% of the total world population in the 1780's), by its
indented coastline, which placed most of the country within easy
reach of water transport; and by the abundance of those natural
resources, taken from the colonies, that proved to be of immense
importance for the new industrial technology. As a centre of
capitalism and the most industrialised empire in Europe, stress was
placed by the large feudal Lords on greater freedom to expand markets,
protect commercial interests and make more gains and profit.

----

1) Roger Charles, Ibid., p. 264

The materialists and owners of production factors, landlords and manufacturers found in Adam Smith's books, the intellectual justification of the policy of laissez faire. He was celebrated as a sophisticated and persuasive advocate of the policies which they wished to pursue. In his observation that "man is led by an invisible hand to promote that which was no part of his intention", Smith made it clear that in seeking out their own expressly selfish and individualistic ends, men are, at the same time, inevitably led by forces over which they have no control (but which rather control them) to secure the common good[2].

Smith saw no contradiction between his ethical approach to the study of economics and his beliefs that economic individualism was a better guarantor of the common good than any form of social supervision. The liberal idea of the autonomous individual who recognises no law superior to his own subjective conscience characterised Smith's school of thought. Sharing the intellectual and utilitarian philosophy of the laissez faire or empiricist philosophers such as Hume, Mill and Bentham, Smith's "Wealth of Nations" exposes an institutional mechanism that acts to reconcile the disruptive possibilities inherent in a blind obedience to the passions alone. This protective mechanism is competition, an arrangement by which men's passionate desire for bettering their condition, is turned into a socially beneficial agency by pitting one man's drive for self-betterment against another's.

---

2) Smith, A., Wealth of Nations., New York, Cannan Edition, 1937, p. 423

Liberal capitalism thus shows as Smith points out, that the
unintended outcome of this competitive struggle for self-betterment
(a sort of survival of the fittest) brings about the "invisible hand"
regulating the economy. He explains how the mutual vying of men
forces the prices of commodities down to their "natural" levels,
which correspond to their costs of production. Moreover by
inducing labour and capital to move from less to more profitable
occupations or areas, the competitive mechanism constantly restores
prices to these "natural" levels despite short-run aberrations.

Finally, by explaining that wages and rents and profits are themselves
subject to this same discipline of self-interest and competition,
Smith not only provided an ultimate rationale for these "natural"
prices but also revealed an underlying orderliness in the distribution
of income itself among workers, whose recompense was their wages;
landlords, whose income was their rents; and manufacturers, whose
reward was their profits [3].

---

3) Robert L. Heilbroner, Adam Smith, Article published in the
Department of Economics, New School for Social Research,
New York, (Cf. Encyclopaedia Brittanica, Vol. 16, (1768),
1982; p. 904, publ. Chicago).

Unlike the Newtonian system with which Smith was quite familiar, the growth machine did not depend on human nature alone for its operation. Human nature and its laws drove it, and human nature was a complex rather than a simple force. The theories of liberal capitalism knew nothing of the conscious restraints of morality from either revealed or natural law. Great evils and injustices resulted out of the competitive and profit-oriented thesis engrained in the theory. Human rights and needs, contempt for Christian social principles and God's law, all these led the materialistic liberalist capitalism of Adam Smith and his followers into greater and greater confusion. Class struggles ensured and a watered earth was made possible for an opposing theory championed by Karl Marx and F. Engels in the name of socialism or communism. Both extreme economic theories have in our time been seen to be built on false premises. We shall expose this in the succeeding pages.

2 . Critique of Liberalism

Whatever achievements or advantages which liberal capitalism brought
about, and there is no doubt that there are many - such as -
greater production of goods of various sorts available to the people;
an increase in the standard of living of people averagely observed;
the guarantee of freedom to the entrepreneur who has free hand and
free choice of his business; the availability of initiative; the joy
in seeing the fruit of one's own hard labour and planning, and many
others, still these advantages are overtaken when we consider what
the common people had to suffer to achieve this end. It is also
questionable if the basis of individualism and materialism accepted
by liberal capitalism can be morally justifiable?

One thing is certain as Roger Charles has mentioned: "Liberalism
does not give chance to the demands of distributive justice" [4].
Distributive justice concerns the distribution of benefits and
burdens among individuals having legal rights within a society,
as it results from the major social institutions - property systems,
public organisations, regulations of wages, profits, the protection
of the person's rights through the legal system, the allocation of
medicine, housing and welfare benefits. Its motto is "to each
according to his merits, needs and due". Burdens, which may be simply
regarded as "negative benefits" have also been included in the
distribution, understood as balancing the various benefits one is
receiving against the burdens he suffers to arrive at an overall amount.

---

4) Roger Charles, op.cit., p. 271

In capitalistic liberalism, too many workers did not recieve enough
from the wealth that they created to support life decently. As Roger
Charles describes: "At the begining of the twentieth century, some 25%
of the adult male wage earners in Britain were recieving barely a
living wage. Overall, one-quarter of the income-earners took two-thirds
of the national income; the manual workers, who comprised the other
three quarters, took only one-third of the income[5].

Liberal capitalism, therefore, bore too harshly on the manual workers and
the ordinary people, not letting them share in the goods which their hands
produced. In the first instance, it treated the industrial and agricultural
workers all too badly, and though it did bring real benefits in material terms
and was modified in theory and practice as time went on, still, Liberal
capitalism's materialistic basis was deficient, believing only in gain,
profit and consumption. It lacked any Christian ethical perspective, and
this is what condemns it before Christians[6].

---

5) Roger Charles, op.cit., p.271
6) We have to mention in this connection the views of Professor Anton
   Rauscher on rigid capitalism where he says: "Entgegen der Annahme, daß
   Arbeitsteilung und freie Konkurrenz am Markt den „Reichtum der Nationen"
   begründen und Not und Elend aus der Gesselschaft vertreiben würden, kam
   es zur Verproletarisierung der Arbeiter, zur Verelendung großer Teile der
   bisherigen Handwerker und der Bauern. Die„Soziale Frage" erschütterte
   die sich entwickelnden Industriegesselschaften und spaltete sie zu
   Klassengesselschaften".
   (Ref. Rauscher, A., "Katholische Soziallehre und liberale Wirtschaftsordnung", In : "Selbstinteresse und Gemeinwohl" (Soziale Orientierung,
   Bd. 5), Duncker und Humbolt, Berlin, 1985,p.283.

The bulk of the criticism of the liberal capitalist system and its
hydra headed forms in our modern times is that it remains, as we
have said, not merely an economic philosophy, but a complete
philosophy of life. It is its poverty in this respect which condemns it
for Christian social principles.

As a philosophy, individualistic liberalism denies the transcendent
dimension, the metaphysical and theological perspective that it had
inherited from its Christian past. In the nineteenth century, it
became clear to everyone that liberalism simply was another word
for materialism.

Besides, further criticism on liberal capitalism proceeds from this
fact which shows that with the growth of the system, profits are
substituted for the virtues of human personality and material values
are made the measure of all things. In practised capitalism, the
smallest possible number of men were imbued with the greatest possible
amount of economic goods, even though the aim of the classical
economists was to seek and arouse the greatest possible number of men
to have their demands for the goods of this earth satisfied to
the greatest possible manner. In this aim however, the question is not
raised as to which purpose and for what meaning is this absurd and
endless consumption and acquisition directed? Why should man's
physical and spiritual abilities be trained to simply demand and
satisfy wants to the extent that waste, over-consumption,
exploitation, accumulation of wealth become a self sufficient end?

This is why Pope Paul VI, while condemning the evils of liberal
capitalism and recognising the human progress which economic
freedom has brought to mankind, seeks to suggest a middle way, by saying
that there must be a purpose for all the accumulation and struggle.
He makes it clear that the idea of a free trade is no longer
equitable given the disparity of economic power between nations.
The Pontiff does not deny the value of competition, but he stresses
the need for planning and central direction too. In other words,
the market economy and the social control should move closer
together and complement rather than oppose each other [7].

---

7) Paul VI, Pope, Populorum Progressio, Encyclical Letter,
     Paragraphs 32 - 33; 56 - 60, (1967), CTS, S273, London.

Catholic social ethics rejected the idea of a totally free and
unbriddled competition, and its articulate exponent is
Pope Pius XI's Encyclical "Quadrage-simo Anno". The Pontiff said:
"The proper ordering of economic life cannot be left to free
competition. From this contaminated source have proceeded in the past
all the errors of the economic individualist school. This school,
ignorant or forgetful of the social and moral aspect of economic
life, held that this must be considered and treated by the State as
absolutely free and independent, because it possesses in free
competition and the open market, a principle of self - direction
better able to control it than any human ingenuity... Free
competition cannot be the guiding principle of economic life...
Free competition has destroyed itself; economic domination has taken
the place of the open market ... the whole economic regime has
become hard, cruel and relentless in a ghastly manner" [8].

Here, it is necessary to mention that the Holy Father was condemning
the liberal capitalism manifested at his time in the early part of
this century. Surely, free competition in our times is not the
same as its classical tone and methods, different even though here and there,
it rears up its ugly head.

---

[8] Pius XI, Quadrage-simo Anno., Paragraphs 88; 109; London, CTS,
Number S 105. (1931).

3. Communist - Socialism and Karl Marx

One of the most dramatic and intellectual personalities to cross the pages of history in the nineteenth century, and one who emerges as one of the greatest men of our epoch (negatively or positively) was Karl Heinrich Marx, a German Jew, born in Trier, Germany in 1818. Marxologists see him as a fascinating figure, the saviour of the exploited labourers and the man who liberated man from God and gave the "coup de grace"to religion. Anti-marxologists on the other hand, consider Marx as a volcanic personality and the evil genius of our time. They see him as a dangerous and revolutionary spirit determined to knock off all established institutions with which he disagrees. So much has been written on the life of Marx that an attempt here would be only by reference [9].

The reactions to the evils of individualism, strongly represented in the evil and oppressive liberal capitalist practices of the nineteenth century gave rise to Marxist socialism, thought out and expounded firstly by Karl Marx and Friedrich Engels, later re-interpreted by Lenin, Mao Tse Tung, Stalin and their successors. [10]
Marx witnessed the crass poverty and injustice which existed in his day in the factories, the exploitation of the labourers, women and children, and the growing class distinction between the haves and the have-nots of his time. His major concern was with the day to day

---

[9] Obiora Ike, Karl Marx on Religion and Christianity - a critical study, unpublished Masters Thesis, University of Innsbruck, Jan. 1981.

[10] It is of course clear that Marx and Engels were not the first to criticise liberal capitalism . Authors before them gave attention to this evil including such pious writers as Adam Müller (1816), Franz Reichensperger (1847),Josef Görres (1838), Bishop Ketteler, Adolph Kolping and the Saint Simonians. (Refer to Höffner,J."Wirtschafts-ordnung und Wirtschaftsethik,Eröffnungsreferat, DBK,Fulda,1985,r.12).

problems of real people. Consequently his major economic
criticisms turned on the society in which he lived, a concern
which was solely economic, but also considered the extent to which
the capitalistic system kept the proletarians from ever fulfilling
their potentials as individuals. Marx referred to this situation
as alienation. By this is meant, a relationship, whereby man
becomes cut off from, out of tune with himself, his family, his
friends, his work and his world. Because of this alienation, man
is not and cannot be a whole, fully developed human being in a
capitalist society.
Applied to the world of work, the worker producing goods for others
is alienated from what he makes. Thus we have alienated labour
in capitalist society[11].

Materialism as developed by Marx and Engels was theoretically and
scientifically aimed at fighting this alienation caused by capitalist
oppression of the workers and the metaphysical interpretation of
the world propounded by the religions. Marxist socialism was
therefore based on the philosophy of the influences which the conditions
of life exert on man. Said Marx: "The philosophers have interpreted
the world in various ways. The point however is to change it"[12].

---

11) Ibid., p. 23 (Refer also to Istvan Meszaros, "Marx's theory of
    alienation", Merlin Press, London, 1970).

12) Marx. K., Theses on Feuerbach, 1844.

It was with Marx and Engels that the critique of the classical
theories of economic liberalism took its shape.

Writing the "Communist Manifesto" with Engels in 1847/8, Marx's
idea was scheduled to re-create the world's economic system into a
non-competitive, classless, stateless society, based on a
scientific-atheistic and materialist - economic and deterministic
world view. The basic view was to create a socialist community
of persons, where "each can contribute what he can and take what he needs".

The "Das Kapital", published in 1867 has been taken as the clearest
expression of Marx's immense scholarship and original literary creation.
It is on the "Das Kapital" that Marx's worldwide reputation or
rejection lies. The book, published in three volumes has been
acclaimed by academicians and economists as a "world classic" which had
at the time of publication, the qualities of style, vision, imagery,
irony and serious economic analysis in its theories of value,
history, politics, money and philosophical reflections. Marx himself
called the book "a work of art".

The "International Working Men's Association" formed in 1864 in London
was a group held together by common political - economic subjection -
all seeking an outlet to channel their opposition to the status quo.
Its English members were against special privile-ges, the French against
Bonarpartism, the Irish against Britain, the Poles against Russia, the
Italians against Austria and the Germans, like all others against
capitalism[13].

---

13) Ike, O.F., op.cit., p. 27

Marx remained for eight stormy years at the helm of affairs and one of the indomitable pillars that held the International together until it was shattered by internal strife and rivalry. It was the experiences he gathered with the colleagues in the International that he processed in the Capital. In all his economic thoughts, four strains of thought are interwoven, namely, a prophetic, moral, historical and revolutionary tone. The author stressed class and violence where necessary.

In the Communist Manifesto, the authors carried the language of revolution which called for the "overthrow of all existing bourgeois institutions", "the rule of the dictatorship of the proletariat", "the abolition of all private property", "the annihilation of all classes", and "the establishment of a classless, stateless, non-competitive society".

Marx's basic views as understood by his life-long friend Engels
was so formulated:

"That in every historical epoch the prevailing mode of economic
production and exchange, and the social organisation necessarily
following from it, form the basis upon which is built up, and from
which alone can be explained, the political and intellectual history
of that epoch; that, consequently, the whole history of mankind
(since the dissolution of primitive tribal society, holding land in
common ownership) has been a history of class struggles, contests
between exploiters and exploited, ruling and ruled (oppressed classes);
that the history of these class struggles forms a series of evolutions
in which, nowadays, a stage has been reached where the exploited
and oppressed classes - the proletariat - cannot attain its
emancipation from the sway of the exploiting and ruling class - the
bourgeois - without at the same time, and once and for all, emancipating
society at large from all exploitation, oppression, class
distinctions and class struggles" [14].

---

14) Engels, F, Preface to the Manifesto of the Communist Party,
January 30th 1888., (See The Great Books, Vol. 50, p.415
Brittanica Great Books, William Benton Publishers, London, 1982).

266

The language here is clear and need no commentary. The starting
point of the Marxist economic analysis was the "Labour Theory of Value",
a concept inherited by the classical economists from Locke and
adapted by Ricardo who argued, with qualifications, that the value
of a commodity depended on the relative quantity of labour necessary for
its production. Marx called the part of the value created which
went to the employer "surplus value" and presented it as theft from
the worker. The commentators do not all agree on the significance of
the labour theory of value as it is used by Marx, but it played a
key role in his predictions of capitalist self-destruction[15].

Profits, according to the theory, are derived from unpaid labour time,
yet, since capitalists are driven by competition to accumulate capital
and thus become more and more efficient in production, capital becomes
concentrated in fewer and fewer hands. As it does so, the profits
of capital are reduced as labour saving machinery replaces the labour
from whose unpaid time profits are derived; hence, the army of the
unemployed grows, swollen by the ruined small capitalist and the
workers displaced by machined.
The fold of goods created by ever more productive capitalist industry
meanwhile finds fewer buyers as more and more are workless, and wages
are squeezed. United in their anger and misery, the masses rise up
in revolt: "the knell of capitalist private property sounds, the
expropriators are expropriated" [16].

___

15) Freedman, R; Marx on Economics, pp. 27ff., 69ff -
    H.W.B Joseph., The Labour Theory of Value in K. Marx, London, 1923
    (See also Roger Charles, op.cit., p.273)
16) Marx, K., Das Kapital, 1:31 (see : Freedman, op.cit., p.170.,
    R. Charles op.cit., p.273);

Marx expounded more on these views when he considered the role of the
capitalist in his labour theory of value. He begins by asking a
question: "But does wage labour create any property for the labourer?
Not a bit! It creates, that is, that kind of property which
exploits wage labour and which cannot increase except upon condition
of begetting a new supply of wage labour for fresh exploitation.
Property in its present form is based on the antagonism of capital
and wage labour... To be a capitalist is to have not only a purely
personal but a social status in production. Capital is a collective
product, and only by the united action of many members - nay, in the
last resort only by the united action of all members of society - can
it be set in motion. Capital is therefore, not a personal, it is a
social power"[17]. And Marx states that with the communist situation,
this will not be so. There will be equality and more justice for
the worker. "Workers have nothing to loose but their chains".
Says he, "In place of the old bourgeois society, with its classes and
class antagonisms, we shall have an association in which the free
development of each is the condition for the free development of all"[18].

The main import of Marx's thinking, therefore, was the thesis that
the capitalist system was bound to destroy itself and give way to
socialism. It is accordingly, stronger in its criticisms in this
direction than in its account of the exact nature of the socialist
paradise. From scattered references to the shape of that alternative,
which we find in Marx, we gather that when production is under the
control of a planned society the market price of goods will equal
their value in terms of the social labour time employed in their
production[19], and prices will be the same as under capitalism, but
the surplus over-value will go to the State, not the capitalist[20].

---

17) Marx K, and Engels, F., Manifesto of the Communist Party., op.cit.,
    p. 426
18) Ibid.
19) Marx, Das Kapital, 3: 10, (Freedman, R., op.cit., p.229)
20) Marx, Das Kapital., 3:3 - 9, (Freedman op.cit., p.230 - 231)

In this state of affairs, money will be abolished; producers may receive
cheques so that they can obtain what they want from the social supplies
of means of consumption, a share corresponding to their labour time.
But such cheques will not be equivalent of money; they will not circulate[21].

"The problem of distribution where production is for use and not for
exchange or profit is to be solved by reserving part of what is
produced for social use - industrial expansion, insurance and
reserves, costs of administration, community services and schools,
health services and employment... Thereafter, the remainder will be
distributed, not according to production input or labour time, but
according to the principle "from each according to his ability, and
to each according to his needs"[22].

This is in part the goal and ambition Marx set for himself, through
which he thought, he would change the world's social and economic
face into a gigantic image that corresponded adequately to his idea
of a perfect society. Karl Marx made it clear that his intention
was to give up idle speculation and to make philosophy speak a
language which corresponded to the practical problems of real men.

Since his death some hundred years ago, mankind has discovered that
they have inherited in this German - Jew, a completely revolutionary
attitude towards looking at the world and the role man is supposed
to play in it. Judged by the number of those who profess marxism
and of countries governed by communist systems, Marx and Engels have
influenced and inspired one of the greatest mass movements of all
times - a movement which transcends national, racial and continental
boundaries.

---

21) Marx, Das Kapital, 2 : 18
22) Marx, K., A Critique of the Gotha Programme, Vol.I,
     (See Roger Charles., op.cit., p. 275).

4 . Critique of Marxist Socialism

It is now a century since Karl Marx died and many things have
happened in the world to allow us objectively consider his theories
and dole out adequate criticism of them. While recognising the
massiveness of Marx's genius, his contribution to the development
of the social and historical sciences and the masterly way in which
he disposed of some of the more obvious weaknesses in the
economic logic of the liberal capitalists, coupled with his method
of analysis of poverty and exploitation, we must also recognise his
limitations.

Karl Marx declared himself a materialist, believing in no religion
and in no transcendent reality outside matter which he called the
"be and end all of all reality". Materialism, as developed
theoretically and scientifically by Engels and Marx was aimed at
fighting capitalist exploitation of the worker and the metaphysical
interpretation of the world, which Marx said was distracting the
workers from fighting for social justice and and equity here in this world.

a) Marx's Economic Utopia:

It is clear today, that materialism, which Marx developed and which
has been given a chance to be practiced, infact above fifty years
(after Lenin's 1917 revolution), has not solved the world's
economic problems, nor has the theory given final answer to the
problem of meaning affecting human existence here on earth.
We shall begin with his economic utopia! The marxist pure communism

contained the following characteristics: "The distribution of
income according to need, no longer according to labour performed,
no classes, no competition, no religion, no God; the State withers
away; very high productivity, so that there is plenty for all;
high socialist consciousness since people work without personal
incentives; No money; a command economy, managed by a free and equal
association of producers; the disappearance of the differences
between occupations so that there is no social distinction between
persons or between town and country; each person does about as much
physical and intellectual labour; the system is worldwide"23[)].

Such was Marx's economic utopia and when we look into the countries
which claim Karl Marx as their founder, often labelled "Communist"
or "Socialist", we discover that Marx's views were simply fanciful
and noble ideas which do not exist in reality and which never may
exist. Many communists today believe that it will never come 24[)].

Marx was as much an optimist about the nature of socialist man as
the advocates of laissez faire were about the nature of liberal
capitalism. Both assumed in their objects of veneration a perfection
of human nature that has not been there since the Fall of Adam, as
the Christian sees it, or since man was overwhelmed by the hubris
that the Greeks saw rooted in human nature. The reality is very different.

---

23) Sargent T.L., Contemporary political ideologies, 3rd edition;
    Dorsey Press, Illinois, 1975., p.79
24) Ibid., p. 106.

Infact, it was the social evils of liberalism that gave rise to
socialism, but this later, in the words of Kamenka, "has raised up
a new metaphysical sovereign - history itself - so that it is able to
exercise, at its whim, unprincipled tyranny". Marxism came into
Russia through a series of events which neither Engels nor Marx
forsaw, and which bore no relationship to their theory of how
socialism will come to be. "It was the social, economic and
political situation existing in Czarist Russia before 1914, and
the effects of this war period, which provided Lenin with the
opportunity to use Marx's theories, or elements of them, as the
intellectual guide to the take over of a Russian revolution which had
already in essentials succeeded. It was the communist party
which saved Marxism from undergoing the fate of many other nineteenth
century philosophies, by turning it into a faith[25].

Although Marx talked of a classless, Stateless, partyless society
(Stalin), the Party in Communist countries, perhaps intoxicated by
its own ambitious programme, nourishes a narcissism, convincing itself
of its own indispensability. The dictatorship of the proletariat
was believed to last for a fairly brief period of transition.
Contrary to Marx's ideas, it looks as if it has become the final stage.
Marx said that economics is the foundation of the entire social
system, and he argued that the superstructure - that is - forms taken
by law, religion, politics, aesthetics, philosophy and so forth are
determined by the economic structure and processes of society[26].

---

25) Roger Charles., op.cit., p.286 (see also Copleston, F., A History
    of philosophy, Vol. 7, p.65)

26.) Marx, K., Preface in the Contribution to a Critique of Political
    Economy., transl. by N.I. Stone, Chicago, 1913., C.H. Herr Co.,
    pp 11 - 12.

For this reason, he has been called an economic determinist. He
overstressed the importance of economic relationships in his
definition of the material nature of things. Even though economics
plays a very vital role in the socialisation process, it is an
exaggeration to narrow the whole process to economics alone.
Now, Marx's basic attack on liberal capitalism are exposed in his
labour theory of value, the doctrine of subsistence wages, and the
theory of surplus value. Generally, Marx used value in the sense of
real costs in labour. Nothing else was considered. In other words,
the value, not the price of any manufactured object was based on the
amount of labour and time consumed in producing it. This is the
labour theory of value. A man has to work for a certain number of
hours or days to produce enough to provide himself with a living.
Obviously, this is one of Marx's weakest points, which has been
contradicted by historical experiences. We need only think of the
work done by machines today which can feed a whole city, although
hardly a single person is at work.

Marx believed that the profit of the capitalist was taken from the
amount produced and above the wages of the worker. This is the theory
of surplus value and can be used to explain more fully the doctrine of
subsistence wages. As the capitalist replaced workers with machines,
he would have to reduce wages to keep up his rate of profit, since
profits came only through surplus value extracted from labour[27].
This view has also been disproved by history and the inherent
miscalculations of economic flow has been highlighted by economic
experts - be they bourgeois or communist.

27) Sargent, T.L., op.cit., p. 80

At last, and above all, the classless, non-competitive society of
equals prophesied by Marx has been denied the citizens in today's
communist States. Instead, the Party and the central governments
have taken up the place of the exploiters and capitalists.
Marx's utopia is without doubt laid bare and his attempt to bring
down paradise here on earth remains an "infantile illusion".
Need we mention the alarming drama that communism which stood up to
fight liberalism ended up fighting itself. There is a problem as
to the legitimate heir and interpreter of Marx's ideas. In various
countries, his disciples claim legitimacy to the right interpretation
of his writings, but the conflicting meanings which they attach to
his thoughts leave the entire communist world in disarray.

The divisions between Moscow, Peking, Yugoslavia, Albania and others
are not merely rumblings of petty grievances of who is more important -
Stalin or Lenin! They are signs of power struggle capable of
destroying communism itself. Chinese 'dogmatism' and Russian
'Revisionism' are the terms of abuse. Surely this is a dilemma for
marxism.

b) Marxist Atheism and Economic Determinism Negates Man's Spiritual Values:

There is yet another point! Materialism as applied in the present
communist States denies and disregards the spiritual values of man.
Since marxism denies without accepting this accusation, the spiritual
values of man, (no religion, no God, no eternal life, no morality,
no freedom, etc. - for all these are regarded as bourgeois creation),
the value of man as an individual, an entity, a person is reduced
to merely "a cog in the ever turning wheel of the State", or
"a merely material and bialogical being". In many marxist States,
the traditional worth of the individual is subjected to an un-
identifiable mass. Man is simply a product of matter without any
future. Commenting on the marxist view of man, Lewis Watt observes that:
"dialectical materialism can neither satisfy the human mind in the
search for a meaning in life, nor offer to the human will motives
weighty enough to counterbalance its egotism. It is infected with
that false humanism which ignores the sinfulness (limitation) of
man. As a system of philosophy, it is a failure; as a substitute
for the christian religion, it is an illusion"[28].

Consequent to what has been said, the individual's freedom of speech,
movement, choice of a state of life and so forth is not evident in
marxist countries. Marx and Engels identified the thing we call
"free-will" as being nothing more nor less than a conscious awareness
of the materialistic forces which impels the individual to act.
This conscious awareness of "natural necessity" makes men think
that they are choosing, when as a matter of fact, they are simply
watching themselves follow the dictates of material circumstances.

---

28) Lewis Watt., Communism and Religion., CTS R 165, London, Avocet Press,
1969, p. 31

Marx and Engels wrote in the "German Ideology." "Circumstances make
men... the social structure and the State are continually evolving
out of the life process of definite individuals, but of individuals,
not as they may appear in their own or other people's imagination,
but as they really are, that is, as they operate, produce
materially, and hence, as they work under definite material limits,
presuppositions and conditions independent of their will" [29].

Engels put it this way: "We do not promise any freedom or any
democracy" [30].

However, the marxists believe that the long term policy of communism
is one of freedom for the masses. In the short run, there is an
attempt to protect the proletariat from "decadent western society".
Therefore, the masses are informed that self-denial is necessary
for survival, that selfishness is treacherous. As such, the liberties
of press and assembly, to read or listen to everything is restricted.
Art, religion, education, science and music come under the groping
yoke of control from the government. Man must be a dutiful
servant to the "Omnipotent State". In such a system, the fountain
of individuality (freedom) runs dry. But the marxist consoles
himself with the theory that these concepts of freedom are products and
concepts of bourgeois capitalists.

---

29) Marx - Engels., The German Ideology, chap. 1, (1845-46).
See Marx-Engels On Religion., Moscow, Progress publ. 1976, p.65 - 72
30) Engels, F., Quoted in Lenin, Selected Works, Vol. 9. p. 242.

Martin Luther King questioned this denial of freedom in socialist
countries of the East. Said he: "The trouble with communism is
that it has neither a theology nor a christology; therefore it
emerges with a mixed anthropology. Confused about God, it is also
confused about man. Inspite of its glowing talk about the welfare
of the masses, communism's methods and its philosophy strip man of his
dignity and worth, leaving him as little more than a depersonalised
Cog in the ever turning wheel of the State"[31].

Harder language was used on communism by Pope Pius XI in his
writings: "... a doctrine full of error and sophistry, contrary to
revelation and reason alike; a doctrine destructive of the
foundations of civil society and subversive of social order;
a doctrine which refuses to acknowledge the true origin of the State,
its true nature and purpose;which repudiates and denies the rights,
the dignity, and the freedom of the human person... all this
is completely opposed to natural ethics and to the will of the
divine creator" [32].

The Pope does not end here. He continues his critique with an
exposition of what he understood the Communist society to be.
"The Communism of today, even more pretentiously than similar
theories in the past, poses as the saviour of the poor. A pseudo-ideal
of justice, equality and brotherhood among workers inspires the whole of
its theory and practice, permeating the movement with a counterfeit
mysticism which, combined with the glamour of illusive promises, both
dupes the masses and fills them with a contagious and vehement enthusiasm...
Briefly, the object is to introduce a new order culminating
in a godless human society"[33].

---

31) King, Martin Luther., The Strenght to Love; Fontana, Chicago, 1963
32) Pius XI, Divini Redemptoris, 1937, (CTS, London, S139), par.21, 45.
33) Ibid., 11, 19.

5. The Social Market Economy

The social-market-economy programme was developed in the Federal
Republic of Germany between the Second World War and the German
currency reform of 1948. Since this period, this concept has served
to express the entire economic political foundations which West
Germany has followed and developed. Its founders include such eminent
personalities as Ludwig Erhard, Alfred Müller-Armack,Alexander Rüstow,
Walter Eucken and Wilhelm Roepke, Franz Böhm to mention just a few .

The situation in 1948 was marked by economic paralysis, the result of
destruction wrought by the war and the devastating effects of repressed
inflation. There were also other elementary problems of production and
distribution, the restoration of the markets for domestic goods and
capital, the need to foster fresh confidence in the currency and the
reintegration of West Germany into a world economy recovering from
the ravages of war. In this situation, there was urgent need to
overcome the existing shortages and general misery facing the masses,
as well as laying the foundations of a future economic direction for
the nation. In 1949, members of the ruling party, the Christian
Democratic Union under chancellor Konrad Adenauer in their party
guidelines known as "Düsseldörfer Leitsätze der CDU", projected this
concept of a social market economy to the public. So, in the first
place we can call it a German economic model.

a) Tenets of the Social Market Economy and role of the State

Principally, the social-market-economy rejects total rigid capitalism
as practised in the nineteenth century,as well as State directed or
planned economy as practised in today's communist societies.
In the words of one of the intellectual founding fathers of this system:
„Sinn der Sozialen Marktwirtschaft ist es, das Prinzip der
Freiheit auf dem Markte mit dem des Sozialen Ausgleichs zu
verbinden"[34]. It is as such a mixed economy.

---

34)Müller-Armack,A., Wirtschaftsordnung und Wirtschaftspolitik,Verlag
Haupt Bern,Stuttgart, 1966,p.243.

The logic of the social-market- economy, which is not very far away
from that of the free-enterprise economy can be summarily be stated
as follows:
"The economy works better for the good of all if productive goods
are mainly owned by private individuals, or campanies and operate,
subject to the laws of competition, in a "free" market.
The owners or managers of companies then respond to the needs of the
consumers through the price system and, according to their efficiency
in responding to those needs, they are profitable and, being profitable , flourish. Firms which are not profitable go out of
bu.siness. Investment decisions are made in the main by private
interests in response to market needs. Government has an economic
role in a mixed economy, but it should be limited as much as possible" 34b).

Nobody who has adequate knowledge of the situation of Western Germany
would deny that the "social-market-economy" has created great material and social benefits for a large number of people as we shall
show later. Added however to the material factors of work in Germany,
we can with modesty also mention as having contributed to this success,
the existence of a particular work-ethic (consider Kant's categorical
imperative and the call to perform 'duty for duty's sake'),and the
kind of social and cultural values that highly extol personal initiative and inventiveness, and encourage savings and its allied virtues.
We can state that the determination to survive, led the founding fathers
of post-war Germany towards this type of economic system, which seemed
to go beyond the one-sided ideological conception of economics.

34b) Rogers,C., op.cit., pp 278 -9

The aim is thereforeto,establish a market economy tempered by social safeguards which are consistent with free-market principles.Rather than distort economic interrelationships by fixing prices and injecting purchasing power, it attempts to adjust undesirable disparities in incomes via a clearly defined income-tax system. It attempts to keep the trading system intact and at the same time achieving a high level of productivity by providing adequate safeguards for free enterprise.

According to Müller-Armack:

> „Das Prinzip des Wettbewerbs als unerläßliches Organisationsmittel von Massengesselschaften ist nur funktionsfähig, wenn eine klare Rahmenordnung des Wettbewerbs sicher ist"[35].

From this, we see that the social-market-economy accepts only a minimum of governmental activity in economics, although it at the same time presupposes the development of a legal framework for the economy which does justice to all involved in the economic process.
In the words of Müller-Armack: "It is quite consistent with market-economy principles to introduce certain safeguards along lines of the American anti-trust laws to prevent any one-sided accumulation of economic power. Under such a social market economy, companies and trade unions will possess the scope which they need for genuine , free negotiations leading to collective agreements, without these being distorted by the intervention of the State"[36].
Certain facts become clearer in this mixed system, namely, the state must protect the competitive order of economics and promote it; the State has only to act as "watchdog" in the capacity of intervening to regulate the social order, not by intervening into the market economy, but by correcting the mistakes of this economy. Therefore, certain laws guiding the citizens and the economy from monopoly, cartel organisations or oligopolies have to be instituted to avoid exploitation of the weaker by the stronger and to guarantee the stability of the market.

---

35)Müller-Armack,A. op.cit., p.244
36) Müller-Armack,A., The social aspects of the economic system,1947; (article published in :Standard Texts on the Social Market Economy, Gustav Fischer, Stuttgart,New York,1982,p.18).

b) Difference to rigid capitalism

The system also seeks to protect and continue the possession of
private property, this time, however, contrary to rigid capitalism,
to make ownership of property spread as wide as possible to the
working classes.

One would presume that the social market economy accepts the basic
economic tenets of liberal economies, even though it tries to give
them a social face. So we speak of "Sozial temperierter Kapitalismus".
This is true to some extent when one considers that like the methods
of liberal capitalism, the social-market-economy accepts the instruments
of price and free entrepreneural competition as determinants of the
market. Demand and supply should therefore not be governed by any extra-
law except that which the market itself accepts, namely price.
What cannot meet consumers tastes disappears from the market. Free
entreprise and competition exist and the weak competitors also fall
out of the market. If the State must intervene in competition, then in
the interest of the consumers,as in the case of Cartel bodies.

There is however a difference to rigid capitalism as Müller-Armack
tries to show:

> "Mit dem Neo-Liberalismus teilen die Vertreter der
> Sozialen Marktwirtschaft die Überzeugung, daß Alt-
> liberalismus zwar die Funktionsbedeutung des Wett-
> bewerbs richtig gesehen hat, die sozialen und sozio-
> logischen Probleme jedoch nicht ausreichend beachtet.
> Im Gegensatz zum Altliberalismus erstreben sie keine
> Wiederherstellung einer Laissez-faire Wirtschaft; Ihr
> Ziel ist eine neuartige Synthese"[37].

Müller-Armack believes that the social-market-economy must distinguish
itself from the liberal market economy of the nineteenth century which,
like the system of central control in the communist societies, should
be a thing of the past. He pleads therefore for a strong social
objective. This social objective is seen in the agreeable and commen-
surable income paid to workers, in income-tax justice,pension funds,
house building allowances, social care expenditure (Soziale Ausgaben),
unemployment allowances, insurance conditions and care for the weak.

---

[37] Armack,A., op.cit., (Wirtschaftsordnung und Wirtschaftspolitik,p.244)

c)Some achievements

The emphasis on the social dimension of the economy has shown that
an economy can serve two purposes, namely, guarantee the existence
of the citizens , as well as provide for the weak and the socially
marginalised. Despite this, there is a constant emphasis in the
social-market-economy on individual responsibility (Selbstverant-
wortung), personal initiative (Eigeninitiative), independence of man
(Sebständigkeit des Menschen) and social responsibility (soziale
Verantwortung).

When one looks back to the beginings of this economic model in Western
Germany, even its opponents would readily agree that it has proved
possible to a surprising degree to create a new basis for the material
existence of the German nation. In certain phases as Müller Armack
writes in retrospect, "there was a tendency to doubt whether it would
be possible to achieve social progress in line with the development of
private enterprise. But looking back over the economy of Germany
since the war, the social-market-economy can be said to have proved
its ability to have at least done a few things"[38].

The market economy has at least resolved the problems of supply con-
fronting an industrial State within narrow geographical limits.
The increase in savings activity in recent years and the efforts to
place property - ownership at the disposal of a broad percentage of
the population, added to the fact that the problems of income and
prosperity can be resolved without State involvement or central planning,
all these are achievements indeed. Further more, Germany, has been
able under its peculiar circumstances and within fourty years to rise
economically and to compete fairly well with the other economic giants.
There is today more automation, better processing methods and better
policy-making methods which have solved the problems of shortage in
the supply of goods. One can even boldly say that many workers have
emerged from the proletariat s ge and we can now talk of'democratisation
of consume; rising standard of living(materially seen)and the holiday "fever".

---

38)Müller-Armack,A.,The second phase of the social-market-economy-an addi-
    tional concept of a humane society,1960 (In Standard texts,op.cit.p.49).

These visible material achievements led Müller-Armack to assert that
"there can be no doubt that the range of technical oppurtunities
not yet exploited is such that there seems to be no visible limit
to continued economic expansion"[39].

This euphoria for progress and economic prosperity led the fathers of
this economic model to think of strategies of maximising their material
wealth and ensuring steady growth in the future. The words of our
author Müller-Armack expresses these facts clearly, namely:
"Über das Erreichte hinaus ist der Gedanke der Sozialen Marktwirtschaft
ein Programm für die Zukunft der deutschen Wirtschaftspolitik"[40].

These include:

1) seeing social-market-economy as a policy for a free society
2) advancing production technology as well as controlling environmental
   pollution
3) provide more skilled labour,more training and study facilities, and
   promote research and science
4) invest in brain power to reach the optimum
5) aim at relative equalisation of incomes and ownership
6) institutional safeguards for the weak and marginalised of the society
7) full employment and steady economic expansion
8) monetary stability
9) encourage self-employment in all its forms
1o) medical facilities modernisation and accident prevention procedures
11) meaningful integration of industries,transport services,residential
    and recreational areas in state planning
12) concentrate social security measures on certain areas of priority
    in order to create a better balance between individual responsibility
    and more effective aid
13) road building schemes to be consistent with overall environment schemes
14) readjustment of budgetary policy, more funds on a more selective
    basis, strenghtening of the public sector... [41].

39) Ibid., p.50
40) Müller Armack, Wirtschaftsordnung und Wirtschaftspolitik,op.cit., p.248.
41) (Refer to quotation 39, Ibid., p.60)

d) Certain critical issues in the social-market-economy

From all that has been highlighted in the preceeding pages, one would without doubt maintain that the the mixed economy of the social-market-economy system has produced various advantages in the productive and distributive sectors. However, we must equally maintain that there is much to be done still,if economy must serve the needs of man and help him towards self -realisation.
Infact,the range of tasks which has to be accomplished for the individual in a free society is incomparably broad and certainly goes beyond what has been achieved so far.
Cardinal Joseph Höffner believes that the system of the social-market-economy and the principles enunciated by Catholic Social Teachings are interestingly agreeable to both schools of thought, eventhough he maintains that certain prerequisites still needs to be fulfilled. Says he:

> "Die Katholische Soziallehre hält die Marktwirtschaft für die richtige Grundform der Wirtschaftsordnung. Sie ist jedoch davon überzeugt, daß ihr ein humanes Leitbild gegeben werden muß"[42).

And he goes on to mention twelve prerequisites which still have to.be fulfilled before a complete agreement would be reached.
First of all, he talks about the "Sachziel der Wirtschaft" or the substantial aim of economics, and maintains that all economics must serve man and not the other way round. Man is the being who must be fully respected and elevated to his full personality through the discipline of economics. How far has this been achieved since the fourty years of social-market-economy ?
Müller-Armack well noted in his analysis of the achievements so far through this system that,"It is no longer the classes who are the problem of society but the individual. It is he who feels inferior to society as a whole and uncertain of himself. Vis-a-Vis society as a whole, the individual is bound to feel that his entry into certain occupations, his advancement and integration into a particular environment are fraught with uncertainties which he cannot gauge properly. Economic cycles,market fluctuations and readjustments of

---

42) Höffner,J., Wirtschaftsordnung und Wirtschaftsethik -Richtlinien der Katholischen Soziallehre; Referat,Deutschen Bischofskonferenz, Fulda,23.9.1985;Hqb. DBK,Bonn,Kaiserstraße 163,Nr. 12. n.24.

production operations harness him to mechanisms which appear ano-
nymous and which he finds hard to understand. He is gripped by
hesitation and an indefinable fear of what await him in his environment, both now and in the future..."[43].

There is no doubt that the social-market- economy increased the
material wealth of many people and elevated their standard of living.
But what is this when the individuals suffer a lack of meaning and end
up as materialists and consumers ? Has economics become an end in
itself or is it still a means to an end, namely, a more humane, more
worthful human existence ? On this again, Cardinal Höffner says:

> "Der Sinn der Wirtschaft liegt weder- rein formalistisch-
> im bloßen Handeln nach dem ökonomischen Rationalprinzip,
> noch im größtmöglichen materiellen „Glück" einer größt-
> möglichen Menschenzahl. Auch wäre es irrig, die Wirtschaft
> als Befriedigung von Nachfrage durch Bereitstellung
> eines entsprechenden Angebots zu definieren; denn dann
> entspräche die Deckung sinnloser oder schädlicher
> Bedürfnisse dem Sachziel der Wirtschaft"[44].

Whatever its material advantages, any economic system which simply
believes in valuing means above ends, or neglecting the main issue
of economics, namely man who must be served by it, has to be called
to question and given a guideline that makes it more meaningful.
In Christian Social Teachings, "Das Sachziel der Wirtschaft besteht
vielmehr in der dauernden und gesicherten Schaffung jener materiellen
Vorraussetzungen, die dem einzelnen und den Sozialgebilden die
menschenwürdige Entfaltung ermöglichen"[44a].
In other words, the social-market-economy must ensure that it does
not consider economics higher than the person.

---

43) Müller-Armack,A., The second phase of the social-market-economy:
an additional concept of a humane economy., op.cit., pp.51-2.

44) Höffner,J., Ibid.
44a)Ibid.,

There are other areas for reflection and critical consideration of
the social-market-economy as seen through the eyes of Social Ethics.
Müller-Armack, himself as one of the founding fathers of this system
considered some of these criticisms himself.
First of all, there is the fear that this system with its strong
accent on productivity, growth, price stability and surplus balance
of external trade leads the citizens to a certain consumerism.
Says Armack:

> "Häufiger ist in den letzten Jahren, zumal angesichts
> des steigenden Lebensstards, das Argument angeführt
> worden, die Soziale Marktwirtschaft liefere den
> Menschen, hier also das deutsche Volk, dem Materialismus
> aus. Zweifellos besteht ein materialistischer Hang
> zu einer immer größeren Güterversorgung, und sicherlich
> werden durch die ständige Schaffung neuer Güter
> Begehrlichkeit und Unruhe bei den Menschen erhöht...
> Vorsicht ist geboten bei der Kritik dieser Wirtschafts-
> ordnung auch auf theologischer Seite, denn auch hier
> sind Vorwürfe erhoben worden, die sich besser an
> eine andere Addresse richten würden. Schließlich ist
> es nur Aufgabe der Wirtschaftspolitik, die Versorgung
> der Bevölkerung zu verbessern, und es wäre falsch, ihr
> ein anderes Ziel zu setzen"[45].

From the above, it has become clear that this system has an inherent
temptation for man's "insatiable appetites", and leads him to demand
ever more and more goods. Müller-Armack accepts this criticism, but he
tries to see it as almost inevitable, over and above that, warning the
discipline of theology to keep its claws off this critique.
Well, theology and theologians did not heed this advice, for Cardinal
Höffner warns:

---

45)Müller-Armack,A., Die Soziale Marktwirtschaft nach einem Jahrzent
   ihrer Erprobung., (Vortrag gehalten vor der Verwaltungs- und
   Wirtschaftsakademie Köln, am 16 April 1959. Veröffentlicht in:
   "Wirtschaftspolitische Chronik",H.2/3 (1959), sowie in: "Studien
   zur Sozialen Marktwirtschaft. (Institut für Wirtschaftspolitik an
   der Universität zu Köln,Untersuchungen.Hrsg. von Alfred Müller-Armack
   und Fritz W.Meyer.Bd.12) Köln 1960.

"Die Marktwirtschaft darf nicht zum Konsumismus führen.
Die Konsumwerbung, die den Käufer sachlich informieren soll,
darf ihn nicht durch suggestive Reizüberflutung verwirren und vernebeln.
und nicht an das versucherische Haben und Genießenwollen
appellieren" [46].

Catholic Social Teaching has always warned of the dangers of over-
valuing material goods to the detriment of spiritual values.
In the writings and teachings of Holy scripture, but also in those
of Popes Pius XI and John XXIII, adequate warnings and references
are made to this situation [47].

Over and above this consumerism, there are other issues that need
reflection.   First of all, it should not be forgotten that many
raw materials used and greedily consumed are obtained from economically and industrially poorer countries, mostly in the"Third World",
at prices below what they should have been if those countries had
been able to include the total costs of the health and social progress of their people. It is as such involved in economic injustice.
Secondly, as Father Schotte shows, "in the distributive sector also,
the market system often encourages a consumption of goods that
leaves the poorer sectors of society untouched, or that tries to
impose itself on peoples and nations in inferior economic conditions
who cannot afford such consumption. When any system creates injustices, it must be corrected by inserting viewpoints regarding values
and goals that transcend mere profit and aim at the total well being
of the human person in society" [48].

Cardinal Höffner mentions several other areas in this connection
where critical questions can be posed on the social-market-economy.
He maintains that the market economy needs to be directed, otherwise

---

46) Höffner,J., Ibid.,

47) Refer: Pope Pius XI, Quadragesimo anno,para.75
           Pope John XXIII, Mater et Magistra,Par.175 ff. (See Math.6,24-34).

48) Schotte,P.Jan,. "Laborem Exercens and the socio-economic issues-
    . a new challenge". (Paper read before the Pontifical Commission
    'Iustitia et Pax', Vatican City, Rome,1982,Nr.9,p.25).

it might end up in liberal capitalism.

He emphasises that the mechanism of the market is not enough for
justice to function fully well in the economy, having in mind the
"invisible hand" theory of rigid capitalism. "Auch die Marktwirtschaft ist steurungsfähig und steurungsbedürftig. Dringende Aufgaben,
die heute im Hinblick auf das Sachziel der Wirtschaft und auf das
Gemeinwohl gestellt sind, lassen sich mit dem bloßen Markt-und Preis-
mechanismus nicht meistern"[49]. In this connection, he goes on to
consider a few areas, namely, the distribution of property to the
broad members of the society,the continual economic growth of the
community without crisis, the solution of the problems of members of
the society who are today unemployed, and in Germany, this number
has reached a record of two-and-half-million people, and the solution
to the problems of ecology [50].

There are of course other related problems which still are tasks for
the social-market economy. They include the right understanding of
the relationship between labour and capital, especially since the
Encyclical letter of Pope John Paul II, "Laborem Exercens" showed
that there is no inherrent contradiction between them, but a strong
interconnection. Following these are those related issues which
concern the hierarchy of values in the world of man, and which place
the economic far below other values, such as, the family, religion
and morals. All these go to show that although, immediate post-war
problems such as scarcity have been solved, supply of goods increased,
there still remain a range of tasks which has to be accomplished for
the individual in a free society, and this is incomparably broader
and certainly goes beyond what has been achieved so far.

No economic system can claim to have solved all problems. But some of
them can claim to have done more than others in comparative analysis.

---

49) Höffner,J., op.cit., p.25

50) Ibid., (In this connection, more details can be obtained from the
    excellent analysis of E.F.Schumacher:"Small is beautiful - a study of
    economics as if people mattered",Abacus,London,.1974).

This is not the place to go into the ideological debate of which
system is better or higher than the other, or which system needs
reform, and which one not. One point can however be held as certain,
namely, that no economic system can refuse reform or change and still
exist for a reasonably long time - no matter with what political
measure the enforcers determine to put it accross. It is in this
connection that the achievements, prospects and problems of the
social-market-economy can be highlighted.

In the words of Professor Anton Rauscher:

"Das Optimum jeglicher Wirtschaftspolitik ist noch nicht
erreicht, wenn bestimmte Ziele verwirklicht sind oder
funktionalen Erfordernissen mit einem verfeinerten Instru-
mentarium entsprochen wird. Darauf macht gerade jene Kritik
an den bestehenden wirtschaftlichen Verhältnissen aufmerksam,
die bis hin zu dem Zweifel reicht, ob die Soziale Marktwirtschaft oder überhaupt ein marktwirtschaftliches System mit
den "säkularen" Herausforderungen von heute fertig werden
könne, mit der Arbeitslosigkeit, mit der Entfremdung in der
Arbeit, mit den Umweltbelastungen, mit der Ressourcenveren-
gung, mit einer Neuordnung der Weltwirtschaft zugunsten der
Länder der dritten Welt,mit dem Konflikt zwischen "Kapital
und Arbeit"... Die gegebene Wirtschaftsordnung könne die
sozialen und politischen Möglichkeiten eines größeren Maßes
an Humanität nicht mehr ausschöpfen"[51].

---

51)Rauscher,A., Salbstinteresse und Gameinwohl (Vorwort),. (Soziale
Orientierung, Bd.5), Duncker und Humbolt,Berlin,1985,p.5.

6 . Summary:

The Catholic approach to work emphasises both freedom and social
responsibility, because both emphasise that man, the image of God
is the worker and the subject of work. To abandon freedom in search
of an earthly paradise as the Marxist socialists do, or to abandon
social responsibility in search of an earthly individualistic
paradise, like the liberal capitalists did, both dehumanises man, who
is, in truth, the end and purpose of every social organisation, not
a means to that end.

It is under this perspective that all criticism to liberalism or
Marxist socialism should be understood. Man must be the Being who is
to be served by the economic structure. He should not be under the
economic structure but above it, directing it and giving it meaning
with his faith and with regard to the future of mankind.
Pope Pius XI made this point clear where he said in his
encyclical letter 'Divini Redemptoris' :

> "We showed, that there can be no hope of saving human society
> from the ruin and disaster to which an ammoral liberalism
> is driving it, unless the economic and social order is
> inspired and guided by the principles of social justice and
> christian charity; no salvation for it is to be found
> in class warfare, in terrorism, or in the arbitrary and
> tyrannical use of power of the State"[52] .

---

52) Ibid., 43

It is in the line of this thinking and tradition that we shall now
analyse the basic views of John Paul II on the relationship
between Capital and Labour. He neutralises the extreme views
taken by liberalism and collectivism and places man in the
centre as the most important factor, infact the deciding factor
in the economic process. Man should therefore not be seen as
divided into blocks. The conflict existing between labour and
capital is an artificial one. It can be disposed of, and the pontiff
does it so nicely, that one cannot help but marvel at his articulate
and clear solution to the problem. It is as such, the solution of
Christian Social Principles to a problem created by economic
determinism and materialism.

PART TWO (II):   Conflict Between Labour and Capital:

1. Introducing the Problem:

In the third part of the Encyclical - still based on the same
criterion which is man - the subject of work - Pope John Paul
deals in detail with the conflicts between the "world of labour"
and the "world of capital". Says he: "In the following part of
these considerations I intend to return to greater detail to these
important questions, recalling at least the basic elements of the
Church's teaching on the matter... the issue of work has of course
been posed on the basis of the great conflict that the age of,
and together with, industrial development emerged between "capital"
and "labour"[1].

The Pope refers to the historical background of this conflict which
"marked and in a sense symbolised the publication of the Encyclical
Rerum Novarum"[2]. Leo XIII's work emerged in the background of
"the unmistakable elements of conflict in the vast expansions of
industrial pursuits and discoveries of science; in the changed
relations between masters and workmen; in the economic fortunes
of some few individuals, and the utter poverty of the masses; in the
increased self - reliance and closer mutual combination of the
working classes; and finally in the prevailing moral degeneracy"[3].

---

1)   John Paul II, LE, n. 11, 1
2)   Ibid., n. 11, 2
3)   Leo XIII., Rerum Novarum, May 1891, par. 1 (CTS, London, S219, 1976,
     p. 7)

Without going over into the historical detail, John Paul assumes
that we are already familiar with the history of this conflict and
with the demands of both sides. And he makes it clear that in his
encyclical, going into details is unnecessary, for they are known
both from the vast literature on the subject and by experience.
Not to go over again the history of these conflicts with all their
alternate events, not to submit an analysis of them, his point of
departure is "to go back to the fundamental issue of human work
which is of such importance for man, constituting as it is, one of
the fundamental dimensions of his earthly existence and of his
vocation"[4]. With this as starting point, John Paul maintains that
the present historical phase makes it urgent and necessary to overcome
the conflicts in the name of the dignity of the worker.
While reaffirming the priority of labour over capital and the means
of production, the Pope explains the reasons that make it imperative
to overcome the conflicts.

---

4) John Paul II, LE, n. 11, 6

2. Exposing the Problem

When he speaks about the conflict between capital and labour,
John Paul clearly states that "opposition between labour and
capital does not spring from the structure of the production process
or from the structure of the economic process"[5].
The conflict originated in the fact that the workers put their
powers at the disposal of the entrepreneurs, and these, following
the principle of maximum profit, tried to establish the lowest
possible wages for the work done by employees. In addition there were
other elements of exploitation, connected with the lack of safety
at work and of safeguards regarding the rights of workers[6].

Labour was separated from capital and set in opposition to it,
and capital was set in opposition to labour, because they were
seen under the same common denominator: both in capitalistic and
collectivistic systems, capital and labour were seen as mere
"production factors" or as "impersonal forces"; and as the
Pontiff says: "the real conflict between labour and capital was
transformed into a systematic class struggle, conducted not only by
ideological means but also and chiefly by political means"[7].

In Laborem Exercens, we have a new major contribution to what the
Church has always claimed to do through its social ethics - namely,
'offering elements of a coherent vision, values and guiding criteria
that aim at making any system responsive to the totality of man's
needs as a human being'. With a sense of great freshness and
relevance, the encyclical attempts to give a new reading of problems
that is adapted to the new times and situations in which mankind
finds itself, without breaking away from the whole tradition of the
social teaching of the Church.

---

5) John Paul II, LE, 13, 2
6) Ibid., 12,1
7) Ibid.

294

In order to find a way out of the dilemma and the labour-capital-
conflict, which is also dividing the whole world into "leftists" and
"rightists", the encyclical offers reference points which are at the
same time elements for an examination of the present situations and
systems.
The same error which was so blattantly committed in the period of
primitive capitalism and liberalism, and which exists in doctrinaire
collectivistic systems, can nevertheless be repeated in other
circumstances of time and place, if people's thinking starts from
the same theoretical and practical premises[8].
He offers three criteria for solving the conflict as we shall now show.

---

8) Schotte, P.J., Reflections on Laborem Exercens., Pontifical
    Commission, 'Iustitia et Pax', Vatican, 1982., Vol. 9, p.25

3. Three Criteria for Resolving the Conflicts Between Labour and Capital

a) The Priority of Labour over Capital

The first criteria mentioned by the Pope in determining and solving
the conflict already mentioned is stated clearly in Laborem Exercens -
namely, THE PRIORITY OF LABOUR OVER CAPITAL. The Pontiff says:
"In view of this situation (present day), we must recall a principle
that has always been taught by the Church: the principle of the
priority of labour over capital. This principle directly concerns the
process of production: in this process labour is always a primary
efficient cause, while capital, the whole collection of means of
production, remains a mere instrument or instrumental cause. This
principle is an evident truth that emerges from the whole of man's
historical experience"[9]. We may therefore speak of 'Laborismus' as
Nell-Breuning shows.
The encyclical further justifies the origin of this principle which
has its roots in the bible. Here, man is called "to subdue the earth",
and as the Pope adds, "we know that these words refer to all the
resources contained in the visible world and placed at man's disposal.
These resources can serve man only through work"[10].

---

9) John Paul II, LE, n. 12 (Nell-Breuning says on this: "Nennen wir die
   bestehende Subjektstellung des Kapitals und Objektrolle der Arbeit
   „Kapitalismus" und die verwirklichende Subjektstellung der Arbeit
   und Objektrolle des Kapitals "Laborismus", dann bedeutet die Aussage
   der Enzyklika eine in dieser Eindeutigkeit bisher nicht vorliegend.
   Option für den „Laborismus"; daran ist nichts zu deuteln oder
   zu drehen". In : Kommentar : 'Der Wert der Arbeit und der Weg zur
   Gerechtigkeit, Herder, Freiburg, 1981, p.120 .

10) Ibid. n. 12,2

Natural resources are not produced by man, they are given to him by the
Creator, as John Paul says: "these riches and resources of the visible
world man finds, but does not create them"[11]. It is only through
human work that these resources can serve man. The means to
transform the riches given by God, and put them at the service of man,
are also the fruit of human labour done in the history of past
generations. "In a sense man finds them already prepared, ready
for him to discover them and to use them correctly in the productive
process... At the beginning of man's work is the mystery of creation.
This affirmation, already indicated as starting point, is the guiding
thread of this document"[12].

If this is so, then there can be no question of what is prior - labour
or capital, because man's efforts, intellect, energy and labour
transforms the means of production, including capital to be what it is.
Since the concept of capital includes not only the natural resources
which man transforms in accordance with his needs (and thus in a sense
humanises them), it must immediately be noted that capital includes
the work of past generations, and are therefore "the result of the
historical heritage of human labour"[13].
Thus the Pope can say that everything that is at the service of
man is the result of work, and with this argument justify the priority
of labour over capital. Says the Holy Father, "it is man that has
gradually developed all the means of production, from the most primitive
to the ultra-modern ones; - from simple instruments for cultivating the
earth to the more complex ones such as machines, factories, laboratories,
and computers. This gigantic and powerful instrument - the whole
collection of means of production that in a sense are synonymous with
"capital" - is the result of work and bears the signs of human labour"[14].

---

11) Ibid.,
12) Ibid
13) John Paul II, LE, n. 12, 4
14) Ibid. n. 12, 5

Need we seek for more points to substantiate what Pope John Paul II
with this perspective has done? He has been able as
Professor of Social ethics, philosophy, as moralist and theologian
to propose a solution to solve the century-long dilemma and conflict
existing between the so-called workers and the so-called owners of the
factors of production. John Paul has been able to show that Labour
precedes Capital, for "the whole collection of instruments, no matter
how perfectly they may be in themselves, are only a mere instrument
subordinate to human labour"[15].

This principle is called by John Paul the "guiding thread"[16]
of Laborem Exercens. This principle emphasises the primacy of the
human person over things, the primacy of the worker over the work
(in the objective sense), and primacy of labour (work in the subjective
sense) over capital. . And in his conviction that his standpoint is
absolutely correct, beyond the limited and partial rumblings of
the liberal capitalists and marxist socialists, the Pope suggests
that "this truth, which is part of the abiding heritage of the
Church's teaching, be always emphasised with reference to the
question of the labour system and with regard to the whole
socio-economic system"... It has to be emphasised because "this truth
has important and decisive consequences"[17].

---

15) Ibid.
16) Ibid.
17) Ibid. n. 12, 6

b) There is no Opposition between Labour and Capital but an
   Inherent Interconnection

Here lies the second criteria proposed by John Paul II towards
resolving the capital - labour conflict. Although capital
(the totality of the means of production by which man appropriates
natural resources and transforms them in accordance with his needs)
is subordinated to the human person, "capital cannot be separated
from labour; in no way can labour be opposed to capital or capital
to labour, and still less can the actual people behind these
concepts be opposed to each other"[18].

The separation of labour and capital is one of the deepest causes
of the ideological conflict tomenting people in all labour
oriented or capital oriented economic systems. In inviting us to go
beyond the boundaries of the opposition between labour and capital,
and between the human beings designated by this concept,
John Paul shows his Christian optimism. "A labour system can be
right, in the sense of being intrinsically true and also morally
legitimate, if in its very basis it overcomes the opposition between
labour and capital through an effort at being shaped in accordance with
the principle put forward ... that of the substantial and real
priority of labour, of the subjectivity of human labour and its
effective participation in the whole production process, independently
of the nature of the services provided by the worker"[19].

---

18) John Paul II., LE, n. 13, 1
19) Ibid.

With his arguments, any emotional support for the opposition
between labour and capital is destroyed and we are asked to go beyond
the limitations of systems which are only materialistic. "Labour and
what we are accustomed to call capital are intermingled; they are
inseparably linked". Those who created a break in this inherent
interconnection set capital in opposition to labour as though they
were two impersonal forces, two production factors juxtaposed in the
same economistic perspective. Here, John Paul does not waste time
to condemn this perspective as a "fundamental error"[20].

His predecessor, Pius XI also took a stand on this issue where he
criticised as false any claim to absolute truth by either opposing
views : "It is entirely false to ascribe the results of their
combined efforts to either capital or labour alone"[21].
In other words, capital and labour are related to each other and should
be understood as interdependent or complementary. "It is unjust that
either should deny the efficacy of the other, and claim all its profits"[22].
The reasons for this appeal are not just due to a tactical nature.
The Pontiffs do not propose a "Third Way" between liberal capitalism
and marxist socialism. John Paul simply asks us to go beyond, to
'push further and deeper, in order to reach human persons while
respecting the destiny assigned to them by God himself'.
In the debate between capitalism and communism, he offers elements
for a critique of both systems, elements that enable each system to
check and correct itself in order to respond to the full demands
of humanity and man's dignity.

---

20) Ibid., 13,3
21) Pius XI, Quadragesimo Anno, A.A.S, XXIII, 1931, p. 195
22) Pius XI, op.cit., (See also: John XXIII., Mater et Magistra,
1961, paragraph 76, CTS London, S259).

He talks of the situation in which the labour versus capital break-up took place. "The consistent image, in which the principle of the primacy of person over things is strictly preserved, was broken up in human thought, sometimes after a long period of incubation in practical living"[23]. In this connection two errors must be mentioned as responsible for the break up and the opposition, namely, "an error of materialism" and an "error of economism".

The error of economism is "that of considering human labour solely according to its economic purpose"[24]. And the error of materialism is that "economism directly or indirectly places the spiritual and personal (man's activity, moral values and such matters) in a position of subordination to material reality"[25].

The Pope critically surveys the errors of both systems, namely liberalism and marxist socialism, which are represented by economism and materialism, and therefore liable to the same charges. For him, "the error of thinking in the categories of economism went hand in hand with the formation of a materialistic philosophy, as this philosophy developed from the most elementary and common phase (also called common materialism, because it professes to reduce spiritual reality to a superfluous phenomenon) to the phase of what is called dialectical materialism"[26].

---

23) John Paul II., LE. n. 13, 3
24) Ibid.
25) Ibid.
26) Ibid.

301

He then goes on to show that this "antinomy" (using Kant's phrase)
between labour and capital - the antinomy in which labour was
separated from capital and set in opposition to it, on the ontic
level, is not justified. Setting both systems against each other brings
about an incomplete picture of the production process and leads
to inhumanism. Says he: "It is obvious that materialism, including its
dialectical form, is incapable of providing sufficient and definitive
bases for thinking about human work, in order that the primacy of man
over the capital instrument, the primacy of the person over things,
may find in it adequate and irrefutable confirmation and support"[27].
In these systems, man is not "first and foremost the subject of work
and the efficient cause of the production process, but continues to
be understood and treated, in dependence on what is material, as a kind
of "resultant" of the economic or production relations prevailing
at a given time"[28].

This criticism is very serious and the realities of our world give
it more objectivity. Whether it is in socialist countries like
Russia, or in capitalist countries like the United States of America,
this antinomy of setting an opposition between labour and capital
ends up in setting human beings against each other. We need not go
far but just think of the threat of a nuclear war between these
two super powers, the lavish war of words already existing in the
media between them, and above all, the attempt by these two countries
to divide the peoples and nations of the world into "For or Against",
"East or West", "Individual or Group".

---

27) John Paul II, LE, n. 13, 4
28) Ibid.

The Pope's appeal is one that comes from the Christian view of the
economic system, based deeply in a theological category of
seeing man as "God's image". This is why the Pope states that there
is an inherrent interconnection between labour and capital since
man is behind both factors. As such, "the only chance there seems
to be for radically overcoming this error is through adequate changes
both in theory and in practice, changes in line with the definite
conviction of the primacy of the person over things, and of human labour
over capital as a whole collection of means of production"[29].

We are thus led to consider the third and last criteria put across
by John Paul II towards the resolution of the economic antinomy
between labour and capital, namely, viewing work as good, meaningful
and creative.

---

29) Ibid. n. 13, 5

c) Human Work is Good, Meaningful and Creative

Human work was considered by John Paul in strong relations to man -
the worker. Since man is "the fundamental way of the Church" and
since the Church "believes in man", John Paul looks at human work
as an activity of man, created in the image of God. Besides, man is
called to work as this corresponds to his vocation, destined by the
creator - "subdue the earth and dominate it". From these
perspectives therefore, work is a man's good, (Labor hominis bonum)
it is meaningful and it is a creative activity which unites man to
his creator and makes him co-creator. Says the Pontiff:

"Even when it is accompanied by toil and effort, work is still
something good, and so man developes himself through love for work.
This entirely positive and creative, educational and meritorious
character of man's work must be the basis for the judgements and
decisions being made today in its regard in spheres that include
human rights"[30].

Such a view of the reality and the value of work enables us to look
with esteem and confidence at human efforts; such a principle is a
premise for attempting solutions in which creativity, initiative,
and commitment to work are not penalised under the glorification
of "non - work" or of the "meaninglessness of work" - a culture,
which at the present time is spreading to the point of becoming the
culture of the meaninglessness of life itself.

---

30) John Paul II., LE, n. 11

A positive view of the meaning and value of human work, whether as
labourer or as owner of capital, "is an act of confidence in humanity
and in its capacity and will to construct a more just and fraternal
world"[31]. This expalins why John Paul II sees work in his analysis as
"a great reality with a fundamental influence on the shaping in a human
way of the world that the Creator has entrusted to man; It is a reality
closely linked with man as the subject of work and with man's rational
activity"[32]. To work is to be human.

4. Conclusion

From the three criteria offered above for the evaluation of the right
understanding of elements involved in human work, namely:
  a) the priority of labour over capital
  b) the inherent interconnection between labour and capital, coupled
      with the absence of opposition between them, and
  c) the nobility of work, its meaning and goodness,
we are led to see what noble contributions that Christian Social Principles
has suggested for the defence of humna rights against any false economic
doctrines which lead to his denegration and personality loss.
John Paul's solution can be regarded as a bold and successful venture
by a Pope whose concern relate to the world of the working man.
Thereby, the antinomy between labour and capital is rendered extravagant
and unnecessary.

---

31) Shottle,P.J., op.cit.,p.26
32) John Paul II, op.cit., Ibid,.

PART THREE (III):   Elements for a Social Ordering of Human Work

1. Introducing the Situation:

From our conclusions in the last section, we are now enabled with
certified criteria to derive elements for a social ordering of
human work. These elements concern primarily the relationship
between State monopoly and private ownership of property including
the means of production; the justification for trade unions and
their relationship to employers associations; the problem of
unemployment; the relationship between direct and indirect employer,
and its relevance in the world of work, in State policy of nations,
and in international organisations, such as the Labour and Food Organisations of the United Nations;   besides these, the problems of
wages, strikes and other relevant rights related to the social
structure of human work will be discussed.

2. The Popes on Private Property and State Monopoly:

We shall attempt here to re-state teachings concerning ownership of
private property and its relationship to State monopoly as thought
out and argumentatively proved by the Popes in the tradition of
Social Ethics. It will be seen, that the right to own private property, including productive goods, is central to the teachings of the
Popes since Leo XIII's famous Encyclical "Rerum Novarum" in 1891.
While criticising rigid capitalism and the abuses it led to, the Popes
do not want to see abolished an institution, which guarantees human
freedom, preserves natural rights and encourages responsible private
initiative. The abuse of a good things in the thinking of the Pontiffs,
should not blind us to the value of that thing in itself.
To remove private property from the hands of private owners and to
place them in the hands of another , namely, the "almighty State", is
to distort the true order of things in the mind of the creator himself.

(i) <u>Pope Leo XIII</u> (1878 - 1903) According to Pope Leo XIII,
"The right to possess private property is derived from nature, not
from man; and the State has the right to control its use in the
interests of the public good alone, but by no means absorb it
altogether... It includes the ownership of productive goods, but
naturally brings with it also an intrinsic obligation to society.
It is a right which must be exercised not only for one's own
personal benefit but also for the benefit of others... The law
therefore should favour ownership, and its policy should be to
induce as many as possible of the people to become owners" [1].

"Whoever has received from the divine bounty a large share of
temporal blessings whether they be external and material, or
gifts of the mind, has received them for the purpose of using them
for the perfecting of his own nature, and, at the same time, that
he may employ them, as the steward of God's providence, for the
benefit of others. "He that hath a talent", says St. Gregory the
Great, "let him see that he hides it not; he that hath
abundance, let him quicken himself to mercy and generosity; he
that hath art and skill, let him do his best to share the use and
utility thereof with his neighbour" [2].

"Is it just that the fruit of a man's own sweat and labour should
be possessed and enjoyed by anyone else? As effects follow their
cause, so is it just that the results of labour should belong to
those who have bestowed their labour" [3].

"Every man has by nature the right to possess property as his own.
This is one of the chief points of distinction between man and the
animal creation, for the brute has no power of self-direction, but is
governed by two main instincts - self-preservation and the
propagation of the species" [4].

1) Leo XIII, Encyclical Letter "Rerum Novarum, 1891,
       (CTS, London, S 219) n. 35
2) Leo XIII, Acta Leonis, XI, 1891, p.114
3) Leo XIII, Rerum Novarum, n. 8
4) Ibid., n. 6

"The socialists, working on the poor man's envy of the rich are
striving to do away with private property, and contend that
individual possessions should become the common property of all,
to be administered by the State or by municipal bodies...
But their contentions are so clearly powerless to end that
were they carried into effect, the working-man himself would
be among the first to suffer. They are moreover emphatically
unjust, for they would rob the lawful possessor, distort the
functions of the State, and create utter confusion in the
community" [5].

(ii) Pope Pius XI (1922 - 1939) - In the words of Pius XI, he writes:
"Let it be made clear beyond all doubt that neither of those who
have taught under the guidance and direction of the Church, have
ever denied or called in question the two-fold aspect of
ownership, which is individual or social according as it regards
individuals or concerns the common good. Their unanimous
assertion has always been that the right to own private property
has been given to man by nature, or rather by the Creator Himself,
that individuals may provide for their own needs and those of
their families, and also that by means of it the goods for the whole
human race may truly serve this purpose destined by the Creator...
A double danger must therefore be carefully avoided. On the
one hand, if the social and public aspect of ownership be
denied or minimised, one falls into "individualism", as it is
called, or at least comes near to it; on the other hand, the
rejection or dimunition of its private and individual character
necessarily leads to "collectivism" or to something near it.
To disregard these dangers would be to rush headlong into the
quicksands of modernism in the moral, juridical and social order,
which we condemned in the Encyclical Letter issued at the beginning
of Our Pontificate [6].

5) Ibid., n. 3
6) Pius XI, Encyclical Ubi Arcano, December 23, 1922

"Let this be noted particularly by those innovators who launch against the Church the odious calumny that she has allowed a pagan concept of ownership to creep into the teachings of her theologians, and who assert that another concept must be substituted, which in their astounding ignorance they call Christian" [7].

"...Men must take into account in this matter, not only their own advantage, but also the common good... History proves that ownership like other elements of social life, is not absolutely rigid... When civil authority adjusts ownership to meet the needs of the public good, it acts not as an enemy, but as the friend, of private owners; for thus it effectively prevents the possession of private property, intended by nature's Author for the support of human life, from creating intolerable disadvantages and so rushing to its own destruction; it does not break down private property but protects it; and far from weakening the right of private property, it gives it new strength; it is plain therefore that the State may not discharge this duty in an arbitrary manner" [8].

"State and public ownership of productive goods is lawful, especially those which "carry with them a power too great to be left to private individuals without injury to the community at large" [8b].

---

7) Pius XI., Encyclical Quadragesimo Anno, 1931, n.45-46 (CTS, London, S 105).

8) Pius XI, Ibid., n. 49

8b) Pius XI., Ibid., A.A.S. XXIII, 1931, p. 214

(iii)   Pope Pius XII, (1939 - 1958) - "The dignity of the human person
        normally demands the right to the use of the goods of the earth,
        to which corresponds the fundamental obligation of granting
        private property to all if possible. It also guarantees the
        conservation and perfection of a social order which makes
        possible a secure, even if modest, property to all classes
        of people" [9].

        "Private ownership of material goods has a great part to play in
        promoting the welfare of family life. It secures for the father
        of a family the healthy liberty he needs in order to fulfil the
        duties assigned him by the Creator regarding the physical,
        spiritual and religious welfare of the family" [10].

        "In defending the principle of private ownership, the Church is
        striving after an important ethico-social end. She does not
        intend merely to uphold the present condition of things as if it
        were an expression of the divine Will, or to protect on
        principle the rich and plutocrats against the poor and indigent...
        The Church aims rather at securing that the institution of
        private property be such as it should be according to the plan
        of the divine Wisdom and the dispositions of nature" [11].

---

9)   Pius XII, Broadcast Message, 24. December 1942; Cf. A.A.S. XXXV,
     1943, pp.19 - 20
10.) Pius XII, Whit Sunday Message, June 1st 1941,
     A.A.S.; XXXII, 1941, p 202
11) Pius XII., Broadcast Message, 1st September 1944;
     A.A.S; XXXVI, 1944, p.253.

(iv)   <u>Pope John XXIII</u> (1958 - 1963) - "Our predecessors have insisted time and again on the social function inherent in the right of private ownership, for it cannot be denied that in the plan of the Creator all of this, world's goods are primarily intended for the worthy support of the entire human race"[12].

"Should man own private property including productive goods? There is no reason for such a doubt to persist. The right to private ownership of goods, including productive goods, has a permanent validity. It is part of the natural Order, which teaches that the individual is prior to society and society must be ordered to the good of the individual. Moreover, it would be quite useless to insist on free and personal initiative in the economic field, while at the same time withdrawing man's right to dispose freely of the means indispensable to the achievement of such initiative... History and experience testify that in those political regimes which do not recognise the rights of private ownership of goods, production included, the exercise of freedom in almost every other direction is suppressed or stifled. This suggests, surely, that the exercise of freedom .find its guarantee and incentive in the right of ownership" [13].

"In the first place it must be stated that in the economic order, first place must be given to the personal initiative of private citizens working either as individuals or in association with each other in various ways for the furtherance of common interests... the principle of subsidiary function must be paramount in all economic relations" [14].

"Private property is a right which constitutes so efficacious a means of asserting one's personality and exercising responsibility in every field, and an element of solidity and security for family life and of greater peace and prosperity in the State"[15].

---

12) John XXIII, Mater et Magistra, 1961, n.119 (CTS, London, S 259)
13) John XXIII, Mater et Magistra, n. 109
14) Ibid., 51 53
15) Ibid, n - 112

(v)   Paul VI (1963 - 1978) - "The Church does indeed defend the legitimate
      rights to private property, but she also teaches no less clearly
      that there is always a social mortgage on all private property,
      in order that goods may serve the general purpose that God
      gave them. And if the common good requires it, there
      should be no hesitation even at expropriation, carried out
      in due form"[16].

(vi) Vatican II, (Gaudium et Spes, 7.1.1965)   - "God destined the
      earth and all it contains for all men and all peoples so that
      all created things would be shared fairly by all mankind
      under the guidance of justice tempered by charity. No matter
      what the structures of property are in different peoples,
      according to various and changing circumstances and adapted
      to their lawful institutions, we must never lose sight of this
      universal destination of earthly goods. In his use of things
      man should regard the external goods he legitimately owns not
      merely as exclusively to himself but common to others also, in
      the sense that they can benefit others as well as himself"[17].

---

16) Paul VI, Encyclical Letter, Populorum Progressio,
    1967, n. 24 (CTS S273)
17) Vatican II, Pastoral Constitution "Gaudium et Spes",
    1965, n.69

"The right of private ownership is not opposed to the right
inherent in various forms of public ownership. But the transfer
of goods from private to public ownership may be undertaken only by
competent authority, in accordance with the demands and within the
limits of the common good, and it must be accompanied by fair
compensation. Moreover, it is the duty of public authority to see
that no one abuses private ownership against the common interest ...
Whenever this social aspect is neglected, property too often becomes the
occasion of greed and serious disturbance, and its opponents are
given excuse to call the right itself to question... Since property
and other forms of ownership of external wealth contribute to the
expression of personality and afford opportunities for social and
economic service, it is a good thing that some access to them should
be encouraged whether for individuals or for communities... Private
property of some control over external goods gives a certain elbow-room
for personal and family independence and can be regarded as an
extension of human liberty. Since also it provides incentives to
responsible work, it is in some sense a condition for civil
liberties" [18].

---

18) Vatican II, op.cit., n. 71

3. Analysis of the Teachings of the Popes on Private Property and
   State Monopoly:

From what the Council Fathers and the teachings of the Popes show
as we have without commentary portrayed in the preceeding pages,
it is clear that there is a big difference between the Church's teaching
on and defence of property, and the understanding of this idea both in
liberal capitalism and in communistic socialism. In the social
principles of christianity, systems based on private property must
provide a good human life for all. If they do not fulfil this
demand, they may as well not waste time claiming the defence or patronage
of the Church.

First of all, Christian Social Principles starts with the person in his
relationship to his Creator, and then proceeds to the horizontal level
where this person meets other persons in society. Without doubt, the
norm by which the Church judges all social institutions is the impact
on the individual personality. Human beings are differently gifted, and
some are particularly gifted with skills called entrepreneurial from
which activity they gain much satisfaction. Social ethics demands that
such individuals be allowed to fulfil their personalities by being
allowed free initiative in using their skills. Thereby, they would
prove more useful to their society given the adequate incentive to
work themselves.

Secondly, it is clear that where the means of livelihood are all
under the control of the State or public authority, it is in practice
impossible on the long run for individuals or groups within
society to oppose state authority on a matter in which the State is the
be all and end all. In such a situation, the individual's personality
disappears and is buried in the collective. "It is the Christian
insight, justified by the scriptures and her experience of human
society over two thousand years, that where the right to own
property does not exist, it is not possible for the other human freedoms
to be maintained" [19].

Thirdly, those societies which took Karl Marx and Friedrich Engels
serious are today discovering that they are working under utopic
presumptions. As can be proved from the examples of Yugoslavia, Rumania,
Hungary, and to some extent the Union of Soviet Socialist Republic,
the State itself is practicing and somehow tolerating private
property now. This is a positive move which shows that they are
flexible and are able to give in to competition and individual
expression, also in economic life. Christian Social teachings feels
justified if this tendency of the Marxist societies continues in the
area of private property. The "Summer 1980" and the phenomenon of
Lech Walesa's "Solidarnosy" in Poland is still to be reckoned with.

Lastly, if the State controlled economies refuse to give in to
full ownership of property including the means of production, it is
difficult to see how the transfer of ownership and the control of all
economic resources to the State will in the end be of more benefit
to their citizens and mankind in economic growth terms. Like someone said:
The contention of the socialists that human needs can be fulfilled
without the use of private ownership is yet to be proved, if it can be
proved at all. There is enough evidence that socialist countries are
now encouraging initiative and giving financial incentives to their people.

---

[19]   Roger Charles, op.cit., p.301

Gaudium et Spes can be summarily looked upon as the document which exposed in a definitive way, the positive advantages of private property, thereby making it impossible for Christian Social Ethics to accept total State monopoly of ownership. This is so because private ownership

    (i)   is an expression of personality;

   (ii)   affords opportunities for economic and social services;

  (iii)   there is evidence from the history of mankind that this institution is "natural" to man in the sense that all ages seem to have found it necessary;

   (iv)   the possession of private property can give a man and his family the security they need;

    (v)   the possibility of increasing one's ownership is an incentive to work harder and so benefit not only oneself in the community;

   (vi)   Lastly, without economic freedom through private property, the other freedoms disappear. Unless we hold on the principle and see it given in effective practice, it is impossible to see how other civil liberties, be it intellectual, spiritual, cultural or political can be realised.

4. John Paul II on Private Property and State Monopoly:

The issue of private property and State monopoly was taken seriously
by Pope John Paul II for he gave adequate attention to the topic.
This is so because, as we have shown in earlier chapters, on this
topic rests the ideological conflict dividing the world and
mankind. It has to be mentioned immediately that John Paul's stand
on the subject has provoked many comments - often contradictory -
especially where he speaks of work and ownership [20].

John Paul says: "When we speak of opposition between labour and
capital, we are not dealing only with abstract concepts or "impersonal
forces" operating in economic production. Behind both concepts there
are people, living actual people: on the one side are those who do
work without being the owners of the means of production, and on
the other side those who act as entrepreneurs and own the means of
production. Thus ownership of property enters from the beginning into
the whole of this difficult historical process" [21].

He poses the problem of the ownership of the means of production -
a problem which has been at the heart of the social question - in
existential terms, that is, in terms of work and of the human person.
The Pope confirms earlier Church teaching on this matter, and he
cites Leo XIII and John's "Mater et Magistra" as illuminating works
on the area. However, John Paul distinguishes himself from these
in his normal originality by making clear from the onset that
"property is acquired first of all through work in order that it
may serve work" [22]. The means of production "cannot be possessed against
labour, they cannot even be possessed for possessions sake, because their
only legitimate title of possession is that they should serve labour,
and thus by serving labour, that they should make possible the
achievement of the first principle of this order, namely, the universal
destination of goods and the right to the common use of them" [23].

---

20) John Paul II, Laborem Exercens, n. 14 (Cf. Jan P. Schotte., "Reflections
   on Laborem Exercens, Pontifical Comm. "Iustitia et Pax", Nr. 9,p.30).

21) John Paul II, LE, n.14

22) Ibid

23) Ibid.

In this way, the Pontiff teaches that ownership should never be understood in a way that could constitute grounds for social conflict in labour. He therefore dishes out doses of criticism on capitalism and collectivism because these systems refused the invitation to "go beyond" their myopic standards of viewing the world's economic systems.

Against collectivism, the Pope asserts the right of private ownership of property and the means of production. He says that many desired reforms cannot be achieved by an apriori elimination of private property and ownership of the means of production. For it must be noted that merely taking these means of production out of the hands of their private owners is not enough to ensure their satisfactory socialisation. They cease to be property of certain social groups, namely the private owners, and become the property of organised society, coming under the administration and direct control of another group of people, namely, those who, though not owning them, from the fact of exercising their power in society manage them on the level of the whole national or the local economy [24].

Even though such a work can be carried out well, it may also be carried out badly, besides offending basic human rights. Therefore he concludes that "merely converting the means of production into State property in the collectivistic system is by no means equivalent to "socialising" that property" [25]. This is a very rational and strong observation. Communism has not succeeded to create a society of equals which it set out to achieve. Rather, it has established

---

24) John Paul II, LE, n. 14
25) Ibid.

a state of imbalance, which although claiming to make all persons
equal, ends up making all unequal and unfree like George Orwell
would like to say in his book - "Animal farm" :
"All men are equal, but (in socialist states) some are more equal than
others".

Also against capitalism, John Paul insists that the right to private
ownership is not absolute - it is subordinated to the right of
common use. Included in the phrase "common use", is not only the
earth's and ocean's riches, but also the riches in space, thereby
opening the Church's social doctrine to a "spatial dimension".
His critique of capitalism is hard for he says that rigid capitalism
continues to remain unacceptable, for the principle which calls for
respect for work demands that the right to private property should
undergo a constructive revision, both in theory and in practice [26].

"Christian tradition" says the Holy Father, "has never upheld the
right to private ownership as absolute. On the contrary, it has
always understood this right within the broader context of the
right common to all to use the goods of entire creation: the right
to private property is subordinated to the right to common use, to the
fact that goods are meant for every" [27].

With such a teaching, the Pope not only refers to the biblical
accounts or Genesis (which says:"All these goods I give to you and to
your children); but also to the theories of Thomas Aquinas; and
the Council Fathers in the constitution "Gaudium et Spes" which upholds
the teaching that "God destined the earth and all it contains for
all men and all peoples so that all created things would shared fairly
by all mankind under the guidance of justice and tempered by charity".
Therefore, isolating these means as a separate property in order
to set it up in the form of "capital" in opposition to "labour" - and
even to practise exploitation of labour - is contrary to the
very nature of these means and their possession.

26) Ibid.,
27) Ibid., LE

St. Thomas Aquinas (c.1225 - 1274), unlike the earlier Christian writers, defended the naturalness of private property, by underlying the positive value of the institution to human nature. Private property was only unnatural in the sense that wearing of clothes was unnatural, namely, that nature did not provide us with clothes and we had to make them to protect ourselves from cold, sun and so on. In the same way, nature did not bestow private property on people, but men have discovered that the best way to fulfil the original gift of God to all was to develope this institution. Private property was not so much unnatural as in addition to nature.

Thomas, Summa Theologica, I-II, q.94, art. 5 ad 3, q.105, art. 2 ad 3.
II - II, q. 57, art. 3, q. 66, art. 2).

In article I of this Question St. Thomas argues that it is natural for man to have dominion over things in the sense of having the power to use them. In themselves material objects belong to God, being made by him, and therefore cannot be brought under man's domination. But since man has a mind which can perceive how things can be made useful to him and a will to bring them into use, and since less perfect things exist for the sake of more perfect, it is natural for man to adapt material goods for his use. In this sense, man can rightly own things. This is the argument used by John Paul in LE, XII (The priority of Part 3 labour). In Article 2 of this question St. Thomas proceeds to consider whether it is legitimate for individual men to own goods. He makes a distruction bewteen 2 powers: that of caring for and distributing things; and that of using them. As regards the first power, he argues that individual ownership is not only lawful but also necessary. He advances 3 reasons - First, the property of one man is better cared for than is something held in common. Secondly, individual responsibility is more efficient than is general responsibility. Thirdly, clear distinctions between what belongs to one person and what belongs to another reduce the risk of quarrels. As regards the second power, he argues that management, while best done by one man, has to be always in the interest of all men. An owner must be ready always to provide for the needs of others. Private ownership does not justify purely private use. Bearing in mind man's duty to grow in humanity and the connection between responsibility and development it can be argued that employing is a more important aspect than is enjoying.

5. John Paul's Concrete Suggestion: Conditional Socialisation and Personalism

Concerning the implementation of these principles, the Pope is
cautiously not suggesting any concrete formula. In fact, the Church
has always refused to fix her teachings on these points in
historical realisations only. Whether this tactics has helped the
world is another matter! However, John Paul proposes as an operational
principle, that concrete formulas be subjected to continual
constructive revisions within a diversity of complementary systems of
private and public ownership. The formula he uses is called
"Socialisation".

"In consideration of human labour and of common access to the goods
meant for man, one cannot exclude Socialisation, in suitable conditions,
of certain means of production" [28]. Such socialisation however,
cannot be realised by an apriori elimination of private property,
nor by making the means of production state property. There is an
in-between which calls for the use of the "Personalist Argument" to
make his point more clear. John Paul says that "any socialisation
of the means of production must take the personalist argument into
account if it is to be rational and fruitful" [29].

Now, the "Personalist Argument" states that when a man works, using all
the means of production, he also wishes the fruit of this work to be
used by himself and others, and he wishes to be able to take part
in the very work process as a sharer in responsibility and creativity
at the workbench to which he applies himself. Inspite of all the
social aspects of work, work remains and is a personal activity.
This worker is a person who desires not only due remuneration for his
work, but demands to know that his work, even if owned in common,
is also something for himself [30].

---

28) Ibid., Thomas Aquinas, Summa Theol., On the Right to Property, II-II,
q.66, arts. 2 and 6; De Regime Principium, book i, chap. 15 and 17;
On the social Function of Property, Summa. Theol, II-II, q.134, art.1
and 3

29) John Paul, II, op.cit. Ibid.

30) John Paul, LE, n. 15

John Paul emphasises that the Church has always expressed the strong convinction that man's work concerns not only the economy but also, and especially, personal values. "The economic system itself and the production process benefit precisely when these personal values are fully respected... Every effort must be made to ensure that in this kind of system also the human person can preserve his awareness of working for himself" [31].

Socialisation therefore, can best be understood, when on the basis of his work, each person is fully entitled to consider himself a part owner of the great workbench at which he is working with everyone else. As such, "nationalisation" cannot be excluded from the economic process when it is necessary and considered by the competent authority to be justified. In general terms, ideal in the world of ownership is "co-ownership or associating labour with the ownership of capital through a number of intermediate bodies with economic, social and cultural purposes, and granted full autonomy with regard to the public authorities" [32].

In all, respect for the human person and his rights must be paramount, and the common good of the entire society remains highest ideals. All throughout his discussion of the relationship between private ownership of property and state monopoly, we discover that John Paul main-ains the basic principle which motivated his encyclical; namely, the primacy of "homo laborem exercens".

---

31)   John Paul II, LE, n. 15
32)   Ibid., n. 14

6. Conclusion:

The position of Christian Social Ethics is that the ownership
of private property goes hand in hand with the virtues of justice
and charity. It belongs to the virtue of justice not to
encroach on the rights of another, even when it means exceeding the
limits of one's own right of property once it is rightfully in one's
possession. The great and principal duty is to give to everyone
what is just and what is his due. "To gather one's profit out of
the need of another is condemned by all laws, whether human or divine"[33].

Charity on its own is the duty to love and care for the other in
the spirit of brotherliness and humanity. It finds its fulfilment
in the person and life of Christ who, as Catholic Theology teaches,
poured out his love for all mankind through his acceptance of the
human flesh and his death on the cross to save man.
With justice and charity, the opposition between labour and capital,
between private ownership of property and state monopoly of the means
of production will disappear.

---

33) Leo XIII, Rerum Novarum, op.cit., par. 17

CHAPTER SEVEN : The Rights of Workers Considered in the Context of
Universal Human Rights

PART ONE (I) :Factors involved in defence of the rights of workers

1. The role of trade Unions :

"One fundamental human right that workers have is that of freely
setting up unions which can genuinely represent them and contribute
to a proper organising of economic life. They have also the right to
participate freely in union business, without fear of victimisation.
This kind of orderly participation, combined with progressive economic
and social training, will increase everybody's awareness of his position
and duties, and make each feel associated according to his capacities
and attainments, with the whole work of economic and social progress
and with universal welfare". (Gaudium et Spes, par. 68).

The Encyclical "Laborem Exercens" has brought out once again, in
the light of twentieth century labour experiences, the importance of
trade unions. It does this within the broader context of human rights
as a whole, and in strict accordance with the earlier reflections
on work as outlined in chapters one and two of the encyclical.
Here, it shows that human work and the dignity of the human person
are related, and work should have a "humanising" function.

Earlier Church pronouncements on the subject were also positive
for "Rerum Novarum" asserted that the rights of workers to form
associations of trade unions for the defence of their legitimate
rights was in order. Likewise did Pius XI in "Quadragesimo Anno"
and John XIII in the famous encyclical "Mater et Magistra"[1] recommend
the association, not only of working men, but also of the employers,
because, "by means of such organisations which afford aid to those
in distress, the two classes of workers and employers would be
drawn more closely"[2]. This recommendation has however earlier

---

1) Leo XIII, Rerum Novarum, par. 36 - 42
   Pius XI, Quadragesimo Anno, Par. 29 - 38
   John XXIII, Mater et Magistra, par. 91 - 103
2) Pius XI, op.cit. par 29.

origins in the bible where the writer says: "It is better that
two should be together than one; for they have the advantage of
their society. If one fall he shall be supported by the other. Woe to
him that is alone, for when he falls he has no one to lift him up"[3].
The book of Proverbs expressed this wisdom more articulately where
it said: "A brother that is helped by his brother is like a strong
city" (proverbs, 18:19). This, therefore, may be described as the
biblical - "raison d' etre" of Trade Unions and Employers Associations,
on which writings by Pope John Paul II, we shall consider now.

a) The Imperative to Form Trade Unions:

John Paul injects from the beginning of his meditation, the element
which emphasises that rights and duties go hand in hand, and the
worker seeking his rights cannot neglect at the same time his duties.
Work is an obligation, a duty, on the part of man because the Creator
has commanded it and because his own humanity requires it; his
relation of solidarity with his fellow man demands it; his connection
to his family and the responsibilities demanded by the nation and
the entire human race imposes it on him[4].

But work is not only an obligation, for there are also rights
deriving from it, which help man to be more man. Leo XIII believed
that these rights which could be obtained through unions would
"furnish the best and most suitable means for attaining what is
aimed at, and for helping each individual member to better his
condition to the utmost in body, soul and property"[5]. Here lies
the importance of trade unions. It is otherwise known as "the

---

3) Ecclesiasticus, 4:9 - 10
4) John Paul II., Laborem Exercens, n. 16
5) Leo XIII., Rerum Novarum, op.cit., par. 42

solidarity of labour" for the realisation of the rights of the
worker. Interests common to all workers and interests that concern
individual professions must be pursued by unions within the context
of the common good of society as a whole. This consideration was
attested by the International Labour Convention, number 87 of 1948 and
the Pope reiterated this position in his known "famous speech"
in Geneva before the International Labour Organisation, where he said:
"Any policy to achieve the common good must be the fruit of organic
and spontaneous cohesion of the forces of society; this is another
form of solidarity - an imperative of social order that manifests
itself through the existence and the work of associations of social
partners. The right to associate freely is a fundamental one for
all those connected with the world of work and who constitute the
work community"[6]. And as if it seems that these words are not
enough to make the point, he expresses himself even more clearly
in his magisterial teaching in the encyclical under revision, making
the fundamental assertion that trade unions are imperative and
indispensable. "The experience of history teaches that
organisation of this type are an indispensable element of social life,
especially in modern industrialised societies"[7].

Many people might, and some really have expressed surprise that
the Holy Father gives unreserved support and encouragement to
worker's unions, and the suspicion has been raised if Karol Wojtyla
was not writing with the developments in his native Poland at heart,
especially, the phenomenon of "SOLIDARNOSZ" led by Lech Walesa
in Summer 1980 but which the polish government banned and even
imprisoned some of its oversize or outspoken members. Otherwise,
how can we explain this unreserved and whole-sale encouragement and
imperative to workers to defend their rights through unions? Are there
advantages attached to trade unions? What are these and what other
reasons, if any does the pontiff have for recommending trade unions?

---

6)   John Paul II, Address to the ILO, Geneva, 15. June 1982, op.cit, p.290
7)   John Paul II, Laborem exercens, n.20

b) Advantages of Trade Unions:

Without going into excessive details, we shall limit ourselves to
a few advantages connected with trade unions and which John Paul
summarily dealt with in his address before the world body. He said:

> "Trade unions have so many advantages. It unites man and
> makes it impossible for any working man to be isolated or
> feel lonely; it expresses the solidarity of all in the
> defence of rights which are rightfully theirs and flow
> from the requirements of their work; it affords a normal
> channel for participating actively in the performance of
> work and everything related to it, while being guided
> at the same time by a concern for the common good"[8].

Trade unions make it possible that workers assume responsibility
for defending the truth which states that a labourer merits a just
wage, and above all, workers are enabled to learn, to be instructed
in the economic methods of operation, and this education helps them
realise the true dignity of human work, solidarity and brotherhood.
The Pope suggests that the struggle of trade unions should be seen
"as a normal endeavour "for" the just good - a mouthpiece for the
struggle for social justice, and for the just rights of working
people... It is not a struggle "against" others"[9].

When there must be opposition and struggle, then because it aims at
the good of social justice, but not merely for the sake of "struggle"
or to eliminate the opponent[10].

---

8) John Paul II., Address to ILO, op.cit., p.291
9) John Paul II, Laborem Exercens, n.20
10) Ibid.

This is an appeal for both those who give job and those who work
to avoid confrontation and seek constructive dialogue and resolution
of problems. "Union demands cannot be turned into a kind of group
or class "egoism", although they can and should also aim at correcting
with a view to the common good of the whole society, everything
defective in the system of ownership of the means of production or
in the way these are managed"[11]. From the aforesaid, we are made to know
that the first and basic character of labour, and the institution
which represents labour, namely trade unions, is "to build a community",
and not to "play politics", struggling for power, or become an
instrument used for other purposes [12]. Trade unions must take full
independence from the political authorities in order to freely
arrive at, in full responsibility, the internal organisational aims and
activities set out by their noble ideals, and thereby escape misuse or the
division which such party political dependence could bring about.
Since solidarity is the watchword of the trade unions, and there
cannot be any solidarity without unity as aim, trade unions must then
be a factor and instrument of unity in the society, not of division.

Having said this, the Pope offers some time, discussing the method
trade unions could use to achieve their legitimate rights, and here,
he does not exclude the use of strikes. We shall therefore discuss
in the next section, the issue of strikes and of just wages for just work.

---

11) Ibid
12) Ibid.

2. The "Right" to Strike:

The strike issue has become an increasingly important one, made
more complex by the structures of modern economic realities, and
the power of "worker - blocks" in the demand for certain rights.
The wage earner has often no other possibility to get his rightful
demands respected and so strike remains the only way open.
There would be no point in the right of association if the right
to use the ultimate sanction that those who work for others have,
was denied to them in pursuing the aims of their association.

Interesting to note in this connection is that the council Fathers
at Vatican II devoted some attention to the problem of strikes, saying:

> "In the event of economic - social disputes, all should
> strive to arrive at peaceful settlements. The first step
> is to engage in sincere discussion between all sides;
> but the strike remains even in the circumstances of today
> a necessary (although an ultimate) means for the defence
> of worker's rights and the satisfaction of their lawful
> aspirations. As soon as possible, however, avenues should
> be explored to resume negotiations and effect reconciliation"[13].

With this statement, the council recognises the right of free trade
unions, which genuinely represent the needs of the workers to
strike if this becomes a last resort. And it is in this context that
Pope John Paul bases his own teaching on the subject. "While
admitting that it is a legitimate means, we must at the same time
emphasise that a strike remains, in a sense, an extreme means. It
must not be abused"[14], since abuse of the right to strike can lead

---

13) Vatican II, Gaudium et Spes, par. 68
14) John Paul II, Laborem Exercens, n. 20

to a complete paralysis of the entire socio-economic life of the
people and would thereby be contrary to the common good of society,
which work represents and which the striking workers epitomise.

Paul VI recognised the impact of this situation and insisted
years ago on certain fundamental laws to be observed, should strikes
become an actuality. He begins with a warning, observing that
"here and there a temptation can arise of profiting from a position
of strenght to impose, particularly by strikes, the right to which,
as a final means of defence, remains certainly recognised, conditions
which are too burdensome for the overall economy and for the social
body, or the desire to obtain in this way, demands of directly
political nature. When it is a question of public services
required for the life of an entire nation, it is necessary to be
able to assess the limit beyond which the harm caused to society
becomes inadmissible"[15].

---

15) Paul VI, Octogesima Adveniens n. 14

a) <u>Problems caused by Strikes</u>:

There is no doubt that the right to strike has always possessed
within it serious anti-social implications in its practice, as
we can concretely prove, since the development of modern
industrial relations in the nineteenth century. There has been
labour laws and its various attempts to rationalise, organise and
set up limits upon which strike action can take place. This attempt
inspite of its good will, has not met with much success.

As I write on this page, the newspaper of today carried with it
two strike-news which go to prove what we have tried above to
demonstrate. The "Stadtanzeiger" of Köln has this to write:
"Mit neuen Warnstreiks haben IG Metall und IG Druck gestern ihre
Förderung nach der 35 Studen-Woche untermauert, auch in Köln.
Laut IG Metall legten rund 5000 Beschäftigte kurzfristig die Arbeit
nieder. Für Köln schwankten die Zahlen zwischen 500 und 1200.
Die IG Druck sprach bundesweit von 5000 Beschäftigten im Warnstreik.
Die IG Metall will, so Vorstandsmitglied Jansen, mit der 35 Studen-
Woche nicht die Regierung, sondern die Arbeitlosigkeit bekämpfen.
Gegenteilige Behaptungen seien dumm und töricht"[16].

---

16) Köln (EB, ap), Kölner Stadt-Anzeiger, G 4237 A, Freitag,
16. März 1984, Nummer 65., Redaktions Bericht
"Warnstreiks vom Metall u. Druck in Kölner Firmen", s.1

And on the Island of Britain, the "traditional" home for strikes,
news came from the same newspaper about recent strikes going on
which has even led to the death of a young man. The news reads:
"Der Streik der britischen Bergarbeiter hat sich am Donnestag
weiter zugespitzt. Fast der gesamte Bergbau in Nordengland und
Wales wurde durch den Ausstand lahmgelegt, mit dem die staatliche
Kohlbehörde NCB gezwungen werden soll, die geplannten Entlassungen
von 21,000 Kumpels zurückzunehmen. Lediglich in 20 von 174 Zechen
wurde normal gearbeitet. Der Arbeitskampf, der vor rund einer
Woche mit spontanen Arbeitsniederlegungen begonnen hatte, forderte
ein Menschenleben. Ein 24jähriger Streikposten starb vor einer
Zeche im Bergbaugebiet der Grafschaft Nottingshamshire nach einem
Handgemenge mit Jugendlichen"[17].

From the above stray news, which is already a daily occurence in
Italy, Nigeria, Brazil, Argentina and many countries of the world,
one wonders if there can be any basis from which strikes can be
justified or condemned, and if, how?

---

17) London (dpa, ap)., Ibid., p.2. The "Donnerstag" referred to
is the 15th March 1984.

b) Justification of Strikes:

Social scientist Roger Charles examined the "Just war" theory and
its criteria, transplanting the same theory to the "just strike" theory.
Admitting that it is extraordinarily hard to give general
guidance which will enable particular strikes to be judged justified
or unjustifiable, he makes bold however to add:

For a strike to be just then, it must be called by proper authority
in a just cause (namely the redress of a grievance and not for any
aggressive purposes), and with a right intention; therefore, it must
use just means in pursuing its just aim; in particular, it must not
cause more evil in pursuit of its claim than the evil it intends
to overcome[18]. So much for the general principles. But here it ends,
for the difficulty arises when it comes to the application.
The actual situation in which a strike takes place is very rarely
one in which the issues are clear enough for the immediate and
successful application of any such general principles.
The magisterium does not say precisely how strikes organised by
unions, shareholders and the other corporate associations should
be carried out, or what immediate action should cause the reaction of
strikes. But the magisterium insists that the end of the common
good be accepted by all the groups, whatever action they undertake.

---

18) Roger C., op.cit., pp. 325 ff.

   (In this case, any strike can be accepted to be justifiable if
   its interest is the common good of those members of society
   affected, and the common good of the greater society is not disturbed).

This position of the teaching authority of the Church however leaves
unsolved the "Why" and "When" and "How" of a strike. Surely, we
cannot expect the magisterium to define who is the proper
authority to call a strike. The relationship between unions, their
officials and their members on the shop floor is one that is
difficult to rationalise satisfactorily. If unions are voluntary
associations, the members only obey their leaders insofar as
they wish, but if they are given corporate status, the members
can in theory be more effectively disciplined. Because of the
problems raised by corporate status, unions here are regarded as
voluntary associations[19].

This has meant that leaders in a country like Britain have very
little in the way of sanctions against members - but corporate
status would not solve the problem either. Leaders have very
little authority to compel members to act against their will.
And where the state itself has tried to use the full weight of the
law under wartime conditions, it has not been able to do so[20]. The
question of effective authority in trade unions is "therefore,
more difficult than it appears at first sight. It cannot be
assumed that trade union leaders can get the men out on strike or
that they can stop them from striking. It depends very much on the
unions, the situation and the mood of the moment"[21].
The German situation is however different, for here, a centralised
trade union system with a central apparatus makes more possible
what British arbitrary trade union system, competing among each other
for gain and power cannot make possible.

19) Weekes Brian, et. al., Industrial Relations and the Limits of
    Law (Oxford, 1975), pp.95 ff.
20) Royal Commission on Trade Unions and Employers Associations
    Report (Donovan Commission, 1968), pp.131
21) Roger Charles., op.cit., p. 328

This difficulty of adequate acceptable criteria is also felt in
the other mentioned factors, such as striking for a just-cause,
with a right intention and with a just means. The researcher
meets a lot of competing results that each criteria has to be weighed
and counter-weighed, and yet an objective answer eludes all the time.
We are naturally led back to the point of departure which calls
that workers and employers with the state work together to avoid
such situations where strikes can originate. There is the call
for a just wage for work done and there is the call for tolerance
and corporate co-operation. While the rights of capital to
organise for profit are defended, and the rights of labour to
organise its own best interests are likewise defended, capital and
labour are not to be seen as naturally antagonistic on a marxist sense,
but ready to seek a reduction of needless conflicts and cooperate
where interests coincide. The Wage organisation is the melting pot.

3. Just Remuneration for Work done (Wages):

> "In every case, a just wage is the concrete means of
> verifying the justice of the whole socioeconomic
> system and, in any case, of checking that it is
> functioning justly. It is not the only means of
> checking, but it is a particularly important one and
> in a sense, the key means". (John Paul II, Laborem
> Exercens, n.19).

With the above quotation, John Paul II brings out one of the basic
economic and social principles guiding the area of human labour.
He does this not in isolation, but in agreement with the earlier
teachings of his predecessors and with the Council pronouncements
as singularly portrayed by the cons-titution of "Gaudium et Spes".
There the council Fathers decreed : "Wages must be paid which will
give adequate scope for living, materially, socially culturally and
spiritually, considering each man's job, his productivity and the
general welfare"[22]. In this statement lies in general, the entire
reason for adequate wage payment and the advantages which such
brings to the society at large and the working man in particular.
No wonder, John Paul sees wages as "the key problem of social ethics".
For him, there is no more important way for securing a just
relationship between the worker and the employer than that constituted by
remuneration for work. And he makes it clear that this remains the
case for all sorts of work contracts, "whether the work is done in
a system of private ownership of the means of production or in a
system where ownership has undergone a certain "socialisation"[23].

---

22) Vatican II, Gaudium et Spes., par. 67 (Cf. Leo XIII, Rerum Novarum,
    ASS, 23, 1890-1, p.649, 662; Pius XI, Quadragesimo Anno, AAS,23,
    1931, p.200
    Pius XII, Christmas Broadcast, 1942, AAS, 35, (1943)p.20.,
23) John Paul II. Laborem Exercens, n. 19

a) Wages - A Test of Justice:

Contractual justice, defined as "justitia commutativa" demands that
the worker receive the work wages which the contract demands, and this
cannot be fulfilled without considering the adequate remuneration
of the imput by the worker in terms of time, energy and risks,
besides productivity which the worker makes available to the market for
consumption by the common society. Here again, we are led to accept the
principle enunciated by the Church Fathers and the magisterium that
"the goods of this earth are for the common use of all". And it is
specifically through wages in a big way that the worker gets his own
share of this universal property.
Justice is therefore demanded for effective distribution and division.

> John Paul says that "in every system, regardless
> of the fundamental relationships within it between
> capital and labour, wages, that is to say remuneration
> for work, are still a practical means whereby the vast
> majority of people can have access to those goods which
> are intended for the common use: both the goods of nature
> and manufactured goods"[24].

It is also to be attested that on the national level, the economic
prosperity of a nation is not, so much its total assets in terms
of wealth and property, as the equitable division and distribution
of this wealth. On this depends the personal development of the
members of the society, the goal which is pursued by the national
economy. Pope Pius XII recognised this truth, as does John Paul
II, for he writes in a Whitsunday message in 1941, during the

---

24) Ibid.

war-appetite period of Hitler's Germany that: "Likewise the
national economy, as it is the product of the men who work
together in the community of the state, has no other end than to
secure without interruption the material conditions in which the
individual life of the citizens may fully develop . Where this is
secured in a permanent way, a people will be in a true sense,
economically rich, because the general well being, and
consequently the personal right of all to the use of worldly goods,
is thus realised in conformity with the purpose willed
by the Creator"[25].

When we consider the real economic situations within nations, and
beyond, on the international level, we marvel and shudder at the
same time with fear at the crass injustices, discrepancies and
dialectical wage differences existing in the world of work. Here,
the class and elitist attitude has not changed much, also because
the states policies have not altered. In Nigeria, for example,
whereas the lowest paid worker following the government white paper
on salary gradings received about one hundred Naira (100 N), the
highest paid workers were counting above sixteenthousand Naira
(16,000 N) a month, and both groups are supposed to go to the same
market, feed the same number of children, and pay towards the
national economy. Interesting to note in this connection is that
more than eighty percent of the working population, in order not to
underestimate, come from the lower cadres of the economic ladder.
Where is the justice of the wage policy? The situation on the
international level is more staggering, for, per capita income
ranged from 5,971 dollars in Switzerland to 88 dollars in Indonesia
and 87 dollars in Ethiopia [26].

---

25) Pius XII, Whitsunday Message, AAS, XXXIII, 1941, p.200
26) G.M. Meier, Leading Issues in Economic Development, New York,
    1976, pp.12; L.W. Phillips, Why Third World, (The Third World Review),
    January 1979. (The quoted books give basic date on 115 middle
    and low income societies).

The prophet Amos issued an indictment on those responsible for the inequitable distribution of wealth and wages where he says: "O you who turn justice to wormwood, and cast down righteousness to the earth... you trample upon the poor and take away from him exactions of wheat... who levy taxes on the poor and extort a tribute of grain... who persecute the guiltless, hold men to ransom and thrust the destitute out of court... Therefore they shall be the first to go into exile, and the revelry of those who strech themselves shall pass away"[27].

He then calls them to repentance, "seek good and not evil, that you may live; and so the Lord God of hosts will be with you". In the distribution of the national economy, regard must be given to social justice and equity. The common good belongs to all men, and policy makers should make it their duty to arrive at this aim, as much as is humanly possible. Pope John XXIII had time to refer specifically to the problem of wages. "We therefore consider it our duty to reaffirm that the remuneration of work is not something that can be left to the laws of the market; nor ought it to be fixed arbitrarily. It must be determined in accordance with justice and equity; which means that workers must be paid a wage which allows them to live a truly human life and fulfil their obligations to family in a worthy manner"[28]. In saying this, his concern is for the poorly paid workers for whom the Church must make an option to defend, normally termed "Option for the poor"! "...their rate of pay is quite inadequate. It in no way corresponds to the contribution they make to the good of the community, to the profits of the company for which they work, and to the greater national economy"[29].

---

27) Amos, Chapters 5 and 6
28) John XXIII., Mater et Magistra, par. 71
29) Ibid., par. 70 (Pope John believes that the productive efficiency of many national economies has been rapidly increasing. Within the limits of the common good, wages too shall increase that the worker may save up more and acquire a certain amount of property, Ibid,n.112)

If strikes are to be avoided with all the damages that it can bring
to the national economy, a fair and just wage must be regulated
in favour of the workers, especially those who have a family.
Infact, John Paul II is very determined in his social ethical
thinking on this subject, for on it rests the justice of the wage
earner and in a broader context, the human rights of the worker.
In a family of seven, the father is often the only worker, supposed
to feed his entire family with the salary of only one man. Often
with an inadequate salary, his wife is forced to leave the home and
abandon the care of the children to also seek for enough money
with the husband to feed the family and bring up the children well.
In such a situation, children are often forced to abandon the home
earlier, without adequate foundation and training for a future, to
look for cheap work in the industries. The family structure, its
decency and integrity is lowered, money determines the nature of
life, and society is forced to contain citizens not properly secured
and well brought up. The nation suffers the consequence as crimes
rise, meaninglessness creeps in and the parole of "No Future" is
placarded by young people everywhere. It is this picture that
John Paul has in mind when he demands that the wage earner, who is
at the same time a family father, be given special consideration by being
paid more. John XXIII understood this problem for he said twenty
years before "we are filled with an overwhelming sadness when we
contemplate the sorry spectacle of millions of workers in many lands
and entire continents condemned through the inadequacy of their
wages to live with their families in utterly sub-human conditions"[30].

---

30) John XXIII., Mater et Magistra, par. 68

b) <u>Elements Towards Determining Just Wage</u>:

With this situation in mind, John Paul II demands that the
family be paramount in wage discussions.

> "Just remuneration for the work of an adult who is
> responsible for a family means remuneration which will
> suffice for establishing and properly maintaining a
> family and for providing security for its future.
> Such remuneration can be given either through what is
> called a 'family wage' - that is, a single salary given
> to the head of the family for his work, sufficient
> for the needs of the family without the other spouse
> having to take up gainful employment outside the
> home -" [31].

Wonderful an idea as this may be, (even though externally impracticable
because of the state policy of nations and population control), the
Holy Father suggests other methods through which this ideal wage
system can be attained, namely, "through other social measures such
as family allowances or grants to mothers devoting themselves
exclusively to their families. These grants should correspond to the
actual needs, that is, to the number of dependends for as long as
they are not in a position to assume proper responsibility for their
own lives"[32]. It is important to assert immediately that certain
nations are already putting into practice these suggestions of the
Pope, even if not in its totality, but at least in some measure.

---

31) John Paul II., LE, n. 19
32) Ibid.

Western Countries like Austria and Germany and even Sweden have
policies which guarantee "social aid" to families, but often, this
social aid, is given not within the wage-contract system, but as
State direct aid to the so called "Kinderreiche Familien",
or "Children-rich families" in literal translation. The future
has still much in stock and it remains to be seen if this principle
put accross by John Paul can be actualised within the wage system.

Pius XI did also demonstrate the advisability in the present
circumstances of modifying wage - contract by applying to it
elements taken from the contract of partnership, so that "wage
earners and other employees participate in the ownership of and
management of the industry and thereby also share in the profits"[33].

Of special doctrinal and practical importance is his affirmation
that "if the social and individual character of labour be overlooked,
it can be neither justly valued nor recompensed according to
equivalence"[34]. In determining wages therefore, justice demands
that account be taken not only of the needs of their families, but also
of the financial state of the business concern for which they work
and of the "economic welfare of the whole people".

---

33) Pius XI., Quadragesimo Anno, par. 63 - 73
34) Ibid.

c) Advantages of Just Wages:

Surely, there are advantages which are inevitable if the rules
governing the game of "wage policies" are observed. Some of these
were outlined by Pope Leo XIII [35], but we shall give a summary
of them here by naming four main advantages:

    (i)   Just wages will guarantee a wider distribution of
property which is in accordance with the "common good"
theory of the Church and also the political institutions.

    (ii)   a greater yield from the land will result, since
workers will definitely engage themselves with interest
in their work and produce their maximum best.

    (iii)   the avoidance of strikes and its attendant consequences,
since most strikes take place in the demand for more
wages and better rights of the working man. Just
wages would mean at the same time minimal strikes,
better cooperation between the various groups engaged
in the labour world, and a solidarity of all working
peoples with the state, be it of trade unions, employers
or public authority.

    (iv)   Lastly, with just wages comes naturally the love
of one's country, greased with a healthy patriotism for
the nation. Thereby, migrants leaving their nations will
drop and unnecessary sufferings for human beings will be
avoided. A healthy society will grow, since the family,
the basic political unit, will be stable and the
common good will prosper.

---

35) Leo XIII, Rerum Novarum, n. 34-35

4. Direct and Indirect Employer

To properly understand the papal pronouncements on the rights and duties of man in relation to work, particular attention must be paid to what John Paul says concerning the "direct" and "indirect" employer. This distinction, which is not without a certain originality - helps to understand more clearly how, at the present stage, the labour relationships and the worker rights are conditioned by a number of factors and external agents that intervene fully, although indirectly, in the network of responsibilities connected with the workers' rights. Such a way of presenting the problem, sheds a new light on the unemployment dilemma and makes clearer the relations of dependence existent in the labour world.

a) Definition of Terms

Who is the "direct Employer"? The "direct employer" writes Pope John Paul, is "the person or institution with whom the worker enters directly into a work contract in accordance with definite conditions"[36].

Who is the "indirect Employer"? The term "indirect employer" indicates a whole series of factors - there are so many - which exert a "determining influence on the shaping both of the work contract and, consequently, of just and unjust relationships in the field of human work"[37].

---

36) John Paul II, Laborem Exercens, n. 16
37) Ibid., n. 16

The indirect employer substantially determines one or other facet of the labour relationship, thus conditioning the conduct of the direct employer when the latter determines in concrete terms the actual work contract and labour relations. In other words, the indirect employer is the "unseen hand" behind many labour decisions. This includes collective contracts, principles of conduct established by national laws, government's labour policies, international economic and commercial connections, the rate and degree of industrialisation of various countries - especially in the third world, multinational and transnational companies, banking systems, and the whole of the world economic and financial policy. In the words of the secretary of the pontifical commission of justice and peace, "all these factors influence not only a company's or a nation's labour policy, but also the objective rights of the single worker"[38].

Hereby, we notice that the "indirect employer" as John Paul says, is "the omnipotent director" of the labour world. He warns however that this role of the indirect employer should not and does not absolve the direct employer from his own responsibility, but only helps us appreciate the complex difficulties and influences facing him in his business conduct[39]. We are thus made to know how much dependent the direct employer is on factors sometimes beyond his direct control. These factors are felt by ordinary workers in their banking systems, work contract, wages, the employment problem and a whole net of rights justly due to the worker.

---

38) "Reflections on Laborem Exercens", Address by the Secretary of the Pontifical Commission of Justice and Peace, 15.9.1981, PCJP, Vol. 9, p.7 , Press Conference, Vatican; (1982).
39) John Paul II, Laborem Exercens, n. 17

John Paul elucidates the complex economic tangles by exposing the fact that the indirect employer is everywhere to be found - in every nation, society and organisation, an influence made possible because of the inter - dependent situation of the modern world realities. Consequently, problems facing one part of the world are easily felt in other very remote parts. An actual example is the rise in oil prices due to Opec's policy of "cartelling and acting jointly", which influence has been felt in mounting inflation in many industrial goods, in the general rise of prices and sometimes in the inability of many poorer nations to pay their depts. This reality is today clearer than ever before as John Paul tries to show.

"It would be difficult to speak, in the case of any State, even the economically most powerful, of complete self-sufficiency or autarky"[40]. He elaborates more on the areas of this dependence, highlighting above all the export and import process which involve the exchange of goods such as raw materials, semi-manufactured goods, or finished products. Accepting this dependence theory as a normal phenomenon in present day world economic reality, John Paul points out that some have misused the situation and have gone into the exploitation of others. Such exploitation, says he, "influences the labour policies of individual states and individual workers who are the proper subjects of work"[41].

---

40) Ibid

41) Ibid.

He then goes on to call names, "scapegoats", who as indirect
employers are capable, and really engage in the exploitation of
others. The multinationals and transnational companies of the
industrialised nations, often, naturally fall into the temptation
as the pontiff remarks. But this should not be! Believing in
profit and big gain, the multinationals "fix the highest possible
prices for their products, while trying at the same time to fix
the lowest possible prices for raw materials or semi-manufactured
goods. This is one of the causes of an ever increasing disproportion
between national incomes. The gap between most of the richest
countries and the poorest ones is not diminishing or being stabilised
but is increasing more and more, to the detriment, obviously of the
poor countries"[42].

With this analysis of the unjust policies of the indirect employer,
specifically, the transnational companies of the industrialised
nations, the Pope shows how this complex web of multifaceted economic
relations transcends the simple national boundaries, laws and
regulations, ascending into a transcendental plane which affects
the international market and the labour policy, not only of the local
countries concerned but also of the world economy.

---

42) Ibid.

John Paul asserts: "evidently this must have an effect on local labour policy and on the workers situation in the economically disadvantaged societies. In this system, the direct employer fixes working conditions below the objective requirements of the workers, especially if he wishes to obtain the highest possible profits from the business"[43]. The individual worker is in such a system left without means to defend his rightful interests alone, and cannot enter into dialogue with his employer (indirect), or participate in decision making at a level where true cooperation resides.

The weaknesses or inefficiencies of the States, nations and workers before the "unseen and omnipotent" indirect employers calls for the voice "from the wilderness" to admonish men to sanity and call for a just, ordered and truly human - orientated labour policy for the good of the entire working world. John Paul II boldly accepts this role which has always been the function of the pontiff in the world. This function must be performed because, "the attainment of the rights of the workers cannot be doomed to be merely a result of economic systems which on a larger or smaller scale are guided chiefly by the criterion of maximum profit and the desire to have[44]. The Holy Father therefore calls on the entire world body represented in the United Nations through such organs as the International Labour Organisation, Food and Agricultural Organisation, State Ministries and other departments who control, manage and have influence as, and on indirect employers, to seek new ways to "achieve full respect for the rights of workers".

---

43) Ibid
44) Ibid

In this attempt, John Paul's aim remains as is seen throughout the encyclical on human work, the defence of the rights of the human person who is an image of God and the key element in the whole of the social moral order; he aims also at balancing the relationship between the workers and the employers, reducing the tensions existing between labour and capital, and thereby achieving a long term aim, namely, the humanisation of work. The achievement of these aims can be realised in three areas as well shall now make evident.

b) The Relationship between - Trade Unions and Employers Association:

> "In business enterprises, it is persons who associate
> together, that is, men who are free and autonomous,
> created in the image of God. Therefore, while taking into
> account the role of every person concerned - owners,
> employers, management, and employees - and without
> weakening the necessary executive unity, the active
> participation of everybody in administration is to be
> encouraged". (Gaudium et Spes, par. 68).

The appeal of the Holy Father to "direct" and "indirect" employers merits special consideration, when we consider the relationship between trade unions and employers associations. And the appeal of the Council Fathers in Gaudium et Spes quoted above, concerning the rights of workers to participate in higher level discussions goes further than simply the "cooperative" idea, seeking to give the workers a place in the deliberations of any organisation about the level of the industry. In fact, various countries have tried in various ways to ensure a more rationalised and overall cooperation of individual workers in industrial performance and in the economy as a whole. What John Paul's encyclical does is to call the attention to this practical approach, in the spirit of good will, cooperation and "right reason".

There are three attitudes which this call involves, namely - the respect for the dignity of the worker; adequate dialogue; and practical approach in policy and principles affecting both parties.

(i) Respect for the Dignity of the Worker - Gaudium et Spes made it clear that in business enterprise, "it is persons who associate together, that is free and autonomous men created in the image of God". Employers must therefore bear in mind that the dignity of its workers is paramount in all work-decisions. The firm must not treat those employees who spend their days in service with the firm as though they were mere cogs in the machinery, denying them any opportunity of freely expressing their legal wishes and views, even if it involves bringing their experience to bear on the work in hand, and keeping them entirely passive in respect to decisions that regulate their activity.

Pope John XXIII commented on this reality when he wrote in Mater et Magistra: "We are in no two minds as to the need for giving workers an active share in the business or the company for which they work - be it private or public. Every effort must be made to ensure that the community is indeed a true community of persons concerned about the needs, the activities and the standing of each of its members"[45]. Very often, decisions affecting the economic and social conditions of the workers are made, not so much within the business itself, but by institutions at a higher level who are ignorant of the situation of the common worker. Sometimes, these institutions are hundreds of miles away, and since it is on these that the future of the workers and their children depend, the latter should be allowed a say in decision-making either in person or through their representatives such as the unions.

---

45) John XXIII., Mater et Magistra, par. 65

(ii) The Call for Objective Dialogue:

The second attitude to be developed has to do with dialogue. The fundamental point in dialogue is that both sides, that is both trade unions and employers associations, should be convinced that there can ba a common truth and common good to be gained by both parties, and that dialogue would help to attain it. Dialogue however is not the question of abandoning one's faith or seeking a victory over the other. Dialogue aims basically at three things, namely:

(i) to discover and understand better the position and identity of the partner in dialogue and his ideas;

(ii) to explain one's own personal standpoint to the partner in the dialogue; and lastly,

(iii) to discover common values which will lead to attaining the common good and co-existence.

To achieve these ends, the partners in dialogue must know that dialogue assumes a common basic attitude of respect for man and a willingness to achieve a compromise from both sides. The difficulties encountered in the search should not limit the attempts, but rather enhance the search for unity. Pope Pius XI spoke out for dialogue thus: "Let employers, therefore, and employed join in plans and efforts to overcome all difficulties and obstacles, and let them be aided in their wholesome endeavour by the wise measures of the public authority. In the last extreme, counsel must be taken whether the business can continue, or whether some other provision should be made for the workers. The guiding spirit in this crucial decision should be one of mutual understanding and christian harmony between employers and workers"[46].

---

46) Pius XI., Quadragesimo Anno., par. 73

In the same way, Leo XII called for dialogue saying:
"Both workers and employers should regulate their mutual relations
in accordance with the principle of human solidarity and christian
brotherhood"[47a]. As such, unrestricted competition in the
liberal sense, and the marxist creed of class warfare, are
clearly contrary to the demands of dialogue, besides being against
man's nature. Dialogue demands that the relations between the
management and employees reflect understanding, appreciation, and good
will on both sides. It demands too, that all parties cooperate
actively and loyally in the common enterprise, not so much for
what they can get out of it for themselves, but as discharging a duty
and rendering a service to their fellow men[47].

John Paul II addressing a group of entrepreneurs in Italy demanded
that dialogue be the basis of cooperation, and called the employers
to give a hearing to the demands of their workers.
"The entrepreneur and managerial staff must do everything in their
power to give a hearing to the voice of the worker in their
employment and to understand his legitimate demands for justice
and fairness, overcoming all selfish temptations to make the
economic factor a law unto itself... Any lack of attention in this
sector is culpable, any delay fatal. So many conflicts and
antagonisms between workers and employers often have their roots in
the unproductive soil of the refusal to listen, rejection of
dialogue or undue postponement of it. Time spent meeting your
employees personally is not time wasted"[48]. Because this is so,
it is not acceptable to see enterprise or industry as one simply

---

47a) Leo XIII, Rerum Novarum, par. 36 - 40

47)   John XXIII, Mater et Magistra, par. 93

48)   John Paul II., Address to Christian Union of Entrepreneurs and
      Managers, (UCID), 24 November 1979, Ref. L'osservatore Romano,
      English Edition, 24.12.1979, Nos. 52 - 53; p.3

in which some issue orders and others take them. So long as unity of
direction is ensured, there must be some way in which all, not only
proprietors, employers and managers, but the wage earner, the trade
unions, should also have a share in management. Further, unity
of direction and dialogue demands that all should have a voice in
management and deliberations concerning the organisations of industry
and if possible, beyond it.

(iii) Applying the Policies and Principles of Social Ethics:
How this can be made possible, brings us to the third and last
attitude which should exist between employers associations and the
representatives of the workers. The first demand concerns
sharing in the ownership of the means of production. Pope John says:
"Every effort must be made that at least in future, a just share
only of the fruits of production be permitted in the hands of the wealthy,
and that an ample sufficiency be supplied to the workers"[49].
John XXIII made this point clearer where he advocated for a
participation in Shares of the companies: "We hold that the workers
should be allocated Shares in the firms for which they work, especially
when they are earning no more than the minimum wage"[50].

This participation of workers in the production process and in
ownership of shares requires of course an attitude of mind which allows
negotiations. The unions and employers must be prepared to
cooperate with one another in a positive way. Roger Charles calls
this pattern "Primary procedural norm"[51]. He maintains that it is
procedural in its concern with the "How" of collective bargaining and,
in all that involves human relations and the attitude of mind of the

---

49) John XXIII, Mater et Magistra, n.77
50) IIbid, n. 75
51) Roger Charles, The development of Industrial Relations in
     Britain, 1911 - 1939; London, (1973), p.28

parties to accept each other as necessary positively, instead of a
half-hearted and suspicion-loaded tolerance of the other. With this
situation, proper observance of agreements reached will be obeyed in
the "primary procedural norm".

The other requirement concerns "substantive agreements"[52] which must
provide satisfactory standards of wages and conditions upon which
the wages are structured, and an existing agreement covering the
provision for worker's rights including adequate health insurance,
social benefits, pensions, and the right to rest from work for a
longer period during each work year. All these require therefore
as basic condition, the method of collective bargaining and co-
operation between the unions and the employers. Such an agreement
helps to limit strikes, general damage to both parties, the industry
and the nation at large. This is as such a consequence to be followed
in theory and practice, if one wishes to avoid the conflicts
that exist in the labour field. Compatible as it is with the
social principles of Christian ethics, this moral demand and call is
as difficult as it sounds to put into practice, and the employer,
manager, worker and the unions are reminded that such difficulties
can be easily overcome, if the common aim of achieving the common
good is placed in the centre and the principles of complementary
respect for each others position is followed up with a reasonable
dialogue.

---

52) Ibid, p. 29

c) State Policy of Nations:

"The political community exists for the common good; this is
its full justification and meaning and the source of its
specific and basic right to exist. The common good embraces
the sum total of all those conditions of social life which
enable individuals, families and organisations to achieve
complete and efficacious fulfilment. It follows that the
exercise of political authority must always be carried out
within the framework of the moral order, and in pursuit of
the common good". (Gaudium et Seps, par. 74).

What is briefly stated above, covers some of the thorniest and most
complex problems in political theory and organisation. This is so
because many political communities have understood the common good
to mean different things. And sometimes, while using policies
which oppress the common good, they present this as in order, thereby
leaving politologists with the dilemma of what is really the common
good. Another problem concerns the fact that many political authorities
and communities came into being in so many different ways as historical
data teaches us. Infact some States came to birth by natural
evolution of a people, some by conquest or revolution, and some by a
mixture of all three.

Attempting to solve the details of these problems escapes the
scope and stuff of this thesis. What is important for our research is
the council's view of the fundamental reason why we establish
political societies. On this matter it is clearly positive. We set up
political communities because we want to find a fuller life through
them. The view of the proper use of political power is also clear
for the framework of the moral order "established by God", the natural
law and the law of the Gospel, which are the demands made by the Church
on all political institutions.

Failing to accept this criteria might lead to a misuse of the
citizens, a neglect of their rights, and as such, a reaction from
the citizens themselves in action of self defence against
government subjection. If the individual and family precede the
state and are given their essential rights and freedoms by God, then
the state may never demand of them a loyalty which acts contrary
to the law of God, or try to remove their rights without incurring
opposition both from the Church and the citizens.

Our task in the following passages is to briefly make clear,
in the light of the preceeding chapters, what the state policy of
nations should be. Pope John Paul II does not introduce anything new
into the subject, but enhances and repeats the earlier teachings of the
magisterium and theologians on the subject.
Jesus taught his disciples and hearers to give to Caesar what is
Caesar's and to God what is God's, a lesson emphatically
repeated by St. Paul and St. Peter in their various epistles[53].

It is not therefore a question of whether the Church recognises
the legitimacy and necessity of the state. It is rather a question
of asking the state to consider the purpose of its existence and
to keep the common good always in the middle of its policy.
St. Thomas Aquinas made this point clear writing that "as for the
state, its whole raison d'etre is the realisation of the common good in
the temporal order. It cannot therefore hold aloof from economic
matters. On the contrary, it must do all in its power to promote
the production of sufficient supplies of material goods, the use of
which is necessary for the practice of virtue"[54].

---

53) Mt. 22: 21; Romans 13: 1 - 4; I Peter 2: 13 - 17;
54) St. Thomas Aquinas, De regimine princip-um., 1:15.

Translated into concrete terms, this exhortation on the state
means that both on national and international levels of action,
policies are to be taken which lead to the good of everybody and
contribute to world peace. The workers, women, children and the
rights of the entire citizens must be protected and promoted.
Terms of employment, the influence of the direct and indirect
employers and the labour relationships are to be regulated and
based on justice and equity, preventing harm to the material or
spiritual well-being of the workers, and making it possible that
their human dignity is not trampled upon [55].

Pope John XXIII considered what this demand called "common good"
means both on the national level and the international level.
On the national level, the demands of the common good include,
"the employment of the greatest number of workers, care for the less
priviledged classes - also among the workers; the maintenance
of equilibrium between wages and prices; the need to make goods and
services accessible to the greatest number; the elimination, or
at least the restriction, of inequalities in the various branches
of the economy, that is, between agriculture, industry and services;
the creation of a development of social services; the best possible
adjustment of the means of production to the progress of science
and technology; the need to make the prosperity of a more human
way of life available, not only to the present but to coming
generations as well"[56].

---

55) John XXIII, Mater et Magistra, n. 20 - 21; Leo XIII, Rerum   Novarum,
    n. 26 - 35
56) John XXIII., Mater et Magistra., n. 78 - 81

These basic ideals enunciated by the pontiff need hardly any more comment for they are so clear and pinpointed. Important however is to ment—ion that to achieve these noble aims which the state should pursue in its policy, individual citizens should be called in to participate in the structuring of the economy. Experience, especially in the industrialised nations of the world has shown that, where personal initiative is not guaranteed by the state, political tyranny is not far-fetched, and in addition, economic stagnation can set in because the individuals do not see themselves fulfilled in a system that does not guarantee their personal initiative and free enterprise.

At the same time, we must add that where the state does not use its good offices to establish equitable distribution of scarce goods, disorder ensues; the state must particularly act with its laws against unscrupulous exploiters of the weak, who are always around to use the slightest opportunity against their fellow citizens.

It should be engaged in the economy as a regulating force, always willing to see that just distribution of goods among the citizens takes place, and making it impossible that extreme poverty and excessive richness or squander should exist side by side. The council described this situation thus: "In the midst of huge numbers deprived of the absolute necessities of life, there are some who live in riches and squander their wealth... luxury and misery exist side by side. While a few individuals enjoy an almost unlimited opportunity to choose for themselves, the vast majority have no chance whatever of exercising their personal initiative and responsibility, and quite often have to work and live in conditions unworthy of human beings"[57].

---

57) Gaudium et Spes., par. 63

What does the state policy of nations demand as necessary for the common good on the international level? Simply put, a narrowing of the gap or contrast existing between economically more advanced countries and the third world nations[58]. This unhealthy situation is created mainly through unfair competition and lack of collaboration or good will for the developing nations. Paul VI in his encyclical on fostering the development of peoples, called for certain policies in this area. He calls for equity in trade relations, fair contract and the avoidance of international competition which automatically places certain nations in the loosing arena[59]. He calls for a world fund otherwise spent on armaments to be used towards the health, intellectual and moral development of peoples, instead of using them to cause wars and to engage in ideological squabblings[60]. Active participation as a social worker in development aid projects in its various aspects is called for[61], including the acceptance to pay higher taxes to the public authorities, or higher prices for imported goods, so that the producer may be justly rewarded[62].

Important though the economic development is, it is not the only or indeed the main indicator of progress from undervelopment. In the words of Paul VI : "development cannot be limited alone to mere economics... It must be complete ... promote the good of everyman, of the whole man - materially, intellectually and spiritually"[63].

---

58) Ibid.

59) John XXIII., Ibid

60) Paul VI., Populorum Progressio, par. 56 - 61

61) Ibid., par. 48 - 54

62) Ibid., par. 47

63) Ibid., par. 14 - 17

Finally on the national and international levels,
subsidiarity as a principle must be observed. Propounded first in
its latest form by Pius XI, the principle of subsidiary function
maintains that "just as it is wrong to withdraw from the
individual and commit to a group what private enterprise and industry
can accomplish, so too it is an injustice, a grave evil and a
disturbance of right order, for a larger and higher association to
arrogate to itself functions which can be performed efficiently
by smaller and lower societies"[64]. Of its very nature, the
true aim of all social activity should be to help members of the
social body, but never to destroy or to absorb them. Put in other
words, "a large and more powerful group must never absorb or
displace a smaller one so long as the latter can act efficiently
on its own".

The above then is an outline of what Catholic ethics expects in
the state policy of nations locally and internationally. The central
fact concerns the common good which refers to "all the conditions of
social life by which men can more fully and readily attain their
personal perfection and fulfilment".

---

64)   Pius XI., Quadragesimo Anno., AAS, XXIII, 1931, p.203

d) International Organisations

(i) The International Labour Organisation (ILO):

The International Labour Organisation is an official international
institution affiliated with the United Nations, but existing even
before the formation of the UN. Historically, the peace
conference of Paris in 1919, fearful of social revolutions among the
populace, set up a commission for international labour legislating
headed by Samuel Gompers, who was then the president of the
American Federation of Labour. The commission acted according to
expectation, and put aside the more ambitious claims for a body with
powers of recommendation to national governments for action by them, in
composition of a tripartite body in which half the representation
would be by government, and one-fourth each by labour and employers[65].

The peace conference adopted these proposals and, by inserting
them in the Treaty of Versailles, thereby set up the ILO.
The ILO was concerned in its first decade primarily with research
efforts destined to promote proper minimum standards of labour
legislation for adoption among member states. They spent time too on
"mutual education programmes" and some form of collaboration among
workers, employers, government delegates and office professional
staff. During the 1930's, the ILO sought ways to combat worldwide
unemployment and economic depression, which unfortunately helped
political adventurists to come up to power and plunge the entire
world in the second world war. During this time, the ILO proposed
extensive international public works, but national decision makers
did not pay heed to it[66].

---

65) Leland Mathew Goodrich; United Nations, article in Encyclopadia
    Brittanica, Vol. 18, /1768), 1982, p. 900
66) Ibid.

   (Besides the International organisations mentioned in detail here,
   we might also add the existence of many other organs of this world
   body interested in securing a fair and balanced relationship between
   nations such as the World Bank, OECD, GATT, and the Lome Convention).

After 1945, the "cold war" followed by the break-up of
European colonial empires, and the claims of the developing nations
placed new tasks in the foreground for an organisation the
membership of which was no longer chiefly that of European,
economically developed states, but increasingly that of the less
developed states. Thus, emphasis was shifted by the ILO to the
area of human rights and to technical assistance, besides the
labour world of negotiations, especially in favour of the countries
in Africa, Asia and South America. It's ideal also moved over to
"Universality of membership". So many countries are today members
of the ILO and by the end of 1971, its membership was 119 nations.
As an organ of the United Nations, the ILO is represented in many
countries with its offices.

The main institute for labour studies is in Geneva, Switzerland,
opened in 1962, and concerned primarily with leadership training for
poorer countries. Offices in Turin engage in vocational training
for different types of enterprise, including co-operatives in the nations
of the third world. The Vatican has intimate connections and interest in
the activities of the ILO, and pays adequate tribute to its activities.

John Paul II, while addressing the 68th session of the
International Labour Conference confirmed this fact where he said:
"If I ventured the International Labour Organisation in
my Encyclical Laborem Exercens[67], I did so both to draw attention to
its many achievements and to encourage it to strenghten its activities
aimed at making work more human... in efforts to give human labour a
truly moral basis consistent with the objective principles of social
ethics, the aims of the ILO are very close to those which the Church
and the Apostolic See are pursuing in their own sphere, with means
adapted to their mission"[68].

---

67) John Paul II, Laborem Exercens, n. 11. Here John Paul speaks
of "the entirely creative, educational and meritorious
character of man's work, the many labour codes prepared by
legislative institutions, and the specialised agency of the
UNO, the ILO devoting their scientific and social activity to the
problems of work".
68) John Paul II, Address to the ILO, 15.6.1982, Geneva,
(Cf. CTS, 1982/7, London, op.cit., p.280).

John Paul goes further to refer to several occasions when his
predecessors expressed greetings and cooperation with the ILO,
referring especially to Pope PIUS XII, John XXIII and Paul VI, who
himself participated in 1969 in the fiftieth anniversary
celebrations of the founding of the ILO; thereafter, he refers to the
fact that the Holy See culminated its support for the organisation
by accrediting in 1967 a permanent observer to the International
Labour organisation.

But why this great recognition for the ILO? John Paul finds
the answer in the unity of objectives of both institutions.
This concerns the area of social justice. "Following its creation in
1919, it undertook to contribute to lasting peace through the
promotion of social justice, as stated by the opening words of the
Preamble to its Constitution: "Whereas universal and lasting peace
can be established only if it is based on social justice..."
The Papal Commission 'Iustitia et Pax' has also this injunction on
its parchment, 'Si vis pacem cole iustitiam' - 'if you want peace,
cultivate justice"[69].

Over and above this identity in social principles, the merits of the
ILO shine forth in its many international Conventions and
Recommendations in respect to international labour standards, so that
Paul VI had to refer to these "new rules of social conduct" to compel
'particular interests to submit to the wider vision of the common good"[70].

---

69) Ibid.
70) Paul VI, Address at the ILO on the fiftieth anniversary of the
    foundation of the ILO, Geneva, 10, June 1969, (CTS, London,
    1982/7, p. 280).

Other areas where the activities of the ILO are seen include the
many activities aimed at satisfying the new needs to which the
evolution of social and economic structure has given rise. They
are finally, reflected in the persistent day-to-day efforts of
the officials of the International Labour Office, and the bodies
it has created to strenghten its activities, such as the
International Institute for Labour Studies, the International Social
Association and the International Centre for Teaching and
Vocational training[71].

The Pontiff feels obliged to express accord and recognition of the
ILO like JOhn XXIII did in 1961. He wrote in Mater et Magistra:
"We must also express here our heartfelt appreciation of the work
that is being done by the International Labour Organisation.
For many years now, it has been making an effective and valued
contribution to the establishment in the world of an economic and
social order marked by justice and humanity, an order which
recognises and safeguards the lawful rights of the working classes"[72].

No wonder that John Paul prays openly for the ILO, speaking on
behalf of the Apostolic See, the Church and the Christian faith.
He prays that the work of the ILO as well as efforts of the workers,
may go on "promoting the dignity of human labour and genuine human
progress", and he ends up with a wish: "May yours be a tireless
contribution to the building up of a civilisation of human labour,
a civilisation of solidarity, and - even more than that - a
civilisation of human love, that man may truly fulfil his destiny as a
human being, as preordained by Eternal wisdom and Eternal Love"[73].

---

71) Ibid
72) John XXIII, Mater et Magistra, n. 103
73) John Paul II, Address to ILO, op.cit, p.291.

(ii) The United Nations Food and Agriculture Organisation (FAO) :

The Food and Agriculture Organisation (FAO), the first of the
permanent specialised agencies of the United Nations to be
founded after World War II, came into formal existence in
October 1945 with the signing of its constitution at a conference
held in Quebec city. The immediate factor leading to its
foundation was the Conference of Food and Agriculture convened at
the request of the president of the United States,
Franklin D. Roosevelt at Hot Springs, Virginia in 1943. In
1951 the organisation was transferred from its temporary
headquarters in Washington, D.C., to a permanent seat in Rome.

The ideas underlying the foundation of the new organisation came
from two sources. First was the International Institute of
Agriculture founded in Rome in 1905. The IIA had been designed
to protect farmers against the effects of sudden slumps and
gluts and was therefore, concerned with information about market
trends and agricultural statistics[74]. A second reason
concerned the League of Nations, which in the period immediately
before the second world war, had been interested in problems
of nutrition and their relationship to health. Both the IIA and
the League, however, had been principally concerned with the more
advanced countries, whereas in the foundation of the Food and
Agricultural Organisation, several of the new and developing
countries took great interest and played an active part. Since
the formation of the FAO was partly an answer to the problems
caused by the second world war, that of feeding vast
populations in countries especially disrupted by the shattering

---

74) Leland Mathew Goodrich., op.cit., p.901-2

economic effects of the war, it was natural that the first few years
should be devoted to trying to help bring about a rapid increase
in the world's overall supplies of food. At the same time, the
member countries had an eye on the possible emergence of surpluses
of some commodities in certain countries should the distribution
system break down or should needy governments not be able to pay
for the food they required.

Finally, an appreciation of the rapid rise in population in
virtually all parts of the world in the immediate postwar period
added urgency to the organisation's activities.
The FAO has a wide range of projects which include agriculture,
nutrition, fisheries, widespread plant and animal control schemes,
such as, the desert locust-control program in the Arabian Peninsula;
Other projects include the eradication of rinderpest, creation of
a European Commission for the control of food-and-mouth disease, a
broad educational programme, training centres and seminars on
subjects concerning food, agriculture and health, coupled with
technical assistance aid to developing nations.

The Council Fathers at Vatican II recognised these problems
facing several economically retarded regions. Vast country estates
are left uncultivated because the majority of people have no
land like it happens mainly in latin America, or have only the
smallest plots to cultivate, all this, when an increase of

productivity is evidently urgent. In the same continent, as indeed elsewhere, those who are employed by landlords to till land rented from landlords are given a wage, or keep, unworthy of men, not decently housed, or they are exploited by middlemen. As is the case in South Africa, blace workers lacking all security, live like serfs that they have practically no chance of acting freely and responsibly because they are debarred from all cultural development or participation in social and political life. "A variety of reforms are therefore required: wage increases, better working conditions, greater security of employment, incentives to work willingly, the redistribution of insufficiently cultivated estates among those able to make them productive"[75].

With the 1970's, developed countries as a whole had a calorie intake of 16% above established standards, while the under-developed countries had 2% below standard[76]. Life expectance was 71 to 48 years at the time.

Recently, the General Secretary of the United Nations, Javier Perez De Cuellar said that the failure to eradicate hunger and malnutrition represented the gravest of the economic and social problems facing the world. "Death from hunger claims thirty (30) young lives every minute", he pointed out [77]. A really shocking information in a world where affluence is still to be found in squandering proportions.

---

75) Gaudium st Spes, par. 71

76) Roger C., op. cit., p. 336 - 7

77) Perez De Cuellar, In "West Africa" No. 3474, 19. March 1983, London, Editor, Kaye Whiteman, p. 621.

With this background, the Food and Agriculture Organisation sets
out with the aim to make greater self-reliance in food as the key
to world food security and stability. But there still remains a
long way to go, as there is still a large gap in food aid
requirements. Many nations lie in the Sahel regions, without water and
food, but with sufficient armaments to fight tribal wars. The
food supply situation of about twenty-four African states exposes the
gravity of the hunger problematic. In this connection, the
Director General of the FAO, Edouard Saouma, speaking recently in
Rome, appealed to the world conscience for aid, emphasising that

> "a significant proportion of the combined population of
> over 150 million people in the 24 African Countries is
> threatened by massive hunger and starvation as a
> result of prolonged drought and other natural and man-made
> causes. In about half of these countries there are well over
> 1.2 million refugees who are among the people most affected
> by the present food crisis"[78].

He confirms that a number of governments from thirty countries
have made substantial increases in their food aid allocations
or are in the process of doing so, but supplies must arrive
immediately to alleviate the suffering masses.

It is this sort of social and economic action that the Vatican
supports. Infact, on 6th March 1984, the Vatican announced the
establishment of a foundation to fight hunger in the eight drought
stricken Sahel countries; the foundation, named "pope John Paul II
Foundation for the Sahel", will concentrate on training local
experts and carry out small development projects. Its initial
budget is raised from funds coming from Roman Catholic churches
in the Federal Republic of Germany, who have already donated about
nine million dollars[79].

---

78) Ibid., (The same report quoted)
79) Ibid.

Infact, Pope John Paul II had occasion to address the
United Nations Food and Agricultural Organisation [80] and to have
made the basic point that his thinking aims at reflecting
upon in a coherent way, namely, "the cause of man, his dignity
and the inalienable rights flowing therefrom". It is
this same aim that the FAO pursues, and for that reason contributes
in no small measure, towards putting into practice, what the
social encyclicals have always called for - namely, a healthy
man in a healthy soul with a healthy body.

---

80) John Paul II, Address to the ILO, op.cit., p.281

(iii) United Nations Educational, Scientific and Cultural Organisation:

UNESCO's activities were intended primarily to be facilitative, through conferences, publications, seminars and through the promotion of research and exchange of information and knowledge, and through technical advisory services, to support, assist and complement the efforts of individual member states.

By the end of the 1970's, developed countries as a whole had a literacy rate of 97% opposed to the underdeveloped countries which had barely 50% literacy[81]. Living in abject poverty and ignorance, many of the world's peoples are not fully sharing in the common good of this world, outlined by the Council to be the possession of all the earth's children.

The Unesco's significance is however limited in the life of many nations. Even the allocation of the total budgets among the neediest members would provide small amounts compared to what is spent by the countries themselves.

In 1945, membership in this organisation was registered to be forty five, but since the 1970's, membership has reached one hundred and twenty seven. A crisis hovers today over this institution of the United Nations as the United States of America threatens to quit the institution. Somehow, the suspicion is ripe that the Unesco has become a platform for ideological misuse, since the power blocs in East and West

---

81) Roger, C; op cit., p. 336

compete with each other on what should be taught where, and which scientific and cultural programmes should be accepted or rejected in the programme. Initially however, emphasis was placed upon strenghtening international culture; establishing clearing houses for the exchange of information, and promoting international professional conferences of scholarly abstracts, symposia, seminars; assistance for developing public library resources in certain emerging countries; fellowships for study in more highly developed areas of the technical world, and basic projects in so-called fundamental education.

Obviously, the Church's interest in such an organisation can easily be understood, since it represents an institution where men of academic standing can meet each other to exchange views on scientific, cultural and intellectual topics. For the Church, the Unesco can become a platform for preaching the gospel of universal love, solidarity and the rights of the workers.

5. Conclusion

There are many who have questioned the legitimacy, nay, the effectiveness of the United Nations and its organs in settling international problems. Critique abounds where the UNO is labelled "a toothless bull dog", or "big for nothing". People believe that it is a "forum for the squander of money without any concrete achievements, except that men in well dressed attire come together, assemble to drink tea and chat, write noble communiques and express wooly condemnations of systems opposed to man". This criticism must not be left unchallenged. Not only does it water-down the real issues, it does not offer any better alternative.

The Papal approval of the United Nations and its organs does not involve an obligation on all Catholics to agree with the assessment it makes of this institution. On such practical matters, says Roger Charles, "we have to make up our minds and political judgements individually. What is incumbent on Christians and all men of good will as a matter of moral principle, is the search for a better world order, and an effective means of supra-national government which respects the rights of individual nations while supplying those services for all nations that they cannot provide for themselves"[82].

---

82) Roger C., op.cit., p. 260

In a world of today, no nation can independently live alone without the others. Interdependence has become absolutely necessary and this is not only reasonable but it is a "conditio sine qua non". If we are exasperated with the United Nations and its organs, we should be seeking better alternatives, not contending ourselves only with criticisms of this institution and its obvious defects and weaknesses. At the present however, it is not apparent that any such alternative to the UNO exists, nor have we grounds to claim that the near future will bring us another organisation.

We are thus challenged to make better use of the UNO, and see it as a starting point, a necessary institution and the only concrete form presently in the world towards creating a more effective future for mankind, and for all nations and peoples.

PART TWO (II)

SPECIAL GROUPS OF WORKERS

1. Women and Work

In chapter IV of "laborem exercens," where the Holy Father talks of
the rights of workers, he devotes sub-sections of his writing to
agricultural workers, the disabled, migrant workers, but it is
surprising that he does not devote a sub-section to the problem
of women and work. Rather, women are considered alongside other
topics under: "wages a   other social benefits ". This is however
not a neglect. The problem of women was always specially treated
by him in various speeches outside the encyclical, and in
various areas within the encyclical itself. He puts an emphasis
on the family life as a natural right and vocation of the human
person, and thereby considers under it the role of women and
mothers, without whom a family cannot be possible.

Women merit pastoral concern in John Paul's teaching because they
play an important role in the family. It is family life that
pre-occupies the Pope when he observes that the woman's role as a
mother is subject to discrimination in some sectors of society
and in certain feminist circles. He refers to women when he talks
of the hardship of human work, saying: "It is familiar to
women, who, sometimes without proper recognition on the part of
society and even of their own families, bear the daily burden and
responsibility for their homes and the upbringing of their children"[1].

---

1)   John Paul II., Laborem Exercens, op.cit., n. 9

And when he talks of the family, like in a sermon he delivered
in his native Poland on his first official visit as Pope, he does
not fail to mention the role of motherhood as essential for women.

> "The reason for the family is one of the fundamental
> factors determining the economy and policy of work.
> These keep their ethical character when they take into
> consideration the needs and the rights of the family.
> Through work, the adult human being must earn the
> means needed to maintain his family. Motherhood must
> be treated in work policy and economy as a great end
> and a great task in itself... giving birth, feeding and
> rearing, and no one can take her place in the home.
> True respect for work brings with it due esteem for
> motherhood. It cannot be otherwise. The moral health
> of the whole of society depends on that"[2].

In accordance with the teaching of his predecessors, Pius XII
and Paul VI, and with Vatican II, John Paul confirms that it is
the Church's glory to have highlighted the equal dignity of man
and woman, both as human beings and his children of God; to
have liberated women from a state of degrading slavery contrary
to nature; and to have reaffirmed the right and duty of both man
and woman to contribute to the economy of the common welfare.
On many occasions, he exhalts the spouse, mother and woman at work
in her multiple activities in the family, industry and agriculture.

---

2) John Paul II., Homily at mass for workers at Jasna Gora,
    (Poland), 6 June 1979; L'osservatore Romano, english edition,
    16.7.1979. No. 29, pp. 3 - 4.

Pius XII wrote in 1945: "Woman has to contribute with man to the good of the "civitas", in which she is in dignity equal with him. Either sex must take the part that belongs to it according to its nature, characteristics, physical, intellectual and moral capabilities. Both have the right and duty to cooperate for the total good of society. However it is clear that if man is by temperament more inclined to deal with exterior affairs, public activities, woman has, generally speaking, greater insight and finer tact to know and solve the delicate problems of domestic and family life, the basis of all social life, which does not prevent some women showing great skill also in every field of public activity"[3].

Commenting on this passage, which has become the traditional position of Popes when they talk about women, many people are of the opinion that such assertions portray nothing less than "male chauvinism". Leo XIII was even more direct on this issue. He wrote:

> "Work which is quite suitable for a strong man cannot
> rightly be required from a woman or child... Women are
> not suited for certain occupations; a woman is by nature
> fitted for home work, and it is that which is best adapted
> at once to preserve her modesty and to promote the good
> bringing-up of children and the well-being of the family"[4].

---

3) Pius XII; Address of 21 October 1945; Quoted in Vol. 5 of
   "The Social Teaching of John Paul II, Pontifical Commission
   "Iustitia et Pax", Vol. 5, Vatican City, 1982, p.25 (Cf.Paul VI,
   AAS, 67 (1975) refers to the passage to the Interventions for the
   international Year of Women).
4) Leo XIII., Rerum Novarum. n.33 (Today, the Feministic Women groups
   blame the role of the church as partly responsible for the lowly
   position of women in society).

Really hard words, unpalatable for women liberation movements, but these are the words which have led to so many decisions concerning women both within the Church and also without, in the various cultures.

John Paul rightly remarks that this demand made of women is a "sacrifice, a humble and monotonous work, but a heroic work too". It is however not enough consolation for women who have emerged in our century as emancipated people, equal to men in all competitive levels, and no more prepared to play the domestic role which men assigned to them earlier, calling it like Leo XIII did, "a natural order".

a) The Attitude of Jesus to Women

Of particular interest in our consideration of women and work is to meditate on the attitude put up by Jesus Christ himself towards women. From the accounts of the New Testament writers, Jesus is portrayed as bold and progressive, very open and tolerant towards women, when one considers the historical and cultural determinants at the beginning of this millenium in Israel and beyond. Women in those times were considered in paganism, but somehow too in Judaism as "possessions, labourers, domestic beings, objects of pleasure, rearer of children. They were subordinated and humiliated in Judaism"[5].

---

5) John Paul, Address to Italian Professional Association of family Collaborators, API - COLF; 24 April 1979, L'osservatore Romano, english edition, 14. May 1979, No. pp. 2- 4.

Jesus always showed the greatest esteem and the greatest respect for woman, for every woman, and in particular he was sensitive to female suffering. Going beyond the social and religious barriers of the time, he re-established woman in her full dignity as a human person before God and man. Otherwise how else do we understand his friendship and sympathy for Martha and Mary [6], how do we recall the meeting with the Samaritan women [7], with the widow of Nain [8], with the adulterous woman brought to him for condemnation by the Tewish hypocrites [9]?

Jesus's attitude towards the sufferings of women and his sympathy for them, his respect for then and an acknowledgement of their worth and dignity are further manifested when we meditate on his healing of the woman who suffered from a haemorrhage [10], with the sinner at the house of Simon the Pharisee [11], and even in the company of his closeest followers, the disciples were women who associated with him and helped the twelve [12]. They accompanied him and served him, and were of comfort to him during the painful way to the cross. And after the resurrection, Jesus appeared to the Holy women and to Mary Magdalene, bidding her announce his resurrection from the dead to his disciples [13].
Above all however, is the case of Mary, a woman who by God's providence became the mother of Jesus, and raised to the dignity of "mother of God Incarnate, Queen of Heaven and of Earth".

---

6) Luke 10:38 - 42
7) John 4:1 - 42
8) Luke 7:11 - 17
9) Jôhn 8:3 - 9
10) Mathew 9:20 - 22,
11) Luke 7: 36 - 50
12) Luke 8: 2 - 3
13) Mathew 28:8

Jesus was a liberator, a sympathisant of woman raising them to
their true dignity.

b) The Attitude of John Paul II to Women

John Paul II tries to follow in the footsteps of Jesus for in an
address to family collaborators in Italy, he stated that
only in the footsteps of Christ can we find true fulfilment
and be sure that we are on the right way.   This reality is
made eloquent where the Pope says: "I say to you: let your
ideal be the dignity of woman and her mission! It is sad to see
how woman has been so humiliated and ill-treated in the course
of the centuries. Yet we must be convinced that the dignity of
man, as of woman, is only found completely and exhaustively in Christ"[14].

With this statement, John Paul shows that as children of God, man and
woman are absolutely equal, as also with regard to the ultimate
purpose of human life, which is eternal union with God.   In
Christ, all men, irrespective of age and sex find salvation and
equality. However, the Pope emphasises that there are roles which
each person plays to bring about the good of the common society, namely
the family. A woman's role should be primarily that of motherhood.

Motherhood does not mean that women cannot work where they
are fitting and capable. As long as this does not conflict with
her role in the family, a woman has all the freedom which the

---

14) John Paul II, Address to Italian Professional Assoc.,
     op.cit.

labour world offers and all the rights or duties ensuing from it.
He writes:

> "It is a fact that in many societies women work in
> nearly every sector of life. But it is fitting that they
> should be able to fulfil their tasks in accordance with
> their own nature, without being discriminated against
> and without being excluded from jobs for which they are
> capable, but also without lack of respect for their
> family aspirations and for their specific role in
> contributing, together with men, to the good of the society"[15].

Added to the above, John Paul has another perspective which helps
us to assess his attitude towards women. "The true advancement of
women requires that labour should be structured in such a way that
women do not have to pay for their advancement by abandoning what
is specific to them and at the expense of family, in which women
as mothers have an irreplaceable role"[16].

John Paul's view is that of one who is concerned with the
upbringing of children and the balanced ordering of the structure of
the human family according to traditional norms. In many
patriarchal societies, (to which the Church belongs) women placed
the role of mothers, carers of the home and the kitchen, and
John Paul does not see why this should no more be the case. If
it is because of finance, the Pope sends word to the organisers
of labour, the State' policy of Nations, direct and indirect
employers, and all those concerned in the world of labour and of

---

15) John Paul II, Laborem Exercens, n.19
16) Ibid.

women to give the role of women priority in their labour
structures. There must be a re-evaluation of the mother's role,
of the toil connected with it, and of the need that children
have for care, love and affection in order that they may develope
into' responsible, morally and religiously mature and
psychologically stable persons! For John Paul, there is the strong
feeling that society has everything to gain if they support
strongly the role of a mother financially and otherwise, instead of
leaving her to the vicissitudes of an insecure economic life,
thereby abandoning her primary care for children. In such a case,
many women who feel insecure would even abandon marriage, abandon
giving birth to children, and surely society might have some
trouble with the future of the human race. This on the other hand does
not mean indiscriminate birth of children without any responsible
parenthood. Says the Pope,

> "it will redound to the credit of society to make it
> possible for a mother - without inhibiting her freedom,
> without psychological or practical discrimination, and
> without penalising her as compared with other women -
> to devote herself to taking care of her children and
> educating them in accordance with their needs, which may
> vary with age. Having to abandon these tasks in order
> to take up paid work outside the home is wrong from
> the point of view of the good of society and of the
> family when it contradicts or hinders these primary goals
> of the mission of a mother"[17].

---

17) John Paul II, LE, Ibid.

From the above, we can see that John Paul insists on the irreplaceable role of mother in the family and society, and asks that labour structures respect these roles, enhancing it and thereby raising the dignity of women.

Moderate and hard criticisms have been expressed on these views of John Paul, as well as those of his predecessors. There is first of all the accusation that he understands the role of motherhood as that which condemns a woman to spend her life in the kitchen, at home, in washing and in domestic activities. It is said that he wishes to keep the woman tied to the home as if this were the only vocation for her, of course with the normal argument that it corresponds to the nature of women.

A second criticism is the fact already projected by many women supporters today, that a man can also stay at home and take care of the children, while the woman goes to work. It has been practised in many situations, and in many cultures and countries, and really, men have also proved that they can do the same work which the woman does in the home.

Why then this insistence that the woman should do the domestic work of the family, and the man the external? Many women who are engaged in external activities have also proved to be more competent than many men, in their managing of the affairs of the State and other related public responsibilities. In many countries today, women are heads of State, ministers and official representatives of their nations in international and national levels.

A third criticism to the papal insistence on the role of
women at home looks down on domestic activities. It is argued
that work in the home is degrading, unfulfilling and sometimes
dehumanising. The orthodox view that women should stay at home
is looked upon as another form of "male chauvinism" which
believes in doing the better job, and leaving the dirty job
to women.

Surely, arguments of this type cannot be shoved away by a wave
of the hand. Not only that they are constructive, they
are also reasonable and serious, and threaten in core, the
postulations of the pontifical teachings on the role of women in the
labour world. We can only add here that on both sides of the
issue, there are positive and negative elements, and history is
daily in the making that we can hardly with all definitiveness
give either party a total support.

It is perhaps necessary to make a reference to the defence put
up by John Paul to the last criticism dealing with domestic work,
where he defends it and looks at it as not degrading, but elevating.
Domestic work, says the Pope, must not be seen as an implacable
and inexhorable imposition, a form of slavery, but as a free choice,
responsible and willed, which completely fulfils woman in her
personality and requirements. Domestic work, in fact, is an
essential part in the smooth running of society and has an
enormous influence upon society[18].

---

18) John Paul II; Address to Italian Professional Association of
    family collaborators, op.cit.

He then goes on to talk to women directly on the dignity of
domestic workers and of work itself in its subjective dimension,
since man stands behind each work, and work, all work has a
dignity, since it is the fruit of man - "the image of God".
John Paul said on this issue: "Domestic work gives rise to the
dignity of your work as family collaborators; your commitment
is not a humiliation but a consecration!

It is a great task, one could almost say a mission... called
"pedagogy of fatigue" which makes it possible to organise one's
services better... I praise therefore all women engaged in
domestic activity"[19].

---

19) Ibid.

2. Agricultural Workers

> "The men who till the land: it is precisely they who
> in fact, feed us. For this reason, they deserve our
> constant gratitude and we owe them lasting memory for
> their work. Respect for their profession requires not
> only that it should find social recognition, but that
> it should also bring farmers due remuneration and create
> adequate conditions for their sustenance and the
> maintenance of their families" -
> (John Paul II, At Angelus, 11,11. 1979, PCJP, Vol.5, p.58).

The Apostolic See has dedicated a great deal of attention to the
areas of agricultural work, and spoken out often in defence of
farmers. This is testified by pontifical documents of great
importance, especially in the writings of Leo XIII and John XXIII[20].

In this section, I shall consider under four perspectives, the
role of agricultural workers and their dignity; then I shall
consider the problems of agricultural workers; attempt a guideline
towards a solution of these problems in accordance with the Social
Principles of the Church; and finally offer with John Paul II, an
attitude which farmers should also have towards their work and
towards the land which they cultivate.

---

20) Leo XIII, Rerum Novarum; John XXIII, Mater et Magistra.

a) Dignity of Agricultural Work and the Rights of Workers:

John Paul II, while continuing his enumeration of the rights of
workers in chapter four of "Laborem Exercens" discusses the dignity
due to agricultural work, a dignity which is to be understood in the
objective and subjective dimensions. For him, the area of agriculture
is a vast sector uniting entire mankind, "not restricted to one or
other continent, not limited to the societies which have already
attained a certain level of development and progress"[21]
Farm work is known to man, in all cultures, in all places and at
all times.

It has to, because on the fruits of agriculture depends man's life,
subsistence and existence on earth. Says the Pontiff:
"the world of agriculture, which provides society with the goods it
needs for its daily subsistence, is of fundamental importance"[22].

In the work of the farm the human personality finds every incentive
for self-expression, self-development and spiritual growth. It
is a work, therefore, which should be thought of as a vocation, as
a God-given mission. For John XXIII, it should be thought of also
as a noble task, undertaken with a view to raising oneself and
others to a higher degree of civilisation[23].

---

21) John Paul II., Laborem Exercens, n.21
22) Ibid.,
23) John XXIII; Mater et Magistra, n. 149

While addressing Indios and peasants at Cuilapan, Mexico during
his first official visit to that vast continent, John Paul II
did not mix words, but very clearly, like his predecessors, give
credit to the dignity of agricultural work, a work which today,
is often looked upon as infradig, dirty and for primitive people.
He said:

> "the agricultural world has great importance and great
> dignity. It is just this world that offers society the
> products necessary for its nutrition. It is a task that
> deserves the appreciation and grateful esteem of all, which
> is a recognition of those engaged in it"[24].

But where does this dignity lie? Simply put,
their dignity lies in the fact that

> "they are living in close harmony with nature - the
> majestic example of creation. Their work has to do with
> the life of plants and animals, a life that is
> inexhaustible in its expression, inflexible in its laws,
> rich in allusions to God the Creator and Provider. They
> produce food for the support of human life, and the raw
> materials in ever richer supply"[25].

As such, it is a dignity that can and must increase with the contemplation of God, contemplation encouraged by contact with nature,
reflection of the divine action which looks after the grass in the
fields, makes it grow, nourishes it; which makes the land fertile,
sending it rain and wind, so that it may feed also animals which help
man, as we read at the beginning of the book of Genesis[26].

---

24) John Paul II., Address to Indios and Peasants at Cuilapan,
    Mexico, 29 January 1979, Cf. L'osservatore Romano, english
    Edition, 12.2.1979, No. 7, p.7
25) JOhn XXIII, Ibid; 144
26) Genesis 1: 29 - 31.

John XXIII maintained that agricultural work carries with it a
dignity all its own. It brings into its service many branches
of engineering, chemistry and biology, and is itself a cause
of the continued practical development of these sciences, in view
of the repercussions of scientific and technical progress on the
business of farming. Besides, agricultural work is a work which
demands a capacity for orientation and adaptation, patient
waiting, a sense of responsibility, and a spirit of perseverance
and enterprise[27].

From what we tried to show above concerning the dignity of farm
work, it follows that basic human rights must derive from it for the
workers. The economic revolution which has changed the world has
been seen precisely as the industrial revolution, yet in truth, it
has been agricultural too. Man's ability to exploit the world's
natural resources through agriculture and mining has raised the
industrial growth. For this reason, agricultural development is a
key factor in modern industrial expansion. For that reason too as
Roger Charles observes, it is the food production capacity of the
human race which, more than anything else, will determine whether
the huge population the world now contains, and will continue to
contain, will be properly nourished. As it becomes a responsibility
towards the world, agricultural workers must be helped to
rise from their oppressed and neglected situation. The depressed
rural world, the worker who with his sweat waters also his
affliction, cannot wait any longer for full and effective recognition
of his dignity, which is not inferior to that of any other social
sector. He has the right to be respected and not to be deprived, with
manoeuvres which are sometimes tantamount to real spoilation, of the

---

27) John XXIII., Ibid.

little that he has. He has the right to be rid of the barriers of exploitation, often made intolerable by the selfish attitudes of owners and policy makers, who shatter his advancement. He has the right as John Paul II says, "to real help - which is not charity or crumby of justice - in order that he may have access to the development that his dignity as a man and a son of God deserves". And in the words of Paul VI, this is a very urgent task.
"It is necessary to act promptly and in depth; it is necessary to carry out urgent reforms immediately, which are deeply innovatory. There is no time to waste any longer... since, the ferment of the Gospel rouses in man's heart a demand for dignity that cannot be stifled"[28].
And John Paul ends up this call for the recognition of the dignity and rights of agricultural workers by saying:

> "This is the great fundamental right of man: the right to
> work and the right to the land. Although economic
> development may take us in another direction, although one
> may value progress based upon industrialisation, although
> the generation of today may leave en masse the land and
> agricultural work, still the right to the land does not
> cease to form the foundation of a sound economy and sociology"[29].

We agree with this view completely.

---

28) Paul VI, Populorum Progressio, n. 32; (Cf. Gaudium et Spes, n. 26
29) John Paul II., Holy mass at Nowy Targ, Poland; 8 June 1979,
L'osservatore Romano, eng. edition, 16.6.1979 No. 29, p.7

b) Problems of Agricultural Workers:

Work in the fields involves great difficulties, because of the
energy and efforts it demands from the farmers, because of the
obstacles it meets with, both in financial, technical and moral
terms, and because of the contempt with which it is sometimes considered.
These difficulties therefore demand a far-reaching action.
The Holy Father gave time towards considering the difficulties
with which agricultural workers are confronted. The flight from
the countryside to the cities is not for nothing, rather it is
its difficult nature which force hundreds and thousands of young
people to flee the villages and look for cheap money, white collar
jobs in the cities and thereby causing problems of 'extensive and
distressing proletarisation, overcrowding in houses unworthy of
human peoples, etc."[30].

Commenting on this situation John Paul says: "Agricultural work
involves considerable difficulties, including unremitting and
sometimes exhausting physical effort and lack of appreciation on the
part of society, making workers feel they are social outcasts and
causing them flee in mass exodus from the country side to the cities
inspite of dehumanising conditions"[31].

Added to the above, many farmers, especially in the developing
nations are not adequately trained in their professions, they lack
adequate equipment and suffer under unjust situations, even though,
they do sometimes contribute to this themselves by practicing
"a certain individualism, whereas a better co-ordinated and united
action could be of great help"[32], for the purpose of defending their rights.

---

30) John Paul II, Address to Indios and Peasants, op.cit.

31) John Paul II, Laborem Exercens, 21

32) Address to Indios and Peasants, Ibid.,

A general question could be asked, in reference to why this flight of farmers and peasants from the villages to the cities? John XXIII gave this question a detailed attention and analysis[33], settling for four basic reasons:

(i) Economic Expansion: As an economy developes, the number of people engaged in agriculture decreases, while the percentage employed in the industry and the various services rises. This truth is simple if we take Nigeria as example. Before the colonial interruption of the normal development of this culture, more than eighty percent of Nigerians were engaged in agriculture, farm work, fishing, hunting etc. With the colonial era and the post independence experiment in the city industrialisation, less this percentage, infact, not up to fourty percent of Nigerians are engaged in farm work of various types. Nigeria has become an oil exporting country, and a food importing country. Interest has changed due to colonial policy from self-reliance and independence to easy and quick money on the short-run but poverty and dependence on the long run.

(ii) City life and Comfort: The desire to escape from the crumped surroundings which offer little prospects of a more comfortable way of life has also led to the desertion of the villages. In the country sides, economiy and social amenities are lacking, there is no progress in making basic amenities available in the villages, simple things like water, electricity, decent food, good roads are regarded as luxuries reserved only for the cities. There is no high life for the young, no comfort, hardly any recreational facilities, and all these naturally lead to flight from the villages, and with it too from farm work.

---

33)   John XXII., Mater et Magistra, n. 124

(iii) <u>Lure of Novelty, Adventure and Easy Money:</u>   Whereas the villages possess little attraction for the youth of the twentieth century, used to being pampered, and often comparing themselves to youth in better-of economic richer countries, the danger is therefore high that departure and migration to the cities will follow. There is the lure of novelty and adventure on the youth. The attractive prospect of easy money, of greater freedom, of laxity and the enjoyment of all the amenities of town and city life, both in day and night, the fact that long respected traditions and cultures are breaking away with the cultural conflict and the colonial heritage, there is no surprise that large numbers of youth are fed up with village life, determined to seek adventure in the cities. Above all, the cities offer chances and opportunities for furtherance of education, acquisition of foreign property and fitting into the parole euphemistically labelled "modern man".

(iv) <u>Contempt for Farm Work:</u>   There used to be a time when farm work was noble, respected and highly regarded in many traditional societies. Today, also in industrialised societies, there is the doubtless fact that farming has become a "depressed occupation". It is inadequate both in productive efficiency and in the standard of living it provides. Farmers are rated as second class citizens, not yet emancipated, primitive and backwards. Their rights are not well guaranteed, they do not receive adequate state support, aid and professional education necessary. Under such a situation, an alternative is to find security, better living and refuge in the cities.

c)   Guidelines Towards Solving the Agricultural Problem:

In Laborem Exercens, John Paul asserts unequivocal support for
urgent action in the area of agricultural work, issuing an invitation
to all those involved in the world of work to rally around the
farmer and agricultural worker. He says: "In many situations
radical and urgent changes are needed in order to restore to
agriculture - and to rural people - their just value as the basis
for a healthy economy, within the social community's development
and promote the dignity of work, of all work, but especially of
agricultural work, in which man so eloquently "subdues" the earth
he has received as a gift from God and affirms his "dominion" in
the visible world"[34].

John Paul refers specifically to certain situations where the
rights of agricultural workers are trampled upon and calls for justice.
He refers to the situation in the developing countries, but also to
the injustices in the industrialised nations, making specific
reference in the case of the former, to millions of people
"forced to cultivate the land belonging to others and are exploited
by the big land owners, without any hope of ever being able to gain
possession of even a small piece of land of their own"[35].
Thereafter, he refers to the lack of forms of legal protection for the
agricultural workers themselves and for their families in case of old
age, sickness or unemployment. In the case of the latter, the
industrialised nations, John Paul says that in these countries, where

---

34) John Paul II, LE, n. 21
35)   Ibid

scientific research, technological achievements and State policy
have brought agriculture to a very advance level, there still
exists an infringement on the rights of workers, when the
"farm workers are denied the possibility of sharing in decisions
concerning their services, or when they are denied the right
to free association with a view to their just advancement,
socially, culturally and economically"[36].

This criticism is topical now, in the face of the unsuccessful
summit meeting of the European Economic Community and the
meeting of agricultural ministers in Brussels in the month of
March 1984. The demand for more rights by different countries for
their farmers and the quota of their sales within the community, and
the protest strikes and marches of agricultural workers themselves
in France, Spain and Italy in the month of January, all go to
prove this indictment made by the Holy Father on the policy makers.
He however does not go so far to say how these urgent
reforms and rights can be realised, but he lets us know that he
agrees with his predecessors on their suggestions to this problem.
John XXIII gave the guidelines.

---

36) Ibid.

(i) Essential Public Services: John XXIII said that "in the
first place, considerable thought must be given especially by
public authorities, to the suitable development of
essential facilities in country areas: roads, transport,
means of communication, drinking water, housing, health
services, elementary technical and professional education,
religious and recreational facilities, and the supply of
modern installations and furnishings for the farm residence.
Such services are necessary nowadays if a becoming
standard of living is to be maintained"[37].

The fathers of Vatican II, considered this matter in their
pastoral Constitution on the Church in the world of today.
They gave support to the views expressed above by John XXIII
and wrote."in view of the special difficulties in production
and marketing in agriculture, country people must be helped
to improve methods of production and marketing, introduce
necessary developments and to achieve fair return for their
products, lest they continue as often happens, in the state
of inferior citizens"[38].

---

37) John XXIII., Mater et Magistra, n. 127
38) Vatican II., Gaudium et Spes, n. 66

(ii)   Gradual and evenly balanced development of the Economy:

If a country is to develope economically, it must do so
gradually, maintaining an even balance between all the sectors
of production. Agriculture therefore must be allowed to make
use of the same reforms in the method and type of production and
in the conduct of the business side of the venture, as are
permitted or required in the economic system as a whole.
All such reforms should correspond as nearly as possible with
those introduced in industry and the various services[39].

Advantages would of course result from this type of
economic policy, especially the fact that it will become easier
to keep track of the movement of the labour force set free
by the progressive modernisation of agriculture. In such a
case, facilities could be provided for the training of such
people for their new kind of work, and they would not be left
without economic aid, mental aid and spiritual aid needed to
properly get integrated into their new social milieu.
The council Fathers referred also in their reflections on the
farmer on this issue, and wrote that it is their first
priority to see that farmers are aided, peasants and other
agricultural workers who are not oppressed by unjust systems
of land tenure, but who, for reasons peculiar to the nature of
agriculture, cannot alone organise themselves sufficiently to
meet the needs of modern production and fulfil their societal
roles as food producers. On the other hand, where the land

---

39)   John XXIII., n. 128

tenure and the general social conditions are so unjust that large
numbers of farmers who get their living from the land are subjected
to inhuman conditions of life and work, reforms are called for,
especially those which deal with better wages for hired labourers,
better equipments to make the work less burdensome, and available
resources to enable a better production[40].

At the 1974 World Food Conference in Bucharest, Paul VI sent an
urgent message to this world body, urging those responsible for
policy to shift emphasis from solely industrialisation to include
agriculture and life on the land too[41]. This message is just
very actual and urgent. It is an emphasis which looks at
priorities and demands that first things come first. A journalist
writing for The Guardian commented on the Holy Father's message thus:
"The Pope argued that nothing less than new orientations were
needed ... a reorientation of first priorities away from ever more
industries to the natural life of agriculture"[42].

As is gradually becoming clearer to citizens of the earth, the world
food problem cannot be solved by relying everlastingly upon the bounty of
the harvests of North America. It can only be solved by "improving the
low acre yields of millions of those who operate small farms in the
developing world". With the staggering number of deaths of
hungry people all over the world, and the rising population of
mankind, men of good will are called to a radical consideration of

---

40) Gaudium et Spes., n. 66 and 71

41) Paul VI, Address to Participants of the World Food and Agricultural
Conference, 9 November 1974; published in L'osservatore Romano,
English Edision, 21 November 1974.

42) Thomas Hartford, Article in "The Guardian", London Newspaper,
18.11.1974

398

the rights and duties of those involved in the world of
agriculture, and those who are responsible in policy making
are made to know that productive efficiency of food and
agricultural products demands incentive and assistance for the
farmers. This can be done by improving productive efficiency
of the small farms, supporting equitable land tenure
and effective cooperation between the farmers, and decreeing a
clear law concerning contracts and wages, encouraging
property and liability laws, integrity in the administration
and accounting of farmers funds and a definite improvement
of government in seeing that justice is done to the farmers.

(iii)   The need for a suitable economic policy on taxation:

To avoid the flight of farmers from the countryside into the
cities, and to encourage youth to pick up the agricultural
professions, a sound agricultural policy must be developed,
if public authority is to maintain an evenly balanced progress
in the various branches of the economy. This is specifically
to be practiced in the area of taxation as Pope John XXIII
suggests. "A taxation based on justice and equity will
proportion burdens to the capacity of the people contributing.
Government should take care of the problems of farmers when
assessing taxation. For example, farmers have to wait longer
than other workers for their returns from the farms, run more
risks both in forms of climate, fire disasters, erosion and
heavy rainfall, and have greater difficulty in getting
adequate capital for their farm work"[43].

---

43)   John XXIII, Mater et Magistra, n. 132 - 133

(iv) <u>Credit Banks:</u>   It is also suggested by the Church's Social
Principles that business people who invest more in industries
than in agriculture pay high interest rates to Credit Banks,
a high rate which agricultural workers cannot afford. The
State is therefore called upon to evolve a special credit
policy [44], and to form credit banks that are orientated
towards granting farmers good conditions of Capital at a
moderate rate.

(v) <u>Social Insurance and Social Security</u>: It is proved that many
farmers and agricultural workers earn less per head other than
workers in industry and the public services. Such a situation calls
for a type of social security and insurance which can be
looked upon from two sides, namely, concerning the agricultural
produce itself, and dealing with the workers and their families[45].
Such a system will definitely make desired and effective
contribution to the overall distribution of natural income based
on the principles of justice and equity, which is the guiding
thread for a peaceful society.

(vi) <u>Price Protection:</u>   The point is also made and this is quite
objective, that a suitable means of price protection is
necessary, given the special nature of agricultural
produce. What this demand involves in its ideal fashion is
that such a price protection should be enforced by the farmers
themselves, with a moderate State supervision if this necessary.

::::

44)   Ibid., n. 134
45)   Ibid., n. 135 - 136

It is to be recalled that the price of agricultural
produce usually represents the reward of labour rather than
a return of invested capital. If the suggestion given is
accepted, and there is no reason why it should not in a just and
egalitarian society, a price for products will be set within
the means of all consumers, since farm produce is intended for the
satisfaction of man's basic and primary existential needs.
Exploitation is to be avoided by the farmers themselves on the
people, and a decent price obtained through the sale of their
farm products would generally raise their social and economic
depression. It will also make it impossible for international
Concerns to dictate the prices of the goods of the workers, as
is the situation at the moment, in international trade.

Prices for goods produced in Tanzania, Kenya,Gabon, El Salvador
to name but a few of the developing nations are pricely
dictated not in the countries where the goods are produced, but
in London, Paris, New York and Bonn. If the Pope's suggestion is
accepted in protecting prices for the farmers products, then
economic ethics and the demands it makes that the rights of workers
protected, might thereby be justified.

(vii) Promotion of Ancillary Industries: "Establishment of industries
and services concerned with the preservation, procession
and transport of farm products should be encouraged"[46].

46) Ibid., n. 14

401

(viii) The Structure of the Farm Unit: As we know, living conditions
for rural workers are not the same everywhere, and the social
position of farmers are also different in the various
countries. It is therefore not easy to lay hard and
fast rules a-priori as to how the structure of the farm units
could look like. The Pope however offers an ideal form of
farm unit, which is modelled on the basis of a community of
persons working together for the advancement of their mutual
interests in accordance with the principles of justice[47].
Reference is made to the kind of farm privately owned and
managed by the family or a group of families. "Every effort
must be made in the prevailing circumstances to give effective
encouragement to farming enterprise owned by the family".
In some countries, especially in strictly communist regions,
this demand is not only obnoxious, but is also impossible,
given the nature of their economic system. But where it is
possible, like in many African countries and tribes where
family farm is the normal agricultural farm, the Pope's
suggestion comes, not as a new teaching, but as a confirmation
of the already existing system.

----

47) Ibid., n. 142

(ix) Professional Organisation: Finally, a last suggestion is made
      in the attempt to make agricultural work more human, and
      to grant to farmers the rights which are naturally theirs in
      labour world. John XXIII makes the point that workers must
      gain in professional organisation and competence, by
      obtaining up-to-date instructions on the latest methods of
      cultivation, preservation of farm goods, and marketing
      of these goods. To realise this noble venture, the assistance
      of experts is necessary[48]. The consequence of such a combined
      effort would lead to the formation of Co-operative
      Organisations, arranged on a professional level, which will
      enable the workers to take an active part, not only in
      defending their rights, but also in participating in the
      general life of the community on political, social, cultural
      and administrative platforms.

      By so doing too, they will be contributing to the common
      welfare of the entire society, as John Paul II pointed
      out to farmers in his attempt to stress the Christian and
      Social function of a well developed, productive agricultural policy[49].
      We are thus led to the final section of the research on
      agricultural work and workers by dealing in the following
      pages on the attitude of workers themselves to the land, but
      also towards each other, not less to God, the giver of life
      and land.

---

48) Ibid., n. 143
49) John Paul II, Holy Mass at "Living History Farms",
    De Moines (USA), 4 October 1979; L'osservatore Romano,
    29.10.1979, No. 44, p.3 - 4.
    Here, the Pope speaks on a three dimensional level -
    Farm work in its relation to man, to God, and among farmers
    themselves.

3. Attitude of Farmers towards the Land

Recalling the life of Jesus as a worker in Nazareth, Pope John Paul
II lists out three attitudes man should have towards the land.
After reaffirming the Church's high esteem for agricultural work,
and recalling that the Land is God's gift entrusted to man to care
of, and to shape in the Creator's mind, a task which involves a
certain vocation and responsibility, John Paul reminds American
farmers how their efforts have been rewarded with abundant crops,
making it possible for millions of people who themselves do not
work on the land, to feed and live. Positive attitudes are
therefore expected of the farmers towards the land, namely:
gratutude, care and generosity.

a) Gratitude:

Workers have to be grateful to God for the land because it helps
them know how much they depend on God. Says the Pontiff:
"From the heavens come rain, the wind and the sunshine.
They occur without a farmer's control or command. The farmer
prepares the soil, and cultivates the crop. But God makes it grow:
he is alone the source of life"[50]. This is really enough reason
for the believer and farmer to give thanks.

---

50) Ibid.

404

b) Care:

Secondly, the land must be conserved with care since it is intended
to be fruitful for generations upon generations. There is present
everywhere today, the risk of irreversible contamination of the
biophysical environment. In the face of this risk, the farmer
is called to "protect and care for the earth". Says John Paul:
"You are the stewards of the most important resources God has given
to the world. Therefore conserve the land well, so that your
children's children and generations after them will inherit
an even richer land than was entrusted to you. But also remember what
the heart of your vocation is: ... In farming, you cooperate with
the Creator in the very important sustenance of your earthly life"[51].

c) Generosity:

Lastly, John Paul demands that agricultural workers be generous.
The Council Fathers at the Second Vatican Council had already made
the point that "the goods of the earth are destined for all men, with
all it contains, so that all created things would be shared
fairly by all mankind under the guidance of justice tempered by
charity"[52]. Says John Paul: "You who are farmers today are
stewards of a gift from God which was intended for entire humanity...
Recall the times when Jesus saw the hungry crowds gathered on the
hillside. He gave his disciples command to give them to eat[53].
Did he not intend the same words for us today?"

---

51) Ibid.
52) Gaudium et Spes, n. 69
53) Mt. 14 : 16.

Certainly these words "give the people to eat" has relevance
also in our own times. In the midst of much suffering, hunger,
destitution, one cannot really justifiably say that one did not
hear the voice that calls us to share our bread with our neighbour.

John Paul therefore concludes:

> "Let us respond generously to this command by
> sharing the fruit of our labour, by contributing to
> others the knowledge we have gained, by being the
> promotors of rural development everywhere and by
> defending the right to work of the rural population
> since every person has a right to useful
> employment"[54].

---

54)   John Paul II, Holy Mass at "Living History Farms",
      De Moines, (USA), op.cit.

4. Technical Workers

> "We have the right and the duty to take account in our
> approach to human work of the various needs of man, in
> the spheres of both the spirit and the body, and to take
> this approach to human work in each society and in each
> system, whether manual or technical...in its relation
> to man - and not the reverse - as a fundamental criterion
> for assessing progress itself".
> (John Paul II, Address to ILO, 1982).

In no other sphere of human work are these words better understood
and applicable as in the area of technical work - the work with and
on nature, through which man actually manipulates, subdues and
dominates the universe. Technical work makes possible the
fulfilment of the challenge and vocation of man in Genesis
"subdue the earth and conquer it" !

When we consider all that man has done in the area of art,
technique and science, we have hardly words to describe the
gigantic progress, achievements and discoveries which man has been
able to arrive at. The reality of today's world with the
electronic and technological revolution, with all its sophisticated
computer memory chips, micro-processors and other mechanisms,
whose consequences are yet only half understood, has brought along
with it, a changed and yet ever changing nature of work and the
work force, new jobs and new skills.

We are on the verge of a productivity increase that is every bit
as dramatic as the shift from an agricultural to an industrial
economy due to this technological wonder. People speak today of
the "moon age", "space age", "nuclear and atomic age" and the "computer
and Robort age". Economists note that high levels of technological

innovation in the past have always resulted in rapidly expanding jobs. The optimists believe that the economy will become more highly skilled, and many jobs will become more satisfying. Computers will be used to perform the unpleasant, repetitive tasks, allowing individuals to pursue more human and fulfilling goals. The standard of living will rise, ensuring a richer life for all.

At the same time, experts are worried that the fruits of the technological age are not so rosy as presented. They believe that the computer age will produce some wrenching changes throughout the global economy. People have learnt how to replace workers with technology, but they do not know how to use technology to put people back to work. Thousands of previously productive workers have been condemned to marginal workers. Technique has brought with it too, a looming crisis in the world of work.

It is surprising that John Paul II, does not devote adequate attention to the problem of technical workers and the world of technology, outside a few stray observations here and there in his famous encyclical, and general principles of work which are generally applicable also to technical workers. John Paul notes that we are "on the eve of new developments in technological, economic and political conditions which, according to many experts, will influence the world of work and production no less than the industrial revolution of the last century"[55]. He goes on to talk about "the widespread introduction of automation into many spheres of production", among many other factors, which new conditions and demands will require a "reordering and adjustment of the structures of the modern economy and of the distribution of work"[56].

---

55) John Paul II., Laborem Exercens, n. 1
56) Ibid.

The consequences of these changes are partly imaginable and the Pope knows this for he says: "unfortunately, for millions of skilled workers, these changes may perhaps mean unemployment, at least for a time, or the need for retraining. They will very probably involve a reduction or a less rapid increase in material well-being for the more developed countries. But they can also bring relief and hope to millions who today live in conditions of shameful and unworthy poverty"[57]. And here the Pope's reference to the world of technical workers ends.

However, this reference to the world of technical work offers us several elements in considering this very important area of human work. On technology and technical workers depends a great proportion of mankind, and on them can man claim a basic way for feeding many of its people, especially in the industrialised nations. The first element to reflect upon deals with the humanisation of technical work. Work has to be made more human in the general idea called "Humanisierung der Arbeitswelt".

Pope Leo XIII and Pius XI had time to refer to this factor in their great social encyclicals, thus: Not only the physical conditions of work are to be adequate, but the psychological conditions, the full involvement of the person in work should be sought. Man's alienation needs to be overcome, he needs to co-operate with others in his work, and he needs to be personally identified and fulfilled through any undertaking in which his labour, by hand or by brain or technique is involved[58].

---

57) Ibid
58) Leo XIII, Rerum Novarum, n.33; Pius XI, Quadragesimo Anno, n. 69.

Technical work is a progress in man's attempt to overcome the
universe, but progress always requires "an evaluation and a value
judgement". One must ask whether a given progress is sufficiently
"human" and at the same time sufficiently "universal"; whether it
helps to level out unjust inequalities and to promote a peaceful
future for the world; whether, in the work itself, fundamental
rights are ensured, for each person, for each family and for each
nation. In a word, one must ask oneself constantly whether the
technical work concerned helps man to become more human and to
fulfil the meaning of his life. If technical work alienates man,
then it is to be criticised and corrected. Although technical
work represents work in the objective sense[59], yet, work has its
highest dignity in the subjective dimension. Work must serve
man and not man serving work. The marxist criticism of capitalism
as alienation can be applied to technical work where it becomes
a sort of alienation too. Capitalism made men experience their
own work and what they produced as something foreign and alien to
them, a force directing them from outside, and this had much truth in
it. If technical work does the same, it ends up as alienation for
the worker, and man, supposed to conquer the earth ends up being
conquered by the earth. Technical work must serve man, not the other
way round. John Paul made the point clearer in his address to
representatives of the International Labour Organisation gathered in
Geneva in 1982:

> "technical work must be the ally of man, enabling
> him to live in truth and freedom in all its fulness,
> to lead a life more worthy of man"[60].

---

59) John Paul II, LE, n. 5
60) John Paul II, Address to the International Labour Organisation,
op.cit., p.284 (Refer: McClellan, D; Karl Marx, London,
1973, p.77).

This brings us to a second element of technical work, namely that
it should help man to achieve meaning in his life. In a homily at
a mass for workers at Jasna Gora, in his native Poland, the
Pope stated clearly that "work is the fundamental dimension of
man's life on earth. Work has for man a significance which
is not merely technical but also ethical. It can be said that
man subdues the earth when by his behaviour be becomes its master,
not its slave, and also the master, not the slave of work"[61].

He goes on to emphasise that the link between work and the
very meaning of human existence bears constant witness
to the fact that man has not been alienated from work, that he has not
been enslaved. In this perspective, work has an inbuilt social
as well as inbuilt personal element. Technical work is not only
necessary to man from its economic use alone, but psychologically
and spiritually too, its fulfills his personality.

---

61) John Paul II, Homily at Mass in Jasna Gora, op.cit.
(Refer also, Laborem Exercens, 4).

411

5. Migrant Workers:

On migrant workers, John Paul is seen to display a sensitivity of
very special fondness and understanding. His speech to
workers in Monterrey, Mexico, forcefully underlines his care
and anxious defence of the rights of migrants. Already at the
beginning of his pontificate, the Pontiff took a trip to Mexico,
the land of "migrants and slums", faced specially with the serious
topical phenomenon of workers who emigrate to look for better
working conditions, like in many other nations of the world.
Says Pope John Paul II,

> "we cannot close our eyes to the situation of millions of
> men, who, in their search for work and livelihood have to
> leave their country and often their family. They have
> to cope with the difficulties of a new environment that
> is not always pleasant and welcoming, an unknown language,
> and general conditions that plunge them into solitude and,
> sometimes, social exclusion for themselves and for their
> wives and children, even when advantage is not taken of
> these circumstances to offer lower wages, to reduce social
> insurance and welfare benefits, and to give housing
> conditions unworthy of a human being"[62].

This speech has interesting elements in it, and it is noteworthy
that John Paul in his encyclical published two years later on human
labour, took out time to consider the problems of emigration of
workers, re-peating some of the views mentioned above. First of all,
the Pope mentions that emigration of workers from one place to
another for a better working condition, or living condition is
"an age-old phenomenon which nevertheless continues to be repeated
as a result of the complexities of modern life"[63].

62) John Paul II., Address to Workers at Monterrey, Mexico,
31. January 1979, (L'osservatore Romano, engl. edition,
19.2.1979. No. 8, pp. 6-7).
63) John Paul II, Laborem exercens, n. 23

Emigration of workers is not new. Human history does not exist
without this phenomenon, and each time, people are motivated by the
survival and existential question. They emigrate because they
want to live. Surely, such a struggle for existence is in the
words of the Pope "in some aspects an evil, perhaps a necessary evil"[64].

Emigration is an evil because it brings with it many discomforts
and inconveniences to the migrant as shown above.
Secondly, it is an evil because "it generally constitutes a loss
for the country which is left behind. It is the departure of a
person who is also a member of a great community united by history,
tradition and culture... in this case it is the loss of a subject of
work, whose efforts of mind and body could contribute to the common
good of his own country, but these efforts, this contribution
are offered to another society which in a sense has less right to
them than the original country"[65]

Besides the already offered reasons which make migration of workers
an evil, there are surely many other factors which also make
migration an evil. This refers to the personality of the migrant who
may get lost in the host country, and suffer uncalculable
psychological damages. It concerns also the children of migrants
born in the host countries, who often suffer as "cultural mulatoes",
living between two worlds, that of their parents and that of the
land in which their parents are "guest workers". If these people
should sometime leave the host country back to their original
nation, the children often look like "fish out of water" when they
are like growing plants plucked out of the earth and transplanted on
a new earth, that they need time to undergo the metamorphosis of their
new environment with all its risks, shocks and even death
possibilities. John Paul is aware of all these evils, as he says,
but despite them, one cannot undermine the right to emigrate to
any place in the world if this becomes a necessity and an
existential reality.

---

64) Ibid
65) Ibid

For John Paul,

> "man has the right to leave his native land for
> various motives - and also the right to return - in order to
> seek better conditions of life in another country"[66].

Mankind is challenged to minimise those factors which lead to the
emigration of workers, or at least to prevent this "material
evil from causing greater moral harm; indeed every possible
effort should be made to ensure that it may bring benefit
to the emigrant's personal, family and social life, both for the
country which he leaves and the country to which he goes"[67].
To realise this noble ethical demand, much has to be done in the
various nations in the area of "just legislation". A just
legislation defends the rights of workers, as well as migrant
workers, and makes exploitation impossible.
Besides, a just legislation, helps to elevate the personality
of the human being, whether migrant or not, because through
the law, the workers rights are protected along with their
personality.

Talking to workers at Monterrey, the Pope mentioned the notorious
fact of the exploitation of workers by employers, who demand
from the foreign workers, maximum efficiency, while deliberately
ignoring not only the current laws on labour, but even the most
elementary respect for the human person and his work.
"Emigration in search for work must in no way become an opportunity
for financial or social exploitation"[68]

---

66) John Paul II, LE, n. 23
67) Ibid.
68) Ibid.

414

John Paul, speaking as an eloquent defender of the rights of the
working man, declares in unequivocal terms that the seasonal worker
also when he becomes a permanent emigrant, "should not be placed
at a disadvantage in comparison with the other workers in that
society in the matter of working rights ... the value of work should
be measured by the same standard and not according to the
difference in nationality, religion or race"[69] as justice and
equity demands.

69) John Paul II, LE, n.23

There is the problem here in Germany called "die Ausländer Problematik",
whereby migrant workers, especially from Turkey, Yugoslavia and
some other southern nations are discriminated against. There is
frequently the talk in the mass media of "Ausländer Feindlichkeit",
"Ausländer Raus" and many of such paroles. All these do not
correspond to the ethics of labour as far as migrant workers are concerned.
One needs to think in this connection also of the thousands of
illegal migrants and workers thrown out of Nigeria in 1982.
The legal reasons apart, there was totally lacking the human aspect.
Faced with this phenomenon, John Paul II offers, like the Church
has always maintained, that the principles to follow, is not that of
allowing economic, social and political forces to prevail over man,
but on the contrary, to place the dignity of the human person
above everything else, and for the rest to be conditioned by it"[70].

7o) John Paul II,. Address to workers of Monterrey, Mexico, op.cit.,

Therefore when dealing with migrant workers as persons,
especially for the defence of their fundamental rights - such
as the right to live with their family, to have a decent housing,
to educate their children, and become integrated in the social
life of the host country - the parameter should always be man's
centrality and the respect of his dignity. It is exactly on
this point that the safest therapy for the old and new ills in
human societies finds a basic solution. The hierarchy of values
and the profound meaning of work itself require that the
fundamental principle be repeated: "that capital should be at
the service of labour and not labour at the service of capital"[71].

---

71) John Paul II, LE, n. 23

6. The Role of the Disabled

Without hiding the fact that the disabled create a difficult
and complex problem for the labour world, John Paul II, hopes that
a "correct concept of labour in the subjective sense be developed,
which will create a situation that makes it possible for disabled
people to feel that they are not cut off from the working world or
dependent upon society, but that they are full-scale subjects of
work, useful, respected for their human dignity and called to
contribute to the progress and welfare of their families and of the
community according to their particular capacities"[72].

Wars, accidents, natural deformities and catastrophes of
different types have brought into the world of work, many
men and women, who are capable of production, but who because
of their deformities, are sometimes neglected, degraded and
rejected as capable of competing in the field of labour. This
rejection and neglect says John Paul should not be, for work counts
more in the subjective sense than in the objective one. It is
man that works and because his dignity is sacred and inviolable,
discriminations carried out against him simply because of his
physical features renders him inhuman and useless.
Says John Paul: "in spite of the limitations and sufferings affecting
their bodies and faculties, they point up more clearly the dignity
and greatness of man"[73]. First man, then the rest!

---

72) John Paul II, Laborem Exercens, n.22
73) Ibid.

The Holy Father addresses national and international communities,
organisations, employers and managers to find out new
avenues of raising to a truly human dignity, the disabled in our
midst, who cannot do the normal daily duties, but who can still
do other things that are useful to society. Those responsible
for work should find new jobs fitted for these unfortunate people,
they have the duty to create avenues to make their burdens
lighter by making them feel needed, giving them opportunities
to be productive, and aiding them to be fully human beings,
inspite of all deformation.

> "Since disabled people are subjects with all their
> rights, they should be helped to participate in the
> life of society in all its aspects and at all the levels
> accessible to their capacities...
> It would be radically unworthy of man, and a denial of
> our common humanity, to admit to the life of the
> community, and thus admit to work, only those who are
> fully functional"[74].

The purpose of the political body is to create a world where no
man is an island, and where each takes care of the other.
The State has its legitimacy in so far as it works towards
the good of all in the community. And the Church can claim to be on
the right path, if like its founder, it concerns itself with the
various problems of the different parts of the human community -
giving to each, within its limits, what it can.
Jesus himself spent his life and time for the poor, the disabled,
the blind and hungry, the lame and even the dead. It is a
challenge therefore, not only to the Church, but also to the State
and to various organisations to take into consideration the
situation of the disabled in the society.

---

74) Ibid.

During the second world war, Germany's Hitler eliminated those
who were sick, imbeciled, deformed or weak, in his idea to create
the "ideal man". This tragedy should not befall mankind a second
time. Man is man, whether sick or not, whether deformed or
healthy; whether man or woman. All those responsible in the
body politic must therefore find time, money, energy and legal
covering to protect the weak and disabled in their society. As the
Pope puts it: "Each community will be able to set up suitable
structures for finding or creating jobs for such people both in
the usual public or private enterprises, by offering them ordinary
or suitably adapted jobs, and in what are called "protected" enterprises
and sorroundings"[75].

Of course, in the carrying out of this task, careful attention
has to be devoted to the psychological and physical working
conditions of disabled people - as it is done for all workers - making
sure that they are justly remunerated in their wages, promoted
according to their possibilities and helped to overcome their
predicament as disabled persons.

This area involving the disabled demands a dignified and noble
idea of the worth of the human person. It corresponds to the general
area of social ethics and covers the rights of the individuals
and the workers. It is encouraging to mention in this connection that
in various nations and Christian organisations, this suggestion of
John Paul II, even before it was proposed had been practiced.
The disabled were aided to become more man, to feel needed and
fulfilled, and these nations and organisations merit the praise
of the magisterium of the Church. Others are invited to join in the task!
The disabled remain for mankind, human beings, whose rights as persons
must be guaranteed and furthered, no matter their deformities, as
long as they can also work and be fitted into the labour world.

---

75) Ibid

7. The Unemployed

a) Introducing the Problem:

In many countries of the world today, a very large number of people
have no alternative but to look at work from the outside; they are
the unemployed. Its symptoms are the same everywhere : layoffs,
locked factory gates, long lines of workers queuing up for
unemployment checks. The most poignant victims are the young who
are searching for their first job and the old who are worried that
they may have lost their very last one. 'Around the world,
unemployment - the worst since the Great Depression - may soon
displace inflation as the industrial world's prime economic nemesis'.

Leonard Glynn, economic correspondent for America's most popular
magazine, Newsweek has this in a collective work to say:
Among the twenty-four affluent nations of the Organisation for
Economic Cooperation and Development, the overall jobless rate
is rapidly approaching double - digit levels; more than thirty one
million workers in the OECD nations are now out of work. Together
with their dependents, their numbers are larger than West Germany's
entire population.. Among less developed countries, up to fifty
percent of the work force is already jobless or only partly employed.
Even in communist nations - where work for all is guaranteed and
unemployment is technically a crime - slower growth is producing
a job squeeze. Many workers, especially in Europe's milder welfare
states, have reconciled themselves to years of dependence on state
and social welfare handouts. The resultant bitterness of "enforced
leisure" underlies both the despair of Europe's "no future" generation
and the scattered outbursts of rioting in such spots as Britain's
dead-end ghettos and the depressed regions of northern France
and Belgium[76].

---

76) Leonard Glynn and colleagues, Jobs - A weary world looks for work,
     in Newsweek Magazine, October 18th 1982, p.44

This research looks at the problem, nature and extent of
employment and describes from the perspective of Social ethics
how the magisterium considers this problem and what contributions
they make towards its solution. We shall carry out this task in
three stages, namely: a statistical data, the stand of John Paul II,
and lastly possibilities towards a solution of the dilemma.

b) Unemployment - a Statistical Data

Statistics can be boring, but they give an overall picture of a
situation, they offer means of showing the trends up or down,
and indicate, in the case of unemployment, what groups of people, how
many, what percentage of the total labour force are affected by
the situation. At the moment, the plight of the people, who
eventhough they are not disabled, have been disabled to work
because of the market situation is painful. The current problem
has been so prolonged and severe that many workers have simply
exhausted their eligibility. Young workers and many women have
"naturally" high rates of unemployment. In the case of youths,
they may be testing the job market or seeking temporary jobs
between periods of schooling or travel, and in the case of women,
they drop in and out of the work force to earn extra cash to
support their families or buy themselves some novelties. At the
same time, seasoned workers who have invested heavily in homes,
skills and local communities are naturally reluctant to accept
the first new job to come along.

In Britain for example, by August 1982, unemployment had risen
to over 3, 1/4 million people; the highest number ever recorded in
the United Kingdom; 13% of the working population, and this is
about twenty five million people who are in the labour force.
It means then that one in seven workers is unemployed[77].
This is a serious problem and we could say that unemployment has
done irreparable harm to the people. It has caused a rise in
crime, divorce, alcoholism, child abuse and many other social problems.
Of course, dating back to two centuries ago, Europeans have heard
scare talk before, when people found themselves permanently out of
work because of machines.

"We are being afflicted with a new kind of disease of which
readers will hear a great deal in the years to come - namely
technological unemployment", wrote Maynard Keynes fifty-two years
ago in his essay "Economic possibilities for our Grandchildren".
A few years ago everybody was saying that we must have much more
leisure. Now that everybody has got much leisure - it may be
involuntary, but they have got it - they are complaining they are
unemployed! The statistical data attached in the following pages
portray the enormity of the situation. The tendency on the graph
is rising, and perhaps, unemployment has come to stay with the
human economic situation, grossly mismanaged by political policies
at the people's expense.

---

77) Cf. Unemployment and the Future of Work; Published by Church of
England General Synod Board for Social and Economic affairs,
Ec. 1982, chapter 2.

422

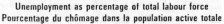

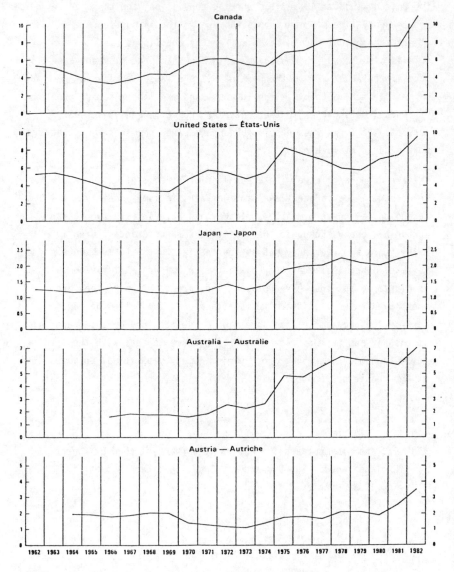

Graph shows unemployment as percentage of total labour force;
Data obtained from the Department of Economics and Statistics,
OECD, Labour Force Statistics (1970 - 81) publ.Paris, 1983,p.53ff

GRAPH 4 — GRAPHIQUE 4

Unemployment as percentage of total labour force
Pourcentage du chômage dans la population active totale

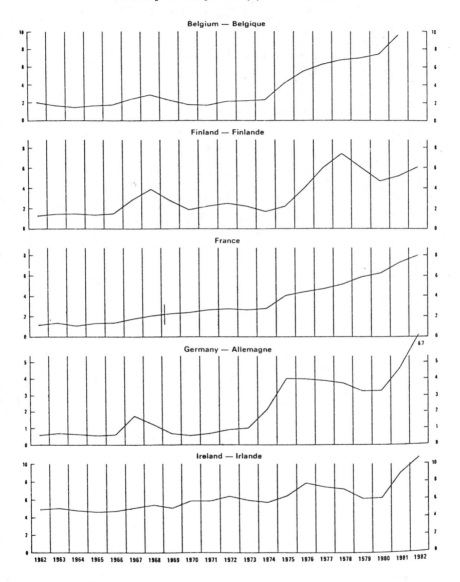

Source : Ibid.,

424

GRAPH 4 — GRAPHIQUE 4

Unemployment as percentage of total labour force
Pourcentage du chômage dans la population active totale

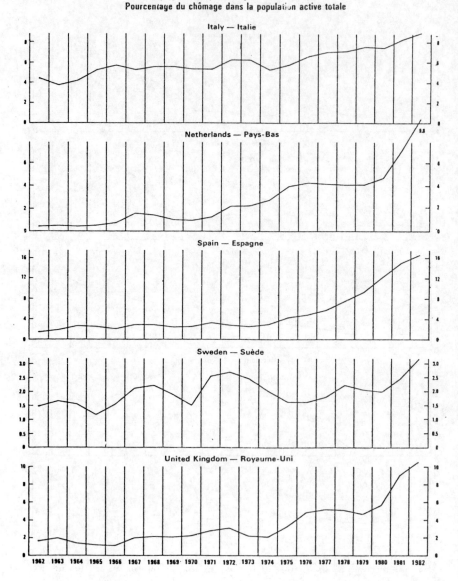

Italy — Italie

Netherlands — Pays-Bas

Spain — Espagne

Sweden — Suède

United Kingdom — Royaume-Uni

1962 1963 1964 1965 1966 1967 1968 1969 1970 1971 1972 1973 1974 1975 1976 1977 1978 1979 1980 1981 1982

Source : Ibid.,

Bundesanstalt für Arbeit
Statistik
Ib2 - 4221

Februar 1984

ARBEITSMARKT-VORMELDUNG

- Gesamtübersicht -

Merkmale	Zahl	Veränderung gegenüber Vormonat absolut	%	Veränderung gegenüber Vorjahresmonat absolut	%	Arbeitslosenquote 1) Berichtsmonat	Vormonat	Vorjahresmonat
Arbeitslose								
1. Arbeitslosmeldungen im Berichtsmonat	289 769	- 184 212	- 38,9	+ 2 311	+ 0,8	—	—	—
von Personen								
68,7% nach vorheriger Erwerbstätigkeit	199 040	- 191 499	- 49,0	- 9 774	- 4,7	—	—	—
6,2% nach vorh. betriebl. Ausbildung	18 071	+ 9 030	+ 99,9	+ 3 620	+ 25,1	—	—	—
25,1% ohne vorherige Erwerbstätigkeit	72 658	- 1 743	- 2,3	+ 8 465	+ 13,2	—	—	—
seit Jahresbeginn	763 750	—	—	- 38 391	- 4,8	—	—	—
2. Arbeitslose am Ende des Berichtsmonats	2 536 593	- 2 715	- 0,1	+ 757	+ 0,0	10,2 3)	10,2	10,4
davon: 60,0% Männer	1 521 946	+ 12 204	+ 0,8	- 16 766	- 1,1	10,1	10,0	10,3
40,0% Frauen	1 014 647	- 14 919	- 1,4	+ 17 523	+ 1,8	10,4	10,6	10,5
davon: 29,9% Angestellte	757 970	- 4 404	- 0,6	+ 50 407	+ 7,1	6,0	6,1	5,8
70,1% Arbeiter	1 778 623	+ 1 689	+ 0,1	- 49 650	- 2,7	14,5	14,5	15,1
dar.: 12,0% Ausländer	303 723	- 1 829	- 0,6	- 13 900	- 4,4	15,2	15,3	15,4
7,5% Jugendliche unter 20 Jahren	189 922	- 1 503	- 0,8	- 26 431	- 12,2	9,0	9,1	10,1
5,6% Schwerbehinderte	142 544	- 376	- 0,3	+ 12 053	+ 9,2	.	.	.
4,2% 59 Jahre und älter	105 939	- 531	- 0,5	+ 8 480	+ 8,7	.	.	.
9,6% Teilzeitarbeitsuchende Arbeitslose	243 357	- 2 658	- 1,1	- 9 240	- 3,7	10,0	10,1	10,4
3. Leistungsempfänger - Monatsmitte -	1 754 681	+ 78 882	+ 4,7	- 19 939	- 1,1			
Offene Stellen								
1. Offene Stellen gemeldet im Berichtsmonat	106 781	+ 15 311	+ 16,7	+ 25 075	+ 30,7			
seit Jahresbeginn	198 251	—	—	+ 43 195	+ 27,9			
2. Offene Stellen am Ende des Berichtsmonats	79 708	+ 9 747	+ 13,9	+ 10 934	+ 15,9			
davon: 45,1% Angestellte	35 963	+ 3 188	+ 9,7	+ 3 636	+ 11,2			
54,9% Arbeiter	43 745	+ 6 559	+ 17,6	+ 7 298	+ 20,0			
dar.: 8,5% nur für Teilzeitarbeit	6 746	+ 482	+ 7,7	+ 742	+ 12,4			
Arbeitsvermittlungen im Berichtsmonat	121 904	+ 14 586	+ 13,6	+ 26 527	+ 27,8			
seit Jahresbeginn	229 222	—	—	+ 42 686	+ 22,9			
Kurzarbeiter - Monatsmitte -	643 615	+ 78 127	+ 13,8	- 504 553	- 43,9			
Teilnehmer an beruflichen Förderungsmaßnahmen .. (Ende 12/83)	209 143	+ 24 683 4)	+ 13,4 4)	+ 7 638	+ 3,8			
darunter waren vorher arbeitslos	100 125	+ 13 721 4)	+ 15,9 4)	+ 22 136	+ 28,4			
Beschäftigte in Arbeitsbeschaffungsmaßnahmen am Ende des Berichtsmonats	52 675	+ 548	+ 1,1	+ 29 065	+123,1			

Saisonbereinigte Zahlen in 1000

Monat	Arbeitslose	Offene Stellen
1.83	2 145	72
2.83	2 207	71
3.83	2 252	75
4.83	2 280	75
5.83	2 298	76
6.83	2 318	74
7.83	2 319	75
8.83	2 323	76
9.83	2 314	80
10.83	2 275	80
11.83	2 242	81
12.83	2 228	81
1.84	2 200	81
2.84	2 200	82

1) Arbeitslose in % der abhängigen Erwerbspersonen (ohne Soldaten) nach dem Mikrozensus von April 1982
2) 9,1 % bezogen auf alle Erwerbspersonen
3) Die Abnahme der Arbeitslosenquote gegenüber dem Vorjahr ist auf die Änderung der Zahl der abhängigen Erwerbspersonen zurückzuführen.
4) Veränderung gegenüber Vorquartal

426

Bundesanstalt für Arbeit
Statistik
Ib2 - 4221 -

Arbeits-Vermittlungen
Februar 1951 bis 1984

Jahr	im Berichtsmonat			seit Jahresbeginn bis Ende des Berichtsmonats		
	insgesamt	Veränderung gegenüber Vormonat		insgesamt	Veränderung gegenüber Vorjahr	
		absolut	in %		absolut	in %
1951	402 459	+ 4 186	+ 1,1	800 732		
1952	333 087	+ 34 703	+ 11,6	631 471	- 169 261	- 21,1
1953	330 720	+ 53 539	+ 19,3	607 901	- 23 570	- 3,7
1954	327 729	- 16 916	- 4,9	672 374	+ 64 473	+ 10,6
1955	424 226	+ 61 191	+ 16,9	787 261	+ 114 887	+ 17,1
1956	339 385	- 6 876	- 2,0	685 646	- 101 615	- 12,9
1957	316 549	- 1 917	- 0,6	635 015	- 50 631	- 7,4
1958	342 604	+ 30 867	+ 9,9	654 341	+ 19 326	+ 3,0
1959	280 992	- 19 527	- 6,5	581 511	- 72 830	- 11,1
1960	333 383	+ 25 916	+ 8,4	640 850	+ 59 339	+ 10,2
1961	281 521	+ 13 004	+ 4,8	550 038	- 90 812	- 14,2
1962	246 148	+ 11 440	+ 4,9	480 856	- 69 182	- 12,6
1963	237 897	+ 25 514	+ 12,0	450 280	- 30 576	- 6,4
1964	233 360	+ 20 255	+ 9,5	446 465	- 3 815	- 0,8
1965	224 143	+ 2765	+ 1,2	445 521	- 944	- 0,2
1966	208 213	+ 21 633	+ 11,6	394 793	- 50 728	- 11,4
1967	179 977	+ 11 169	+ 6,6	348 785	- 46 008	- 11,7
1968	230 480	+ 18 707	+ 8,8	442 253	+ 93 468	+ 26,8
1969	220 279	+ 3 406	+ 1,6	437 152	+ 5 101	- 1,2
1970	229 495	+ 15 723	+ 7,4	443 267	+ 6 115	+ 1,4
1971	214 017	+ 22 194	+ 11,6	405 840	- 37 427	- 8,4
1972	198 030	+ 18 831	+ 10,5	372 229	- 28 611	- 7,0
1973	210 111	+ 18 672	+ 9,8	401 550	+ 24 321	+ 6,4
1974	181 477	+ 16 647	+ 10,1	346 307	- 55 243	- 13,8
1975	159 221	+ 10 546	+ 7,1	307 896	- 38 411	- 11,1
1976	161 724	+ 5 379	+ 3,4	318 069	+ 10 173	+ 3,3
1977	184 107	+ 25 657	+ 16,2	342 557	+ 24 488	+ 7,7
1978	157 565	- 6 550	- 4,0	321 680	- 20 877	- 6,1
1979	166 096	+ 12 274	+ 8,0	319 918	- 1 762	- 0,5
1980	155 764	+ 5 703	+ 3,8	305 825	- 14 093	- 4,4
1981	131 567	+ 20 954	+ 18,9	247 180	- 63 645	- 20,8
1982	115 380	+ 16 443	+ 16,6	214 317	- 27 863	- 11,5
1983	95 377	+ 4 218	+ 4,6	186 536	- 27 781	- 13,0
1984	121 904	+ 14 586	+ 13,6	229 222	+ 42 686	+ 22,9

Bundesanstalt für Arbeit
- Statistik -
Ib2 - 4221/4301
Germany (West)

Arbeitslose, offene Stellen und Kurzarbeiter

Vergleich zum Vormonat

Februar 1948 bis 1984

Jahr	Arbeitslose				Offene Stellen			Kurzarbeiter		
	Bestand am Ende des Berichtsmonats		Veränderung gegenüber Vormonat		Bestand am Ende des Berichtsmonats	Veränderung gegenüber Vormonat		Bestand am Ende des Berichtsmonats	Veränderung gegenüber Vormonat	
	absolut	Quote	absolut	in %		absolut	in %		absolut	in %
1948	476 353	3,4	- 5 618	- 1,2	.	.	.	.	.	.
1949	1 068 885	7,4	+ 106 019	+ 11,0	.	.	.	.	.	.
1950	2 288 368	13,5	+ 87 882	+ 4,0	108 304	+ 19 213	+ 21,6	.	.	.
1951	1 948 422	11,8	- 165 131	- 7,8	135 434	+ 28 930	+ 27,2	54 969	- 26 297	- 32,4
1952	2 172 973	12,5	+ 66 137	+ 3,1	109 500	+ 20 012	+ 22,4	175 706	+ 35 073	+ 24,9
53	2 060 651	11,6	- 20 576	- 1,0	123 636	+ 27 044	+ 28,0	142 762	+ 20 770	+ 17,0
1954	2 275 347	12,6	+ 58 104	+ 2,6	119 673	+ 23 991	+ 25,1	111 651	- 2 922	- 2,6
1955	2 000 102	10,7	+ 24 943	+ 1,3	156 918	+ 25 087	+ 19,0	46 807	- 23 836	- 33,7
1956	1 982 469	6,7	+ 592 134	+ 42,6	174 316	+ 6 791	+ 4,1	33 707	+ 4 431	+ 15,1
1957	1 222 789	6,1	- 378 773	- 23,7	212 996	+ 49 526	+ 30,3	45 417	- 1 061	- 2,3
1958	1 418 192	6,8	- 115 365	- 7,5	213 342	+ 41 170	+ 23,9	48 993	+ 12 466	+ 26,8
1959	1 203 311	5,7	- 242 197	- 16,8	237 872	+ 67 094	+ 39,3	75 210	- 20 578	- 21,5
1960	581 440	2,7	- 102 857	- 15,0	395 708	+ 77 654	+ 24,4	6 885	+ 1 641	+ 31,3
1961	321 910	1,5	- 100 834	- 23,9	559 041	+ 96 744	+ 20,9	6 791	+ 3 090	+ 83,5
1962	273 789	1,2	- 12 609	- 4,4	576 062	+ 49 350	+ 9,4	5 760	- 2 430	- 29,7
1963	416 889	1,9	+ 6 842	+ 1,7	496 899	+ 42 502	+ 9,4	33 316	+ 17 249	+ 107,4
1964	304 690	1,3	- 32 807	- 9,7	585 871	+ 85 170	+ 17,0	5 455	- 733	- 12,4
1965	291 236	1,3	+ 4 902	+ 1,7	608 512	+ 45 112	+ 8,0	1 879	+ 344	+ 22,4
1966	235 816	1,1	- 33 032	- 12,3	591 548	+ 43 551	+ 7,9	6 148	- 2 228	- 26,6
1967	673 572	3,1	+ 52 416	+ 8,4	275 531	+ 20 464	+ 8,0	343 718	+ 103 558	+ 43,1
1968	589 707	2,8	- 82 910	- 12,3	364 838	+ 61 643	+ 20,3	27 611	- 6 455	- 18,9
1969	374 126	1,8	- 5 541	- 1,5	624 735	+ 74 516	+ 13,5	2 691	- 919	- 25,5
1970	264 080	1,2	- 22 186	- 7,8	788 373	+ 65 603	+ 9,1	2 416	- 117	- 4,6
1971	254 753	1,2	- 31 418	- 11,0	668 503	+ 47 334	+ 7,6	62 908	- 1 044	- 1,6
1972	368 952	1,7	- 6 612	- 1,8	501 626	+ 40 967	+ 8,9	206 977	- 107 221	- 34,1
1973	347 053	1,6	- 9 299	- 2,6	569 958	+ 47 907	+ 9,2	16 198	- 1 323	- 7,6
1974	620 154	2,7	- 340	- 0,1	330 659	+ 23 107	+ 7,5	309 264	+ 41 345	+ 15,4
1975	1 183 501	5,2	+ 29 206	+ 2,5	246 236	+ 25 173	+ 11,4	956 514	+ 55 962	+ 6,2
1976	1 346 723	5,9	- 4 267	- 0,3	208 539	+ 17 921	+ 9,4	493 278	- 250 043	- 33,6
1977	1 213 741	5,3	- 35 177	- 2,8	224 464	+ 22 533	+ 11,2	281 211	+ 12 393	+ 4,6
1978	1 224 309	5,4	+ 10 811	+ 0,9	223 841	+ 19 145	+ 9,4	250 599	- 574	- 0,2
1979	1 134 060	5,0	- 37 293	- 3,2	266 894	+ 29 104	+ 12,2	166 950	+ 32 036	+ 23,7
1980	992 520	4,3	- 43 999	- 4,2	312 593	+ 30 368	+ 10,8	101 558	+ 5 467	+ 3,5
1981	1 299 919	5,6	- 8 646	- 0,7	239 282	+ 11 174	+ 4,9	373 765	- 27 743	- 6,9
1982	1 935 316	8,1	- 14 438	- 0,7	132 034	+ 9 886	+ 8,1	587 167	+ 48 492	+ 9,0
1983	2 535 836	10,4	+ 48 761	+ 2,0	68 774	+ 6 946	+ 11,2	1 148 168	- 43 615	- 3,7
1984	2 536 593	10,2	- 2 715	- 0,1	79 708	+ 9 747	+ 13,9	643 615	+ 78 127	+ 13,8

Verhältnis Arbeitslose : offene Stellen Februar 1984 = 1 : 31,8 (Januar 1984 = 1 : 36,3)

Bundesanstalt für Arbeit
- Statistik -
Ib2 - 4221
Germany (West)

Abgang an Arbeitslosen

Februar 1961 bis 1984

Jahr	im Berichtsmonat					seit Jahresbeginn bis Ende des Berichtsmonats				
	insgesamt	dar. Vermittlungen von Arbeitslosen in Beschäftigung über 7 Kalendertage		Veränderung gegenüber Vormonat		insgesamt	dar. Vermittlungen von Arbeitslosen in Beschäftigung über 7 Kalendertage		Veränderung gegenüber Vorjahr	
		abs.	in %	abs.	in %		abs.	in %	abs.	in %
	1	2	3	4	5	6	7	8	9	10
1961	291 346	.	.	+ 81 396	+ 38,8	501 296	.	.	.	.
1962	189 016	.	.	- 2 516	- 1,3	380 548	.	.	- 120 748	- 24,1
1963	171 169	.	.	+ 18 555	+ 12,2	323 783	.	.	- 56 765	- 14,9
1964	185 052	.	.	+ 28 295	+ 18,1	341 809	.	.	+ 18 026	+ 5,6
1965	134 174	.	.	- 6 652	- 4,7	275 000	.	.	- 66 809	- 19,5
1966	153 133	.	.	+ 36 709	+ 31,5	269 557	.	.	- 5 443	- 2,0
1967	198 432	.	.	+ 38 873	+ 24,4	357 991	.	.	+ 88 434	+ 32,8
1968	255 390	.	.	+ 51 553	+ 25,3	459 227	.	.	+ 101 236	+ 28,3
1969	147 087	.	.	- 5 625	- 3,7	299 799	.	.	- 159 428	- 34,7
1970	135 701	.	.	+ 15 157	+ 12,6	256 245	.	.	- 43 554	- 14,5
1971	152 479	.	.	+ 29 748	+ 23,6	275 810	.	.	+ 19 565	+ 7,6
1972	170 590	.	.	+ 28 413	+ 20,0	312 767	.	.	+ 36 957	+ 13,4
1973	157 703	.	.	+ 7 528	+ 5,0	307 878	.	.	- 4 889	- 1,6
1974	207 397	.	.	+ 25 883	+ 14,3	388 911	.	.	+ 81 033	+ 26,3
1975	248 849	.	.	+ 19 895	+ 8,7	477 803	.	.	+ 88 892	+ 22,9
1976	272 145	.	.	- 9 555	- 3,4	553 845	.	.	+ 76 042	+ 15,9
1977	302 144	.	.	+ 44 345	+ 17,2	559 943	.	.	+ 6 098	+ 1,1
1978	254 706	.	.	- 15 699	- 5,8	525 111	.	.	- 34 832	- 6,2
1979	276 279	.	.	+ 26 180	+ 10,5	526 378	.	.	+ 1 267	+ 0,2
1980	260 831	.	.	+ 19 683	+ 8,2	501 979	.	.	- 24 399	- 4,6
1981	254 389	.	.	+ 39 065	+ 18,1	469 713	.	.	- 32 266	- 6,4
1982	282 605	56 536	20,0	+ 52 936	+ 23,0	512 274	99 816	19,5	+ 42 561	+ 9,1
1983	238 697	47 316	19,8	- 12 263	- 4,9	489 657	89 453	18,3	- 22 617	- 4,4
1984	292 484	65 091	22,3	+ 8 825	+ 3,1	576 143	120 108	20.8	+ 86 486	+ 17,7

Bundesanstalt für Arbeit
Statistik
Ib2 - 4221 -

Germany (West)

Zugang an Arbeitslosen

Februar 1961 bis 1984

Jahr	im Berichtsmonat			seit Jahresbeginn bis Ende des Berichtsmonats		
	insgesamt	Veränderung gegenüber Vormonat		insgesamt	Veränderung gegenüber Vorjahr	
		absolut	in %		absolut	in %
1961	190 512	- 139 370	- 42,2	520 394	.	.
1962	176 407	- 61 548	- 25,9	414 362	- 106 032	- 20,4
1963	178 011	- 151 997	- 46,1	508 019	+ 93 657	+ 22,6
1964	152 245	- 89 680	- 37,1	394 170	- 113 849	- 22,4
1965	139 076	- 85 998	- 38,2	364 150	- 30 020	- 7,6
1966	120 101	- 87 263	- 42,1	327 465	- 36 685	- 10,1
1967	250 848	- 158 244	- 38,7	659 940	+ 332 475	+ 101,5
1968	172 480	- 177 756	- 50,8	522 716	- 137 224	- 20,8
1969	152 628	- 102 297	- 40,1	407 553	- 115 163	- 22,0
1970	113 515	- 101 121	- 47,1	328 151	- 79 402	- 19,5
1971	121 061	- 113 383	- 48,4	355 505	+ 27 354	+ 8,3
1972	163 978	- 83 953	- 33,9	411 909	+ 56 404	+ 15,9
1973	148 404	- 78 886	- 34,7	375 694	- 36 215	- 8,8
1974	207 057	- 109 320	- 34,6	523 434	+ 147 740	+ 39,3
1975	278 055	- 159 278	- 36,4	715 388	+ 191 954	+ 36,7
1976	267 878	- 141 416	- 34,6	677 172	- 38 216	- 5,3
1977	266 967	- 149 815	- 35,9	683 749	+ 6 577	+ 1,0
1978	265 517	- 127 678	- 32,5	658 712	- 25 037	- 3,7
1979	238 986	- 175 742	- 42,4	653 714	- 4 998	- 0,8
1980	216 832	- 194 052	- 47,2	627 716	- 25 998	- 4,0
1981	245 743	- 159 844	- 39,4	651 330	+ 23 614	+ 3,8
1982	268 167	- 207 394	- 43,6	743 728	+ 92 398	+ 14,2
1983	287 458	- 227 225	- 44,1	802 141	+ 58 413	+ 7,9
1984	289 769	- 184 212	- 38.9	763 750	- 38 391	- 4,8

c) Analysing the Causes of Unemployment

The job crisis has no single cause - nor any quick and evident cure.
Lothar Ross maintains that "there are no simple monocausal
explanations" and we might add, there are no easy mono-solutions
to complex problems.
So is it in the area of unemployment. Pope John Paul II repeated
this position before the International Labour Organisation in
Geneva, where he said: "As we know, the causes of unemployment
indeed are many and varied. One of these causes may lie in the
improvement in the instruments of production which progressively
curtails the direct share of man in the production process.
This involves us a new antinomy which may well set human labour
against "capital"[78]. Thus we face a new problem!

The classical economic theory that dominated in the nineteenth
century assumed that the economy was self-regulating and that if
only economic forces were given full play then in time there
would be employment for all. The state's job was to make sure
that the various parts of the naturally working economic system
were working without hindrance. It was believed that it was
not possible in normal circumstances to have a state of
equilibrium below the level of the full employment of capital
and labour as a result of their being insufficient demand for the
goods that could be produced. Any such fall away from the level
of full employment of capital was temporary and due to the
hindrances on the working of the natural laws of supply and demand.
The experience of mass unemployment in the inter-war years and
the theories of economists such as Keynes brought about a change
in mind and heart and readjustments in public policy.

---

78) John Paul II, Address to International Labour Organisation,
op.cit, p. 288

In the period between 1914 and 1939, the experience of mass
unemployment and the degradation it brought to those affected
by it bred in the western nations and on their leaders a
determination to find another way. Although the original
assumption of the market economy was and is that the system
of demand and supply works independently of any concerted
government action, this assumption has been modified in the light
of the needs of present day economic realities.

Lord John Maynard Keynes (1883 - 1946) was concerned with the
unemployment and argued against the classical theorists
that the economy did not necessarily operate at the level of the
full employment of labour and resources[79].

He suggested that the state needed to intervene in order to
encourage consumption, initiate public and private investment and
lower the rate of interest[80].

His thesis provided the theoretical justification for a policy
of state action to manage the economy by managing demand. In the
last ten years, under the experiences of inflation and faltering
economic growth, the Keynesian analysis[81] has been increasingly
challenged, and the policies based on it have been proved
to have its problems too.

It is being suggested therefore by economists that full employment,
as we have known it, is not possible without inflation, and that
there is a natural rate of employment consistent with constant
real wage costs. The key to expansion without inflation, therefore,
is moderate expansion of money supply, popularly called
"monetarist" theory[82].

---

79) Roger C., op.cit., 268; R. Freedman, Marx on Economics, London,
1962, p. 146
80) D. Dillard, The Economics of J.M. Keynes, London, 1966, p. 327
(Roger, c. ibid.
81) Keynes, J.M., Theory of Employment, Interest and Money, 1936
82) Friedman M. The Optimum Quantity of Money and other Essays, London,
1969, Refer also his other book "Unemployment and Inflation", London
1975.

Besides what we have tried to analyse above, there are many other
reasons why unemployment has become the order of the day in our own
times. Its immediate trigger was the recession that followed
OPEC's drastic 1979 - 1980 oil price increases[83].
Western governments adopted severely restrictive monetary policies
to avoid repeating the inflationary prop of the 1970's.
Those policies did curb inflation, but they also sent interest rates
soaring, stymied investment and prolonged the economic downturn.
Thousands of financially weak companies went under, and many
firms that survived did so only by imposing massive layoffs.
The workers, in short, were casualties of the battle against
inflation[84].

Above all, there is the dilemma of technology with all its problems
especially in the area of employment removal. As unemployment
increases, the switch from people to machines shows no sign of
abating. As Harry Anderson remarks: "In many basic industries, the
American worker has simply priced himself out of world markets;
in other words, his employer must rapidly automate in order to meet
emerging competitive threats from abroad. The question from
manufacturers is whether they are going to reduce their workers by
twenty five percent by putting in robbots, or by hundred percent
by going out of business.

The answer is obvious. With more than 13,000 workers already on
layoff, General Motors Corporation announced that it planned to
buy 14,000 industrial robbots over the next ten years... As analysis
shows, those new machines will be able to replace 40,000 to 50,000
workers when they are installed"[85]

---

83) Leonard Glynn and Co., op.cit., p.44

84) Ibid.

85) Harry Anderson and colleagues, "Jobs - putting America back to
     work", Newsweek magazine report, 18 october, 1982, p.38.

Modern technique creates a whole set of new problems and
sometimes produces unemployment. Pope John Paul II does not however
bury himself in pessimism. Technology has also its positive sides.
For him, "it opens great possibilities that ask of the worker
increasing qualifications, as also the contribution of his human
capacities and his creative imagination"[86].
Technology of course does create new jobs: people have to make, sell,
service new machines and operate them, and other have to sell their
houses, food, stocks and bonds. However, the full impact of the
technological ery is still to be really assessed. No one can say
for sure where technology is leading or how it will be applied in
the future. As far back as 1970, for example, no forecaster could
have predicted the impact of the microprocessor: it had not been
invented. And it is to be added however, that even if
technology does create new jobs today, as well as it removes, though
more, there is no assurance that the future will be bright as far as
technology and human labour is concerned. If history is any
indication, technology will eventually open up new industries that
no one has ever dreamed of yet. But as long as machines are applied
to jobs currently performed by human beings, people will inevitably
lose their jobs.

There are other causes of unemployment, for example, the creation
of an "academic proletariat". There are in certain redundant
areas of the labour world, so many overqualified candidates, and in
economic principle, if supply is more than demand, there will be a
fall in price. As long as many people refuse to give birth
to children in the western societies, there will be problem of a job
position for many people who are currently studying in the universities

---

86) John Paul II., Address to Workers at Jalisco Stadium, Mexico,
    30.1.1979, L'osservatore Romano, english edition, 12.2.1979.,
    No. 7, p.11.

to become teachers. Whom will they teach? They need a retraining
in jobs or else, they will finish their courses to find
themselves in the line of the jobless.

There is the secondary reason, which is no less important,
that people who are already having a high level of wage, say
a couple, also continue to work, both man and woman, instead of one
person staying at home to look after children, since the partner
earns enough salary. Rather, a young married couple do not want
to give chance for children in the family. But they want to have
more cars, more material goods, more houses, more possessions and
a very high living standard, when at the same time, many other
citizens of the same society have no jobs, even if the single
wage earner in a family of six or seven, where the rest do not have
work, is jobless. This situation is strongly reflected, when it is
proved that many women, whose partners earn fat salaries, also take
up paid jobs, and this all, at the expense of a society suffering
unemployment as our statistics show.

Finally, there is the strong reason that politicians and policy
makers are not showing very serious and radical signs for concern
and for the stopping of unemployment beyond modest government
schemes for job creation, training and retraining. As Anthony Sampson
remarks in an article titled "The spectre haunting the West",
saying that "politicians still find it hard to think seriously
about how their societies might be reorganised to cope with
diminishing employment or to try to answer the question: "What
happens when the work ethic runs out of work?" They have shown
themselves quite unable to bridge the gap in thinking about the need for
leisure on the one hand and the rise of unemployment on the other"[87].

---

87)   Sampson A., The spectre haunting the West, Newsweek, 18.10.1982, p.51

He goes on to make the hard point about the laxity of politicians
who have refused to face the basic truth concerning this "evil".
"The only logical solution to long term mass-unemployment
lies in a redistribution of work and leisure; Hard times have
concentrated the minds of many people, from company chairmen to
self-employed loners, on how to use one person to do the work of two"[88].
In the easy years of the economic boom, many company executives
built their empires by adding unnecessary staff; in the hard years,
they judge their success by the numbers they can fire.

In the face of all this problematic, there is a challenge from
Eastern Europe and the communist countries where unemployment is
technically impossible.

> "As a new generation in Western Europe is confronted by the
> prospect of long term mass unemployment, the politicians
> will face a second challenge - a challenge from Eastern
> Europe. However authoritarian, inefficient and
> unattractive the Eastern European regimes may be, they
> can somehow boast that they offer one benefit that
> Western Europe does not : the guarantee of job. The job
> may be minimal, uncomfortable and outdated; but if the West
> cannot face up to the problem of creating jobs, this
> promise from the East will inevitably begin to look
> more attractive to younger people who see no likelihood
> of work in their own country in their lifetime"[89].

---

88) Ibid.
89) Sampson, A.,, Ibid.

436

d) John Paul II on Unemployment - An Ethical Perspective:

In the fourth part of the encyclical, Laborem Exercens, where he examines the rights of workers, John Paul shows special concern, as indeed many men of good will, with the problem of unemployment which contradicts the basic principle that man has a God-given right and a vocation to work. Unemployment is an evil, says John Paul for many reasons, and when it reaches a certain level, can become a real social disaster[90]. Work is a right of every human person. It is one of the inalienable rights; it is a great and fundamental right of man, especially, the right to work and the right to the land[91].

In todays world, the reality presents a world where the right to work, does not necessarily entail the right to a job. Of course, it is not possible to create jobs out of nothing, nor is it possible to create jobs to manufacture goods which people do not want at prices no one can, or will chose to afford. However, it is the mind of many experts that unemployment as we have it today is curable. It is partly a problem deliberately or forcefully created out of a system of economic theory, handed down from the liberal naturalistic school, which influences are still with us. Otherwise, how can we explain that many countries in the communist countries do not know unemployment in large numbers, since they do not have it in their countries as is present in the West?

90) John Paul II, Laborem Exercens, n. 18
91) John Paul II, HOly mass at Nowy Targ, Poland, 8.6.1979, L'osservatore Romano, english edition, 16.7.1979, No. 29, p.7

John Paul regards unemployment as an evil, especially when it
affects young people "who after appropriate professional
preparation fail to find work, and see their sincere wish to work
and their own responsibility for the economic and social development
of the community sadly frustrated"[92]. Something has to be done
urgently!

In an address he delivered to a group of Christian Workers with the
title "The Right to Work and to Social Justice", the Pope said among
other things:

> "...In the first place, it is my earnest wish that
> work may be a real right for every human person.
> Today, the national and international situation is so
> difficult and complecated, that it is not possible
> to oversimplify. But since we know that work is life,
> serenity, commitment, interest, meaning, we must wish
> everyone to have it. He who has a job, feels he is
> useful, sound, engaged in something which gives his own
> life value. To be without job is psychologically
> negative and dangerous, particularly for the young
> and for those who have a family to support.
> Therefore, while we must thank the Lord if we have work, we
> must also feel the grief and distress of the unemployed and,
> as far as is in our power, endeavour to meet these painful
> situations. Words are not enough! It is necessary to help
> concretely, in a Christian way! While I appeal to those
> responsible for society, I also address each of you
> directly: commit yourselves, you, too, in order that
> everyone may have work!"[93].

---

92) John Paul II, Laborem Exercens, n. 18.

93) John Paul II., Address to a Group of Christian Workers; "The Right
to Work and Social Justice", 9 December 1978; L'oservatore
Romano, English Edition, 20 December 1978, No. 52, pp.4, 7.

This then is the view of John Paul on the problem of
unemployment. The right to work, which is also a duty, has to be
promoted and protected by society, even if it conflicts with other
potential rights. But the civil community should not confine
itself solely to protecting rights of workers, but should at the
same time see to it that the necessary economic and social
conditions are created to guarantee everyone the concrete exercise
of these rights. This requires that workers be prepared to play
an active part in economic life, according to their qualifications,
and through professional training adapted to the needs and
possibilities of the economy; but even more so, by a personal
promotion to such a cultural level as to be prepared for
further adaptation and change, wherever needed.
The plague of unemployment is the dreadful consequence of the
denial of such a right, and it is a serious problem of modern times,
for which the Holy Father has often expressed much concern.

John Paul stresses that there must be as a matter of state policy,
social security and financial assistance for the unemployed. He
writes in 'Laborem Exercens': "The obligation to provide
unemployment benefits, that is to say, the duty to make suitable
grants indispensable for the subsistence of unemployed workers and
their families, is a duty springing from the fundamental principle of
the moral order in this sphere, namely, the principle of the
common use of goods, or, to put it in another and still simpler
way, the right to life and subsistence"[94].

Respect for such a right is the responsibility of all those who
belong to a given society and act through the state structures, but
it is also the duty of the whole international community.

---

94) John Paul II, LE, n. 18

e) Elements Towards Solving the Problem of Unemployment:

Today, there is a call for action to revitalise the economy and
create jobs for people. In the past, many governments did not
give adequate attention, or coordinated and
coherent sense of purpose towards eliminating the problem of
unemployment. Workers were hired or fired depending on the flow
and ebb of the business cycle, and the labour scrambles to get -
and to hold on whatever it can, or to dispose of that which
does not make gain.

This attitude is no longer enough. Infact, the threatening
economic crisis cannot be taken for granted. The profound
changes at work in the job market require a new era of cooperation
among all sectors of society, a rigorous attention to preventing
the economy and human pain of sweeping dislocation. Any
effective agenda for creating jobs will demand sacrifices on many
fronts and action on a wide range of nagging problems.

To this complex problem there are admittedly however, no easy or
ready-made answers - none, certainly or uniformly applicable in
all situations and in all regions. It is the duty of ethics
to direct the attention of governments, employers - both direct and
indirect, to make the problem and its solution a priority number
in their line of action. In all, social responsibility
should be the leading motive.

Pope John Paul does not claim to be an expert in economic disciplines, and he certainly believes that the total suggestion for the eradication of the unemployment problem has to come from economists and those who have responsibility in the name of the people to make decisions for the common good. He however offers some guidelines for action[95]:

(1) Rational planning on a global scale;

(2) International co-operations;

(3) Creative efficiency;

(4) Discovery of the just proportion between the various types of work .

(5) Adequate systems of training and education·

These are the paths indicated by John Paul's encyclical to achieve the respect of the right to work for those who plough the earth, for the workers in industry and services, as well as for those dedicated to intellectual, scientific or artistic achievements. The unemployed must be put back to work. And John Paul uses a word, which in his homeland Poland, symbolises all that is necessary to stand against state oppression of the workers which it is supposed to support. He speaks out the word several times - SOLIDARITY!

Unemployment can be solved because it is often a man-made problem. The solution however lies in solidarity with work, in other words; "in accepting the principle of the primacy of human work over the means of production, and the primacy of the industrial worker and individual over production requirements or purely economic considerations.

We have the first and ultimate criterion in the planning of employment; solidarity with work must be the overriding theme in any search for a solution and it opens a new field to man's ingenuity and generosity"[96].

---

95) John Paul II, LE, n. 18

96) John Paul II., Address to the International Labour Organisation., op.cit., pp. 288 - 289.

CHAPTER EIGHT

TOWARDS A SPIRITUALITY OF HUMAN WORK

PART ONE (I):   Historical Background

1. Introducing the Situation:

When attempting a reflection on Human Work, and some elements for
a christian social ethic of labour, we should never lose sight of
the context and perspective in which a "Theology of work"
has developed in its historical phase, through antiquity, the
middle ages and continuing into our time. Infact, when John Paul
offers an Encyclical devoted to the "Social Question" especially work,
he ends his reflections with some elements for a "spirituality of work".

But John Paul does not start his analysis with society as such,
nor with sociological or economic details, rather he goes back to the
roots, and begins his meditation in a historical perspective with
the Bible as the point of departure. Convinced that Human Work
is "a fundamental dimension of man's existence on earth", and
taking into consideration the conclusions of the natural and physical
sciences towards humanising work, the Church, - and John Paul makes
this very specific both in his Magisterial Writing
"Redemptor Hominis" and in "Laborem Exercens", teaches that man
"is the fundamental way for the Church" as revealed in the Bible.
Thereby, what is a conviction of the intellect becomes for every
believing Christian, a conviction of faith[1]. When referring to the
human person, and by shedding light on his life and problems,
the Pope seeks to express "the eternal designs and the transcendental
destiny which the living God and the Creator and Redeemer, has linked
with man"[2].

_____

1)   John Paul II, Laborem Exercens, n. 4
2)   Ibid.

Thus man, created "in the image and likeness of God", who is at the same time, a father, mother, citizen of a nation, member of the Christian Community and of the world body, participates in God's creative activity. Man subdues the earth to put it at the service of man in honour of God and for the good of humanity[3].

Within the context of a catechesis concerned mainly with the proclamation of the Good News, and aimed at sustaining and developing faith and sensitivity for man's spiritual existence, and within the limits of his own capabilities, man continues to develope and to complete creation as he advances further and further in the discovery of the resources and values contained in the whole of creation[4]. This situation locates human work in the historical perspective, and we shall now devote some short references to earlier background towards a spirituality of work.

In his considerations and reflections concerning a theology and spirituality of human work, Pope John Paul II offers three basic areas where such a reflection can be fruitful. He looks at human work in its Genesis context where God is at work , taking out from it the invitation to man to work namely:

(a) Work as a sharing in the activity of the Creator;

(b) Christ - the man of Work, and lastly,

(c) Human work in the light of the Cross and Resurrection.

We shall conclude the chapter by setting out some accents for practical action in the area of work, a Christian ethic of work, or rather said, a "Theology of Human Work".

---

3) Genesis, 1: 28, LE, n. 4

4) Genesis 1: 28 ff ; LE, n. 25

2. The Genesis Account and Spirituality of Work in Antiquity:

The first two chapters of the book of Genesis depict God himself
as a "worker" "at work", creating the world, moulding man
from the ground with mud, walking in the garden of Eden, dividing
the waters, bringing light into existence out of darkness, creating
the trees, the birds of the air, the animals, etc., and giving to
man charge and control over the whole of creation to continue the work.

"In the day that the Lord God made the earth and the heavens, when
no plant of the field was yet sprung up - and there was no man to
till the ground - then the Lord God formed man of dust from
the ground, and breathed into his nostrils the breath of life; and
man became a living being. And the Lord God planted a garden in
Eden, in the East; and there he put the man whom he had formed"[5].

This biblical account is in the judaic - Christian tradition the basic
point of departure for any "Theology of man, and consequently
of work". Tilling the soil as is here depicted was an activity in
which man was engaged before the Fall, and in this context,
manual work is not to be seen simply as a result of the Fall.
Quite the contrary as the genesis story shows, for God gave to
Adam and Eve a garden to cultivate, delight in and tend, and it
was only after they had acted contrary to God's will and fallen from
grace, that the activity of tilling the soil became attended
with pain and suffering.

---

5) Genesis, 2: 4b - 8

Lothar Roos understood this ambivalence of the world of work, as
a good, but also a hardship where he writes: "Gegenüber einer
anthropologisch unrealistischen Überbetonung der
Arbeitslust und des Arbeitsglücks bis hin zu Vorstellungen einer
Selbsterlösung des Menschen durch Arbeit weiß die biblisch-
christliche Ethik um die Ambivalenz der Arbeit. Sie betont
deren Zwangschrakter (Thomas von Aquin: "Sola enim necessitas
victus cogit manibus operari"), ihre "drückende Mühe, sieht aber
darin auch etwas für den Menschen Wertvolles "bonum arduum"[6].

With this basic background, we can definitely assert that the original
injunction by God to man to till the earth, to work as part
of God's plan for him before the Fall, and the work which is for
him a penance as a result of his Fall - both these elements come
together in the Christian Theology of Work, and this insight is borne
out by the facts of experience. Work helps us attain fulfilment
and personal satisfactionof our needs, enriching our lives
with beauty and enjoyment. Through work, the disorders of a sinful
world can be brought under control, and man participates with God
in the work of creation. But at the same time, work entails an
element of real hardship and difficulty. Whether as a result of
"Original Sin" or as a result of whatever predicament man finds
himself because of the reality of work, pain and toil in this life
cannot be escaped.

Pope Leo XIII made the interesting point in this regard where he said
that the difficulty of work is a reminder of the consequences of
original sin: "Even had man never fallen from a state of innocence,
he would not have been wholly unoccupied; but that which would have
been a free choice and his delight became afterwards compulsory, and
the painful expiation of his disobedience"[7].

---

6) Roos, L., Theologie und Ethik der Arbeit., Communio, Internationale
   Katholische Zeitschrift, 13 (1984) 97-115, p. 102
7) Leo XIII., Rerum Novarum, par. 14 (Cf. also Genesis 3:17 "cursed be
   thee earth in thy work; in thy labour thou shalt eat of it all the
   days of thy life).

For the Jews in antiquity, manual work was held in great respect,
since it was evidently a way of obtaining the necessities for living.
Classical Rome and Greece did not give manual work all the honour
it merited, as the Jews did[8]. There was in the jewish situation
of the time, nothing incongruous in the person of Christ the
preacher, being a carpenter, the son of a carpenter and at the same
time a Rabbi.

Jesus' disciples were mainly manual workers - fishermen, tax-collectors,
hand workers. In the time of St. Paul, hard work was a sign of
good Christian example. He linked the effectiveness of his ministry
with his ability to earn his own living, exhorting his hearers
to be devoted to work, and to give good example with their diligence
at work. "He who does not work, should not eat"[9] became a law
binding the believers. In all that has been highlighted above,
work in the Genesis account and in antiquity had two sides: -
a positive one, which linked all work as a co-operation with God in
the work of creation, helping man also towards his own physical
and intellectual satisfaction; on the other side, work was looked
upon as a difficult task and necessity, a punishment as the book of
Genesis portrays: "cursed is the ground because of you; in toil you
shall eat of it all the days of your life; thorns and thistles it shall
bring forth to you..."[10]. And this predicament of man has since
been elevated by the Church to a "Theology of Work".

---

8) Roger C., op.cit., p.314
9) Ephesians, 4:28., I Thesalonians, 4:11
10) Genesis, 3:µ7

3. From the "Pastoral Constitution" to "Laborem Exercens"

It is later in the writings of Pope John XXIII and in the
"pastoral constitution of the Church in the world of today",
that this reality gained more attention, for in these later
documents, the spiritual situation of the world of work became
alarmingly terrifying, seeing that the question of meaninglessness
and a lack of a religious or ethical perspective led many workers
and business entrepreneurs to a loss of orientation and
direction. People spoke much of the crisis of work called the
"Sinnkrise der Arbeit";
There were also other related problems, namely, what Lothar Roos
characterises as "Der Übergang von der Industrie zur Dienstgesselschaft",
die "Ablösung der Arbeitsgesselschaft durch die Beschäftigungsgessel-
schaft", die "Freizeitgesselschaft", die "Wertunsicherheit", die
"Zukunftsangst", and what he finally calls the "Wirtschaftgesselschaft"[11].

In such a situation of crisis of work, a problem or rather and
better said, a question arises: "Do we not work too much and for many
false aims?" It is in the face of all these conflicting and
sometimes alienating systems that the pastoral constitution and
the teachings of the Magisterium, especially in the area of a
spirituality of work gains its importance as we shall now consider.

---

11) Ibid., p. 97

Not without reason is the Pastoral Constitution, officially
adopted and signed on.7. December 1965, regarded as
"De Ecclesia in Mundo Huius Temporis" - "On the Church in the
world today". The world the Council has in mind is "the world of
men, the entire human family, its whole environment; the
world which is the theatre of human history, marked with man's
industry, his triumphs and disasters"[12].

This world, which is a changing world, a modern world, has brought
with it many pluralistic tendencies. It is a world where one can
say with the writer: "The old Order has changed, giving place
to the new" in all dimensions, be it political, cultural, social,
religious or economical. Lothar Roos describes the time sorrounding
the "Pastoral Constitution" as a period of "geistige
Großwetterlage".

In this changing world, the crisis of human existence and meaning,
the claim to autonomous behaviour without any moral or traditional
background had increased. The Council Fâthers had exactly this
crisis in mind when they wrote their Constitution, for they said:
"In our time men are moved to admiration at their own inventions
and power, yet often wonder anxiously about the way the world is
developing, about the place and function of man in the universe, about
the direction of individual and collective effort, about the
final purpose of things and of men"[13].

---

12) Gaudium et Spes, n. 2
13) Ibid, par. 3

448

Especially worthy of mention in this period was the development of
many of the sciences, both the natural and speculative sciences,
without any sound ethical-philosophical-theological background,
thereby neglecting the basic question of meaning[14]. It is in such
a world-changing-situation that the "Pastoral Constitution" emerged
with its call for a relationship between Ethics and Theology on the
one hand, and its positive attitude towards the earlier points raised
in "French Theology" in the post war period. In this connection,
Roos maintains that exactly here did the Council Fathers set
up a strong accent and emphasis, namely: "Da das Ganze der
menschlichen Existenz nach christlicher OUberzeugung nie ohne den
Bezug des Menschen zu Gott interpretiert werden kann, wenn der
Mensch nicht sein Bestes und Eigentliches bereits in dieser
Welt verfehlen will, können der Mensch und die mit seiner Person
existentiell verbundenen irdischen Wirklichkeiten, und dazu gehört
auch die Arbeit, nicht ohne das "Licht des Evangeliums" voll
ausgeleuchtet werden. Solches Vorgehen verdrängt nicht die
menschliche Vernunft, sondern setzt sie voraus"[15].

From the aforesesaid, we can now assert that human reason remains a
basic "specificum" of man the believer. In trying to develope
such a "Theology of Work" like the Fathers at Vatican II attempted,
there is a call for the other sciences, both the human and social
sciences, besides the natural sciences, to aid the "Theology of work"
and help man arrive at a "Theological Anthropology".

---

14) Lothar Roos., op.cit., p.100 - 101
15) Ibid.

According to Professor Roos: "Die Gestaltung irdischer Verhältnisse
läßt sich nie in "direkter Aktion" vom Evangelium her ohne die
Vermittlung einer sozialwissenschaftlich-philosophisch arbeitenden
Sozialethik vornehmen... Insofern fragt eine "Theologie der Arbeit",
wie sie mit und nach dem Zweiten Vatikanischen Konzil entfaltet
wurde, nach den Konsequenzen einer theologischen Anthropologie für
die Ethik und über deren Vermittlung für die Ökonomie der Arbeit, wie
sie sich aus einem "integralem" Humanismus ergeben"[16].

Having arrived at this theological anthropology, man, the believer, is
made to look up to Jesus Christ, the "new Adam" and son of God, who
purifies and makes all things new in the Order of God's plan for man's
earthly and eternal salvation. The "Pastoral Constitution" understood
this very well for it maintains that "the mystery becomes clear only
in the mystery of the incarnate Word. Adam, the first man, was a
type of the future, that is of Christ our Lord"[17].

In the same vein, Pope John XXIII, Father of the Council wrote in
"Mater et Magistra" concerning this theological anthropology saying:
"We must affirm and reaffirm most strongly that this social doctrine is
an integral part of the Christian conception of life"[18].
It is in the context of this Christian anthropology, which has
Christ as the middle and aim of the universe, that the Pastoral
Constitution may be understood, and thereby too, its teachings on the
area of human work and economics in general. Man has always tried
to enlarge the scope of his life by work and skill, by means of
science and technology, extending his mastery over almost all nature.
In the course of this development, man now gets by his own industry many
benefits for which at one time he looked mainly to heavenly powers.

---

16) Ibid

17) Gaudium et Spes., par. 22,1., Romans 5:14., Tertullian, De carnis
resurrectione, 6: PL 2,282; CSEL 47, p. 33, 1. 12 13

18) John XXIII, Mater et Magistra, n. 222

PART TWO (II): John Paul II - Elements for a Spirituality of Work

1. Basic Views:

In the final section of his Encyclical on Human Work, Pope John
Paul II offers a synthesis of the elements leading to a spirituality
of work. It is significant that the Holy Father would often
approach a worker's audience in a purely religious key. And as a
justification for this attitude, he does this so that
"the work of the individual may be given the meaning which it has in
the eyes of God and by means of which work enters into the
salvation process"[1].

At the centre of this spirituality, the Pope sets three elements:
above all, work, any work even the most common activities of the
daily life of man has to be understood as "sharing in the activities
of God the Creator"[2].

Secondly, the constant point of reference must be the person of Jesus
Christ, the man of work[3]; and thirdly, human work is to be seen
in the light of the cross and the resurrection of Christ. As
John Paul says: "By enduring the toil of work in union with Christ
crucified for us, man in a way collaborates with the son of God
for the redemption of humanity... In work, thanks to the light that
penetrates us from the Resurrection of Christ, we always find... as
if it were an announcement of the new heavens and the new earth in
which man and the world participate precisely through the toil that
goes with work"[4].

---

1) Laborem Exercens., John Paul II., par. 24
2) Ibid., n. 25
3) Ibid., n. 25
4) Ibid., n. 27

This third section dealing with the cross and resurrection of
Christ is significant, taking into consideration the events of
13th May 1981, when the Turk, Ali Agca made an unsuccessful attempt
to assassinate John Paul on his way to announce this
Encyclical, thereby postponing the publication to some four months
afterwards. This Encyclical, we can rightly say, bears the mark
of the cross and the personal suffering of its author. But this
personal suffering has become a symbol of success and of
redemption, not only for the author of 'Laborem Exercens', but also
for entire world of work, for christendom and for all men of good will.

We shall now examine these criteria offered by John Paul II
and end it up with some evaluative perspectives and consequences
for the worker, who is at the same time a believer.

2. Work as a Sharing in the Activity of the Creator

In several chapters in the earlier part of this work, we made
efforts to portray the meaning of work and its social dimensions
and structures, stressing the important point in each juncture of
the considerations that human work is a continuation of the
creative work of the Creator. It is this element that John Paul
highlights in chapter five of 'Laborem Exercens' and in other
speeches which he delivered elsewhere.

Addressing workers at Jalisco Stadium in 1979, the Pope said:
"Friends, workers, brothers, there is a Christian conception of
work, of family and social life. It contains great values, and
demands moral criteria and norms in order to direct those who believe
in God and in Jesus Christ... Work is not a curse, it is a blessing
for man from God who calls man to rule the earth and transform it,
in order that the divine work of creation may continue with man's
intelligence and effort"[5]. This view, which is repeated often
in Laborem Exercens' shows how deep John Paul sees man's role in
God's work. Starting off with a biblical reflection on the text
of Genesis 1:28, which remains a constant point of reference
throughout the encyclical, John Paul presents man in the tradition
of the Church as created to God's image, and therefore, man shares
through his work in God's activity, and gives a personal contribution
to the realisation of the providential plan in history.
John Paul wishes to authenticate this truth and he bases his
arguments on the Sacred Scripture and the Second Vatican Council[6].

---

5) John Paul II., Address to workers at Jalisco Stadium, Guadalajara,
   Mexico., 30 January 1979; Osservatore Romano, english edition.,
   12 February 1979, No. 7, p. 11
6) Genesis 2ff., Revelations 15,3; Gaudium et Spes, par. 34, AAS 58
   (1966 pp. 1052 - 1053).

Says the Pontiff, "This description of creation, which we find in the
very first chapter of the Book of Genesis, is also in a sense
the first "Gospel of work". For it shows what the dignity of work
consists of: it teaches that man ought to imitate God, his
Creator, in working, because man alone has the unique characteristic of
likeness to God. Man ought to imitate God both in working and also
in resting, since God himself wished to present his own creative
activity under the form of work and rest...as the words of Christ
attest: My Father is working still and I am working"[7].

The contents of this "Gospel of work" was given particular
prominence by Jesus Christ, who through his words, his parables and his
life as a simple worker, has truly lived in practice, what he
proclaimed in his teachings to be the "Gospel of work". It is that
same attitude which Pope John Paul II imitates, when he refers to the
"Gospel of work" with a lavishness of biblical quotations and
references to the various Constitutions of "Lumen Gentium" and
"Gaudium et Spes", thus laying the milestones of a spirituality
of work, the elaboration of which is the special duty of the
magisterium and the exposers of the "Gospel of work".

This work, referred to often above is not just a specific type
of human activity, but as the Council teaches, "the most ordinary
everyday activities" which men and women perform for themselves,
their families and the entire society. They can justly consider
that by their labour they are unfolding the Creator's work, consulting
the advantages of their brothers and sisters, and contributing by
their personal industry to the realisation in history of the divine plan[8].

---

7) John Paul, LE, n. 25
8) Gaudium et Spes, par. 34

When this happens, man will discover his limitedness and his need
for God's loving aid and protection. Man will also be better in a
position to understand that his achievements are not
solely his, but that they are aided by God's almighty power.
Such an attitude in the world of work will limit man's rivalry and
competitive attitude towards God, since he will recognise like the
Psalmist put it, and later confirmed by Jesus, that "without God
man cannot do anything". This teaching is a consequence of the
spirituality of work, which avoids pride and presumptuousness
on the side of man, just because of his achievements through work.
If the human person knows that his work and achievements is only
a participation in the work of the Creator, he will channel all
his thoughts and actions towards him.

As the Council Fathers said: "Far from thinking that works produced
by man's own talent and energy are in opposition
to God's power, and that the rational creature exists as a kind
of rival to the Creator, Christians are convinced that the
triumphs of the human race are a sign of God's greatness and the
flowering of his own mysterious design..."[9].
Therefore, by their competence in secular fields and by
their personal activity, elevated from within by the grace of Christ,
man will work vigorously in his labour, through technical skill,
and civil culture to perfect God's designs and the light of his
word

9) Dogmatic Constitution on the Church, Lumen Gentium, 36; AAS 57,
   1965, p. 41 (Cf. Laborem Exercens, n. 25)

3. Christ - the Man of Work

The writer of the Acts of the Apostles began an introduction of
his book with the sentence "Jesus began to do and to teach"[10].
Exactly, with this viewpoint does John Paul II portray the
world of work, and introduces Jesus as a man of work.
Whether it was in his lifestyle some two thousand years ago, or
in his teachings, parables, references, Jesus Christ always showed
special relationship with the working man, with work itself.

As John Paul says: "In his parables on the kingdom of God,
Jesus Christ constantly refers to human work: that of the shepherd,
the farmer, the doctor, the sower, the householder, the servant, the
steward, the fisherman, the merchant and the labourer...
He speaks of the various forms of women's work, compares the
apostolate to the manual work of harvesters or fishermen and refers to
the work of scholars too"[11].

In the preceeding chapter, we tried to show that through his work, the
human being and worker participates in the creative work of
renewing the earth together with the Creator.
Exactly in the life and person of Jesus Christ, the man and worker
in Israel is this attitude epitomised. As John Paul said:
For Jesus not only proclaimed but first and foremost fulfilled by his

---

10) Acts of the Apostles, 1:1
11) John Paul II, LE, n. 26 (Ref.Jn. 10:1-16; Mk 12: 1-12; Lk 4:23;
    Mk 4:1-9; Mt 13:52; Mt 24:45; Lk 12:42-48; Lk 16:1-8; Mt 13:45-46 ;
    Mt 13:47-50; Mt 20:1-16; Mt 13:33; Lk 15:8-9; Mt 9:37; Jn 4:35-38;
    Mt 4:19; Mt 13:52).

deeds the "gospel", the word of eternal Wisdom, that had been
entrusted to him. Therefore this was also the "gospel of work",
because he who proclaimed it was himself a man of work, a
craftsman like Joseph of Nazareth. And if we do not find in his
words a special command to work - but rather on óne occasion a
prohibition against too much anxiety about work and life - at the
same time the eloquence of the life of Jesus is unequivocal
he belongs to the "working world", he has appreciation and respect
for human work. It can indéed be said that he looks with love upon
human work and the different forms that it takes, seeing in each one
of these forms a particular facet of man's likeness with God, the
Creator and Father[12].

The point is clear Jesus Christ himself was a man of manual labour,
the "son of a carpenter" and an employee in the service of
St. Joseph in his workshop in Nazareth.

From this fact that Jesus was a man of work, John Paul reduces
elements for a spirituality of work. First of all, the Christian
has to see the positive sides of work as a joy and a fulfilment,
and therefore as a means of glorifying God. Since God has given
to man talents to develope, we must make honest use of these
talents. Man cannot be so alienated either by conditions or by
the nature of his work from seeking and finding God through that
work - so seeking and finding his own personal fulfilment.

---

12) John Paul Ii, LE, n. 26 (Ref. Mk. 6:2 - 3; Mt 13:55; Mt 6:25 - 34)

The more one gains fulfilment from the nature of the work, the more it accords with God's plan, but the Christian who has to spend his time in doing work of a "less congenial nature, while seeking means of improving his situation can still find Christ in the service of others in that work"[13] Christ himself condescended to do simple menial jobs, ending up a carpenter. Thereby, he has raised the dignity of human work, since also, it is the dignity of man that is in question. This explains why the Pope said that the "value of work was given special prominence by Jesus Christ, the son of God who chose to spend his life as a workman".

With this understanding, the Christian should not be possessed of that snobbery which regards only certain kinds of occupation as really worthy of man's dignity. Inevitably, there are certain jobs or professions which stand in the eyes of society as higher in public estimation than others. Says Roger Charles: "This 'league table' of respect for work is in itself innocent enough and, in its way, necessary, but it must not lead to lack of respect for those who have neither the talent nor the opportunity for the more highly regarded occupations and to do what are necessary tasks, upon which those engaged in more respected professions rely. This very fact, that we all rely on each other - should prevent any underestimation of the human value of all honest work, wherever it stands in the scale of social estimation"[14].

John Paul II goes further in an address to Italian workers to say that "where man sweats, works and suffers, Christ is present. I may say I have come to seek his presence here among you, who expend your tiring labour here as he once did in the workshop in Nazareth"[15] Work has to be the means in order that the whole of creation may be subjected to the dignity of the human being and son of God.

---

13) Roger Charles, op. cit. p. 315
14) Ibid.
15) John Paul II, Address to Workers in Pomezia, Italy, 13 September 1979; Osservatore Romano, English Edition, 1 October 1979, No. 40,pp.3-4

4. Human Work in the Light of the Cross and Resurrection

> "The law of the Cross is engraved on man's work. It is
> with the sweat of his brow that the farmer works. It is
> with the sweat of his brow that the Iron worker works.
> It is with the sweat of his brow - the terrible sweat of
> death - that Christ agonises on the Cross ... Through the
> Cross man has been able to understand the meaning
> of his own destiny, of his life on earth".
>   (John Paul II to workers at Nowa Huta).

Already in 1979 while visiting his native Country Poland, John Paul II
looked at work to be inseparably bound up with the Cross, but also
the resurrection of Christ. The above statements he made to
industrial workers had been repeated in many other incidents and
speeches, not less in the Encyclical "Laborem Exercens".

In this document, John Paul considers human work in the light of the
Cross and Resurrection of Christ. He says that "it is another
aspect of human work, an essential dimension of it, profoundly
imbued with the spirituality based on the Gospel"[16]
There is no work without toil, or rather, all work is associated with
the cross, with the sweat of man's face, and with the consequent joy,
of course that flows from getting ideas put into action through work.

All work, says the Pope, whether manual or intellectual, is inevitably
linked with toil. Toil or the cross cannot be separated from man's
work. Christ cannot be separated from his cross. To work is
therefore in a way, to participate in Christ's Cross, if this work is
understood theologically. As John Paul II made clear in the Nowa
Huta homily: "Christ remains before our eyes on his Cross, in order
that each human being may be aware of the strength that he has
given him: "he gave them power to become children of God" (Jn. 1:12).

---

16) John Paul II., Laborem Exercens, n. 27
17) John Paul II., Homily at mass at Nowa Huta, op.cit.

This must be remembered both by the worker and the employer, by
the work system as well as by the State, the nation, the Church"[17].
Seeing work in conjunction with the Cross has a theological backing
in the book of Genesis where Yahweh is quoted to have said:
"Cursed is the ground because of you; in toil you shall eat of it
all the days of your life"[18].

This toil spoken of in the book of Genesis and connected with
human work here on earth, marks the way of all humans, wherever
you may find them and has since become the basis of the work-ethic
and the spirituality of work, found in Catholic Theology.

John Paul makes this point more explicit for he says:
"Through toil - and never without it. On the one hand this confirms the
indispensability of the Cross in the spirituality of human work; on the
other hand the Cross which this toil constitutes reveals a new
good springing from work itself, from work understood in depth and
in all its aspects and never apart from work"[19]. In a way, this
is proclamation of the Gospel of work. This Gospel of work, helps
people to form a spirituality of work, where men will come closer
to God in their work, and participate in his creative and redemptive
work of salvation for all men. This Gospel of work is the Gospel of the
Cross.

The Christian in the words of John Paul II "finds in human work a
small part of the Cross of Christ and accepts it in the same spirit
of redemption in which Christ accepted his Cross for us. In work,
thanks to the light that penetrates us from the Resurrection of
Christ, we always find a glimmer of new life, of the new good, as
if it were an announcement of "the new heavens and the new earth" in which
man and the world participate precisely through the toil that goes
with work"[20].

---

18) Genesis, 3:17
19) JOhn Paul II, LE, n. 27
20) Ibid.

With this perspective, we can as believers and Christians really say, that
the problems being raised today about human labour are deeply engraved in
the Gospel, and they cannot be fully solved without the Gospel.
Christ will never approve that man be considered, or that man consider
himself, merely as a means of production, or that he be appreciated,
esteemed and valued in accordance with that principle. The Cross
and suffering of Christ opposes any form of degradation of man, including
degradation by work. In fact, it was through the Christian doctrine
which teaches us to adore the son of God made man for love of men,
even becoming an artisan himself and the son of a carpenter that
human labour was elevated to a higher dignity. Under this criteria, work
exists for man and not man for work. If this were not so, man
would become a slave again, but in and through Christ, man has become
God's collaborator. Through the Cross man attains a higher stage -
he participates in the fruits of the Cross, namely the Resurrection.

John Paul announced this "Gospel of Work", a sort of "Theology of
the Cross" and admonished his audience of workers thus:
"Let us go together, pilgrims, to the Lord's Cross; with it
begins a new era in human history. This is the time of grace and
salvation. Through the Cross man has been able to understand the
meaning of his own distiny, of his life on earth. He has discovered how
much God has loved him. He has discovered, and he continues to discover
by the light of faith, how great is his own worth. He has learnt to
measure his own dignity by the measure of the sacrifice that God
offered in his son for man's salvation"[21].

----

21) John Paul II, Homily at mass at Nowa Huta, op.cit.

By becoming incorporate with the mystery of the Cross through
baptism, Christians participate in Christ's work of redemption[22].
Therefore, if labour, in God's original plan, prior to the fall
of Adam, provided man the joy of sovereign dominion over the
earth and all creation, this labour, did not as participation
in the process of redemption after sin, remain free from suffering
and purification.

"The price of sin is death", says the gentile preacher Paul, but
man has been saved through Christ's salvific offering on the Cross.
As Paul says again in his letter to the Romans: Christians
participate not only in the mystery of death, but also in the mystery
of Christ's resurrection[23]. In this way, the Cross of labour is
heartened by the eschatological beginning of future glory and
happiness. Therefore, when man through his human work participates in
the creative and redeeming action of the word of God made man
this labour becomes for Christians, simultaneously both suffering and joy.

The Holy Father refers to this point in "Laborem Exercens" where
he writes: "In a sense, the final word of the Gospel on this
matter as on others is found in the Paschal Mystery of Jesus Christ...
The Paschal Mystery contains the Cross of Christ and his obedience
unto death... It also contains the elevation of Christ, who by
means of death on a Cross returns to his disciples in the Resurrection
with the power of the Holy Spirit"[24]. Because the grave is empty,
as he is "risen from the dead according to the Scriptures", Christ
is now as the Fathers of Vatican II made clear in the "Pastoral
Constitution", at work in people's hearts.

---

22) Romans 6:5
23) Romans 6:4
24) John Paul II, LE, n. 27

"He animates, purifies, and strenghtens those noble longings too
by which the human family strives to make its life more human and to
render the whole earth submissive to this goal"[25]. This type
of earthly progress is wordly and actively encouraged by the
Fathers of Vatican II, for the fruit of hard labour, the sweat of
human work should not go unrepaid - now and hereafter. Through his
labour man creates a new earth, eventhough, "the expectation
of a new earth must not weaken but rather stimulate our concern
for cultivating this one. For here grows the body of a
new human family, a body which even now is able to give some
kind of foreshadowing of the new age. Earthly progress must be
carefully distinguished from the growth of Christ's kingdom.
Nevertheless, to the extent that the former can contribute to
the better ordering of human society, it is of vital concern
to the Kingdom of God"[26].

---

25) Gaudium et Spes, par. 38
26) Ibid., 39

5. Conclusion:

John Paul's spirituality of work is a summon to "go beyond" all
boundaries in treating the "Social Question of Human Labour".
A Christian must go beyond all that a human analysis can offer
and transcend the given in the reality of God's endlessness, in
the "Gospel of work". This we find in God's word which is written
in the Scriptures - words - expressed in the Incarnate God as
seen in the life of Christ. John Paul invites us to approach the
"Social Question" in the perspective of the Creation by God, but
also in the perspective of the passion, death and resurrection of Christ.
By so doing, all problems of Social Justice, and the reordering of
the world of human work""to make work more human" are thus transferred:
they take heed on two noble Fronts, namely:- the theology of the
Creation and of Christology. This is John Paul's contribution
and it is worth consideration, for its depth, its seriousness
and its offer towards solving the "Social Question".

John Paul's desire is to enter into the interior part of the working
world, in order to rediscover it and to give back human and spiritual
authenticity to labour. Infact, when addressing an audience
of workers, it has been remarked that he never fails to mention their
immense reserve of kindness, their openness to God, the relation
between Cross and Work, the Paschal Mystery, the peaceful cooperation
between workers and employers, and the eschathological foundation
of every multiform working activity. "Open up to God" he would say
to workers - everywhere he had opportunity to address them. "God
loves you; Christ loves you"[27].

---

27) John Paul II; Address to Workers and Peasants at Monterrey,
Mexico., op.cit.

Or, as he would say to Italian workers: "Work does not imply only
a human relation, it also has a transcendent and religious aspect.
Manual and intellectual work is part of a wider activity, which is
the moral one: the objective to which it is directed is man "in his
entirety, in his dignity, in his... immortal destiny"[28].

For this fundamental reason, John Paul testifies like his predecessors
too have done in the great Social Encyclicals beginning with Leo XIII,
that the religious co-efficient is no alienating element, but a
necessary one, "to provide a better solution to the human relations
which spring from the industrial organisations, and to correct
"the basic failings of every system which views human relations
in places of work as purely economic"[29]. As John Paul also says
in his first Encyclical as Pope of Rome:

> "Only by giving again a moral and Christian sense
> to human labour conceived and exercised as a vocation,
> will it be possible to set the conditions for a
> better quality of life for all in this stage of
> history"[30].

Yet, the Pope warns that when serving man also in his temporal
dimension, the Church does not act outside the purpose of her
mission, which, according to the liberating anthropology of the
evangelical message, is still to help him become a better man, more
conscious of his dignity, rights and duties, socially responsible,
creative and useful, free from any form of bondage and oppression,
constantly directed to the higher values of spirit, faith, hope
and justice [31].

---

28) John Paul. Address to Workers of Pomezia, Italy; 13.9.1979.
  L'Osservatore Romano, English Edition, 1.10.1979, No. 40, pp.3-4
29) John Paul, Address to the Authorities of the Polish People's Republic,
  at the Belvedere, Warsaw, 2.6.1979; L'Osservatore Romano, Eng.ed.
  No. 24, 11.6.1979., p. 4
30) John Paul II., Redemptor Hominis, n. 22
31) Msgr. R. Rossi, The Social Teaching of John Paul II, PCJP, Vol.5, p.35.

SECTION THREE

THE RELEVANCE OF "LABOREM EXERCENS" TO POST-COLONIAL NIGERIA

CHAPTER NINE : Applying the Social Principles and Ethical
Propositions of Laborem Exercens to Nigeria

PART ONE (I) : Towards a True Understanding of the Meaning and
Value of Human Work

"Nigeria has been blessed by the creator with a rich
human potential and with natural wealth. Such gifts,
received in humble gratefulness, are also a constant
challenge, for the goods of this world are given by the
creator for the benefits of all. Public authorities
are entrusted with the sacred assignment to channel
these riches to the best interests of the people, that
is, for the betterment of all and the future of all".[1a]
        John Paul II in Nigeria, 1982.

"Man alone is adapted to work. Only he works and in
working fulfils his life on earth. Wherefore, work
bears man's signature, the distinctive mark of his
human nature, the mark of a person who is acting
within a community of persons, a mark which reveals
him as he truly is and constitutes to a certain
extent his very nature".
        John Paul II, Laborem Exercens, n.1

1a) John Paul II, Speech to President Shagari in Government
     House, Ikoyi, Lagos, 12.2.1982, Published in Daily Times,
     Special Edition, 1982.

1. A New Value and Meaning of Human Work:

A true understanding of the meaning and value of human work
demands that we consider work in its threefold dimensions and
threefold functions as John Paul tries to show. Regarded from the
point of view of its external effects, work has a threefold
dimension which extends through time. Man procures his daily
bread by work; he developes the technical arts and sciences
by work; and he raises the standards of civilisation by work[1].
Each of these ends he seeks for his family, his nation and the
whole of mankind as it continues through time. As he benefits
from the work of past generations, so also he works for the
benefit of generations yet to come[2]. Work is thus a transitive
activity: it originates from the human subject and is directed
towards an external object[3]. However, it does not
follow from this that work's external purposes are of the first
importance, necessary though it is that all should be pursued.
The second Vatican Council teaches that "as human activity
proceeds from man, so is it ordered towards man'.

---

1) John Paul II, Laborem Exercens, n.1
2) Ibid., n. 16
3) Ibid, n. 24

2. The Person:

The emphasis here is on the human person, the individual.
Most people do not realise it, but it was Christianity that
first brought person into focus. In pre-Christian Greece, for
example, person (prosopon) referred to the mask worn by actors
in plays. This mask was the kind that had a frown or a smile cut
into it so that the actor's voice could speak through it.
Essentially, it was a 'front' hiding the reality behind it.

In Roman times, this came to be called a per-sona, literally,
that through which the sound comes. But with the advent of
Christianity, we find increased attention to the concept and
reality of person, as the one behind the mask. Gradually
with the unfolding of the doctrine of the Trinity, philosophers
and theologians were forced to think through the meaning of what
it is to be human and what it is to be a person.

Of course, it is one thing to know the meaning of person
as a whole and free and intelligent being, but quite
another thing to see the practical implications of that
understanding for everyday living. Human wisdom accumulates only
too slowly, and it took centuries for men and institutions to
work out in practice a genuine respect for the dignity of
persons - a dignity that we too often take for granted today.

An example here will do: For centuries, women and slaves were
viewed as things among things, as household property, as chattels.
Because only the free man was regarded as a person, and women and
slaves were not free, they had no rights. With the conquest of the
New World, this same view obtained vis-a-vis the Indian,
and often Indians were slaughtered with no compunction, much as one
would kill a wild animal, to talk less of the treatment meted
out to Africans during the slave trade era and in the colonial and
neo-colonial situations.

Vatican Council II gave adequate stress on the meaning of
person in the Document 'Gaudium et Spes'. The Council Fathers declared:

> "There is a growing awareness of the exalted dignity
> proper to the human person, since he stands above all
> things and his rights and duties are universal and
> inviolable, for the beginning, the subject and the goal
> of all social institutions is and must be the human
> person"[4].

It is with Christianity, then, that focus is given to the meaning
of person as what is most sacred in the cosmos.
And the richness of the meaning continues unfolding as John Paul's
analysis of the meaning and value of human work shows.
The essential purpose of man's work is more to perfect himself
than to change the world in which he lives. Although it
is true that when man was put into the world he was charged with
the task of changing it, his first care in carrying out his task
is to bring about his own growth in humanity. This is the
"fulness of his vacation which is worth more than any external
riches that can be garnered"[5].

In changing the world, man supplies the material for human progress,
but that material cannot of itself bring about human progress.
Hence the Pope's description of man as 'the subject of work'.
The work is his, it is an expression of his being. Not only
does it originate in him but always it is referred back to him.
Work is 'man's good, his human nature's good'[6].

---

4) Gaudium et Spes, n. 26
5) John Paul II, LE, part 5, Section 26, paragraph 122
6) Ibid., part 2, section 9.

3. All Work is Valuable:

Such a concept practically does away with the very basis of the
differentiation of people into groups according to the kind of
work done: industry or agriculture, manual or intellectual work,
services or research, white-collar or business management; all
those involved in these activities are workers in the fullest
sense of the word. There is therefore in the world of work, no
small man or big man, and no class work, for every man and woman
is a 'homo Laborem Exercens', a human being at work, who gives work
its primary basis and value. What the encyclical says about work
applies to all people. Are we then not called to go beyond the
'workers' question, and to make it the question of the human person
who seeks through his work "to realise his humanity, to fulfil
the calling to be a person that is his by reason of his very
humanity"[7].

The encyclical does not ignore the conflicts but it does not take
the notion of class as a basis to indicate a way towards a solution.
Tensions and conflicts exist, but they do not find an adequate
analysis in the notion of class, nor do they find a just solution
in the systematic class struggle. In the past, the notion of class
was seen as the central dimension of the social question. Today,
we must insist on the world-wide dimension of the Social Question.

From the aforementioned, it follows that although different kinds
of work can have different objective values put upon them, no
differentiation may be made between the poeple who do these
different works. All men are alike in their likeness to God and

---

7)   Ibid., Le, n.6.

therefore all work is to be appraised alike according
to the dignity of the subject of it, the man and person
from whom it proceeds. It follows also that whatever the
material result for which the worker strives, that purpose
has no final significance in itself. The true purpose of any
kind of work is man himself. We must take care that work
is not turned against man[8].

But work is not only refrained to the person doing it.
Infact, person involves not only our own unity and integrity,
but it points to the need of community. Here we learn who we
are by the other revealing us to ourselves. This mystery of
the 'other person' entering into my personhood is such that he
can bring out the best in me or the worst in me. So we can
speak of this other person in psychological language as the
'alter ego'. He it is, who in his relationship to me has,
as Heidegger says, a 'concern for', rather than a 'use of' me.

8) Kirwan, J; Introduction to Laborem Exercens - Study Edition,
    CTS, London, 1984, p.iii - iv.

4. Work is Corporate:

Pope John Paul II did not hesitate to tell Nigerian workers
this truth during his visit to Nigeria in 1982.

> "Work is also man's way of helping his neighbour",
> said he. "One person's work affects another
> person, and together workers help to build up the
> whole of society. Those who work can say:
> When we work conscientiously, we make a real contribution
> towards a better world. Our work is an act of
> solidarity with our brothers and sisters"[9].

Here, human work is seen to be cooperative. The man at work
reaps a harvest which others worked for. Every man lives in a
state of dependency: First of all upon God, who gives him all
gifts; and then upon his fellow men who have worked before him
and who now work with him to develope the potential of those gifts[10].

Everything that is used in work is itself the product of work.
This is true of the natural resources which men have transformed
to fit their purpose, it is true of the machines which men have
made and continue to make, and it is true above all of the
inheritance of technical knowledge and skills which make all else
possible. The world of work is really the entire world, and in
this sense, work offers the appropriate areas for social
integration on the family level, national level and on the
international community, all of which are to be seen as open
towards the whole of humanity.

---

9) John Paul II, in a sermon at mass in Lagos Cathedra, Nigeria
   on 16.2.1982. Documented in Daily Times special edition, p.68
10) John Paul II, Laborem Exercens, n. 13, 14. (see also John 4:38)

The work of which John Paul II speaks is very different from
an all too commonly held idea of work. In the Pope's
vision, work possesses the property of community building;
to the world it seems often to be a source of strife[11],

Work, says the Pope, is a fundamental dimension of man's
life on earth[12]; work for the world is an activity
which becomes less and less necessary, perhaps rightly so,
that man may have time for more important things.

Echoing the Bible, John Paul says that "man is born to work
as well as called to it, that work is for man and that it is
a lifelong activity which man must pursue"[13]. In the wisdom
of the world leisure is more important.

---

11) John Paul II, LE, n. 20
12) Ibid., n. 4
13) LE, n. 1

5. Summary:

In a society in transition and change, we must be alert to
those things that tend to relegate a person to a place lower
than is rightfully his. We must be on guard continuously
against the forces of depersonalisation which flows
readily from a materialistic and computerised mentality.

This guard must be extended also to institutions, even to
the Church herself. We cannot forget that institutions are
also touched by the reality of sin and on occasion,
misidentify the common good with that of the vested interest.

We must keep constantly before our minds the words "the sabbath
was made for man", and also be able to say: "work is made for man".
A similar problem exists in a technological society which tends
to want to manipulate the entire earth and every living thing
within it, as Gabriel Marcel points out. Technology produces
mixed blessings. In transforming nature, it often pollutes
nature. Man's current role as a worker is less in creating the
product than in servicing the machine which accomplishes that end.
Here, as in war, man may be viewed as more expendable than the
equipment he runs.

Today, influenced by the propaganda of technology, we have even
become accustomed to comparing the eye to a camera, the heart to
a pump, and the brain to a computer. In this lies a subtle
danger, for in each case we have compared the maker to what he has
made, a clear case of 'putting the cart before the horse'.
The central vision therefore which we must always consider in our
discussions about human work is the role of the person and his dignity.

PART TWO (II): Towards the Social Ordering of Human Work in Society

1. On Ownership and Property:

When considering the topic of work, the practice of ownership
of property stands as an essential point, for without it,
that is to say, without appropriation by man of the gifts of
nature, work cannot be effective. In the Social principles of
Christianity, and in the practice of many traditional
cultures, including Igboland, possession is not considered a
breach with the natural order of things.

Infact, to own a good, to have possession and full title
to dispose at will over something is regarded as normal and natural.
Ownership of property is the necessary first step in the process
of bringing the earth into subjection. For without it, man
can neither have tools nor materials on which to use tools.
He can neither have enough initiative to produce, for we have
seen in sections one and two of this thesis that the 'personalist'
argument is central to any ordering of work. Work is primarily
for the unique individual person, who can only work if he is
satisfied with the order, structure and fruits of his work.
Thus property comes into existence through work for the sake
of work[1].

---

1) John Paul II, LE, n.12

475

Property can be justified only when it is put at the service of work
for the good of all. Whenever property fails in this, it loses its
justification, whatever be the regime under which the goods of the
earth are appropriated.
Whether ownership be private or public, communal or collective, it
must never obscure the fact that at the begining of work, there stands
the mystery of creation. This is the 'fount and head' of the argument
for property and ownership[2].

An economy is good to the extent that it keeps in view the good of
every individual; this is in keeping with the first principle of the
moral order affecting material goods, which emphasise that all men have
a right to use the goods of this world because all have a right to life
and livelihood[3].

It follows that the claim that ownership confers absolute and untouchable
rights is utterly unacceptable. Ownership has its rights, but they are
always subordinate to the right of all men to use what the earth's
resources and men's industry provide, and they must be examined and tested
in the light of that superior right[4].

---

2)For further reading on this topic, see the interesting pamphlet written
   by Joseph Kirwan: "Introduction to Laborem Exercens - Study edition",CTS,
   London, 1984.
3)This is an explication of the teachings of the scholastics, especially
   of St. Thomas Aquinas.
4)John Paul II., LE,n.14 (Immediately after the Second World War in totally
   damaged Germany,many undernourished, homeless and propertyless war-survivors
   looked up to the Church for moral direction. Cardinal Frings, Archbishop
   of Cologne declared that it wasn't a sin under the winter cold to steal food
   or coal to get through the winter. Colonians call this "fringsen" - a
   local adaptation of the permission under Cardinal Frings on the use of goods).

This principle governs the distribution of property - the wider the diffusion, the better, even where ownership is in some sense common. It governs the ways in which property may be used, as also the relationship between those who have property and those who have not. It governs also the questions of employment and wages. It must not be assumed that such examination and testing will necessarily lead to the abolition of private ownership of the means of production. Merely to transfer those means from private to collective or State ownership is no guarantee for a satisfactory distribution. This is so because the men who administer what is owned publicly are just as likely to misuse what they control[5].

What is called for is a just society where everyone can live a life worthy of a human being. Unnecessary amassing of wealth at the expense of the masses is unjust and must be condemned. Besides, workers must at least have a right to participate and control the work they do through ownership of property. It may be that today's needs would best be met by some form of joint or communal ownership, as John Paul says. However that may be, no government or type of ownership can be acceptable which does not afford to the worker scope for working 'on his own account' -namely, 'in re propria', as the latin text words it[6].

---

5) John Paul II, Ibid, n. 14.
6) Ibid, n. 15.

This implies that where ownership is in some sense communal,
it is the individual worker who must acquire "full entitlements
to co-ownership of the immense workbench at which he stands"[7].

John Paul reminds us that St. Thomas Aquinas preferred private
ownership of the means of production principally for this reason,
although St. Thomas emphasised clearly that the 'goods of this
earth cannot be left to only a few priviledged persons',
but must inspite of all private ownership, be placed at the
disposal of all, especially the poor, weak and oppressed.
It is for this reason that the Pope draws a sharp distinction
between collectivism and what he calls 'the social gathering
together of the means of production for all to use'[8].

Infact, the call to private initiative has gone high
especially in the context of developing nations. One of the
answers I got from a questionnaire I distributed asking
for suggestions on how to solve the problems of ownership and
development in the villages came from Dr. Helmut Schmidtmayr,
an economist from Vienna.

---

7) Ibid, n. 14,
8) Ibid. n. 14.

He asked:

> "Why can't it be possible for private initiative
> to take care of watering the land, raising the crops
> that could nourish people and sharing the profits
> together?... "There must be a way out, the formation
> of "corporate private initiative" (and what else is
> the church?) that would help people liberate themselves
> from perpetual dependence for everything on the State.
> Israel's secrecy to survival in the de-sert, was among
> all else, water wells, digging of ditches and
> irrigation, and behold greens grew in the desert!
> Why could Israel do all that? The secret well
> understood lies in "collective private initiative, not
> just waiting for the government. Nigerians should not
> say: It doesn't work here".

However, such a noble suggestion must be pragmatically effected
through capital. And here lies the basic problem.
Paul VI criticised those who hawk capital from the masses thus:

> "It is unacceptable that citizens with abundant incomes
> and resources should transfer a considerable part of this
> income abroad purely for their advantage, without care
> for the manifest wrong they inflict on their country by
> doing this"[9].

---

9)   Paul VI, Populorum Progressio, n. 23 - 24

Infact, voices are now everywhere heard with the same proclamation.
Tugendhat, as well as Father P.J. O'Mahony refer to this
situation, where they jointly say: "Those who own wealth in
money form (finance), are on the one hand morally bound to invest
it so that the whole community may benefit from the use of
their wealth, and those who control these funds are to be subject
to moral control. In this principle is contained the whole
modern demand for social responsibility by great companies -
a responsibility hard to ensure because of the very scale and
complexity of their operations"[10].

The African societies may find in these social principles,
elements, which originally existed in traditional African
societies, but which today have, in the face of colonial and
neo-colonial tendencies disappeared or changed into materialistic
categories. First man, then the rest. Laborem Exercens can help
Nigeria in this quest.

---

10) Refer to work by C. Tugendhat: 'The Multinationals, London,
     1971, Quoted by P.J. O'Mahony, Multinationals and Human
     Rights, Great Wakering, Essex, England, 1980.

2. Liberal Capitalism Rejected

We were able to expose the history of early capitalism in
Europe and the attendant evils consequent to it in section one
of this research. We also saw that the conflict between
capital and labour is misleading and dangerous for any sound theory
on human work since both of them are ideologically remote-controlled.

When we see the glaring inequality between the 'haves' and
'have-nots' in the Nigerian society of today, we are inevitably
forced to re-assert the basic principles of 'social ethics'
which sees in liberal capitalism an evil, because in it, the
material result of work is ranked above man, who himself is the
worker. In such a way, the biblical order is reversed, and man who
is called to subdue the earth, becomes a mere instrument
subdued by the products of his work. This, says John Paul is what
should rightly be called capitalism: a use of the word which
is different from many other meanings which have been given to it[11].

Capitalism, as Pope John Paul defines it, separated labour from
capital resources and opposed one to the other as though there
were no essential difference between them[12]. This fault
was the consequence of a practical materialism which assumed
that increasing wealth was the prime purpose of an economy, whereas
in fact it is only a means, albeit an important means to an end.
Man himself, whom wealth should serve, is the end and he was ignored.

---

11) John Paul II, Laborem Exercens, n. 7
12) Ibid., n. 13

In this connection, let us listen to John Paul talking directly
to Nigerians in Nigeria during his visit their in 1982.
The Pontiff said:

> "The human person must always be the ultimate measure
> of the feasibility and the success of an economic or
> social programme. Progress therefore cannot be
> separated from the dignity of the human person, nor
> from the respect for his or her fundamental human
> rights. In the pursuit of progress, total progress,
> anything must be rejected that is unworthy of the
> freedom and the human rights of the individual
> and of the people as a whole"[13].

This rejection of capitalism is clear when we see that man,
the worker is often subordinated not only to the things he produces,
but also to the instruments he uses in the process of production,
above all to money and capital. This distortion must therefore
be utterly eradicated if the social economy is ever to be right.
That a man should be the master of the instrucments he uses is
of the first importance. Modern Nigeria has a lot to learn
from this.

---

13) Speech on reception by President Shagari at State House,
    Ikoyi, Lagos on Friday, February 12, 1982, published in
    Daily Times, special edition., pp 5 - 6

3. Errors of Marxist Socialism Rejected:

The criticism of capitalism is also valid for marxist socialism, for it is also based on a materialistic world view. Infact says John Paul II, and we in Africa already know that quite well:

Marxist socialism offers no escape in the search for a new world order. It is itself materialistic, in theory as well as in practice. Marx's man is a thing which emerges from the prevailing methods of production. Such a thing will not be seen as the subject of work[14].

This being so, a shift in ownership from individual to collective, State control, is unlikely to bring about the necessary change in attitudes. The man at work is likely to be treated still as a means only and never as an end of the entire economic process[15].

In Marxist socialistic societies, the struggle between the working classes and the owners of capital resources will go on in the sense that State officers become 'disguised capitalists'. The first encyclical on the social question by Leo XIII titled 'Rerum Novarum' talks of an explosive class struggle. John Paul II accepts the truth of that judgement. And that history of exploitation is 'by no means over yet'.

Says Joseph Kirwan: "that real conflict is not to be confused with the imagined conflict erected by the ideologies of 'scientific socialism' and communism. Neither Leo XIII nor JOhn Paul II nor any of the Popes who came between ever sought to deny the strength of the forces which marxist theory or its manipulation harnesses for its ends. What all have said, and John Paul says it here more clearly than did any of his predecessors, is that Marxism is largely divorced from reality"[16].

---

14) John Paul II, LE, n.13 (Refer also Kirwan Joseph in his introduction to the English translation of Laborem Exercens, CTS, London 1984, p.iv/v)

15) John Paul II, LE, n. 14

16) Joseph Kirwan, op.cit., p.v.

Marxism sees 'class' as the product of property which is the
root of evil, and seeks to create a self-consciousness in one
class, the proletarian working class, that will lead to the utter
elimination of the enemy class, the bourgeoise. This programme
as we saw, presupposes 'the collective control of the means of
production so that, by their transfer from private hands to the
community, human labour may be protected from private
the perverse exploitation to which it easily falls prey"[17].

Herein lies the errors of marxism which is essentially the
same as that which was made before it, and which still exists today
in hydra-headed form, namely liberal capitalism.

The practice of 'rigid capitalism' differs not so much from the
theory of Marxism. Marxism takes the contradictions which liberal
capitalism set up between labour and capital, where none should
exist, and makes it part of its own system by its process of
collectivisation, which, whatever might be said in theory, does
not in practice change the false relationship between workers
and capital resources which is the root cause of the class
antagonism. In the search for an ideology for Nigeria, as well as
for many African and developing nations, reference must be made to
this fundamental error, so that nations do not exchange one
form of colonialism with another, albeit, a more totalitarian one.

Developing nations must take note of this fact which John Paul
emphatically mentions in Laborem Exercens, namely:

> "the place of labour in the system can be right... when it
> eradicates completely the contradiction between labour and
> capital resources... It is necessary to bear in mind that the
> 'error of early capitalism can be repeated... wherever man...
> is not treated as the subject and author and therefore, as the
> true purpose for which the whole process of production is
> carried on"[18].

---

17) John Paul II, LE, n. 11
18) Ibid, nn. 13.7

4. In defence of the Rights of Workers:

It is a basic and clear fact that human work is not confined alone
to paid employment. Work has many other aspects and possibilities,
such as self-employed activity, private business, research and study.
Nonetheless, John Paul II gives a major part of his attention to
considering the problems faced by those workers who depend on the
use of their labour to sustain their existence, that is, those who
work for wages, especially, those who can offer only a service of
relatively low objective value. In marxist terms, the proletariat.
With regard to the effects of economic change, the Pontiff remarks
that the specific task of the church is to defend the rights to
dignity of the wage earners.

> "It is not for the church to analyse scientifically the
> consequences that these alarming changes may have on human
> society. But the Church considers it her task always
> to call attention to the dignity and rights of those who
> work, to condemn situations in which that dignity and
> those rights are violated, and to help to guide the
> above-mentioned changes so as to ensure authentic progress
> by man and society"[19)]

It is very clear that the weakness of employees, especially lower
groups of workers makes them vulnerable vis-a-vis their employers,
as the examples we showed in chapter eight of this thesis clearly
portrays.

---

19)   John Paul II, LE, n.1

Throughout his treatment of the relationship which should
obtain between a worker and the instrument he uses, it is
clearly the vulnerable wage-earner who is at the forefront of
the Pope's mind. Any man can be guilty of making an idol of the
work of his hands, but only the wage-earner who must work for a
living and that of his family can be robbed of his dignity
by others[20], and only he can be compelled to behave as though
his tools constituted a being somehow superior to himself[21].

Leo XIII remarked in 'Rerum Novarum', when a man has no property
of his own on which to work, he must work on the property
of another. The mutual dependency of men forbid therefore that
anyone should be forced into a position where he cannot make
his contribution and cannot exercise his right to the use of goods
which are intended for everybody. From this arise certain
inalienable rights for a worker.

---

20) Ibid., n. 9
21) Ibid, n. 13

a) Right to Just Wage for Work done:

The right to paid employment which belongs to those who have
no property of their own on which to work carries with it a
right to a living wage. Everyone whose livelihood depends upon
work for wages and who does the best he can in the best employment he can find, is entitled in equity to receive in payment for
his labour, sufficient enough to guarantee the needs of himself
and his family. Such a Wage is the test for a proper functioning
of a wage economy[22].

Infact, it is through work that a man can receive adequate wages
which enables him to begin a family. As work 'constitutes a
foundation on which to build the family life which is a man's
natural right and vocation', so also does it pervade the
educationally activity of the family. Work, wages and family
are knit together, for work is one of the ways by which everyone
"becomes a human being", and "becoming a human being" is a pre-eminent
purpose of all educational activity, the family, which is the
primary source of education, is always to be reffered to in any
questions regarding work. Says John Paul II, 'the family is
made possible by work and is the first school of work'[23].

In the context of Nigeria, enough information and cases abound
where workers were not paid their salaries at all for the work they
have done, not only in private sectors, but also by government and
other big corporations. In reality, the military coup of New-Years
eve, 1984 against the democratically elected government of President
Shagari, had, in the words of putschist General Buhari, one strong
reason, namely: "workers being owed salaries in arrears"[24].

---

22) John Paul II, LE, n. 19 (I considered this problem exhaustively in
    section one, chapter three of this work, Refer for full details).
23) Ibid., n. 9
24) General Buhari's speech after the coup to the nation: on Radio and
    Television, January 1, 1984, quoted in West Africa, London,
    9.1.84, p. 57

It is important to state here that "In arrears" is a mild way of
putting the case. Many wage earners, especially teachers and
civil servants had not received their salaries for more than
four to six months in various states, and this has been happening
for years in various Nigerian States, and it still
continues to happen.

There is in recent times the allegation that some workers, who
plead to be paid their salaries are either sacked, suspended
or subtly oppressed. How then can a worker feed his family?
How then can a worker himself survive? How can he support the
nation and identify himself with national objectives, when his
basic rights are denied him? These are very serious questions
for any government worth its salt. We dare not venture into the
area of creating jobs for workers, as cases in chapter eight has
enlightened us. This is the true situation, its consequences are
obvious to us, as armed robbery is on the increase, as well as
bribery, official and street corruption, neglect of duty for lack
of remuneration, broken homes, and total frustration and depression.

John Paul II did not mix words on this issue when in his often
quoted visit to Nigeria in 1982 he said in a mass for workers at
the Holy Cross Cathedral Lagos:

> "All who work, whether they are single or married, well-
> skilled or not, have important rights and responsibilities.
> For example, each one has the right to proper pay and to
> reasonable working hours, including time for holidays.
> And work should never hinder the exercise of one's
> religious freedom. Work is for man, not man for work.
> So work must not be allowed to dehumanise the person
> who does the work"[25].

---

25) John Paul II, in Nigeria, sermon at mass in Lagos for workers,
16.2.1982, Daily Times special edition, p. 68

b) Role of Mother:

The housewife does not earn a wage as she stays at home and
cares for the family. But the work she does is of more
importance than is that of many of those who work outside the
home. Hence the Pope's insistence on the need for a re-evaluation
of the role of the mother in the family. Society is the loser,
not the winner when lack of income compels a woman with little
children, to take paid employment to the detriment of her
children's upbringing[26].

Education by immediate family relations is far better off,
psychologists will tell us, than mercenary education by outsiders.
Worse still, is when a society for lack of money and adequate wage
for the family earner makes it impossible for a husband and wife
to beget children, since this is coupled with the financial
situation. Such an example depicts a 'dying society'.
In this context too, husbands are challenged to respect their wives and
consider the work they do at home as equally reasonable and
noble. When this done, such newspaper reports like "Soldier throws
wife from storey-building for failure to prepare him pounded
foo-foo yams will cease to exist[27].

---

26) John Paul II, LE, n. 19
27) This flashy but shocking story is published in the Sunday New
     Nigeria Newspaper, No. 92, 27.2.1983, p.1.

c) The Handicapped, Migrant Workers, Old and Weak:

> "In Nigeria, you have the beautiful cultural value of
> the extended family system. The sick and the old are
> not abandoned by their children, their nephews and
> nieces, their cousins or other kindred. The umbrella
> of charity has root for all. This is a precious
> heritage that must be maintained"
>> John Paul II, speech to the sick in Onitsha, 1982.

The situation of the handicapped, the weak and sick, the old, the
migrant workers is one which cannot be left untouched, not only
because these are human beings with rights and responsibilites,
but especially, the care of these people is a task and a call of
the Gospels - the voice of God, directing and encouraging mankind
to take care of their weaker neighbours. The prophets always
reminded each generation of this obligation, as Isaiah clearly
announces and later on repeated by Jesus in his first public
Ministry in the temple in Jerusalem:

"The spirit of the Lord is upon me, because he has annointed me
to preach good news to the poor. He has sent me to proclaim
release to the captives and recovering of sight to the blind, to
set at liberty those who are oppressed, to proclaim the
acceptable year of the Lord"[28].

How is this task viewed in Nigeria, by official government policy,
private or group organisations, and by individuals?
It is clear today that traditional African societies have changed
greatly from its community orientated structure to individual
oriented, as a consequence of the cultural meeting-point between
British utilitarianism and Nigerian receptivity to change.

---

28) Isaiah, Chapter 61:1-2; Luke chapter 4:18

There is today in Nigeria a great pressure on earlier forms of
life, on the family, the large families, on village life-style and
on traditional values. The weak, old and sick, are, in course
of recent developments sometimes cut off from the extended family.
The abondonment and solitude of these members of the community
is of course, something totally un-african. This is why a
revival of original values is called for. There is a mounting
neglect of the weak, the sick and the immigrant workers.
Only recently, the National President of the Nigerian Civil Service
Union, Mr. David Ojeli, called on the government to establish a
National Social Security Scheme to provide temporary financial
relief for the unemployed and the weak[29].

Such a scheme would cater for the unemployed, the retrenched, the
sick, the orphans and handicapped, and all those marginalised by
society. This call which is only recent, and so far as
I know, it has not been concretely accepted, shows that Nigeria
has no Social Security Schemes for its people.
It is a test of true government to guarantee the rights of all
its citizens, not only the strong, but especially the weak.

No wonder John Paul II called on priests and bishops to identify
themselves with the poor:

> "The priest must identify with the poor, so as to be able
> to bring them the uplifting gospel of Christ"[30]

The Pope criticised and rejected "domination over the weak,
callousness towards the poor and handicapped, embezzlement of
public funds"[31]

---

29) West Africa, published in London, ed.Kaya Whiteman, 27.8.1984,
    p. 1752.
30) Pope John Paul II, speech to priests in Enugu, 13.2.1982,
    Daily Times special edition, p. 12
31) Ibid., p.6

Certain consequences flow from these assertions, especially,
fom the basic tenet that citizens must be guaranteed a
dual claim to life and to livelihood via work for their merited
wages.

Suitable employment must be provided for all who need it
and are capable of it. Thus, handicapped people must be enabled
to make what contribution they can, and people must be allowed
to migrate in search of employment[32].

There are however policies adopted by government in recent times,
which do not guarantee the security of aliens, nay, opposed to it.
The headlines of newspapers flash the news thus:

27,000 Immigrants Expelled: (West Africa, 28.1.1985, p.190)

"A total of 27,045 illegal immigrants were expelled from Nigeria
between January and October 1984, as announced by the Minister for
Internal Affairs, General Mohammed Magoro. He said 1,000 extra
immigration officers were being recruited and that all immigration
personnel would be trained to use firearms..."

12,000 Aliens Expelled: (West Africa, 7.5.1984, p. 993)

About 12,000 illegal aliens have so far been repatriated to their
various countries by the Nigerian authorities, since the
current exercise started this year. Thousands of other aliens who
entered the country without valid papers are now being held
all over the federation, preparatory to their repatriation, ...
The Minister contented that the Federal Military Government was
not in favour of taking illegal aliens to court to complete the
process of their deportation because this was cumbersome and costly,
pointing out that this was why the authorities preferred
repatriating the illegal aliens... The ideal thing is to turn back
aliens who do not possess valid papers at the port of their entry..."

---

32) John Paul II, Laborem Exercens, n. 23

1,000 Teachers Dismissed: (West Africa, 1.10.1984, p.2010)

"The Lagos government has dismissed alien teachers from its
service numbering 1,016, as reported by the State's Schools
Management Board. The board explained that the dismissal was to
allow qualified Nigerians gain employment as teachers, noting that
it was unwise to keep aliens in jobs for which there
were qualified Nigerians who were unemployed".

The Illegal Immigrants - 2 Weeks Notice: (The Guardian, Nigeria, April, 25, 1985

"In two weeks time - unless wiser counsel prevails - Nigerians,
and indeed the entire world community, would be treated to an
unnecessary spectacle of national self-centredness. Some
70,000 foreigners, mainly from neighbouring sister states in
West African sub-region, would be then either have left the country
or been sent packing in an exodus reminiscent of Shehu Shagari's
1983 pre-election expulsion order. These foreigners - referred to as
"illegal aliens" because they do not possess valid travel
residence documents - were last week given up to May 10 1985
to leave the country".

In the face of these expulsions of immigrants into Nigeria, what
has Christian Social Principles to offer the government as
a basic guideline to action in the face of Nigeria's economic
recession, which is the primary reason for the repatriations?
Let us first of all listen to what the Editorial of Nigeria's
National Newspaper, the "Guardian" said on this issue:
It states that the expulsions are unnecessary. "First, a significant
proportion of the immigrants affected can, strictly speaking, be
considered as refugees. Many of them are either victims of the
drought now ravaging the Sahelian belt of West Africa and of the
collapse that has become the fate of some African state economies.

If other non-Africans can feel so moved by these calamities as
to donate aid for the survival and rehabilitation of these refugees;
if countries as poor as Ghana and Burkina Faso can honourably
accept the responsibility of rehabilitating and providing them
with vocational training as well as absorbing them into the
host country, then surely Nigeria, with its relatively
more buoyant resource base, should at least be able to do even better.

There is something not quite large-hearted about the expulsion and
the question it raises is the same eternal one: Who is my
neighbour? It touches the heart that people who have fled
their land, of want, for succour, are being asked to go. It
negates the spirit of oneness and of one people; it makes us
uncomfortable. It is unlike us, and it runs counter to the
proverbial African hospitality..."[33].
Wise words and good counsel by the 'National Guardian'.

Christian Social Ethics maintains quite evidently that 'man has
the right to leave his native land for various motives -
and also the right to return - in order to seek better conditions
of life in another country'[34].

In fact, human history does not exist without the phenomenon of
migration of workers from one place to another for a better working
condition of work and life. Of course, and John Paul makes this
point, emmigration is "in some aspects an evil, perhaps a necessary
evil"[35].

---

33) The Guardian, Nigerian Newspaper, Lagos, April 25, 1985

34) John Paul II, LE, n. 23

35) John Paul II, Address to workers at Monterrey, Mexico, 31.1.1979;
    (published in L'osservatore Romano, English edition, 19.2.79,
    No. 8, p 6-7)

Emmigration is an evil because it brings with it many discomforts and inconveniences to the migrant as shown above. Secondly, it is an evil because it "generally constitutes a loss for the country which is left behind".

It is the departure of a person from his own tradition, history and society, a loss of a subject of work, whose efforts of mind and body could have contributed to the common good of his own country, but these efforts, these contributions are offered to another society which in a sense has less right to them than the original country"[36].

This is why the problem of emmigration of workers becomes an international problem, and therefore subject to international law. The principle to follow is not that of allowing economic, social and political forces to prevail over man, but on the contrary, to place the dignity of the human person above everything else - in other words, to place the issue of Human Rights at the centre.

---

36) John Paul II, LE, n.23 (Refer to Chapter three of this thesis where the issue of Migrant workers was handled).

d) <u>General Duty to Prevent Unemployment</u>:

The situation of the unemployed is a problem which affects the
entire society. Why should some people have work and others not?
There is the teaching of the Church on the "Common Use of Goods",
frequently repeated by the Magisterium, and which has become
the basis for the urgent call for full employment for all citizens
willing and able to work[37].

The Council Fathers gathered in Rome for the Vatican Two declared:
"God intended the earth and all it contains for the use of all men
and peoples, so created goods should flow fairly to all, regulated
by justice and accompanied by charity. Whatever forms property
may take according to legitimate custom and changing circumstances,
this universal destiny of the earth's resources should always
be borne in mind. In his use of them, man should regard his
legitimate possessions not simply as his own but as common in the
sense that they can benefit others as well as himself. But
everybody has a right to share of the earth's goods sufficient for
himself and his family... Since so many in the world suffer from
hunger, the Council urges men and authorites to remember that saying
of the Fathers:

'Feed a man who is dying from hunger - if you have not fed him, you
have killed him'. Each as far as he can must share and spend his
wealth in coming to the assistance of these suffering individuals"[38].

_____

37) St. Thomas Aquinas, Summa Theologiae, II-II, Q. 66 (See also
        John Paul LE, n. 14; Gaudium et Spes, n. 69)
38) Gaudium et spes., n. 69

The right to the 'common use of goods' means in the first instance,
the right to employ. Those who have the power over the means
of production must make them available for work. This
implies making them suitable for use, no easy task when rapid
changes have caused large-scale obsolence of tools and machines.

Pope John II recognises the heavy chronic disease called
unemployment, and of course he knows that it cannot be prevented
at times when large rapid changes in methods of production and
directions of world trade disrupt an economy[39].
He recognises also that mistaken policies can lead to similar
situations[40].

Yet whatever be the cause of lack of opportunities for employment,
unemployment is always an evil which calls for a remedy.
There is of course, an obligation to come to the aid of those who
are unemployed, but provision of adequate maintenance is not enough.

There is thus a duty laid upon all who can influence events to
prevent that utter dependency which is the result of
involuntary unemployment of people who depend upon employment
and the wages thereof for their livelihood and the support of
their families.

---

39) John Paul II, LE n. 18
40) Ibid.

497

Leo XIII in his encyclical on the 'Social Question' -
Rerum Novarum - remarked, that when a man has no property
of his own on which to work, he must work on the property
of another. The mutual dependency of men forbids that anyone
should be forced into a position where he cannot make his
contribution and cannot exercise his right of use of goods
which are intended for everybody.

This duty therefore, of doing all that can be done to prevent
such unemployment springs directly from the first
principle of the moral order, namely the principle of
"the common use of goods"[41].

All eyes would definitely turn to the State which has the
responsibility of legislating on the necessary re-organisation
methods which would enable investors and private initiative
to act, besides that which the State itself must do in
creating jobs. However, it is clear that the State and public
authorities cannot be asked for more than they can give
without excessive overcentralisation.

The free initiative of individuals and groups, of corporate
groups and business groups has a major part to play in
creating jobs. To neglect this moral demand is to offend against
the obligation which demands that "all men have a right to the
common use of the goods of this earth".

---

41) Refer to Laborem Exercens, John Paul II, n.18

e) The Call for an Independent Trade Union of Workers:

> "Men who are fully engaged in various trades and
> professions have a right to form groups or societies,
> called trade unions, to defend their vital interests
> wherever their rights are in question".
>> John Paul II, LE, n. 20

We have been able to expose the fact that wage earners are condemned
to various types of oppression, overtly, subtly and covertly.
Their wages are not paid, or badly paid; their rights to adequate rest
are not guaranteed; and when jobs are got, these are tied at
disadvantageous terms. Of necessity, employees are fully
caught up in work which they are virtually doomed to take
and they stand in urgent need of some means by which they can
defend themselves. This need gives them the right to form trade
unions[42].

From what was said of the Nigerian Labour world in the previous
chapter, we are certainly moved to seek for ways to resolve the
lack of defence of rights of peasant workers, civil servants,
and all workers both in the private and public sectors. Although
this right to form trade unions was explicitly defended
by Pope Leo XIII in his 'Rerum Novarum' (and his teaching has been
reiterated by all his successors), John Paul II is the first
Pope explicitly to defend trade unions as fighting organisations for
the defence of fundamental workers' rights. He accepts that there
is a likeness between today's unions and the medieval guilds of
craftsmen, to which they have been often compared, but he points also
to an important difference between them. Unlike the craftguilds,

---

42) John Paul II, LE., n. 20

the trade unions have grown 'out of struggle of the workers
and of the whole world of labour, particularly the men
who were doomed to mechanised factory work, to defend their
just rights against the entrepreneurs and the owners of the
means of production'[43].

Their primary function is thus to go on struggling in their just
cause. It is not a battle against others. Even if in
controversial questions it takes on a character of antagonism
to others, it does this for the same of social justice. It is
not a class warfare; it is not fighting for fighting's sake,
nor does it aim at the elimination of the adversary. The unions
only seek their rights[44].

Such a struggle by the unions for the full rights of workers
ought not be a thread to community or the right order of values.
Rather, the unions engaged in it form a necessary element in
the ordering of society, their aim being to bring back into the
community of work all those who have been excluded from it by
a false view of the nature of work and of man, who is himself the
subject of work. John Paul II believes that before all else,
'work has the property of bringing people together, and it is
in this that its social power consists. It is evidently a force
for holding a community together"[45].

The Pope then goes on to state the basic reason why trade
unions must exist within a nation, he justifies its independence
from all political parties, even if they should have their
political opinions objectively, and he calls them to be
realistic of the limitations imposed by the nation, when they
make their demands.

---

43) Ibid
44) Ibid
45) Ibid.

Says the Pontiff, and this is important for the Nigerian labour
market: "Therefore, by reason of this principal
characteristic of every kind of work - that in every type of
society 'labour' and 'capital' resources are utterly
indispensable components of the process of production -
an association which men form to vindicate the rights which arise
of necessity out of what they do, remains a constitutive
element of social order and solidarity among men which may
not be ignored"[46].

Having established the reason for their existence, there is a
warning that in the defence of such rights of workers, account must
be taken of the just claims of others, and trade unions ought
always to distinguish clearly between what it asks for
in defence of its own members, and what it recommends for general
social welfare, political stability and economic prosperity,
governed by the cultural determinants of the society.

The Pope talks of 'prudent concern for common good'.
Thus, while trade unions must obviously have a voice in politics,
they ought not to be committed to any political party. The struggle
for power which characterises political parties is not their
business[47].

The trade unions best serve the needs of the common good by
attending to the education and self-education of their members,
their aim being to encourage among them a desire to
become more completely human.

---

46)   Ibid

47)   Ibid.

This invitation of the Pope on the world of work is an invitation
to avoid petty bickerings and unnecessary class selfishness
to 'go beyond' the simple notion of selective solidarity to the
notion of 'solidarity for human rights'. In such a call and
perspective, the Nigerian worker, employer, government and
other corporations can rightly learn and hope for new
movements, a new spirit in the labour world, 'of solidarity of
the workers - with the workers, and for the workers'.

In this connection, there is a legitimacy to strike on the side
of the working peoples. Of course, the strike is an instrument
which may be used as a last resort in self-defence, but its
very legitimacy sets limits to its use. Strikes must never be used
for party political ends, nor may they go so far as to disrupt
essential services or paralyse social and economic life, if this
can be avoided. The employer should therefore listen to the
legitimate demands of the workers, while the workers must also
see the limitations of the employers. There is in this
invitation to 'go beyond', an invitation to enter into 'DIALOGUE'.

Dialogue aims first of all at reaching a clearer understanding
and a deeper awareness of one's own identity, thanks to the
challenge of the partner. But it does not stop here.
Dialogue helps in understanding too the identity and problems
of the partner in discussion and his ideas.
Lastly, dialogue helps both partners discover common values,
settle differences amicably and work together for the good
of man and the progress of the nation, locally and internationally.

5. Agriculture must be given priority of attention:

a) Background Information:

Before the development of Nigeria's petroleum industry by the
British colonial government, agriculture was the mainstay of
Nigeria's economy. Infact in the pre-colonial days, more
than ninety percent of the population were engaged in agriculture,
be it in the farm, in cattle rearing, hunting, or fishing.

After the introduction of oil, the economy changed hands from
an almost self-reliant agricultureal country to an OPEC country,
with all the neglects this new economy brought the people.

From 1960 until 1970, agriculture made up more than sixty percent
of the country's GDP. It fell down to 22.5 percent of the GDP
in 1977, and today, in the lack of adequate statistics,
Nigeria must import rice, maize, wheat, meat, oil, and all sorts
of food to feed its growing population.

A lot of reasons account for this declining role of agriculture
in the economy. In the pre-colonial days and just immediately
after independence, emphasis was given to agriculture as the
basic provider of food, although during the colonial days,
the governments failed to stimulate productivity significantly.

Then came the 'school days' as condition for being civilised.
Many young people left their villages to the big cities in search
of the "new" from Europe. The problem of 'rural-urban drift'
has had a negative effect on agricultural productivity in Nigeria.

The young tend to abandon their villages and their old parents
for the attractions of the towns, leaving behind them, an
ageing agricultural work force. New agricultural work-force
has been resisted, new trades have developed (and almost every
other person is a business man or trader), and mismanagement
of funds given out for agricultural developments is rampant.
The problem of technology plays a role too. In the words of the
then Federal Commissioner for Industries, Dr. R.A. Adeleye:

"It should not be assumed that all is well on the industrial
scene; On the contrary, the government is acutely aware that
a lot has to be done. The weakest link in the chain of our
efforts is the low state of development of our technology, our
knowledge and our managerial skill... Nigeria does not yet
produce the most basic tools and machinery, let alone the
sophisticated machinery required for complex industries"[48].

---

48) Adeleye, R.A., Federal Commissioner of Industries, 1978, in
     "New African Year Book, 1979, op.cit. , p-261.
     In section Two of this work, we considered the state of
     agriculture in primitive society. Much of this has not
     changed for the small farmer.

b) Lack of Serious Government Initiative

There has not been a very genuine attempt by the governments
of Gowon, Murtala/Obasanjo and Shagari to raise the low stand of
agriculture in the country. And it is clear that their leanings
to easy money which comes from the oil business and the
petro-dollars resulting from it, has not given them enough push
to make their "lip-service" programmes a reality.

Nigerians heard a lot about 'Operation Feed the Nation',
'Green Revolution', 'Otu Olu Obodo', and all such big jargons,
but nothing concretely came out of it. Inspite of all public
pronouncements, Nigerians imported food to the tunes of
millions of tonnes from Europe and America, that the Ports of the
country were overfull, and the food could not even be
offloaded as they stayed on the high seas, and a lot got spoilt.
Malnutrition set into the country!

Inspite of all public incentives, the subsistence farmers, who
make up about fifty percent of all Nigerian farmers today
were not adequately incorporated into National Development.
They have become increasingly impoverished while the rest of the
economy has been commercialised. Meanwhile, those farmers who
grow cash crops (either for export or for internal use) have
not been granted the necessary support to increase their
productivity. They do not have the necessary capital for
expansion. They lack the needed technology for such a change;
and above all, some of them who are illiterate have married
more wives or built new houses in the exceptional cases where
a little capital was granted them.

Nigeria's agragrian underdevelopment, like in many other
developing nations, has still the signature of its
colonial legacy, and this is not unconnected with the industrial
developments in Europe in the 19th century.

To counteract the excessive dependency of many developing nations,
the United Nations Body in charge of 'Food and Agricultural
Organisation' (FAO), in union with many other charitable
institutions, coupled with the principles of Ethics propounded in
the social encyclicals, have taken adequate steps to abridge the
over-dependence for food and nourishment on the developed nations.

Pope John XXIII expressed his views in 'Mater et Magistra' thus:
"Many countries, especially those in the developing nations use
primitive methods of agriculture, with the result that, for all
their abundance of natural resources, they are not
able to produce enough food to feed their population,
whereas other countries using modern methods of farming, produce a
surplus of food. It is therefore obvious that the solidarity of
the human race and christian brotherhood demand the elimination as
far as possible of these discrepancies"[49].

The Pontiff continues by demanding that justice and humanity
demand from those countries which produce consumer goods, especially
farm products in excess of their own needs, to come to the
assistance of those other countries where large sections of the
population are suffering from want and hunger. "It is nothing
less than an outrage to justice and humanity to destroy goods
that other people need for their lives"[50].

---

49) John XXIII, Mater et Magistra, n. 154
50) Ibid., par. 161

It is important to point out that Pope John calls for justice
to be effected. Justice is not charity. Justice means the
virtue which calls on each to allow the other his rights.
In other words, the Pontiff is accusing the nations of the
industrialised world that they are depriving the developing nations
their rights to life and livelihood, if they continue to keep
back technological and financial aid which justice demands that
these nations offer the developing nations.

He warns the developed nations that such an aid should never be a
blackmail, whereby the developing nations are indirectly forced
to dance to the music of the giver nations. "The underdeveloped
nations have their time honoured customs and traditions...
In helping these poorer nations, the more advanced communities
must recognise and respect this individuality. They must beware
of making the assistance into their own national mould"[51].

The only permanent remedy for the poor nations on the other hand,
is to make every possible means of providing the citizens
with the scientific, technical and professional training they need,
and to put at their disposal the necessary capital for speeding up
their economic development with the help of modern methods[52].

_____

51) Ibid, par. 169 - 170
52) Ibid, par. 163.

c) What must be done:

In the developing nations, such as Nigeria, the question of
agrarian reform is first of all crucial, while the problem
of making agriculture efficient are immensely more complex and
fundamental than in the more sophisticated societies of the West.
Urgent steps must therefore be adopted by the state policy
in four areas:

> (a) There must be aid to farmers for the consolidation
>   of their farms into larger units.
>
> (b) Modern methods of re-afforestation, irrigation and
>   land clearance must be introduced.
>
> (c) Market subsidies for fertilisers, fuel and other working
>   tools should be provided.
>
> (d) Scientific tools, services from government and the
>   provision of low interest loans by banks and co-
>   opératives for farmers, besides subsidy for
>   agricultural products should be provided.

These are pressing demands, and it is also a matter of justice
for the farmer, the peasant and the worker.

Nigerian economic planners must realise that the time has
come when the country must be placed back on the path of
agricultural independence. Small farmers must therefore be
supported, as well as the big farmers. If the small farmers are
supported, they can adequately feed their families and count
contribute also the excess to the community; unemployment will
decrease as many more people may find joy and satisfaction in
farm work - since it will become a rewarding job, and the fruits of
the earth will be maximised, so that, from Nigeria, other
neighbouring countries who live on the suburbs of climatic and
geographically unfavourable conditions will be helped.

Pope John Paul recognises this fact, as we tried
in section one of this thesis to show. The fruits of the farmers,
for the Pontiff, is exceedingly important, for on it
depends the subsistence and feeding of millions of people the
world over. Attempt therefore should be honestly made to
defend their legitimate rights when possible, through the
activities of legal experts. Today, the reality in many
developing nations depicts the opposite.

Agricultural workers in countries of Latin America, South Africa,
and in many Islamic states are reduced to the level of mere
labourers working for others, and getting nothing substantially
adequate in return. Says the Pope:

"There is a lack of forms of legal protection for the
agricultural workers themselves and for their families in case of
old age, sickness or unemployment... Legal titles to possessions of
small portions of land that someone has personally cultivated
for years are disregarded or they are left defenceless before the
'Landlords and land hungry' more powerful individuals and
groups"[53].

This is a serious breach of the demands of legal and social
justice, and a neglect of the rights due to the workers.
Something must be done both on individual and on state level.
Infact, radical changes are needed in order to restore to
agriculture - and to rural people - their just value as the basis
for a healthy economy within the social body as a whole.

---

53) John Paul II, LE, n. 21.

Unfortunately, even in the so-called developed nations,
farmers do not have it all too easy though. Inspite
of their advanced technological and scientific stand in the
agricultural fields, there are legislations by government
which retard their equality with other workers on the
hours of work, the energy expended, and the remuneration
merited after such an arduous task.

Like the Pope says: "The right to work (on the farms) can be
trampled upon when the farmers are denied the possibility
of sharing in decisions concerning their services, or when they
are denied the right to free association with a view
to their just advancement, socially, economically and culturally"[54].

The question of the farmer and agricultural work can be summarised
and granted solution under two perspectives as the Pope suggests:

   (a)   To proclaim and promote the dignity of work,
        especially of agricultural work, because through it,
        man subdues the earth, feeds the nations and praises
        the beautiful work of nature made by the creator.

   (b)   By reversing all those negative influences which
        impede the progress of agricultural work, and thereby
        allowing the workers through education, financial
        support, encouragement and incentives to form
        co-operative unions, made up of a group of farmers -
        with all rights, priviledges and responsibilities.

---

54) John Paul, Ibid.,

PART THREE (III) Towards a Spirituality of Work in National and
Private Work in Nigeria

1. Basic Views:

It has been sufficiently shown that religion plays a very
important role in the life of the African. Nigerians, for
example, are a very religious people, both in the traditional
religions and in the missionary religions, whether christian or
islamic. A.G. Leonard records that "it has been stated time
out of mind that the African is generally religious, of whom it
can be said that they eat religiously, drink, work, bathe, and
dress religiously"[1].

Inspite of the changing situation in which Nigeria today finds
itself, (and there is no doubt that the religious world-view
described above is also touched) Nigerians are when
modestly described - a religious people. This is so, not just
because of the proliferation of christian churches and sects
everywhere in alarming proportions; not just because
of the proposedly increasing number of moslems, as well as
christians; but, (and this is a private opinion) because the
African world in its cultural, economic, political and social
aspects has been for centuries permeated by the core of religious
phenomena.

In the giving of names to newly born children, in death, birth,
work, marriage ceremonies, kindred relationships, trade and
manufacture, agriculture and heritage, religion continues to
give meaning to the African world[2]. J.S. Mbiti's book,
"African religions and Philosophy" does not even demarcate between

---

1) Leonard, A.G,, The Lower Niger and its Tribes., Frank Cass and
   Co. Ltd. 1968, p. 429
2) In section two of this thesis, much research material was exposed
   to lend credence to the thesis being proposed here. Refer to
   section two for a detailed account especially chapter 5, 6 and 7.

these two, but considers African philosophy and world view as religious, and African religions as philosophy.

It is on this ground and in unity with the propositions offered by John Paul II towards a spirituality of work, that we shall now consider what relevance has Laborem Exercens to offer to the Nigerian Labour world, the national Ethical code of labour, as well as private work understanding. A detailed description of John Paul's spirituality of work in chapter Four of this dissertation has already been fully undertaken. What is here attempted is to adapt such a spirituality of work to the Nigerian labourer, whether Catholic or not, for as the Pope himself says, the contents of the Encyclical 'Laborem Exercens' is addressed among all else, "to all men and women of good will".

2. Spirituality of Work

The vision of work brought to us by Pope John Paul II begins with
the biblical account of man's creation. After having created all
other things, God at last created beings like unto himself
and gave man the specific task of completing and perfecting
the work of his creation[3].

In his reflections on work and spirituality, John Paul
adverts to this point again and again. It is cardinal
to his argument, and all else in his encyclical hinges on it,
so that nothing from his assertions can be fully understood
apart from this. Man's duty to work is a duty to imitate God,
because he alone of the visible creation is like to God.
Being like to God, man's nature is commensurate with the task of
bringing the earth into subjection[4].

In Nigeria, all the various religious groups, and also those
outside the religions would agree with this basic tradition of
the role of man in God's world. Not only that he has reason,
man is seen in many African cosmological traditions as the being
who continues the work of creation already begun by God.

John Paul says nothing above this as such. If the non-
christians already accept this special role of man, then we must
see in our labour and toil, in all human work, a participation
in the creative work of 'renewing the face of the earth'.

---

3) John Paul II, LE, n. 25
4) Ibid., n. 2 (see also: Genesis: 2,4b-8).

Although we mentioned in earlier chapters the various aspects of work, namely, its creative aspects, its necessity, corporate dimension, unifying aspect but above all, the salvific aspect of work, this latter aspect gives all work its full meaning. The sense of participation in God's activity should permeate the most ordinary of human activities. When by his work, a man provides for his family, he is 'unfolding the creator's work'.
When a man consults the interests of his neighbours he contributes to the fulfilment of the divine plan.

As men extend their control over nature, they widen correspondingly the range of their responsibilities and their duty to help others grow with their ability to do so.

Quoting from the Vatican Council, the Pope points out that by our work, we "unfold the creator's work, consult the interests of our brothers and sisters, and contribute to the fulfilment in history of the divine plan"[5].

---

5) Ibid, n. 25

3. <u>The Example of Jesus Christ:</u>

In a religiously pluralistic world, man remains always the being
who professes through religion, his humble acknowledgement of
God's greatness. Religion must serve man to reach God, and
reach him fully. And man must be fully man through his religion,
for if his belief were to alienate and destroy him, such a belief
would not correspond to an 'uplifting religion' for the good of man.

If there is no Marxism without Marx, then even more - though
in a very different way - there can be no Christianity without
Christ.

In the historical narration of the life, death, resurrection and
ascension of Christ, we are given an insight into the life of
the 'Incarnate Word'. It is this historical Jesus whom Pope John
Paul II places in the middle of his reflections. Both for
Christians and non-christians, Jesus has become in person the
great sign, the signal of God's nearness to man; His proclamation
and his conduct confirm him as the annointed one of God.

His Gospel which was a message of grace, hope, freedom, love and
joy was lived convincingly by him who proclaimed it,
accompanied by striking charismatic deeds, cures of sicknesses
and expulsion of demons, all seen as eschatological signals of
the coming of God's kingdom.

In Jesus, as the bible shows us and history confirms, theory and
practice coincided inextricably in such a way, that today, both
Christians and non-Christians see in this man from Nazareth, Gods
work among men, as he is believed to be 'the Way, the truth and Life'.

John Paul points out that Jesus himself was a man of work, and
thereby has elevated work to a salvific activity -
when performed according to God's Will. John Paul states that Jesus
issued no special command to work, but rather warned us against
too much concern for worldly goods, for we may thereby lose our souls.
Likewise, Jesus warned against too much concern about the
future, as is recorded in St. Mathews gospel[6].

Work can be said to be truly and effectively man's good only
when it is done for the love of God, as Jesus Christ did, who
bids us to do all work to the glory of God and the good of our
fellow men who have need of it.
Man's nature is directed towards the love of God and neighbour
and it is the signature of this loving person that is stamped
upon his work.

Thus work extends far beyond working for a living and far beyond
helping others to do so. Even, were there no physical hunger
in the world, there would always be room for intellectual,
moral and spiritual development, for civilisation in the best use of
that term. Putting the matter another way, man's work is not so
much concerned with the economy as with the good of every single
person[7].

---

6) Mathew 6:25; "...Don't be anxious about your life, what you shall
   eat or what you shall drink, nor about your body, what you shall
   put on. Is not life more than food, and the body more than clothing?
   Look at the birds of the air: they neither sow nor reap...
   yet your heavenly FAther feeds them. Are you not more worth than they?
   Seek ye first the kingdom of God and all these things shall be yours".
7) John Paul II, LE, n. 24

Therefore to become truly operative, work has to be infused with
its own spirituality. It is always a personal action in which
the whole person, body and soul participates. Since it is to the
whole man that is directed the word of the living God, man must
be guided by faith, hope and charity to ensure that
'work is in practice given the meaning which it has with God',
and thus brought 'into the work of salvation like other things with
which that work is entwined'[8].

Here, we can say that work helps us attain fulfilment and personal
satisfaction of our needs, enriching our lives with beauty and
enjoyment. Through work, the disorders of a sinful world can be
brought under control, and man participates with God in the work
of creation. But at the same time, work entails an element
of real hardship and difficulty. Whether as a result of
'original sin' or as a result of any other predicament, paid
and toil cannot be escaped in the world of work, but the example
of Jesus Christ has shown that behind all cross lies the
resurrection.

On the other hand, man's domination of the world may be neither
individual nor external merely. If work is to be effective, it
must be co-operative in both aims and methods, while the dominance
over nature that it seeks must be in the first place man's
dominance over himself. Only thus can man bring himself with all
else back to God[9].

Both individually and communally, man subdues the earth, properly
speaking, only when he is in no way dominated by either the things
he makes or by the process of making them. Man must show at all
times that it is he who dominates. For a new Nigeria, these
elements contained in a spirituality of work can be very useful and
salvific: namely, work sanctifies, saves and fulfils; work is a
participation in the creative work of God; work makes us friends and
brothers of Jesus Christ, when we participate in his cross and
resurrection and thereby become fully man and children of God.

---

8) Ibid., LE, n. 24
9) Ibid, n. 25.

CHAPTER TEN: Final evaluation

> "Only the united efforts of the citizens under
> enlightened leadership can overcome difficulties
> such as Nigeria now has. Only the harnessing of
> all the forces for the common good, in true respect
> of the supreme values of the spirit, will make a
> nation great and a happy dwelling place for its people".
>
> - John Paul II, in Lagos 1982 (Speech to President).

We have now come to the last chapter of this work, and we shall attempt in
the form of summary, to evaluate some of the issues already raised in the
preceeding chapters.

Three steps will be undertaken in the venture, namely:

(1) to present in summary form, the value, meaning and social structure of
human workwith reference to"laborem Exercens" with an aim at underlying
its relevance for post-colonial Africa, in our context - Nigeria;

(2) to refer to certain unsolved questions in the Encyclical, with an aim at
contextual argumentation in the cause of Africa;

(3) to present a challenge to the Nigerian Church in its ministry of evangelisation by pointing to the tasks ahead;

It is historically important to mention here that after this work had been
officially handed over to the University of Bonn as dissertation in June 1985,
but before its publication, a military coup occured in Nigeria in the early
hours of 27th August 1985 and took over power from the oppressive and brutal
government of General Muhammed Buhari and his cliques, ending almost two years
of tyrannical and alienating governmental rule. The new government under
General Gbadamosi Ibrahim Babangida merit special mention here since their
policies and actions since inception go a long way to confirm many of the views
already stated in Section One, Chapter Four of this work. Infact, this new
government has already styled itself the "Government for human rights", and has
in many speeches attempted to rectify the misuse of power by its predecessor.
Unfortunately, we cannot go into details here to show the extent of this impact.
Such a task may be the duty of another research in the near future.

1. What Nigeria can learn from Laborem Exercens: (Summary)

A detailed exposition of the relevance of Laborem Exercens
in the context of a post-colonial African society has already been
undertaken. Here we repeat once again, the basic tenets, namely:

a) It is a man's duty to work. It is by his work that he must
procure his daily bread; by his work that he must contribute
to the continuing development of the technical arts and sciences;
by his work - of particular importance, this - that he must
help to raise ever higher moral and cultural standards of the
society in which he shares his life with the human family.
In so far as we fail in realising this, we frustrate our lives and
fail in what we owe the common good, offending against the virtue
of social justice which bids us to do habitually whatever is
necessary for the common good. Since it is man's duty to work,
Nigerians may need to change their attitude to work, which
since the colonial experience has become exteriorised. Work should
not simply mean "Meal thicket", but must be more for a country with
the potentialities to elevate Africa.
Work must be understood as necessary, creative, corporate, painful and
redemptive.

b) Man alone is adapted to work. Indeed, work is one of the
signs by which man is distinguished from other living creatures.
Although active in sustaining themselves, animals cannot be said
to work. Work is a fundamental dimension of man's existence on
earth, and through work fulfils his life on earth. Wherefore,
work bears man's signature, the distinctive mark of his humanity
and nature, the mark of a person who is created in God's image
to act within a community of persons. We must keep always before
our eyes the subjective nature of work. First man, then the rest.

If we do this we shall never neglect or deny the threefold
external purpose of work, namely family, nation and mankind; nor
shall we neglect the dignity of the working person and unique
individual.

c) The Encyclical Laborem Exercens extols the unique worth,
value and dignity of man, and asserts that economics must serve man,
not otherwise. Man's special relationship to God his creator and
his endowment with reason, Faith and an eternal soul make
him superior over work itself, the objects of work and
the tools and equipments used as working materials. Such an
attitude will help rescue Nigeria and entire Africa from the
the impending economic secularism or materialism facing modern
nations.

d) The conflict between labour and capital is superfluous
and based on false views of man. The undoubted source of the
conflict lay in the fact that when the workers offered
their labour for sale, they put their powers at the disposal of
a class of entrepreneurs who were led by the principle that
profit should be maximised and tried strenuously to establish
the lowest possible wage for the work done.

Apart from this, men's work was abused in other ways for the sake
of profit, among the evils being the neglect of safety
precautions and of provision for the health, living conditions of
the workers and their fundamental human rights as well as their
families. The Pope offers the basic thesis that there is a
priority of labour over capital, and at the same time no inherent
opposition between both. While recommending the sharing of profit
between capital and labour, the Pope warns that both capitalism and
socialistic communism, that is, between economism and materialism
have erred in setting mankind in an antinomy of ideologies to the

left and right. Nigeria must reject all ideologies whether to
the left or to the right. African policy-makers are thereby
helped to strike a balance between rigid capitalism and extreme
collectivism. We must maintain the primacy of man over things
including ideologies.

e) The 'personalist argument' is offered as a valid alternative
to all forms of work which deprive the worker participation
in the means of production, or bureaucratise his personality.
As the document points out, the man who works rightly
expects something besides a fair wage for his labour. He wants
also to have the process of production so arranged that he
works, even on something which is owned in common, he can be aware
that he is working 'on his own account'. This awareness
is extinguished by excessive bureaucratic supervision which
centralises everything and makes the worker feel that he is
just a cog in a huge machine directed from above; nay rather, that
he is for more reasons not just a mere instrument of production
rather than the true subject of work endowed with an initiative
of his own. Failure in this respect inevitably does incalculable
damage to the running of the economy, harm which is not confined to
economic consequences but has for its first victim man himself.

f) On the ownership of private property, Laborem Exercens
maintains that this right is a natural one and is in order with the
will of God. Ownership of property, whether individually owned or in
the hands of the community as title holder must be strictly
differentiated from rigid capitalism or extreme collectivism.
Christian tradition has never held that the right to ownership is
absolute and untouchable, rather, the right has always been
understood within the broader context of the right which is ommon
to all men to use the goods of the whole of creation. The right to
private disposal is plainly subordinate to the right of common use
of goods that are intended for all mankind. In the context of Nigeria,

we are guided from the above assertions to learn that one man cannot live in super - abundance when the entire masses around him live in poverty and squalour. An adequate method of distribution of the goods of the nation must be undertaken to ensure that the majority of the citizens have their rightful share in the nation's resources.

g) Laborem Exercens rightly points out to African leaders as well as workers and employers everywhere, that some of our problems in labour and productivity are controlled by factors beyond the workers and his direct employer. Such factors which cause dependence in economic relations may be social attitudes and institutions, domestic labour policies as well as international trade policies and relations, multi nationals, and other economic determinants which need adequate examination. Policy makers and economic experts are thus helped from the Pope's research to know where the problems lie and to take necessary steps to curb them for the good of the worker.

h) The rights of the worker are inalienable. By guaranteeing him these rights, the charter of the United Nations which calls for the respect of human dignity and guaranteeing of human rights are recognised. In the words of the Pope:
"As the Magisterium of the Church has pointed out several times, especially since the publication of "Pacem in Terris", respect for this great body of human rights constitutes the primary condition for peace in today's world: peace within states and social groups as well as between states. The human rights that flow from work fall into the broad context of these principal rights of the person" (LE, n. 26).

Among the many rights of the workers which any serious nation
must guide and guarantee are: the right of citizens to work;
the right to just wages for work done; the right to form trade
unions for the defence of workers rights from all sorts of
exploitation; the right to strike when this becomes inevitable;
the right to own property and to participate in the ownership
of the means of production; the rights to various social
benefits and insurance such as health, education, leisure and rest,
pension and old age, protection against threats to personality
and property; rights to practice of religion, freedom of
movement, speech, thought and existence.

Other rights include the protection of women from chauvinistic
elements of exploitation; guaranteeing the rights of migrant
workers, technical workers, the disabled and unemployed; and
last but not least, protecting the dignity of agricultural
work by granting farmers essential support, services, loans and
encouragement.

In a developing nation such as Nigeria, official state
policy must be aimed at achieving the full realisation of these
rights for the common good of all its citizens.

i) Finally, the spiritual orientation offered by Laborem Exercens
confirms and elevates the traditional African conception of
work, which if properly understood, contributes to the development
in Africa, as well as in other continents, the conception of work as

a God-given vocation to help in creation. Work will thus be understood as a human obligation in the complex meaning of the word, for the Creator has commanded it and man cannot live and grow in his humanity without it. Properly understood, work has before all else the property of bringing people together, uniting them in the oneness of God's supremacy. For through work, man cares for his family and those closest to him; he cares for the wide range of his human society, that is, the nation which is his mother, and the whole human family of which he is a member.

2. Some unsolved questions:

a)"Laborem Exercens" and the "Third World":
The debth originality and profound thoughts contained in the
Encyclical Letter "Laborem Exercens" has already been discussed
in detail in the preceeding chapters of this work.
The document has generally been described as a positive contribution
to the world of human work, which in the context of the industrial
revolution in Europe, led to the so-called "Social Question"[1].

A critique of the document is difficult to make, keeping in mind
that many of the suggestions and reflections of the Pope have
their foundation in the belief that the rights of man do not
come from the generosity of the State or the benevolence of any other
institution but from the hands of God.

There are however certain unsolved questions which the African reader
might ask, and which of course arise from contextual argumentation.

First of all, the document can be regarded as an Encyclical that
is not specifically directed to the situation of workers in many
of the countries of the "Third World". Infact, "Laborem Exercens"
is not an encyclical on the "Third World" unlike "Populorum Progressio" before it.
In "Populorum Progressio", Pope Paul VI devoted attention specifically
to the "development of those peoples who are striving to escape from
hunger,misery,endemic diseases and ignorance; of those who are
looking for a wider share in the benefits of civilisation and a
more active improvement of their human qualities; of those who are
aiming purposefully at their complete fulfilment"[2].
In a word, Paul VI seeks to rally the thoughts of men to recognise
that solidarity in action at this turning point in human history
with the masses of people in the "Third World" is a matter of urgency.

1) Roos,L., Laborem Exercens-Sinn und Sozialgestalt der menschlichen
   Arbeit;Hrg.Kath.sozialwiss.Zentralstelle,Mönchengladbach,Nr.86,
   Verlag Bachem, p.3.
2) Paul VI., Populorum Progressio,26.3.1967,par.1;(CTS No.S73,London).

In "Laborem Exercens" however, it is not the "Third World" or
its specific problems that has paramount consideration, but the
world of human work, dictated and directed by Europe and the
Super-powers, even though not exclusively limited to these areas
alone.   Pope John Paul II's Encyclical directs attention to the
technological and highly industrialised nations, and these are
the specific audience.   Where elements touching on the"Third World"
are referred to, these are done in a general manner.
John Paul II writes:

> "We are celebrating the ninetieth anniversary of the
> Encyclical Rerum Novarum on the eve of new develop-
> ments in technological,economic and political condi-
> tions which, according to many experts, will influence
> the world of work and production no less than the
> industrial revolution of the last century.   There are
> many factors of a general nature: the widespread intro-
> duction of automation into many spheres of production,
> the increase in energy costs and raw materials, the rea-
> lisation that resources are limited, the problems of
> environmental pollution, and the emergence of peoples
> who, after centuries of subjection, are demanding their
> rightful places among the nations"[3].

We must of course give credit to the approach adopted by John Paul
in "Laborem Exercens".   And we do not of course expect the document
to treat all problems of the world or to repeat the teachings of his
predecessors, if these have in their own times, touched on the problems
of the "Third World".   An exhaustive exposition of the contents of
the document has already been undertaken in preceeding chapters, and
elements adaptable for Nigeria, as well as many other nations of the
"Third World" have been analysed and recommended. However, we must
maintain that the urgent problems facing African nations today, as

---

3) John Paul II., Laborem Exercens,1,3.

well as other developing nations concern poverty, undernourishment, exploitation and ignorance. "Laborem Exercens"is not specific enough with reference to these problems. Infact, these are not its themes. Contextually seen,"freedom from misery, the greater assurance of finding subsistence,health and fixed employment; an increased share of responsibility without oppression of any kind and in security from situations that do violence to human dignity; better education - in brief, to seek to do more, know more and have more in order to be more"[4] these are the basic and urgent problems facing many nations in the developing world. And to these problems, John Paul has no concrete answer in the aforesaid document.

The"Social Question" cannot be completely reduced to the problems of workers in Europe or elsewhere and to the false understanding of the place of human work in human life and societies. In as much as these are very relevant, many Africans had expected that the Pope direct more attention to their peculiar realities.
The problems of capitalism and communism to which "Laborem Exercens" devotes adequate attention is not in reality the specific problems of Africa even though it might be relevant in the face of ongoing developments in the world of work.
The antinomy between Labour and Capital, the problems raised by "laborism", the world of automation, computers and roboters, the criticism on Economism and Materialism, the confrontation facing the ideological blocks on the East-West axis, all these are basic problems which do not primarily concern the dialogue facing the northern and southern hemispheres. Life is inconceivable without a strong economic basis, but this is the dilemma of large populations of the globe. The transfer of vast resources from the rich to the poor countries is a matter of simple justice, not of almsgiving. The"Social Question" today must refer to the inhuman situation of millions of people who are condemned to die in hunger, poverty and squalour, more than to simply appeal to the rich nations to reconsider their concept of human work.
4) Paul VI, Populorum Progressio,par.6.

Pope Paul VI referred to this crass inequality in the distribution
of the world's goods where he says that "the rich peoples enjoy
rapid growth whereas the poor develope slowly. The imbalance is on
the increase: some produce surplus foodstuffs, others cruelly lack
them and see their exports made uncertain...There is also the scandal
of glaring inequalities in the exercise of power. While a small
restricted group enjoys a refined civilisation in certain regions,
the remainder of the population, poor and scattered, has almost
no possibility of acting responsibly and on their own initiative,
and these often live and work in conditions unfit for human beings"[5].
The arguments projected by Paul VI here is that meaningful faith
must take place within the context of the total human situation, in
the quest for social and spiritual justice. His' is a call for a
change from passivity to involvement, from theory to practice, from
the past to the present, from abstraction to reality.
Strangely enough, while a small group of the human family enjoys a
standard of living unknown to the world in the past, most of the
human family eke out a precarious existence and almost fourty-thousand
people die each day from sheer starvation. The basic human right to
eat, to health, literacy and mobility are denied to millions of
people in countries of the southern hemisphere[6].

The point being made here is that there is an urgent need to devote
more attention to the peculiar sociological,psychological and politico-
economical situation of African nations. Any reader of"Laborem
Exercens" from the African perspective might have missed this
attention. African Christians expect more attention paid to them.
After all, the Encyclical "Mit brennender Sorge" was written to the
German nation at a peculiar situation in their history.
A burning and much discussed question concerns the situation of the
workers in many countries of the world, especially in Africa, and
many Christians from this continent expect some document to be

---

5) Paul VI,Populorum Progressio,par.6-7.
6) Patick O'Mahony., The fantasy of human rights,Mayhew-McCrimon,
London,1978,p.25.

written by the Church's Teaching Office with suggestions
towards overcoming present difficulties. If the Church does
not guide and participate in the process of finding justice
for these people and making life more worthwhile for them, She
has no way of influencing the final outcome. The Christian
concern for human rights ought to be translated into practical
terms in the struggle of the African towards emancipation from
the evil effects of colonialism, neo-colonialism and continued
exploitation both from inside and outside Africa.

In the arguments for contextual social ethics, the basic point
has to be made that people cannot be seperated from the situation
in which they live. There is a close relationship between the
human group and their environment. In reality, we can never understand the people of the "Third World" if we seperate them from
the appaling circumstances in which they live. In our times however,
problems have arisen on whether the Social Teachings of the Church,
considers adequately, the problems,prospects and peculiar contextual
situations of the various countries. What of the problems of
identity and differences ? Although Pope John XXIII stated that
the principles of Social Ethics are of universal validity[7] ,how
orthodox is this claim when we consider that most of the contents
of the teachings take their background information in certain areas
from the social,economic and political situation of Europe, thereby,
measuring the activities of other nations from the European standard.
Recent events give credit to this observation as conflicts and
tensions mount further in the distorted relationship between the
so-called "Theology of liberation" and "Catholic Social Teachings"[8].

Infact, observers see "Laborem Exercens" as a document borne out
from the author's personal experiences in his homeland.

---

7)John XXIII, Mater et Magistra,n.22o

8)Höffner J,. Soziallehre der Kirche oder Theologie der Befreiung?
  Bonn, Hrsg. Deutsche Bischofskonferenz,Kaiserstraße 163,1984.

  Roos,L., Befreiungstheologien und Katholische Soziallehre I and II ;
  Verlag J.P.Bachem,Hrsg.Kath.Sozialwiss. Zentralstelle,Mönchengladbach,12o.

  Sacred Congregation for the Doctrine of Faith,Libertatis nuntius.,
  "Instruction on certain aspects of the Theology of Liberation",1984.
  (CTS,London,Do 560 1985).

b) Contextual argumentation

One criticism levelled against the document is that it is a
work written with situation of the native land of the author in
mind. The Pope, John Paul II is polish and nationalist,
and his country Poland exists in the communist block of nations -
and the Warsaw Pact. It is a nation which has suffered
persecutions after another from almost all European kingdoms
throughout history. After many attempts to freedom,
in the summer of 1980, a large group of polish workers and the
masses in Poland led by Lech Walesa and supported by the
Catholic Church of Poland formed a Trade Union of
Workers (SOLIDARNOSC) for the defence of the rights of
the working classes and the general rights of man in Poland.

With the ensuing battle that followed between the
communistic puppet government of Poland and the masses of the
working classes supported by the over 85 percent Roman
Catholic population and religious hierarchy, the former Head of
Government Edward Gierek had to resign and a military man
General Jaruzelski assumed power, banned SOLIDARITY,
imposed martial law in the country, clamped down the
striking leaders of the new movement and put thousands into
prison.

Russian invasion was anticipated and international East-West politicking
and cold war was threatened. John Paul II, who himself had become Pope in
1978, and had since visited his native Poland in 1979 and 1983 spoke out
several times on these issues. It is not there-fore unimaginable, if the
document "Laborem Exercens" - "On Human Work" - came out under these circumstances, first of all, as an encouragement to the masses of Polish people in
their search for basic worker "rights", and secondly, as a guideline for
action, both for government and for official policy and action.
This explains why Jesuit priest and professor for Christian Social Principles
in Frankfurt, Joseph Walraff made certain statements which depict his seemingly
unsatisfied expectations in the document.[9]

Infact, the term "Solidarity" appears many times in the Encyclical and more
than twenty times in a speech delivered by the Pope to the International
Labour Organisation on 15 June 1982 in Geneva. The Speech itself bears the
caption:"The Way of Solidarity".
In this speech, the Holy Father repeats over and over again what solidarity
of the workers must be and why it must be so. Says he:

> "Solidarity - solidarity is an imperative of the social order,
> the kind that manifests itself through the existence and the
> work of associations of social partners... Ladies and gentle-
> men, I have tried transcending systems,regimes and ideologies
> for regulating social relations, to suggest to you a way - the
> way of solidarity, solidarity of the world of labour"[10].

---

9) In an interview in the "Manager-Magazine, Nr.12/81, in pages 130 - 134,
   Professor Walraff states in page 131: "Diese Enzyklika ist nach meinem
   Eindruck kein Weltrundschreiben, sie ist vor allem ein Rundschreiben an
   Polen, mit einigen Gesichtspunkten für die westliche Welt gleichfalls nicht
   falsch sind, jedoch wenig akut".

10) John Paul II, Address to the ILO in Geneva; Published in the "Pope Teaches",
    CTS, London,1982/7, pp.278 - 291.

But one may ask: why does the Holy Father choose to talk and to
overemphasise the issue of solidarity? Is it not connected with the
historical happenings in his country? However, no matter how the
answer goes, it has to be maintained that the contents of the document
has applicable relevance for other societies within and outside
Europe, even though they may not be equally actual at the same time.
In Igboland for example, solidarity at work is a normal way of life
which does not need to be taught the Nigerian Igbo from outside.
This fact was sufficiently shown in the first three chapters of this
work, where the issue of solidarity was regarded as a way of life
embedded in the traditional culture. In this sense, the call to
solidarity is not new to the African. It is a confirmation of practice.
"Laborem Exercens" can therefore be regarded as a document which
lacks a certain pluralistic view of human work. It's concepts and
contents have primary relevance to the world of the author, even
though its applicability extends beyond Europe. This later is not
its point of departure, but it is referred to generally in application.

In a commentary written to introduce "Laborem Exercens" to the
reader, Oswald von Nell-Breuning says:

> "Bei der bis hierhin verfolgten Lehrentwicklung handelt
> es sich um eine geographische Erweiterung des Gesichts-
> kreises von einem engem Kreis besonders fortgeschrittener
> Länder auf Weltweite, womit von selbst auch eine Menge neuer
> Sachfragen in den Blick und damit in die Kirchenamtlichen
> Dokumente gelangte"[11].

From the aforesaid, it has now become clear that contextual argumentation has always been sought in the development of the Social Principles
of Christianity. Africans therefore have not only a right, but
also an obligation to develope a contextual "social ethics".
This is based on the teaching that christianity seeks to be at home
with every culture and is not tied down to any. While the Gospel
breaks across the frontiers of nations and either fulfils or judges

---

11) Oswald von Nell-Breuning,"Kommentar zur Enzyklika Laborem Exercens",
op.cit., p.1o9

them, each people must be able to formulate an indegenous response
to God's invitation through the Gospel, a response that can be
reflected in theological formulations, celebrations of the
liturgy and in practical Christian witness [12].

During his historic visit to Uganda in 1969, Pope Paul VI challenged
African theologians, bishops and christians to develope an authentic
African christianity . He spoke on adaptation of the Gospel
and the Church to African culture. In his speech, the Pope said
among others:

> "Must the Church be European,latin,Oriental or must
> the Church be African?... It is granted that the mode of
> manifesting this one faith may be manifold, hence it
> may be original, suited to the tongue,style,character,
> genius and culture of the one who professes the faith.
> A certain pluralism is not only legitimate but desirable.
> An adaptation of the Christian life in the fields of
> pastoral,ritual,didactic and spiritual activities is not
> only possible, but is even favoured by the Church...And
> in this you may, and you must be an African Christianity"[13].

In the growing Churches in Africa today, this challenge by Pope Paul VI
demands careful reflection by the theologian and Christian who must
always keep in mind that the theology of incarnation makes it
possible for man to venture a direct dialogue with God as Father.
This challenge involves an assessment of the material already
assembled in original studies of African culture, with the basic
question of how they can be seen as standard material on which
the Christian message has to be born. There should be no room for
arrogance or cultural superiority thinking, for we are merely stewards
who should place our talents in seeing that the fruits of economic
growth and development are shared by all.

12)Pius XI, Evangelii Praecones,par.89

   Canaan Banana,. The Gospel according to the Ghetto.,Mambo press,
   Zimbabwe,1980p.75.

13) Paul VI., Le Voyage de Paul VI en Ouganda,Vatican City,1969,pp.64-6.

c) <u>Sin and the problem of structures</u>:

Another unsolved question in the Encyclical letter "Laborem Exercens" concerns the problems related to the personalist argument, the sinfulness of man, and the influence of structures on man's life. John Paul II believes that by setting work in its right order, and by teaching people the right meaning of human work, many evils present today in society will disappear, as evil is primarily a product of sin , and the avoidance of sin the begining of true liberation. Not only in "Laborem Exercens",but also other public speeches and documents[14], John Paul discloses that sin is the basic distorting factor in God's creation, perpetuating injustice,uproar and disorder in the world of men. He therefore calls for a deep conversion of the heart and a change of will from evil to good. Even though he accepts the methods of argumentation posed by Social Teachings, namely personalist and structural reform, he believes that the reform of the mind is more important since it is in man's free will to do or undo. The Encyclical Letter "Dives in misericordia" of John Paul II brings out this point very well, when its first sentences begin with a quotation from the apostle Paul where he writes:

> "You were dead because of your sins and offenses,
> as you gave allegiance to the course of this world,
> following the prince of the power of the air, the
> spirit that is now at work in the sons of disobe-
> dience. Among these we all once lived in the passions
> of our flesh,following the desires of body and mind,
> and so we were by nature children of wrath,like the
> rest of mankind..."[15]

There is no doubt that sin is the root cause of disorder in God's quiet world as John Paul shows. However, in recent times, the debate has begun on whether a change of mind alone is sufficient to renew

14)John Paul II, Redemptor Hominis,March 1979

   John Paul II.,Dives in misericordia,3o-November 1980

   John Paul II.,Reconciliatio et paenitentia,2.December 1984

15)Ephesians,2:1-4

the face of the earth. Infact, it is becoming clearer daily that
there is more to be said on the question of injustice and disorder
in the world, also on the situation of poverty in the "Third World"
than simply sin as root cause. How do we explain away those painful
situations which force man to act as he does in a particular context?
Sin and conversion or change of mind alone cannot really solve
the problems of todays suffering humanity. The change of structures
also play a very important role. The poor of the world have
found that with all their rights, their votes and the respect to
their human dignity given back to them, still they remain poor.
At the basis of many human grievances, there is the same socio-
economic issue of poverty caused by a system that continues to
subdue its victims.   Besides this, there are other natural forces
which act to keep human beings marginalised and below average.

First of all, many nations where there is hunger lie geographically
in the desert or environmentally unfavourable situations. The personalist argument cannot be seen here to be the cause.
Then, there is the problem of ignorance, peculiar cultural and
religious mentalities inherent in certain peoples which continue
to keep them low. It is not sin that caused these.
The system in which men live play a very vital role. In many African
nations for example, political freedom and independence from colonial
rule has been obtained, but they are not accompanied by economic and
social equality. Infact, Nigeria as well as other countries
inherited at colonial independence, an economy structured to
depend on the economy of the richer nations. These nations are still
struggling in vain to rise out of their present malaise, and inspite
of the genuine efforts of many of their leaders, their economies
still lag far behind. Colonialism has come and gone, but the
structures it laid are still there, determining the fate of future
generations yet unborn.
For example, tribalism in Nigeria seems indelible, as well as the
recent problems of "Federal Character" and the attendant corruptions
inherent in it. They are all upshots of colonial rule.

To this might still be added other structural problems:
- exploitation of resources at cheap local labour;
- monoculture as economic forms in certain societies, where peasants
  spend their time and lives cultivating tea,cocoa, coffee,oil, and
  other goods which they do not need, in order that the State may
  import goods for the elite or pay its debts in the international
  markets for technical advise recieved from the raw material buyers;
- migrant labour situations and seasonal farming problems due
  to climate and poor agricultural soil;
- imbalance in export and import relations between nations;
- the fact that many poor people have resigned to their fate and
  accepted the inhumanity and humiliation in which they find themselves
  thereby internalising their poverty as a normal course of life,
  together with the system that produced it;
- Lastly, many industrialised nations frown at technological transfer
  because thereby, they may loose their power over the poorer nations
  who must remain consumers if the market is to remain stable.

In our day and generation, we are witnessing the great scramble by the
superpowers and their allies to control the raw materials, the
seas and the air which belong to all men as of right.
It is clear that many of these structural systems and problems arise
from uncontrollable circumstances, and it would be one-sided to
look at sin as the main cause. There is the popular proverb which
says : "Give a man a fish and you feed him for a day. Teach him
how to fish and you feed him for life".
In this connection, one realises the complications contained in the
story told by Patrick O'Mahony that "while Helder Camara was
giving soup to the poor, the government was happy, but when he
stressed that, if structures were correct, there would be no need
for such a project, the government became hostile. The solution is
not only to work on the soup, but also to work on government"[16].

16) Patrick O'Mahony, The fantasy of human rights,op.cit., p.25

d)"Laborem Exercens" and the concrete human realities:
Another criticism levelled out on the document is that
Laborem Exercens considers certain topics which it treats in a
very general manner. It is not concrete enough, as examples
on topics concerning ecology, technology transfer, and specific
solutions to fundamental economic problems are left unsolved, or
are simply generally considered.

It is said that Laborem Exercens exposes problems but does not
say how they can be solved. And John Paul II justifies this
attitude: He writes: "It is not for the Church to analyse
scientifically the consequences that these changes may have on
human society"[17].
The criticism however remains that the problems are not solved.

The point   has been said by people who can be taken very seriously[18]
that the document does not bring in many new innovations, but
repeats old truths already formulated in the New Testament and by the
early Church Fathers, as well as the teachings of earlier
Popes on the social question of human work, and of Vatican Two. The
Pope it is said, says things which any other average man would say.

His teaching that it is man's duty to work, the unique worth of the
individual and man's dignity,his stress that the antinomy between labour
and capital is superfluous, the emphasis on ownership of property,the
rights of workers, among others are not new.

17) John Paul II, LE, n. 1, 4.
18)   Oswald von Nell-Breuning., op.cit., p.1o9

That the role of man is central in the world of work is a
teaching long stated by the earlier church Fathers, as well as
the humanists of our time. His definition of work, the views
on communism and capitalism are not new.
The rights of man were long outlined in the Evangelium , the
Charter of Human Rights of the French revolution, the
American revolution and the United Nations, as well as the
constitutions of various nations.

John Paul II himself says on this lack of complete originality:

> "It is certainly true that work, as a human issue,
> is at the very centre of the "Social Question" to which,
> for almost a hundred years, since the publication of
> Rerum Novarum in 1891, the Church's teaching and the
> many undertakings conncected with her apostolic
> mission have been especially directed. The present
> reflections on work are not intended to follow a
> different line, but rather to be in organic connection
> with the whole tradition of this teaching and activity"[19]

And on this too, Professor Oswald von Nell Breuning adds:

> "...Diese Lehrentwicklung fand Johannes Paul II bereits
> abgeschlossen vor. Demzufolge darf man - rein stofflich
> betrachtet - in seiner Enzyklika "Laborem Exercens"
> an aufregend Neuem nicht viel erwarten"[20]

---

19) John Paul II, LE, n. 2,1
20) Oswald von Nell Breuning, op.cit., p. 109

It must however be made clear here that inspite of this criticism,
John Paul II's Encyclical on human work still contains certain
things that are new, if not in content, then at least from its
basic "Fragestellung" (questioning), and its point of departure.
This has been adequately explicated in the earlier chapters,
but we can repeat it here in the words of Prof. O. von Nell-Breuning
thus:

> "Neu ist in dieser Enzyklika etwas ganz anderes und sehr
> viel wesentlicheres. Indem sie vom arbeitenden Menschen
> und seiner Arbeit schlechthin handelt, gelangt sie zu
> einer Blickfeld-erweiterung ganz anderer Art, die zu einem
> Wechsel des Ansatzpunktes führt, der seinerseits
> wiederum weittragende Folgen nach sich zieht... Ihren
> Ansatz nimmt sie nicht von den zeitgeschichtlich aktuellen
> Mißständen, sondern genau von der entgegengesetzten Seite,
> von den anthropologischen Konstanten, das heißt von der
> Personwürde ausnahmlos jedes einzelnen Menschen und von
> dem daraus sich ergebenden personalen Charakter jeder Art
> von menschlicher Arbeit. Man kann es so ausdrücken:
> der bisherige Ansatz ergab Sozialkritik; mit dem neuen
> Ansatz dieser Enzyklika tut die Kirche den Schritt über die
> Sozial-Kritik hinaus"[21]

Lastly, there is the criticism that the views of man portrayed in
Laborem Exercens, John Paul's theological anthropology, his
christological anthropocentricm, and his ecclesiological anthropocentrism, coupled with the"noble views and sentiments" on the
worth of the person, the ideal world of work, the search for an
egalitarian, peaceful, and Christian society - all these are regarded
as "pious sentiments", somehow utopian, and are as such not
realistic in this world.

---

21) Ibid., p. 110

John Paul's spirituality of work, his elevation of all work to a
state of grace, his identification of work with the cross of Christ,
his lack of emphasis for leisure or rest and free-time, and his
over-emphasis of work as a task, a vocation of man, a must
all these fall withing the boundaries of some critic.
People believe that the Holy Father's good will and intentions
blinds him to the daily reality of man's world - a world full of
sin, crime, greed and oppression, so as it was in the beginning with
reference to the story of Cain and Abel, and as it is also now in
our time.

It is therefore held by many that the Pope has done his job of
preaching the good news and drawing man's attention to do good.
On the other hand however, it is believed that the world will
always be drawn to evil, to greed, to crime and to sin.
Need we however stop the proclamation of the good news because
man is prone to sin? Is there no conversion? Has the world no hope?
No salvation? What is then with the coming of the prophets and
the incarnation of Jesus Christ?

These are questions which inspite of all call to the reality of
the human condition, inspite of all criticism of the "pious
sentiments" of the Pope, still demand that the "Good News" be
proclaimed in season and out of season. This is therefore a
strong justification for the contents of 'Laborem Exercens' and
for all involvement of the Church in the problems of man, namely in
the "Social Question".

3. Christian Social Principles - A Challenge to the Nigerian Church

> "The Church has always had the duty of scrutinising
> the signs of the times and of interpreting them in
> the light of the Gospel. Thus in language
> intelligible to each generation, it can respond to
> the perennial questions which people ask about this
> present life and the life to come, and about the
> relationship of the one to the other". (Gaudium et Spes, n. 1)

Vatican Two challenged the entire Church, both hierarchy and
laity to scrutinise the signs of the times and interprete them
in the light of the Gospel. This call is based not only on the
biblical vision of discipleship, but also on Church tradition of
Social Teaching, coupled with reasoned reflection on the
political and economic realities of today. This challenge is
as such a task for the Nigerian Church - a task that corresponds
to the threefold functions of preaching, teaching and healing.

The political and economic realities of the Nigerian society
has been sufficiently highlighted in the preceeding chapters of
this work.   In the face of such a transitory society - with
all its problems in the social, cultural, political and economic
spheres, what is the role of the Church? In what does the
challenge of Vatican Two consist for the Nigerian Church of
our time?

Simply put, the challenge is a call for a change from dogmatism to
involvement, from simple theorising to practice, from the past to
the present, and from abstraction to the realities of the moment.
It is only then that the Church will not only teach from the pulpit,
but she will accompany the people,learn with them in the peasant fields,
in factories,co-operatives and assure them of the liberating powers of
the Gospel . It is a challenge to influence change or be changed ourselves

a) The Church is called to be a community of disciples,
a community which commits itself to solidarity with its
members, especially with the poor and those who suffer from
the sinful structures created by human societies. Using
the language of the Pastoral Constitution on the Church
in the Modern World, the Fathers of Vatican Two wrote:

> "the joys and hopes, the griefs and anxieties of
> the people of this age, especially those who are poor
> or in any way afflicted, these too are the joys and
> hopes, the griefs and anxieties of the followers
> of Christ"[22].

In one word, the task of the Nigerian Church today is that
of the Fundamental Option for the Poor.
Biblical perspectives on wealth and poverty form the basis for
what is called "the preferential option for the poor".
This option challenges the contemporary Church to speak out
boldly for those who are defenceless and poor and to access
social institutions and policies in terms of their impact
on the poor. Dealing with poverty therefore is an
imperative of the highest order in our times.

---

[22] Gaudium et Spes, n. 1.

b) The Nigerian Church is challenged to defend human worth
and dignity, to call for a just economic order and to
insist that all persons have rights in the economic and
political spheres. The Nigerian Church must insist that
society has a moral obligation to take the necessary steps
to ensure that no one among us is hungry, homeless,
unemployed or otherwise denied what is necessary to live
with adequate dignity. In a country with just about
10% rich people and more than 60% poor, the Church cannot
keep quiet. Today in Nigeria, there is, as has already
been shown in the preceding chapters, unequal distribution
of income, education, wealth, job opportunities and
other economic goods as well ad discrimination on the
basis of religion, sex, tribe, and other arbitrary
standards. In such a situation, the Nigerian Church must
call and act for social justice and for distributive
justice too. It is the duty of the Church to make it clear
that the dignity of the human person is the criterion against
which all aspects of economic life must be measured.
This dignity can only be realised in relationship and
solidarity with others.

c) The Church must stress three spheres of economic values
in Nigeria: namely

-   that the economy must enable people find self-
    realisation; fulfil their material needs through
    adequate remuneration; and enhance unity within the
    family, the nation, and the world community.

- that meeting human needs and increasing participation should be priority targets in the investment of wealth, talent and human energy. In other words, the fulfilment of the basic needs of the people is of the highest priority, namely, water medicine, light, roads, food, schools, transport, jobs.

- that management and workers should develope new forms of partnership and co-operation, such as co-operative ownership of the means of production, and worker participation in ownership and decision making, thereby broadening the sharing of responsibility in economic society.

d) Of much importance is the political area. The Church in Nigeria must insist that government is not a reserved right of any group of people, because they have the power of the gun or the economic power alone, but government is a right for every individual. Therefore, democracy which allows participation for all citizens and checks dictatorship has to be supported. Above all, the Churches in Nigeria must remind the government of its basic duties towards the citizens, its moral obligation and the reason for its continued existence, namely:

- that of protecting basic rights as guaranteed by the Constitution, the United Nations Charter on Human rights and the Organisation of African Unity charter for Human rights.

- ensuring economic justice for all

- enabling citizens to strike a balance towards these ends by encouraging individual intiatives and social responsibility.

However, while Christian Social Principles provides a positive affirmation of the role of government, it does not advocate a "statist" approach to political or economic activity. The principle of "subsidiarity" is the primary norm for determining the scope and limites of state and government action.

e) Finally, all the moral principles that govern the just operation of any socio-economic endeavour apply to the Church itself and its agencies and institutions. All Church institutions, both the hierarchy and individual Christians in Nigeria, as elsewhere must realise that the Church as a community can make very important contributions to achieving greater economic justice. This can only be done if we have adequate knowledge of the Social Teachings of the Church. In the words of Pope John XXIII, we shall conclude this thesis:

> "It is therefore our urgent desire that this doctrine be studied more and more. While we note with satisfaction that in many Institutes it has been taught for some time and with outstanding success, we urge that such teaching be extended by regular, systematic courses in Catholic schools of every kind, especially in seminaries. It is to be inserted into the religious instruction programmes of parishes and of Associations of the Lay Apostolate. It must be spread by every modern means at our disposal: daily newspapers, periodicals, popular and scientific publications, radio and television.

The laity can do much to help this diffusion
of Catholic social Teachings by studying it
themselves and putting it into practice,
and by zealously striving to make others understand
it. They should be convinced that the best
way of demonstrating the truth and efficacy of
this teaching is to show that it can provide
the solution to present-day difficulties..
They will thus make converts of those people
who are opposed to it through ignorance of it.
Who knows, but a ray of its light may one day
enter their minds"[23].

---

23) John XXIII, Mater et Magistra, nn. 223 - 225.

B I B L I O G R A P H Y

Achebe,C., Things Fall Apart, Heinemann, London (African
          Writers Series), c 1958.

Achike,O., Nigerian Law of Contract,Nwamife publishers,
          Enugu, 1982

Adams, J., Remarks on the country from Cape Palmas to the
          River Congo, London, 1923

Afigbo,E.A., Ropes of Sand - Studies in Igbo History and
          Culture, University Press Ltd.Ibadan and Ox-
          ford Press, London,1981

    -     Economic Foundations of Pre-colonial Igbo Socie-
          ty., (Publ. in Nigerian Economic and Social
          History), University of Ife press,Ile Ife,1978

    -     The indegenous political systems of the Igbo.,
          Publ. in Tarikh, Vol.4,No.2,1973

    -     The Warrant Chiefs - Indirect Rule in South-
          Eastern Nigeria., London,London, 1972

    -     Pre-colonial links between S.E.Nigeria and
          the Benue Valley,University of Nigeria,
          (unpublished paper pp.1 -29),Nsukka

Altaf Gauher(ed)., Talking about development; Third World
          Foundation for Social and Economic Stidies .,
          London,1983

Amadi, E., Ethics in Nigerian Culture, Heinemann, London, Ibadan
          1982

Anene,C.J., Southern Nigeria in Transition-1885 to 1906,
          Cambridge,1966.

Anigbo,O.C., Commensality and Social Change in Ibagwa Aka,
          Unpublished Doctoral Thesis, University of London,
          1979.

Aquinas,T., Summa Theologiae, I-II,q.94

Aquinas,T., regimine principum ,1:15

Arinze,A.F., The Encyclical Laborem Exercens in the context
of Africa, (paper at symposium: From Rerum
Novarum to Laborem Exercens- Towards the
year 2ooo), Rome, 3-5.April 1982, Pontifical
Commission "Iustitia et Pax",Vatican City.
-         Sacrifice in Igbo Religion., Ibadan University
ress, Ibadan, 1970
-         The Christian and Politics., publ. in Nigeria,
1982
Basden,T.G., Niger Ibos, Frank Cass,London,1938 (rev.ed.1966)
-         Among the Ibos of Nigeria,Frank Cass, London,
ev. ed. 1966
Beer,C.C., The Politics of Peasant Groups in W.Nigeria.,
Ibadan University Press, Ibadan, 1976
Booth,E., What the Council says about Economic and Social
Affairs; Catholic Truth Society,London,Do 374
v.Nell-Breuning., Arbeitet der Mensch zuviel? Herder,
Freibourg,1985
-         Worauf es mir ankommt- zur sozialen Verantwortung,
Herder, Freibourg,1983
-         Gerechtigkeit und Freiheit, Europa Verlag,Wien,
-         Soziallehre der Kirche, Europa Verlag , Wien,1983
Brian, W et al., Industrial Relations and the limits of Law,
Oxford,1975
Caroll, D., York Notes on Arrow of God, Longman,London,1980
Chenu,M.D., Die Arbeit - ein Entwurf,Würzburg,1956 (The
original text is in French:"Notes sur la theologie
du travail., Paris,1955).
Chubb,T.L., Ibo Land Tenure, Ibadan Univ.Press,1961
Chukwudum,M.A., Nigeria: The Country in a Hurry, John West
Publishers, Ikeja,Lagos, 1981.
Cicero, . De Officis, 1,42
Coreth, E., Grundfragen des menschlichen Daseins - Einfüh-
rung in die philosophische Anthropologie.-
Tyrolia Verlag, Innsbruck

David, J., Theologie irdischen Wirklichkeit (in Fragen der
          Theologie heute; Hrsg.v.J.Feiner und J.Trutsch
          und F.Böckle), Einsiedeln,1957
Dillard,D., The Economics of J.M.Keynes,London,1966
Donald D. Hartle., Archeology in Eastern Nigeria,Nigerian
          Magazine 93,June,1967
Dunn,A.T., Notes on Things Fall Apart (Chinua Achebe),
          York Press, Longman,Essex,1981
Elias,T.O.S., The Nature of African Customary Law., Man-
          chester University Press, 1956
     -    Nigerian Land Law, 4th edition,London,1971,publ.
          by Sweet and Maxwel (originally published under
          the title : Nigerian Land Law and Custom,Rout-
          ledge and Kegan Paul,london,1961 (rev.ed.1966)
     -    Groundwork of Nigerian Law., Manchester,
Equiano,O., The interesting narrative of the life of Olaudah
          Equiano or Gustavus Vassa, c1794, edited by Paul
          Edwards: "Equiano's travels, London.
Evans-Pritchard., The Nuer,publ. 1940, London
Ezeanya,S.N., A Handbook of Igbo Christian Names, Port-
          Hacourt, Nigeria, 1967
Fage,J,D., A History of West Africa, Cambridge,London,1969
Fagothey,A., Right and Reason - Ethics in Theory and Practice,
          CVM Company, St. Louis, 1959
Firth, Primitive Polynesian Economy, 1939
Flint,E,J., Nigeria and Ghana, New Jersey, 1966
Floyd,B., Eastern Nigeria - A geographical review,London,1969
          Macmillan press.
Forde,D and Jones,G,I., The Ibo and Ibibio speaking peoples
          of south-eastern Nigeria; Int. African Institute,
          London,1950
Forsyth,F., The making of an African Legend- the Biafra Story,
          London, 1969.,
Fortes,M, and E.E.Pritchard, African Political Systems,
          Oxford University Press, London, 1940
     -    The Dynamics of clanship among the Tallensi,
          Oxford University Press for the International
          African Institute, 1945.

549

Friedman,M., The optimum Quantity of Money and other Essays,
          London, 1969
Gauhar,A., (ed) Talking About Development,. Third World
          Foundation for Social and Economic Studies,
          London, 1983
Gluckman,M., Politics,Law and Ritual in Tribal Society,
          Blackwell,Oxford,1977
Green,M.M., Igbo Village Affairs, Frank Cass,Ltd., London,1964
     -    Land Tenure in an Ibo Village in S.E.Nigeria.,
          Humphries, London,1941
Hives, F. ., Juju and Justice in Nigeria, London, John Lane,
          1930
Harris,J.S., Some Aspects of Slavery in South East Nigeria,
          Journal of Negro History,27:1 January 1942
Heck,B (ed)., Arbeit-Ihr Wert, Ihre Ordnung,. (mit einer
          Ansprache von Papst Johannes Paul II), v. Hase
          und Koehler, Mainz,1984.
Hengsbach,F.,Die Arbeit hat Vorrang - eine Option Katholischer
          Soziallehre; (Reihe Arbeiterbewegung und Kirche),
          Grünewald Verlag,Mainz,1982
Höffner,J., Christliche Gesselschaftslehre., Verlag Butzon
          und Bercker, Kevelar,c 1978
Horton,W.R.C., The Ohu system of slavery in S.E.Nigeria.,
          Journal of Negro History,21.1.1942
Ike,O.F., Karl Marx on Religion and Christianity - a critical
          study, (unpublished masters thesis, University of
          Innsbruck), January 1981
Iloanusi,O,A., Myths of the creation of man and the origin
          of death in Africa, European University Studies,
          Peter Lang, Frankfurt/M 1984
Isichei,E., A History of the Igbo People, Macmillan Press,
          London, 1976
     -    A History of Nigeria, Longman, Nigeria,London, 1984

Jeffreys,M.D.W.,The Umundri traditions of origin., African
          Studies, Vol.15,No.3,1956
Joseph,H.W.B., The Labour Theory of value in Karl Marx,.
          London,1923

Keynes,J,M., Theory of Employment,Interest and Money,1936
Killam,G.D., The Novels of Chinua Achebe,African publishers,
        New York,1969
King,M.L.Jnr,. The strenght to love,Fontana,Chicago,1963
Kimminich,O., Subsidiarität und Demokratie- Schriften der
        Kath.Akademie in Bayern,Patmos Verlag,Düsseldorf,
        1981
Kirk-Green,A.H., Crisis and Conflict in Nigeria, London,O.U.P.
        Two Volumes,1971
Kirwan,J., Introduction to Laborem Exercens-Study Edition .,
        Catholic Truth Society,London,1984.
Klein,W.and Krämer,W (Hg)., Sinn und Zukunft der Arbeit -
        Konsequenzen aus Laborem Exercens., Mathias
        Grünewald Verlag, Mainz (Reihe Arbeiterbewegung
        und Kirche)
Klose,A.,(ed) Katholische Soziallexikon (über 1oo Mitarbeiter),
        Tyrolia Verlag, Innsbruck,1964
Lander,John and Richard., Journal of an expedition to explore
        the course and termination of the Niger, 2, N.Y.
        Harper,1837
Leonard,A,G., The lower Niger and its tribes, Frank Cass and
        Co. Ltd, 1968, London.
Liversage,V., Land Tenure in the colonies,Cambridge university
        Press,1945
Lugard,F.D., The Dual Mandate in British tropical Africa,
        London, Blackwood,1922
Maine,C.K., Ancient Law,1959 (ed)
O'Mahony,P.J., The Fantasy of Human Rights,
    -       Multinationals and Human Rights, Great Wakering,
        Essex,England,1980
Marx,K., Das Capital,Vols. I -3 (Publ. by Progress publ.Moscow)
    -       A critique of the Gotha Programme,Vol I
    -       Critique of political Economy, translated by N.I.Stone
        Chicago,1913,C.H.Herr company.
    -(with Engels): The German ideology81845 -6),Progress publ.

Mbiti,S.J., African Religions and Philosophy, Heinemann,
        London, 1969
Meek,C.K., Law and Custom in the colonies,London,Oxford
        University press,1968
    -    Law and Authority in a Nigerian Tribe - A study
        in indirect rule,with a foreward by the Lord Lugard,
        Humanities Press, c 1937
    _   Ibo Law (From essays presented to C.G.Seligman,
        London, Kegan Paul and Co., 1934
Meier,G.M., Leading issues in economic development, New York,
        1976

Messner J., , Die Soziale Frage - im Blickfeld der Sozialkämpfe
        von gestern - der sozialkämpfe von heute - der
        Weltentscheidungen von morgen., Tyrolia ,
    -    Ethik - Compendium der Gesamtethik., Tyrolia,
        Innsbruck
Mieth,D., Arbeit und Menschenwürde, Herder,Freiburg,1985
Mill,S.J., On Liberty, (1859) Schields,CV,ed. Liberal Press,
        New York, 1956
Njaka,N,E., Igbo Political Culture,Evanston,North-West Univ.
        Press, 1974
Northcote,W,T., Anthropological Report on the Ibo speaking
        peoples of Nigeria, Part I, Law and Custom of the
        Ibo of Awka neighbourhood., London, 1913
Northrup,D., The growth of trade among the Igbo before
        1800.,
Nwabara,N,S., Iboland - a century of contact with Britain,
        1860 - 1960., Hodder and Stoughton, London, 1977
Nwankwo,A., Can Nigeria Survive ? First Dimension publ,Enugu,
        1981
Nzomiwu,J.P.C., The Moral Concept of Justice among the Igbos ·,
        (unpublished Doctoral dissertation),pontifical
        Universitas Laterana, Academia Alfonsiana, Roma,
        1977

Ogbalu,C.F., Igbo Institutions and Customs, University
          publishing Company, Onitsha,1973

biechina,N,E., Amos Tutuola and Oral Tradition. Published In:
          (prescence Africaine,New Bilingual edition,
          No.65, 1965).

Okoro,N,M., The Igbo belief in man's continued existence
          after death - its influence on the society.,
          Unpublished doctoral thesis, Rome,1971.

Omoniyi, A., The Judicial system in Southern Nigeria 1854 -
          1954., Longman, London, 1977

Ottenberg,S., Ibo receptivity to change., (publ. in receptivity
          and change in African cultures), W.R.Bascon and M.J
          Herskovits (ed),University of Chicago, 1959.

Rauscher,A., (Hg) Die Arbeitsgesselschaft zwischen Sach-
          gesetzlichkeit und Ethik; (Mönchengladbacher
          Gespräche), Köln, Verlag Bachem, 1985.

-         9o Jahre Rerum Novarum (Mönchengladbacher Gespräche
          Köln, Bachem, 1982

-         Rauscher, A, and Roos, L., Die soziale Verant-
          wortung der Kirche - Wege und Erfahrung von
          Ketteler bis heute, Bachem, Köln, 1977.

Richards,I,A., Land,Labour and Diet in Northern Rhodesia,
          London, 1939, Oxford University Press for the
          International African Institute.

Robertson,D.H., Money, London, Nisbet Cambridge Univ.Press,1922

Rahner,K., Kirche und Staat, in Staatslexikon,6th ed.
          Freiburg/Br. 1967 - 1970, Vol. 4

Roger, C.,The Social Teachings of Vatican Two - its origin
          and development, Oxford, Plater publications,
          1982

-         The development of industrial relations in
          Britain 1911 - 1939., London, (1973).

Roos, L., Sinn und Sozialgestalt der menschlichen Arbeit.,
    Hg. Katholischen Sozialwissenschaflichen Zentral-
    stelle, Mönchengladbach; Nr. 86, Verlag,Bachem,1982
-   Humanität und Fortschritt am Ende der Neuzeit.,
    Hg. BKU , Nr. 24, Bachem Verlag, Köln, 1984
-   Ordnung und Gestaltung der Wirtschaft - Grundlagen
    und Grundsatze der Wirtschaftsethik nach dem II
    Vatikanischen Konzil., Bachem -verlag,Köln,1971

-   (mit Rauscher): Die Soziale Verantwortung der Kirche -
    Wege und Erfahrungen von Ketteler bis heute., Bachem,
    Köln, 1977
Rücker,K,J., Personalität,Solidarität,Subsidiarität - Grund-
    positionen Katholischer Soziallehre,(Dokumente,
    Manuskripte, Protokole),aksb,Bonn,1980
Sargent,L,T., Contemporary political ideologies., 3rd ed,
    Dorsey Press. Illinois,1975
Shapera,I., The Khoisan Peoples of Southern Africa, London,
    Routledge and Kegan Paul,1930
Schalter R., Private Property- The History of an Idea.,
    London,1951
Schasching,J., Katholische Soziallehre und modernes Apostolat;
    Tyrolia Verlag, Innsbruck, 1956
Schreiber,W., Die Botschaft des sozialen Friedens - Beiträge
    zur gesselschaftspolitik, Nr. 23, Hg. BKU, Bachem
    Verlag, Köln,1984.
Shaw, T. , Igbo Ukwu - an account of archeological disco-
    veries in eastern Nigeria, London, 1970
Shorter,A., African Culture and Christian Church - an intro-
    duction to social and pastoral anthropology-.
    Geoffrey Chappman, London, 1973.
Smith, A., Wealth of Nations., New York, common edition,1937
Smock,D, and A., Cultural and political aspects of rural
    transformation: a case study of Eastern Nigeria.,
    Praeger publ. New York, 1972

Sofola,J,A., African Culture and African Personality - What makes an African African ? ;African resources publ. co., Ibadan, Nigeria,1973.

Troelstch,E., The Social Teaching of the Christian Churches, London, 1930

Uchendu,V,C., The Igbo of South-Eastern Nigeria.,Holt and Rheinhart and Winston, New York,1965.

R.de Vaux., Ancient Israel, N.Y. 1961

Watt,L., Communism and Religion.,Catholic Truth Society, R 165, London, Avocet press,1969.

Weber,M., The Protestant ethic and the spirit of capitalism., Talcott parsons, (19309, 1958

Wheare, J., The Nigerian Legislative Council, Vol.IV, Faber and Faber, London.

Wieschoff,W,H.A., Social significance of names among the Ibos of Nigeria., (In:American Anthropologist,Nr.2, Vol.143), 1941

SUPPLEMENTARY LITERATURE:

Banana,C., The Gospel according to the Ghetto., Mambo Press,Zimbabwe,1980.

Baumeister,R,(Redakteur) Die Soziale Marktwirtschaft erneuern-Arbeit - Wachstum - Umwelt.,(Studien zur politischen Bildung) v. Hase und Koehler Verlag,Mainz.

Ejiofor,U.L., Equitable development in Nigeria - A case study of the second national development plan in Nigeria with proposals for the third., Publ. by "Institute of Church and Society",1976 (CS/1) Ibadan,.

Heatley,R., Poverty and Power- The case for a political approach to development and its implications in the West., RVA Zed Press,London,1979.

Höffner,J., Soziallehre der Kirche oder Theologie der Befreiung? Hsgb. Sekretariat der Deutschen Bischofskonferenz, Kaiserstraße 163, Bonn, 1984-

555

Höffner,J., Wirtschaftsordnung und Wirtschaftsethik - Richtlinien
        der Katholischen Soziallehre; Erröfnungsreferat bei der
        Herbstvollversammlung der Deutschen Bischofskonferenz in
        Fulda,23.9.1985;(Hgb. Deutsche Bischofskonferenz,Bonn,Nr.12)
Lappe´,M.F and Collins,J., World Hunger- Ten Myths., Institute for
        food and development policy,San Francisco,c1979 (1982)
Müller-Armack,A., Wirtschaftsordnung und Wirtschaftspolitik, Paul
        Haupt Bern Stuugart,1966 (1976).
 -      The Social Aspects of the Economic System,1947 (article
        published in:"Standard Texts on the Social Market Economy"),
        Gustav Fischer,Stuttgart,1982
 -      The Second Phase of the Social Market Economy - An additio-
        nal concept of a human society,1960 (article like above)
 -      Die Soziale Marktwirtschaft nach einen Jahrzent ihrer
        Erprobung., (Vortrag gehalten vor der Verwaltungs und
        Wirtschaftsakademie,Köln am 16. April 1959.,veröffent-
        licht in "Wirtschaftspolitische Chronik",H.2/3,1959)
Rauscher,A., Katholische Soziallehre und Liberale Wirtschaftsauffassung.,
        Artikel in:"Soziale Orientierung", Band 5:Selbstinte-
        resse und Gemeinwohl,Beiträge zur Ordnung der Wirtschafts-
        ethik., Hgb. von Anton Rauscher, Duncker und Humblot
        Verlag,Berlin,1985.
Roos, L., Die Ordnung der Arbeit nach der Enzyklika "Laborem
        Exercens": Sozialethische Grundaussagen und rechts-
        politische Anregungen., (Artikel in "Renovatio",G 4080 F)
        Heft 1,March 1983, Verlag J.P.Bachem,Köln.
 -      Befreiungstheologien und Katholische Soziallehre I and II,
        Hgb. Katholische Sozialwissenschaftliche Zentralstelle,
        Mönchengladbach, Nr. 119 and 120.
Sacred Congregation for the Doctrine of Faith., "Libertatis nuntius":
        Instruction on certain aspects of the Theology of Libera-
        tion., Rome 1984 (CTS London, Do 560,1985).
Schneider,L., Ist die neue Sozialenzyklika "Laborem Exercens"
        laboristisch ? Hg. Deutsche Kolpingsfamilie,Kölping Verlag,Köln
        1983.

Basic Church documents, speeches,articles,
publications and other related documents to
Human Work and the entire Social Question:

Pastoral Constitution, Gaudium et Spes, of 7.12.1965; In:
AAS,58 (1966),1o25 -1120.
- Leo XIII., Rerum Novarum, ASS 23, (1890 -91)
- Pius XI,. Quadragesimo Anno., 15.5.1931; AAS 23, (1931).
- Pius XI., Divini Redemptoris,19.3.1937; AAS 29 (1937)
- Pius XII., Christmas Broadcast,1941; AAS 34 (1942).
-Pius XII., Christmas Broadcast, 1942, AAS 35, (1943).
Pius XII., Whitsun Broadcast,1941., AAS 44 (1941).
- John XXIII., Mater et Magistra., AAS, 53,(1961) 15.5.63.
-John XXIII., Pacem in Terris., 11.4.1963 , AAS 55 (1963).
Paul VI., Populorum Progressio, 1967, CTS,London,S.273.
- Paul VI., Address to the ILO on the 50th anniversary of
the foundation of the ILO, Geneva, 1o.6.1969,CTS 1982/7

- John Puul II., Laborem Exercens, (On Human Work), engl.
  edition, London, Catholic Truth Society, 1981, Tee and W,.
- John Paul II., The Way of Solidarity., Address to the International Labour Organisation., Geneva,15.6.1982; CTS London,
  1982/7.
-John Paul II., Address to workers at Jalisco Stadium, Gua-
  dalajara- Mexico; 3o.1.1979; In. L'osservatore Romano,
  english edition,12.2.79, No. 7.(Henceforth, OR, english edition)
- John Paul II., Address to workers at Monterrey - Mexico;
  31.1.1979; OR,19.2.79,No.8
- John Paul II., Address to Indios and Peasants at Cuilapañ
  Mexico, 29.1.1979,; OR, 12,2,1979,No.7
- John Paul II., Homily at mass for workers at Jasna Gora;
  Poland, 6.6.1979, OR, 16.7.1979, No.29

-John Paul II., Address to workers of Pomezia, Italy,13.9.79;
  OR,1.1o.79; No.40.
- Address to Italian Professional Association of Family
  Collaborators; (API COLF), 29.4.1979, OR. 14.5.79,No.20.

- Address to General Assembly of the United Nations; 2.1o.
  1979; OR, 15.1o.79, No.42.
- To college of.Cardinals,22.12.1979,OR,14.1.1980,No.2
- To world conference on Agragrian Reform and on rural
  Development, (FAO), 14.7.1979, OR, 23,7.79., No.30
- To Pilgrimage of students from the Archdiocese of Naples;
  24.3-1979, OR, 2.4.79, No.14
- To pilgrimage of workers from Genoa, 2.4.79, OR, 9.4.79;
  No. 15.
-To participants at the convention of the Italian Federation
 of Knights of Labour, 15.5.79; OR 12.5.79,Transl.PCJP.
- To a group of Christian workers: The Right to work and
  to Social justice", 9.2.78, OR, 2o.12.78, No.52.
- To christian union of Entrepreneurs and Managers (UCID),
  24.11.1979; OR, 24.12.79, Nos. 52 -52.
- Homily at mass at "Living History Farms"- Des Moines,
  USA, 4.10.1979, OR, 29.10.79. No. 44
- Homily at mass at Nowy Targ- Poland, 8.6.1979; OR16.7.79
  No.29
- Homily at mass for the "Day of the Railwaymen" - Engine
  Depot, Rome Shunting station; 8.11.1979; OR,1o.12.79,No.5o.
- Wednesday Audience, Theme: "There is no love without justice"
  8.11.78; OR, 16.11.78, No.46
- Greetings to Priests engaged as Diocesan Delegates in the
  Pastoral of Labour; 25.4.1979, OR 26.4.79; PCJP
- Angelus - sunday 11.11.1979; Italian ed. 12-13. Nov.79;
  transl. into engl. PCJP.
- Sunday Angelus, 15.7.79; OR 23.7.1979, No. 30.
- Homily at mass in Holy Cross Cathedral, Lagos to Nigerian
  Workers; OR, March to April 1982, special edition.
- Extracts from address to young people attending the 1982
  meeting for friendship among the people's in Rimini,29.8.
  1982; Publ. in "The Pope Teaches, 1982/9, CTS, London.

- John Paul II., Speech to President Shagari and members
  of the Nigerian Government in Government House, Ikoyi,
  Lagos, 12.2.1982; Publ. in Daily Times , special edition.
- Sermon at speech to priests in Enugu, Nigeria, 13.2.1982.

- John Paul II., Redemptor Hominis., 1979.
- Familiaris Consortio., 1980
- Paul VI.,Evangeli Nuntiandi, 1975.

Documents and working papers of the Pontifical commission
for Justice and Peace: (CIJP or PCJP).
- The Church and Human Rights, 1975, Vatican Press, CIJP
- The Universal purpose of created Things,1977, Vatican press.
- Self reliance by Rev. Heckel, SJ,1978, Vatican Press,CIJP
- The struggle against racism, by Rev. R.Heckel,SJ,1979,
  Vatican Press, CIJP.
- Jan, P.S., Laborem Exercens and the soci-economic issues -
  a new challenge-. PCJP, Vatican city,1982,Nr.9
- Land,D., Social Praxis - the teaching of the Church; publ.
  Doctrine and Life, AFER.
- Texte zur Katholischen Soziallehre - Die sozialen Rund-
  schreiben der Päpste und andere kirchliche Dokumente -
  mit einer Einführung von Oswald von Nell-Breuning,SJ,
  Hg. KAB,1977, Kevelar.
- Okolo, B.C.,African Church and the signs of the Times, Afer,

- Schotte,J.P., Reflections on Laborem Exercens, 1982,
  Vatican Press, 1982.
- Romano Rossi ., Human Labour, Vatican press, 1981.
- New Catholic Encycloped   , New York, McGraw Hill.

- Roos. L.. Theologie und Ethik der Arbeit., Internationale
- Kath. Zeitschrift   13, 1984, 97 - 115-

Documents and Publications
on Nigeria

Catholic Education in the service of Africa; Report of the
Pan-African Catholic Education - Conference,Leopoldville
16 -23 August 1965., Turnai, Casterman,1966.
Easter Joint Pastoral letterby the Catholic Bishops of the
East Central, Nigeria,Onitsha,Tabansi press,1971.
The Catholic Church in an independent Nigeria: Joint Pasto-
ral letter of the Nigerian Hierarchy, October 1 1960, Iba-
dan, Clavarianum Press, 1960 .
Civic and political responsibility of the Christian: Joint
pastoral letter by the Nigerian Catholic Bishops, 10 Febru-
ary, 1979.
The Constitution of the Federal Republic of Nigeria, 1979 .
The East Central State of Nigeria Public Edicts, nos.25,
26 and 27 of 1974.
The Federal Republic of Nigeria National Policy on Educa-
tion, 1977.
The Nigerian Handbook, 1978 -1979; Issued by the Federal
Ministry of   Information, Lagos.
The Third National Development Plan of Nigeria, 1975 -1980.
Africa Studies Review,Vol.26,nos.314, sept-Dec. 1983.
Jones, I,G., Report of the position , status and influence
of chiefs and natural rulers in the eastern region of Nigeria,
Enugu,1957.
Traditional,social and political structures of East Central
State, Government publishers, Enugu,No.WT 189/373/

Eastern Nigerian region- policy for lands; paper No. 3
of 1955, (Enugu Government Printers,1955).
Green Revolution - Insurance against Hunger- published
by the Federal Ministry of Information, Lagos, July 1982

Obasanjo, O., Foundation for stability., Transcript of a
Television Interview from 16 - 18 January 1979. Federal
Ministry of Information, Lagos, 1979.

Hartle,D., Archaelogy in Eastern Nigeria, Nigerian Magazine, Nr. 93, June 1967.

Aguagbaja Village Union Constitution, Umana-Ndiagu, signed: 1.9.1984; Liberty Press printers, Nsukka, 1984.

Oath agreement sworn on behalf of all Aguagbaja Village Union citizens, and signed by 10 signatories of the ten big families, 1.9.1984.

Nigeria: Background Information, publ.by the External Div. office of the President, Lagos, 1981.

Awolowo, O., 1947, and Abubakar Tafawa Balewa : Speeches republished in "The Punch"; Nigerian Newspaper,Friday,12.12. 1982, Vol.8,No.13, 819

Seminar Report : Nigeria in Transition - a critical examination of the main political,economic and social asoects of the Nigerian society; Kaduna,11 -13 september 1979, Federal Government Printers; 1210/480/ (OL,29971).

The Guardian, London Newspaper, 18.11.1974
The Guardian, Nigerian Newspaper,Lagos,25.4.1983
Daily Times, Lagos Nigeria,24.5.1984
Sunday Times, Lagos,7.10.1984
Talking Drums, publ.in London,(ed.Elisabeth Ohene) 4.6.1984;

West Africa magazine, publ.in London, editor: Kaye Whiteman, 9.7.84;21.1.1985;2.4.1984;94.1984; 7.1o.1984; 1.3.1985; 3o.4.1985; 3o.1.1984; 15.1o.1984; 27.2.1984; 7.1.1985; 9.4.1984; 9.1.1984; 29.1o.1984; 6.8.1984; 23.7.1985; 3.12.1984; 28.5.1985; 23.4.1984; 3o.4.1984; 2o.2.1984; 26.3.1984; 13.2.1984; 18.6.1984;27.8.1984; 5.11.1984; 24.9.1984;

- The Church and Nigeria's Social Problems (Pastoral Letterof the Nigerian Bishops), 1972, CSN, Lagos.

New Africa Yearbook,1979, IC Magazine Ltd. London, publ.
Affif Ben Yedder.

Nachrichten aus Nigeria, published in Bonn by the Nigerian
Information and cultural centre; Bonn, No.1; March 1985.

Other Newspapers:

Der Spiegel, Hamburg, 1981,Nr. 39.
Frankfurter Rundschau, 16.9.1981
Emma- 1981, Nr. 12
Manager Magazin, 12/81,
Newsweek, American Magazine,January 24.1983; "All work and no
play - The world's youngest labourers"; special report.
Newsweek,18. 1o.1982, "The spectre haunting the West".

Kölner Stadt-Anzeiger, G - 4237,A, Freitag,16.3.1984,Nr.65.

Report of the Donovan Commission, London 1968; Royal Commission
on Trade Unions and Employers Associations.

Employment Policy in Germany - challenges and concepts
for the 1980's. Federal Employment Institute, Bundesanstalt
für Arbeit, N-rnberg, 1978.

Webster's Third New International Dictionary of the English
Language, (1768), Vol.I, A - G., Encyclopedia Brittanica,
Inc, Chicago, London. copyright 1981 revised edition;
by G.and C. Meriam Co.
The Communist Manifesto, 1848., Marx and Engels.,

Signs: Journal of Women in culture and society,1982,Vol.7,
Nr. 3, University of Chicago.

OECD, Department of Economics and statistics, Labour Force
Statistics, 1970 -1981; published in Paris, 1983..

Statistisches Bundesamt, Wiesbaden, Fachserie Internationale
Monatszahlen.
BMWI Tagesnachrichten der Bundesminister für Wirtschaft;
in Nr. 8529, vom 17.2.1984.

Bundesanstalt für Arbeit ., Statistik 1b2 4221/4301.

21